Balie Peyton
of Tennessee

Balie Peyton of Tennessee

Nineteenth Century
Politics and Thoroughbreds

WALTER T. DURHAM

Hillsboro Press
PROVIDENCE PUBLISHING CORPORATION
FRANKLIN, TENNESSEE

TENNESSEE HERITAGE LIBRARY

Printed in the United States of America

08   07   06   05   04   1   2   3   4   5

Library of Congress Control Number: 2004110407

ISBN: 1-57736-323-X

Published for the Sumner County Historical Society and the Sumner County Archives, 155 East Main Street, Gallatin, Tennessee, 37066.

Cover design by Hope Seth

Cover image of Balie Peyton courtesy of Mrs. Mabel Neal.
Cover image of thoroughbreds Beeswing and Newminster by Allen Haynes.

HILLSBORO PRESS
an imprint of
Providence Publishing Corporation
238 Seaboard Lane • Franklin, Tennessee 37067
www.providence-publishing.com
800-321-5692

To those who consult history
when formulating public policy

CONTENTS

PREFACE AND ACKNOWLEDGMENTS

MOST SERIOUS POLITICAL BIOGRAPHY IS PROPERLY RESTRICTED TO PERSONS of outstanding public achievement, but a study of selected lives of the near great often can be comparably productive. This is especially true as we follow the development of representative government during the early years of the Republic. In pursuit of that belief, I have chosen the life of Balie Peyton, a nineteenth-century Tennessee attorney, congressman, politician, diplomat, turfman, and eternal Unionist. In his career he mingled with presidents, generals, and foreign heads of state; with diplomats, congressmen, and senators; with governors, state legislators, and other aspirants to public office at all levels. Although I have followed him in those relationships, this book is primarily the story of his life, not a study of the times in which he lived.

His career demanded the acquaintance and respect of many. Andrew Jackson was Peyton's neighbor and fellow racehorse enthusiast. James K. Polk was his nemesis in congressional politics, but often the president's brother, William H. Polk, and Peyton were political allies. Peyton defected from the Jacksonians to lead the new Tennessee Whig Party as it captured the statewide vote for Hugh Lawson White against Martin Van Buren in the presidential election of 1836. After moving to New Orleans, he made public appearances and speeches there, in Tennessee, and elsewhere for William Henry Harrison's victorious campaign in 1840. He campaigned to deliver Tennessee to Henry Clay over James K. Polk in 1844. He was a key player in positioning Zachary Taylor to accept the Whig nomination and victory in the election of 1848. A founder of the Constitutional Union Party in 1859, he was state elector for the Bell-Everett ticket in 1860. Tennessee Military Governor Andrew Johnson frequently called him in for counsel and special assignments in 1862 and 1863.

Peyton was a product of the western frontier and the personal violence that marked the lives of his family and many fellow settlers. His competitive nature found outlets in the separate but sometimes overlapping worlds of politics, the turf, and the practice of law. At an early age he was attracted to horse racing and breeding thoroughbreds, both of which had been introduced into the area only a few years before his birth. He attained international recognition as a turfman when he promoted the Peyton Stake race at Nashville in 1843. He was frequently mentioned in national racing and thoroughbred publications from 1835 until after the Civil War.

Balie Peyton's greatest talent was public speaking; he was a superb orator. A great deal of what we know about him is distilled from his reported public speeches and, because of this, I quote freely from them.

Until 1865, Peyton was part of a Southern society in which human bondage was legal and widely practiced. Like other planters, he bought and sold slaves to work his farm and stud.

The greatest disappointment that Peyton researchers encounter is the lack of information about his personal life. Very few family letters have survived, and we are left wondering about the details of his apparently happy married life, prior to the premature death of his wife, Anne, in 1846. Existing information offers no satisfactory answers to questions prompted by the long absences that separated him from his four children or why he remained single after Anne's death.

Peyton did not preserve his papers nor did he keep the stingiest records of his profession. Fortunately for the biographer, his subject's public stature was of sufficient interest to newspaper editors that they often mentioned him in their columns. Much of this story of his life is taken from newspapers in Nashville, New Orleans, San Francisco, New York, and Washington, D.C.

Although he did not preserve his incoming correspondence, many of his hundreds of outgoing letters are found in the collections of others. The David Campbell Family Papers in the William R. Perkins Library of Duke University and the John J. Crittenden Papers in the Library of Congress are two of the richest caches of Peyton material. His speeches and debates in the House are reported in *Gales and Seaton's Register of Debates in Congress*, volumes 10–13. His career as a diplomat is reconstructed primarily from a reading of State Department Despatches to and from ministers to Chile, 1849–53. Mrs. Mabel Neal of Indian Trail, North Carolina, graciously shared Peyton family photographs and letters from the papers of her late husband, Charles Peyton Neal.

Important research assistance came from many sources, among which were the Tennessee State Library and Archives, the Jean and Alexander Heard Library at Vanderbilt University, the Tennessee Historical Society, and the Nashville Room at the Ben West Public Library of Metropolitan Nashville and Davidson County, Nashville; the Williams Research Center of the Historic New Orleans Collection, the Notarial Archives Research Center, the New Orleans Public Library, the Jackson Barracks Military Library, and the office of the U.S. District Attorney,

Eastern District of Louisiana, New Orleans; Southern Historical Collection, University of North Carolina, Chapel Hill; the William R. Perkins Library, Duke University, Durham; Special Collections of the University of Virginia Library, Charlottesville; the Virginia Historical Society, Richmond; the National Archives and the Library of Congress, Washington; McClung Historical Collection of the Knox County Public Library System and the University of Tennessee Archives and Special Collections, Knoxville; The Huntington, San Marino, California; the Bancroft Library of the University of California, Berkeley; the California State Library, Sacramento; the San Francisco Public Library; Sumner County Archives, Volunteer State Community College Library, photographer Allen Haynes, and historian Kenneth Thomson, Gallatin, Tennessee; Calhoun County Clerk, Lavaca, Texas; Cumberland University Archives, Lebanon, Tennessee; Chattanooga-Hamilton Bicentennial Library, Chattanooga, Tennessee; the Historical Society of Pennsylvania, Philadelphia; John W. Marshall, Memphis, Tennessee; and Mrs. Peyton Cockrill Lewis, Washington, D.C.

I am indebted to State Librarian and Archivist Edwin S. Gleaves and attorney Nathan Harsh of Gallatin for helpful readings of the entire manuscript. Professor Joseph G. Tregle of New Orleans; Professor James S. Holliday of Carmel, California; the late Professor Sam B. Smith of Nashville; and Vanderbilt University Professors Jacque Voegeli and the late Simon Collier read selected chapters and offered constructive suggestions that significantly improved the book.

My research assistant and secretary Glenda Brown Milliken has calmly worked through the research, writing and rewriting, a pattern that she and I have followed on many prior manuscripts. Dimples Kellogg's copyediting was essential and the regular encouragement of my wife, Anna Coile Durham, kept me ahead even when distractions competed for my time.

The staff of Hillsboro Press of Providence Publishing Corporation has been unfailingly helpful. I sincerely appreciate editor Nancy Wise's commitment to producing a quality product. The cooperation of the Sumner County Historical Society and the Sumner County Archives made publication possible.

I have enjoyed the help of many, but the responsibility for the end result must rest on my shoulders and mine alone.

Walter T. Durham
Gallatin, Tennessee
July 1, 2004

Balie Peyton
of Tennessee

FROM CRADLE TO CONGRESS
1803–1833

The birth of a baby on the western frontier of 1803 was an especially exciting time for its family and neighbors. Large families were desirable, and most saw the arrival of a newborn as a good omen. So must it have been for John and Margaret Hamilton Peyton[1] when their sixth son, Balie[2], was born November 26 on their Station Camp Creek farm in Sumner County, Tennessee.[3]

The local Indian wars had ended just eight years before. Balie's mother well knew—and he would soon know—that the last Indian raid to claim the life of a white settler in Sumner County had resulted in the death of his grandfather, Robert Peyton, on June 7, 1795.[4] No stranger to violence, she looked anxiously ahead to her new son's overcoming the hardships of frontier life, growing into manhood, and taking his place among the leaders of the region.

Margaret Hamilton Peyton remembered that her father, Capt. John Hamilton, had participated as a British colonial soldier in the disastrous attack on the French at Fort Duquesne in 1755. More recently she had seen her husband wounded in violent encounters with American Indians who resisted the settlement of their hunting grounds in the area that later became Middle Tennessee. John had narrowly escaped with his life in a skirmish in 1782 at Peyton's Creek near Kilgore's Station, had been seriously wounded at Defeated Creek in 1786, and had been a militia participant in the Coldwater Expedition against the Chickamauga in 1787.[5]

Balie was of the first generation of his family born west of the Appalachians. His mother had come to the Cumberland country with her parents in the settlement parties of 1780. His father had reached the new settlements in 1782, after spending the three prior years in Kentucky. Margaret and John met sometime thereafter, were married in 1790, and settled on a 640-acre farm that adjoined her father's place of similar size in Sumner County. John Peyton paid the state of North Carolina at the rate of ten pounds for every one hundred acres.[6] As one of the settlers of 1780 who survived the darkest period of Indian resistance, John Hamilton had received his property as a preemption grant from that state.[7]

Although the violence that had beset his frontier forebears would surely affect Balie's life, so also would the throbbing rhythm of hoofbeats, sounded by thoroughbred horses that exercised on his father's farm and on the race paths of Middle Tennessee.[8] The love of horses and horse races never left him.

The practice of breeding horses for racing had come to Balie's neighborhood in the late-1790s when Dr. Redmond Dillon Barry introduced bluegrass to the farms in the Station Camp Creek watershed. The new grass, with its high calcium content, built strong bones in the animals that grazed it. In 1799, Dr. Barry brought the notable stallion Gray Medley from the stables of North Carolina Governor Ben Williams to stand at William Donelson's farm about fifteen miles southwest of Gallatin. It was the first time that the services of a thoroughbred stallion had been offered to most Tennessee breeders.[9]

The combination of fine blood lines and bluegrass pastures moved Tennessee into the forefront of American racing during the antebellum period. For the next 150 years, a carpet of bluegrass covered the undulating fields that stretched along most of the twenty-seven miles between Gallatin and Nashville. The vista was so impressive that owners of an electric trolley line built in 1913 to connect the two cities called it the "Bluegrass Line." The route passed the breeding grounds of some of the great American thoroughbreds of the nineteenth and early twentieth centuries.[10]

Balie's idyllic childhood on the sprawling family farm was interrupted, at the age of eight, by his mother's untimely death on October 12, 1812. John Peyton suddenly had sole responsibility for his ten children. In addition to Balie, there were four sons older than he, Robert Holmes, John Hamilton, William Randolph ("Ran"), and Ephraim; a younger son, Joseph Hopkins; and four daughters, Angelina Belle, the oldest, Rebecca H., Evalina, and Sarah H., the youngest. John Peyton never remarried. The children received maternal care and counsel from their grandmother, Rebecca Holmes Hamilton, until her death a few years later.[11] Angelina Belle, age fourteen when her mother died, assisted with the younger children until she married in 1818 and later moved to Texas.

John Peyton built the family residence on the Station Camp farm sometime prior to his wife's death. No drawings or written description of it have survived, but local traditions suggest it was a two-story brick house of the Federal style typical of the Tennessee frontier. It would have had a central hall with one or two rooms on each side at both first- and second-floor levels and probably an ell at the rear. The kitchen would have been located in a separate building nearby. A few years after his father's death in 1833, Balie added a white-pillared veranda.[12]

Just before his mother's death, older members of the family began talking about a second war with Great Britain. Balie was proud to ride with his father the three miles to Gallatin where he saw his brother John Hamilton Peyton in one of the four companies of Sumner County volunteers that set out for Natchez in early December 1812 in response to the president's call. Less than a year later, he accompanied his father to see yet another group of volunteer companies depart for war in the South. Balie's experience was of a different sort this time; his family had just been notified that his brother John had died in military service in Alabama.[13]

There was celebration in their neighborhood in 1815 when a messenger from Nashville rode an exhausted mount into Gallatin to announce that General Jackson and Tennessee-led Americans had defeated the British at the Battle of New Orleans. Balie never forgot it. The rider's news included word that the enemy General Edward Michael Pakenham was dead and his army had evacuated Louisiana. The death of Pakenham was of special interest to the Peytons and their neighbors because he had been a college classmate of Dr. Barry twenty-five years earlier in Dublin.[14]

In Professor John Hall's classes at Transmontania Academy in Gallatin, however, young Balie heard more about Thermopylae than New Orleans. As his students worked to master the English language in its spoken and written forms, Hall strongly emphasized classical studies.[15] A fellow student at Transmontania was Balie's first cousin, Ephraim Geoffrey Peyton, who had come from his home in Kentucky to live with his uncle while attending the academy. In 1819, Geoffrey left school and went with an older brother to Mississippi where six years later he received a license to practice law in that state.[16]

By the time he reached his mid-teen years, Balie was attending school across the river at Maj. George McWhirter's Hickory Ridge School in Wilson County.[17] He boarded in the home of a local family.

But horse racing competed for his attention. Years later he recalled, "I received more whippings as a boy for running off from schools to go to horse races than for all other causes put together."[18]

His presence at school in Wilson County was probably the reason Balie was not with his brother Robert Holmes, their father, and their cousin Ephraim Geoffrey Peyton at a confrontation with their neighbor James McKain on March 15, 1817. Robert Holmes abruptly terminated the conversation by firing two pistol shots that wounded McKain. A grand jury indicted Robert on October 10, 1817, for assault with intent to commit murder, but the courts moved too slowly for McKain. In a second altercation, he wounded Peyton by firing a bullet through his body on April 11, 1818. Like McKain before him, Peyton survived. The grand jury indicted the assailant, charging him as Peyton had been charged earlier.

Neither defendant had been brought to trial by the latter part of 1818, and hostility between the two had become so aggravated that Peyton petitioned the court for a change of venue in the case against him because McKain had "systematically cultivated prejudice" against himself and the Peyton family.[19] Lawyers for both sides ultimately dropped their cases, and both defendants went free.

Relations between the neighboring families were strained for many years thereafter. It was Balie's first encounter with a streak of violence in his own family, but there was another event three years later. Angelina's husband, Jonathan C. Peyton, who was their first cousin, killed Stephen W. Thompson when he intervened in a fight between Thompson and one of the Peyton brothers on November 30, 1821. Angelina learned of the killing when Jonathan rushed home to persuade her to flee with him from certain prosecution. They were across the state line in Kentucky by the next morning, the beginning of a long, slow journey that ended in Texas where they settled.[20]

Balie spent much of each year on the Station Camp Creek farm. There he heard his father speak frequently of Andrew Jackson whose plantation was only a few miles down the river. Before the general's victory at New Orleans, most talk had been about the Peytons' and Jacksons' mutual interest in racehorses, but in later years, it had turned to politics. The Peytons applauded the appointment of Jackson as governor of the territory of Florida in 1819, but they hoped he could maintain their shared interest in breeding thoroughbred horses.

While studying under Hall and McWhirter, Balie was a classmate of Jo. C. Guild, another Sumner Countian.[21] The two students shared an undying interest in thoroughbred racehorses, and it soon became the basis for a lifelong friendship.

After completing the schooling available at Hickory Ridge, Peyton and Guild prepared for careers as attorneys-at-law. Balie studied principally in the Gallatin law offices of A. B. Shelby and Judge John J. White. Joining Peyton at Shelby's office, Guild read for a year and then moved to Nashville, where he finished preparation for the bar in the office of attorney Ephraim H. Foster. Both young men were subsequently licensed to practice law and were received into the Gallatin bar. Guild opened his office in 1822; Balie hung out his shingle in 1824.[22]

Talented as an orator and disarmingly quick in debate, Peyton passed over any potential that he might have cultivated as a legal scholar or theoretician. From the beginning he was a trial lawyer whose bailiwick was the courtroom. He depended more on discussion and debate to instruct him than on legal tomes and the published reports of court cases. His arguments employed a direct frontier logic based on rational thought, common sense, and skillful presentation.

During their early years at the bar, Peyton and Guild mixed their love of horses with the demands of their profession. They not only rode for pleasure, but also depended on their horses to deliver them to the court-houses in neighboring counties where they practiced in the periodic sessions of the district circuit court. When at home, both boarded at Capt. Jack Mitchell's hotel in Gallatin.[23]

At the conclusion of a session of circuit court in Carthage during the latter 1820s, Peyton and Guild decided that, while en route home the next day, they would stop for the races at Hartsville. Not expecting to race him, Guild rode their partnership horse Old King to Hartsville. Upon arrival, local race fans so bantered the young attorneys that they agreed to run Old King in a one-mile race against a horse in regular training owned by one Cook Lewis. Even though he had been ridden eighteen miles that morning, Old King won the race to his owners' delight.[24]

Later they were challenged to race Old King against a heavily muscled quarter horse. Aware that their horse could not match such an adversary at 440 yards, they successfully proposed a greater distance that would shift the advantage to Old King. They also won agreement for the horses to carry 140 pounds each, clearly above the customary weight of jockeys. With thirty days to prepare Old King, the partners worked him hard. Secretly, they perfected their plan to have 140-pound Peyton in the saddle on race day when they would feign inability to find a jockey of that weight, only to have Balie volunteer to ride at the last moment.

Shortly after the race began, the opposing jockey tried to force Old King off the track and into the woods. Resisting skillfully, Peyton responded further by striking the rider in the face with his crop. Old King finished far ahead of the quarter horse, and the judge awarded him the purse, ruling that the fouls exchanged by the jockeys had no effect on the outcome. Guild never doubted the results because he regarded Peyton as the best rider in the state.[25]

The friendship of Peyton and Guild prospered. When the latter was married to Katherine Blackmore on December 19, 1826, Peyton was a member of the wedding party.[26] Like her husband and Peyton, Katherine was a first-generation Sumner Countian. Her parents were George and Elizabeth Neely Blackmore, both of whose families had reached the Cumberland settlements by the early 1780s.[27]

While attending court at Carthage in the mid-1820s, Balie met local attorney Robert L. Caruthers[28] with whom he developed another life-long friendship. He was a member of the wedding party when Caruthers married Sarah Saunders[29]of Sumner County at her father's home on the Cumberland River near Hendersonville. On the day after the winter ceremony, Balie rode horseback with the wedding party to Lebanon. The weather was so severely cold that they had to gallop their horses from house to house and stop to warm. Peyton and Miss Sally Van Horn of Gallatin, with the two best horses of the lot, led the way.[30]

While still in his twenties, Peyton was fascinated by the opportunities for breeding thoroughbred stock for racing. He first brought the outstanding racing stallion Rattler to Sumner County and stood him at the farm of G. W. Parker, husband of Balie's sister Rebecca. Shortly afterward he introduced local breeders to the Virginia-bred thoroughbred Anvil, a successful sire he had purchased in Maryland.[31] The arrival of Rattler and Anvil foreshadowed the development of a nationally recognized stud at the farm on Station Camp Creek. It also reflected increasing investments at other nearby studs, such as the importation of "the distinguished English Race Horse" Leviathan to the stables of George Elliott in December 1830.[32]

With maturity Balie realized that he would have more to deal with than lawsuits and horses. Responding to his father's need for financial assistance in 1825, he joined two other men and made a surety bond of four thousand dollars for the elder Peyton to guarantee payment of two court judgments of two thousand dollars each against him. The three guarantors accepted a mortgage on John Peyton's 640-acre home place to secure their interests.[33]

Balie established a professional friendship in 1828 in the courts of Nashville with Henry Alexander Wise,[34] a young attorney from Virginia.[35] Both admired Andrew Jackson, and at slow times each must have shared with the other his dream of a career in politics beyond the local scene.[36]

After coming to Nashville during the late summer of 1828, Wise married Ann Jennings, daughter of Obadiah Jennings, a local Presbyterian pastor, on October 8. They accepted an invitation to spend their honeymoon as houseguests of Rachel and Andrew Jackson at the Hermitage. Rachel had invited them because Henry was a native of Accomack County, Virginia, home of her mother's family. The bride, too, was from the same part of Virginia and, like Rachel, a Presbyterian.[37] But Virginia connections aside, what better reception into Jacksonian politics could one have than to be feted at the board of the next president? What better way to become a Jacksonian unless, like Peyton, you shared the old general's enthusiasm for thoroughbred horses?

At the beginning of the new year, 1829, Balie was practicing in the Nashville firm of "Peyton and Childress, attorneys at law," located on Cedar Street next door to "Foster and Fogg."[38] The pair dissolved their partnership by the end of 1829; George Campbell Childress opted for a stint in journalism before relocating to Texas in 1835, and soon afterward he was chairman of the committee that drafted the Texas Declaration of Independence.[39] Peyton continued to practice in "all of the courts of Davidson, Sumner and some of the adjacent counties" in 1830.[40]

Although he had been "an associate and particular friend" of Eliza Allen since childhood, Balie was not present at her marriage to Governor Sam Houston on January 22, 1829, at Allendale, the Allens' family home just south of Gallatin. Local people knew that Eliza's father coveted the marriage of his daughter to the thirty-five-year-old governor of Tennessee, whom he correctly gauged as a rising star in the political West. In the typical pattern of small town life, Gallatin folk discussed the marriage thoroughly, but gave it their approval.

Peyton and his Gallatin neighbors were totally unprepared for the sequence of events that began on April 11 when Eliza returned to her father's home from the Nashville hotel where she and Houston had been living. Behind she left an empty room and a note to her husband, telling him she could no longer be his wife. Outraged local public opinion immediately placed blame for the abrupt breakup on Houston, and a mob burned him in effigy on the Gallatin public square.[41]

Shortly after her return, Peyton visited Eliza at Allendale. There he commented that he could not believe that she had been "fickle and cruel, to a noble man like Houston." In response she pledged him to secrecy and explained she had left Houston because "he was a demented man . . . crazy." Elaborating on the astonishing allegation, she said, "He is insanely jealous and suspicious. He required me not to speak to anyone, and to lock myself in my room if he was absent even for a few minutes [even] when we were guests in my own Aunt's house."[42]

Eliza told Balie that on one occasion Governor Houston had locked her in their hotel room early in the morning and absented himself until late at night. He had made her a "prisoner . . . without food; debarred from the society of my relatives; and a prey to chagrin, mortification, and hunger."

Acknowledging that she had been wooed and won by Houston's "brilliant conversation and his handsome and commanding presence,"

Eliza confided to Balie, "I parted from Governor Houston because he evinced no confidence in my integrity; and had no respect for my intelligence, or trust in my discretion." Balie kept Eliza's account in confidence until both she and Houston died.[43]

Although he was not at the deliberations in April 1830, Peyton concurred with the findings of a Gallatin citizens' committee that investigated the details of the Allen-Houston marriage, exonerated Eliza of wrongdoing, and judged her character untainted by the experience. The investigators believed her to be "an innocent and injured woman."[44]

Sometime in the latter 1820s while attending court at Carthage, Peyton met a beautiful brown-eyed young woman who soon became the focus of his life. Anne Alexander Smith had come from her family home in North Carolina to join her brother Charles E. and his family in Smith County. She was the only woman Balie ever loved and the only one whose hand he asked in marriage.[45] The attraction was mutual, and on May 20, 1830, the handsome Balie[46] and Anne were married. They set up their home on John Peyton's Station Camp Creek farm.[47]

During the following December, Anne and Balie traveled to North Carolina for an extensive visit with the Smith family at their home near Granville City. Returning overland in January 1831, Balie and his pregnant wife had a very trying journey across the mountains to Sumner County. Two of their slaves, crossing with them, experienced frostbite on their toes, but fully recovered in a few weeks.[48] Notwithstanding the severe conditions of the crossing, Anne successfully delivered their first child, Emily Turner Peyton, on April 8, 1831.

The happiness caused by the birth of their daughter was dampened by the death of Anne's mother a few days later in North Carolina. Her brother Samuel wrote to relay the sad news of their mother's fate. Acknowledging receipt of the letter, Balie noted to another family member, "Anne takes it very hard."[49]

In 1831, Balie was not only a new father but as a major in the Sumner County Militia, an attorney, a horseman, and a planter, he was a rising local political figure. When certain Gallatin leaders had conducted a public meeting to protest the 1828 "tariff of abominations" and to elect delegates to an antitariff convention in Philadelphia, Peyton rallied those of opposing views at a second mass meeting held three days later. He drafted the resolutions that ultimately were adopted, although local public opinion was divided on the issue.

Addressing the crowd, Peyton spoke like a veteran. He warned that the resolutions adopted at the antitariff rally, if unanswered, might "have a

Anne Smith Peyton   *Balie Peyton*

tendency to mislead the public mind—produce discord in the ranks of the Republican party—embarrass the administration of the general government and weaken the banks of the *Federal Union.*" Defending President Andrew Jackson's position on the tariff, he declared that Vice President John C. Calhoun's introduction of states' rights into the issue strongly indicated he countenanced the doctrine of nullification and was willing to let it lead where it would, even to dissolution of the Union and civil war.[50]

Peyton's resolutions declared that an antitariff convention was "inexpedient and ought not to be sanctioned by the state of Tennessee." Maintaining that representative government was competent to deal with tariff issues, he concluded:

> We have entire confidence in the wisdom, integrity and firmness of the president of the United States, and that we may safely rely upon him and the Congress without the intervention of political assemblies, representing [more] often the views of a junta of political aspirants and malcontents than the great body of the people.[51]

Peyton and the voters of Sumner County were strongly in the president's political camp. By election time in November 1832, Jackson's strength had so solidified that only 10 votes were cast against him in the county and 728 were in his favor.[52]

In August 1832 at a Gallatin rally, Peyton spoke against the national bank and espoused the cause of the new state bank for which a local friend, Eastin Morris, had been elected president by the legislature eight months before. Most present voted overwhelmingly to endorse the new state bank, implicitly rejecting the Bank of the United States.[53]

The decision of former governor William Hall[54] of Sumner County to stand aside from possible reelection to Congress from the Sixth District[55] in 1832 caused Peyton and Guild to look self-consciously at each other. Which would seek Hall's vacated seat? No one knows how they reached the decision for Peyton to run, although in a recollection of the event, Guild suggests that he had the better established practice and that he "yielded, and urged his old and longtime friend" to undertake the canvass.[56] Years later, Peyton recalled that Dixon Allen, a member of the legislature who was expected to be the Jackson candidate, declined to run and appealed to him to take his place.[57] The support volunteered by Guild and Allen was all that he needed to announce for Congress.

The contest in the congressional election of August 1 and 2, 1833, was between the thirty-year-old Peyton and Col. Archibald W. Overton of Smith County. Both were Jacksonians at a time in Tennessee when there were as yet no other political parties of significance. Warning Overton that Peyton was a formidable candidate, Guild cautioned, "When you meet him upon the stump, without disparaging your oratory, you will hear it thunder, and you will witness the forked lightning jumping from crag to crag!"[58]

Believing that he had strong support at home in Sumner County, Peyton agreed to meet Colonel Overton on Defeated Creek in Smith County for the opening debate of the campaign. It was an unmatched opportunity to address the people of his opponent's home county on their own ground, but at a historic site that he could exploit. For their meeting Balie had chosen the warpath and battlefield of 1786 where his father, two of his uncles, and their party had been surrounded and attacked by Indians.

The two candidates met on the agreed day, and Peyton launched into a patriotic discourse that ignored current public issues. Beginning with the Declaration of Independence, he led his listeners through the principal battles of the American Revolution to the establishment of the free and independent United States of America. He then took up the trials of the pioneers who crossed into Tennessee to claim the lands of the Indian inhabitants.[59]

Peyton said that settlement of the area was successful only because the pioneers had blazed "their way over the Alleghenies with a tomahawk in one hand and a rifle in the other." Praising their courage and endurance, he reminded the audience that they were gathered upon the creek where his father and uncles had been wounded during an attack by Indians. He went on to say that this attack threatened the lives of a larger group of pioneers who made their escape because the Peyton brothers had skillfully covered their retreat.[60] He recalled the frontier volunteers' assault on Nickajack in 1794, an aggressive but unauthorized exercise that he said brought an end to the local Indian wars.[61]

Having praised the accomplishments of those who had won the West for the present inhabitants, Peyton offered himself as a descendant of one of those old pioneers and asked the voters to elect him to Congress. The crowd liked what it heard and raised cheers that echoed up and down the creek.[62]

Colonel Overton's speech, addressing issues of the day, was dull by comparison. He later scoffed that Peyton had scared the crowd and himself into believing that there was an Indian behind every tree. "I shuddered," Overton said, "I felt the entire assembly would be massacred.

Josephus Conn Guild

In fact, Defeated Creek ran red with blood all the time he spoke."[63] But scoffing did not get votes. Balie had kindled the fires of patriotism in his neighbors' breasts, and the flames burned bright enough not only to win the day for him but also to light his way down the campaign trail.

A month later Peyton attended a Gallatin mass meeting where he seconded resolutions offered by Judge John J. White to endorse President Jackson's nullification proclamation. His western views envisioned a larger Union in the years ahead, but he believed it essential to prevent a fragmentation that would leave the separate pieces much weaker than the whole had been. Balie clearly put himself on the side of the Union, a stance that he would never abandon. Those present adopted Judge White's pro-Union resolutions with few dissenting votes.[64]

Peyton focused much of his campaign effort on Jackson County, where he was not as well known as in Sumner and Smith. Traveling tirelessly, he professed to have visited every man in the county and to have shaken the hand of every woman. During the campaign, the numerous Hogg family in and around Hartsville became Peyton voters when he carried the baby of one of their women in his arms from Dixon Springs to Hartsville while on horseback, the young mother following on her own horse. He was unaware that his opponent, Colonel Overton, had been asked to accommodate the mother and child on his way to Hartsville but had declined because of the press of time.[65]

If Balie needed encouragement to sustain his campaign for Congress, it came in the person of Balie Peyton Jr., born at home on

April 23, 1833. With an infant son and a two-year-old daughter, the father faced increased family responsibilities.

On the days of election, August 1 and 2, 1833, the voters of the Sixth Congressional District chose Balie Peyton to be their congressman by a vote of 4,510 to 1,621 over Overton. Each of the three counties gave him decisive margins.[66] He had done little to earn the office, but a vigorous campaign highlighted by compelling oratory carried the day for him over an older, less-aggressive candidate. Peyton became one of the thirteen-member Tennessee delegation to the House of Representatives, a group that included such political stalwarts as John Bell, James K. Polk, Cave Johnson, David Crockett, and Luke Lea.[67]

Before the excitement of the election had abated, Balie was called to the bedside of his seventy-eight-year-old father who was critically ill with "dropsy of the chest." In the late afternoon of August 20, 1833, John Peyton died.[68] Calling for the payments of all his outstanding debts, John's will specified that, at the request of his older children, the net proceeds from the sale of his property be divided among his three youngest children: Rebecca H. Parker, Joseph Hopkins Peyton, and Sarah H. Peyton. The will impacted Balie heavily; it not only made him executor of the estate but also required him to purchase the Station Camp Creek farm and the old Keefe place, a second tract of about 250 acres. He was to pay for the first at the rate of ten dollars per acre and the second at eight dollars per acre, about the going market price.[69]

Within a period of three weeks, Balie had won election to the U.S. Congress, become executor of his father's estate, undertaken an obligation of approximately eight thousand dollars to pay for the lands purchased from his father's estate, and assumed management of the farm. He did not dislodge his three brothers who lived there but employed the two older ones who were available to assist with the agricultural and horse-breeding operations.

Prior to his own election, Peyton had upheld the president in his support of John Henry Eaton's desire to return to the U.S. Senate, where he had served from 1818 to 1829. Eaton had just resigned from the president's cabinet after he and Jackson had tried unsuccessfully for two years to win social acceptance of his wife, Peggy, the target of rumors alleging sexual improprieties. Felix Grundy, another Jackson friend and former congressman, was the incumbent senator.

Led by Gallatin businessman and former Congressman Robert Desha Jr., several local voters brought pressure to bear on the Sumner County legislative delegation to agree to vote for Grundy, and Peyton was enraged.[70] He took up the cudgels in defense of Eaton. Expecting that Desha would try to neutralize him when he next addressed a local audience, Peyton was prepared when the two appeared together before a large crowd at Gallatin on September 26. Assuming his "highest military attitude," Desha rallied his forces and endeavored to intimidate Eaton supporters "by saying that he would look upon it as a direct attack upon his honor and his veracity for anyone to support Major Eaton."[71]

Peyton could not brook Desha's haughty attitude. Although he did not seek a violent confrontation with his adversary,[72] Balie warned that Desha had "tyrannized over the people of Sumner County long enough" and that he "should not at any peril" attempt "to bully" him. Reminding Desha that the president and the nation were then making a "great struggle . . . to save the Union," he argued that "physical power [and] mere brute force ought to yield to reason and patriotism."[73] The persuasive power of Peyton's oratory during the exchanges with Desha and two other Grundy speakers convinced most of those present. They voted to instruct Sumner County legislators to vote for Eaton.[74]

Although the stern response to Desha angered the former congressman's friends, it further solidified Balie's stand as an unqualified Jacksonian. And that was the rock on which he built his first canvass for Congress.[75]

Balie was irate when he learned that friends of Grundy had won commitments from members of the legislature to vote for him against "whomsoever" might be offered for the U.S. Senate. They secured the legislators' promises by assuring them that the whole activity was only a deserved tribute because Grundy had no intention of being a candidate for reelection. Yet Grundy emerged soon afterward as a candidate with commitments that Peyton regarded as fraudulently obtained.[76]

Convinced that the president wanted the legislature to elect Eaton to the Senate, Peyton rejoiced when, unable to reach a decision, the legislators postponed the election until the first session of the next general assembly, to be convened on September 16, 1833. The postponement put the decision in the hands of the electorate as most seats in the assembly would be contested in the election that preceded the next session. Candidates could not avoid the question: How will you vote for U.S. senator?[77]

The choice was not made until two months after Peyton's election to Congress. On October 7, the legislature elected Grundy on the fifty-fifth ballot after Eaton had circulated a letter asking that his name be withdrawn.[78]

Balie had done his best to fulfill what he thought were the president's wishes. Mixed signals had emanated from the White House as the campaign progressed, and Grundy may well have been Jackson's choice. The president's preference aside, Peyton had, for the moment, incurred the wrath of the politically powerful Senator-elect Felix Grundy, hardly an ideal way to begin a first term in Congress.

CHAPTER 2

JACKSONIAN CONGRESSMAN
1833–DECEMBER 1, 1835

Arriving in the nation's capital[1] to present his credentials to the first session of the Twenty-Third Congress,[2] Peyton found the national bank controversy raging. On September 23, 1833, the president had appointed a new secretary of the Treasury who immediately began complying with his wishes to remove the government's deposits from the Bank of the United States and place them in various state banks. Removal of the deposits prompted renewed opposition charges of a presidential power grab, and President Andrew Jackson's political friends rallied to his side.

Among the first to take the floor of the House at the beginning of the new session was the eager but inexperienced Peyton. Elected as a Jacksonian, he was ready to defend the president. During the debate about the propriety of withdrawing the deposits, Peyton objected to treating the matter hastily. The opposition was trying to frighten the American people into a rash act, he said, but there were many charges against the national bank, charges that the bank's supporters should admit or yield to investigation. He insisted that withdrawals from the national bank by the secretary of the Treasury during the two months prior to the meeting of Congress had been necessary to prevent the bank from withdrawing $9 million from the general circulation of the country.[3] Jackson's friends in Tennessee received accounts of Peyton's

16

remarks with pleasure and urged him to continue his attacks on the national bank.

The House of Representatives heard the confident young orator again on January 16 and 17, 1834, when he fervently advocated pensions for the surviving western frontiersmen who had participated in the local Indian wars of 1780–95. Balie had been greatly annoyed when a Rhode Island congressman cast doubt on their patriotism because they had fought the Indians in "petty feuds and private wars" instead of fighting the British. Proud to trace his origin "to that race of men," Peyton said that his father and fellow frontiersmen fought the Indians because the British had incited them and made allies of them against the colonies. It was as patriotic for Daniel Boone to resist Indian attacks as it was for Washington "to resist the civilized armies of Great Britain," he argued.[4]

Denied pensions because records to substantiate their claims were incomplete or missing, the frontiersmen were truly soldiers of the Revolution. Peyton asserted:

> If you cannot spare for those who lack the means of living, be it so; the West will feed her patriarchal soldiers. . . . Let the war-worn soldier . . . look to the West; it is what his country has done in the hour of her peril and day of her distress.[5]

Returning to the bank deposits debate on February 5 and 6, Peyton blasted the opposition's effort to characterize Jackson as a despot comparable to Caesar or Shakespeare's Richard III. That anyone could liken the president's action in the bank matter to Richard III's murdering his brother's children during their innocent sleep indicated that the accuser's imagination was "horribly distempered." It was equally ridiculous to compare Jackson to Caesar, who drove relentlessly to consolidate power, ever using military force to secure his position. He pointed out that Jackson, when victory was won in 1815, disbanded his armies and retired to his farm.[6]

It was easy for Peyton to see that Representative George McDuffie of South Carolina had resurrected the names of some of the greatest tyrants of human history in an attempt to liken Jackson to them. He saw just as easily that most of South Carolina's opposition to the president was prompted by the issue of nullification.[7]

The bank represented a concentration of wealth and power in the hands of a few—outside the government—that Peyton regarded as a dangerous threat to the governing process. Even as the debate raged, the U.S. Bank directors were using public monies to lobby for the bank's interests and to discredit the president. Responding to their claims that the bank had taken no part in the politics of the country, Peyton declared with pardonable exaggeration:

It is a fact, notorious to the whole world, that the bank has its candidates for every office from a watchman in the cities up to the President of the United States; it has vast sinking funds for its advocates and counsellors at law. . . . It has its presses and its dependents all over the country.[8]

On March 28, 1834, when the Senate passed two resolutions censuring Jackson for removal of the federal deposits from the Bank of the United States, his allies in the House prepared to take offsetting action. His inexperience in office notwithstanding, Peyton was a leader in the debate that on April 4 led the House to adopt four resolutions exonerating the president from the Senate's charges.

Andrew Jackson

Two weeks later Peyton drafted resolutions that upheld the president and asserted further that the Senate's censuring resolutions "infringed upon the rightful and legitimate powers and prerogatives of the House of Representatives." The reason? "Congress has the power, *by law*, to select the places of depositing the public money, and providing for its safe-keeping," he answered. His resolutions were in response to proposals made by his friend Representative Henry Wise of Virginia that had the effect of casting "a solemn censure upon the President" and further injected the House into the conflict between the Senate and the president. He reasoned that if the House was going to get into the conflict, it should "meet the question fully," hence his provisions about ultimate House control of the deposits.[9]

The first-term congressman was astounded when Henry L. Pinckney of South Carolina called a man "gallant" for making a personal attack on the president. Conceding that he did not know how Pinckney defined *gallantry*, Balie knew what gallantry was not:

When an individual had approached a man, who extended his hand to him with the welcome of a friend, and gave that man a dagger, he deserved to be called anything but gallant. The assailant of a revolutionary soldier [Jackson] deserves infamy, and not praise.[10]

Agreeing that it was both "unprecedented and inexpedient for the two houses to engage in answering or praising each other," Peyton said

that it was even more repugnant to good judgment for the House to try
the president "without notice, without a hearing, without arraignment."
The overwhelming power of the national bank was leveraged against
Jackson. He said:

> He is struggling against an institution which would crush any other man,
> and against an array of party strength more powerful than any ever
> witnessed in this country; and we are asked [by the Wise resolutions] to
> cease our legislative pursuits, and join the Senate in hunting him down.[11]

Wise continued to push his resolutions asserting congressional
authority to exercise custody of public funds not disbursed under appropriations by law. Debating the issue, he and Peyton so wearied their
colleagues that they voted 115 to 79 to lay the resolutions and amendments on the table.[12]

Speaking on another issue, Peyton said that a bill to authorize the
sale of public lands at $1.25 per acre would not be helpful to Tennessee
because there were no unsold lands in the state worth that much. Shortly
before the vote was taken, he charged that the act amounted to governmental abuse of certain poor families who were squatters on public land
that they had improved. Notwithstanding his opposition, the House
passed the act on June 13.[13]

Consideration of a bill to authorize the construction of forts to
protect deep-water harbors along the eastern coast gave Peyton another
chance to establish himself as a formidable debater. Taking the western
view that the proposed fortification system was a waste of money, the
Tennessean declared that he opposed killing the bill "by piecemeal" but
favored "beheading it at once."[14]

The security of the nation against foreign foes was not provided by
"lofty battlements and towers," Peyton elaborated, but it "lay in . . . high-
minded brave, patriotic men." He could not imagine an enemy placing
itself before one of our forts as it "sought to invade our land." Surely, he
reasoned, "they would challenge an undefended point," of which there
would be an endless number unless the secretary of war was proposing "to
defend the whole country with a wall." He would rely on "the citizens—
the militia of the country" because they were able "to protect their own soil
and, if they failed, forts and walls" would be of no value. He agreed with
Representative Seaborn Jones of Georgia that the cost of garrisoning the
forts would quickly surpass the cost of constructing them.[15]

During this session, Peyton frequently visited the stables in Washington
where the president and Maj. T. P. Andrews of the U.S. Army were

training racehorses. At the invitation of Andrew Jackson Donelson, Jackson's private secretary, he timed "all of the 'trial runs' of the stable." Peyton was present on the day before the spring race meeting for their final preparations and rode out onto the track with the president and Vice President Van Buren to see the horses being saddled and mounted.

When one of the horses became so unmanageable that his jockey could not mount, President Jackson flew into a rage. Denouncing the trainer for the horse's bad deportment, he turned on Peyton, who was standing a stride away from the timer's station, and scolded him for being out of position. "Why don't you take your position there? You ought to know where to stand to time a horse!"

Peyton noticed that Jackson and Van Buren had taken convenient but safe positions at the rear of the stand, but when the nervous horse continued his antics, Van Buren moved to the edge of the track. The president shouted, "Get behind me, Mr. Van Buren, they will run over you, Sir!" And the vice president complied with his instructions as promptly as Balie had before him.

The story of Jackson's instructions to the vice president at the track became a popular anecdote for the Hugh Lawson White campaign against Van Buren for president two years later. It was told as an illustration of Jackson's sponsorship and "fatherly protection" of the man he chose to succeed him.[16]

Thoroughbreds in the president's stables were not the only racing attractions that caught Peyton's eye during the spring of 1834. At the Central Course near Baltimore he saw the six-year-old Trifle win easily in a four-mile race. Just over eight years later he would have Trifle as a brood mare at his Station Camp farm.[17]

Crying more urgently for his attention was another race, the contest for Speaker of the House of Representatives. Faced with choosing between two fellow Tennesseans, Peyton chose his colleague John Bell over James K. Polk. With Peyton's help, Bell was elected Speaker on June 2, 1834.[18]

Balie had reassured other congressmen that his close political friend would be an evenhanded Speaker. The candidate would continue supporting the views of the administration but "would feel it [his] duty to award to all parties their parliamentary rights," he explained.[19]

At home during the summer, Peyton joined the newly elected Speaker, the Jacksonian intimate John Eaton, and Congressmen David W. Dickinson and John Forester for a visit to the Hermitage to assure the president that Bell was going to support him. The meeting accomplished little because Jackson doubted that the Speaker would stand up against the national bank interests; he had not done so in the past.[20]

Polk's friends hoped the choice would make trouble for Peyton with the voters at home, but that turned out to be wishful thinking. The congressman discouraged any potential voter unrest by suggesting that Polk had been too intimate with the nullifiers. Bell's election seems actually to have improved Balie's standing in his district.[21]

Although the president had supported Polk for the speakership, he did not break with Peyton over the issue. In fact, he turned to Balie in September to care for a pair of his prize fillies in Tennessee. Mixing horses and politics, Jackson wrote from the Hermitage where there was illness in his family but from whence he was about to return to Washington: "I am gratified at your flattering prospects, and am happy the fillies are safe under your care & control—and wish you success against *all* opponents."[22] Balie was not in further communication with the president prior to the destructive fire that swept through the Hermitage on October 13.

Newly appointed to the standing committee on foreign affairs,[23] Peyton returned to the capital for the second session of the Twenty-Third Congress. His arrival in Washington coincided with planning by the opposition, by then known as Whigs, to thwart the nomination of Martin Van Buren, Jackson's choice to be the next president.[24] Believing that his "messmate" Tennessee Senator Hugh Lawson White[25] was a better Jacksonian by far than the vice president, Peyton joined the opposition. Gathering at Peyton's Washington residence on the evening of December 29, the Tennessee congressional delegation voted eleven to none to endorse Senator White for the nomination. White and the three Van Buren men in the delegation, Senator Felix Grundy and Congressmen Polk and Cave Johnson, did not attend the meeting. The eleven drafted a very circumspect letter reminding the senator that his name was being "frequently mentioned as a suitable person" to succeed President Jackson and asking what were his "wishes and determinations." Replying by handwritten message, he said that no one should turn down the office if offered by the people. He made it clear he was willing to run but also willing to have his name withdrawn, should his friends so judge.[26]

Peyton and his associates of the December 29 conclave distributed copies of their letter and White's response so that the "correspondence" appeared in newspapers throughout the country.[27] Delighted that the senator had responded favorably, Balie was proud that the letter written in his quarters had been the instrument that moved White into the presidential race. The senator had previously turned deaf ears to endorsements by certain members of the Tennessee legislature and delegates attending the state constitutional convention of 1834. But the

John Bell

exchange of letters launched the campaign and, alerted by their congressional delegation, the Alabama legislature quickly declared for White. The early momentum caused leaders in other states to consider him seriously as a possible nominee. Peyton encouraged his Tennessee political friends by assuring them that White's prospects were brighter with every new day.[28] Later the Van Buren campaign began to call the original gathering in Peyton's quarters a "caucus" and referred disparagingly to White as "the caucus candidate."[29]

While spreading the word for White, Peyton attended the public rally in Washington on January 8 that celebrated the anniversary of Jackson's victory at the Battle of New Orleans and his more recent retirement of the national debt. Balie toasted three great achievements by the president: "The battle of New Orleans, the veto of the United States Bank charter, and the payment of the national debt, proud epochs in American history."[30] On January 16 Peyton left the House long enough to appear before the U.S. Supreme Court where he was admitted as a practicing attorney and counselor.[31]

Although he had been a loyal Jacksonian, Peyton had not been able to bring himself to support Martin Van Buren, especially against a Tennessee candidate. He had supported Jackson as president and as a friend, but he was unwilling to accept the Old Hero's choice for the next president. During the contest then taking shape, Peyton had unhesitatingly supported White and moved ever deeper into the ranks of the opposition. As a Whig, he was on a collision course with Jackson.

By early February 1835, Congressman James K. Polk reported to a friend in Tennessee that Peyton, John Bell, John B. Forester, and David W. Dickinson of the Tennessee congressional delegation were associating almost exclusively with members of the opposition. He recognized that the White candidacy invited further defections that threatened to break up Jackson's Republican Party. He predicted that long before election time Henry Clay would become a candidate, but that did not come to pass.[32]

Resolutions introduced to secure the election of the president and vice president by the direct vote of the people were before the Congress, brought by friends of the administration. The question grew out of the presidential election of 1824 in which Jackson received a majority of the popular vote but lacked a majority of the electoral votes. Decided by the House, the election thwarted the will of the general electorate.

On February 25, Peyton spoke at length on the subject in the House. Calling on members to act during the present session and overcome the obstacles placed in their way, he reminded them that the resolutions had come with the president's recommendation. But times had changed since the resolutions were first introduced, he explained, and now the professed congressional proponents were opposed to them for partisan reasons. Their immediate plan, he said, was to assure their party had only one candidate for president so that he could gain the nomination without dividing the party. Then with the party's unity and its overpowering strength, he could win election handily. If successful, that strategy would make election by the House a moot issue.

Urging the House to take up the question, Peyton promised that he was ready to "cooperate with any and every gentleman in making these resolutions [as] perfect as possible." Seeking to avoid partisan debate, he focused on the matter at hand, which he said was supported by the president and by Senator White. But the votes were not there, and the resolutions failed to pass.[33]

For the remainder of the short session that ended on March 3, Peyton rarely engaged in debate. He was present, but he spent his time analyzing his role in the rising candidacy of Hugh Lawson White and reconciling that with his own reelection campaign the same year. He decided that he would be a candidate and would campaign for White as much as his own race would allow.[34]

Stopping on the way home in Granville County, North Carolina, his wife's home country, Balie accepted an invitation to speak at a public dinner given April 2 at Oxford to promote White for president. Because he had not publicly abandoned his hope of having White nominated by the Jackson party in preference to Van Buren, he devoted his speech to drawing parallels between the strength and integrity of Jackson and White. He portrayed White as more likely to follow in Jackson's footsteps than the candidate from New York.

Peyton began by establishing his relationship with the president:

> I claim to be one of the most humble, yet one of the most ardent of Gen. Jackson's friends. . . . I was early taught to revere him as one of the patriarchs who achieved our frontier independence; I was born, raised and now live within a few miles of the Hermitage. . . . He and my father toiled together in the same common cause, they went through the [Indian] wars side by side, and they were ever after friends. . . . My brothers were volunteers in his army.[35]

Insisting that all Jacksonians faced the choice of Van Buren or White, Peyton reviewed the latter's public service in detail. White's public life reflected integrity, courage, and vision. He had acquitted himself nobly as state legislator, judge, and U.S. senator. When Balie described the senator's carefully drawn but moderate views, he might have been describing his own.

> His political creed was formed in the school of Jefferson. He is a state's rights man; but does not go so far as some . . . in the South. He is in favor of a strict literal construction of the Constitution of the United States, confining the action of the Federal Government within the expressly delegated powers; at the same time he is in favor of Congress exercising for the general good all the powers which are clearly conferred, yet he does not go so far as some . . . in the North.[36]

Peyton's candidacy for reelection attracted the attention of the Jackson-Van Buren political forces in Tennessee. Hoping to forestall the congressman's return to Washington, editor Samuel H. Laughlin of the newly established Nashville *Union*, a Van Buren paper, believed that if Sumner County could persuade David Burford of Smith County to run, he could win. The widely discussed possibility that Balie and Jo. C. Guild would find themselves as opposing candidates for Congress became increasingly unlikely as the Van Buren leadership thought that Guild would serve them better as a surefire winner for legislature "than by running a doubtful race for Congress."[37]

A few weeks later Gen. William Hall, an avowed Van Buren supporter, declined to oppose Peyton. Although he had not been able to field a candidate by May 30, Laughlin tried to reassure his political friends that Balie could be beaten. "Nothing but absence of opposition," he said, "and having many personal friends, can reelect Peyton."[38] Earlier, Samuel Gwin (active Jacksonian, son of the Methodist preacher James Gwin, and brother of the first full-term U.S. senator from California, William McKendree Gwin) had predicted from Gallatin that Balie would be "opposed, and that successfully," but it did not happen.[39]

For some time, Peyton had known that there was no likely prospect that White or anyone else could stop the Van Buren steamroller. He continued to try to wrench Jackson and Jacksonians away from the old party crowd. Yet he understood well that the only hope to stop Van Buren was an opposition vote strong enough to deny election to any single candidate and thus throw it into the House of Representatives.

Five days before the Baltimore convention unanimously nominated Van Buren for president,[40] Peyton was at home in Sumner County, resigned to the outcome. It had been so predictable that opposition forces stayed away. No delegation of any persuasion from Tennessee appeared, and the chair permitted a Tennessean who was a chance visitor to cast the state's votes for Van Buren.[41]

Nonetheless, Peyton kept Van Buren in his political gun sights all the while. When Hardy M. Cryer, a thoroughbred breeder and friend of both Jackson and Peyton, questioned the latter's interpretation of Van Buren's stand on internal improvements, the congressman craftily recommended that he, "as one of Mr. Van Buren's supporters for the Presidency," should petition his candidate to make a full, clear, and public statement of his position on the issue. It was something Van Buren had avoided. Peyton said that he, too, earnestly wanted to know how the nominee stood on this and eagerly awaited his response to Cryer. Should Van Buren be elected, Peyton said that he would support him and his administration wholeheartedly if they followed the policies of Jackson's administration. He made it clear, however, that he would not tolerate the slightest deviation from what he called "the great cardinal points of national policy."[42]

During the summer, Balie not only campaigned throughout the three counties of his congressional district but also filled a heavy statewide schedule of appearances for White. The most intense scrutiny from the Van Buren people came later when he, George Washington Barrow, and Luke Lea accompanied White and John Bell into Maury County, home of James K. Polk. After their initial visit on October 1, the group returned on the nineteenth and twentieth. Disturbed that his district had been made "the theater of operations by White and Bell," Polk declined an invitation to appear with them to represent Van Buren's views on public policy.[43]

Greatly pleased by the administration party's inability to field a candidate against him, Peyton won reelection and a reassuring complimentary vote on August 5 and 6, 1835.[44] There is no report of the total votes cast because in the state election returns for the Sixth Congressional District, only the votes of Sumner (1,463) and Smith (2,067) are reported, with the Jackson County vote shown as "missing." Because Peyton was extremely popular in Jackson County, the complimentary vote for him there must have been as substantial as it was elsewhere.[45] After a few days at the farm, he resumed an active role in White's campaign for the presidency.

Balie was one of several speakers at the White "festival," touted as the biggest public event in Nashville since the visit of General Lafayette.[46] Staged in the Vauxhall Garden on October 8, the rally brought out a huge crowd. Reviewing the record of the last session of Congress, Peyton was contemptuous of the maneuvers of Van Buren partisans in that body. He denounced them and everyone else who attempted to injure the political character of White and Bell. His remarks prompted a toast by editor

George Washington Barrow: "*Balie Peyton*. Genius and eloquence have bestowed their gifts upon him. As a public man he has always been true to Jackson; no less so to White, and always for his country."[47]

When both houses of the Tennessee General Assembly passed resolutions on October 16 and 17 recommending Hugh Lawson White for president, Peyton was elated. Support for White in Tennessee was building impressively.[48] But it was far from unanimous. The presence in the Van Buren camp of two of his best turf friends, brother-in-law Thomas Barry and Jo. C. Guild, was a constant reminder that there were competent and able men on the other side.[49]

During the summer of 1835, Peyton met a Vicksburg, Mississippi, attorney with whom he later developed a cordial relationship as a fellow Whig. The chance meeting occurred when the Peyton family was visiting Louisville, Kentucky. After Balie had registered his wife and two children at the Galt House, Emily and Balie, ages five and three, were running up and down a corridor of the hotel. They suddenly stopped when a man stepped in front of them and pinned a diamond breast pin on the boy's shirt. Mrs. Peyton demanded that the children return it, but they came back to report that the gentleman insisted that the young man keep it as a "present."

Shortly afterward, young Balie's father received a scrawled note from the man who had made the gift. It was an invitation from Seargent S. Prentiss to visit him in his room. Presenting himself at once, Balie Sr. found Prentiss "surrounded by a party of friends." He introduced his guest, "apologizing at the same time for what he was pleased to term the liberty he had taken." His courtesy and hospitality impressed Peyton.[50]

The meeting had brought together two of the South's foremost orators. They discovered their mutual forensic talents in due time and subsequently enjoyed appearing together to address political audiences.

Earlier in the year, while Congress was yet in session, the January issue of the *American Turf Register and Sporting Magazine* published a list and description of the eleven breeding horses at Peyton's stud near Gallatin. The listing was a great advertisement for his thoroughbred breeding operation, but the March issue of the magazine was even more generous. It included a lithograph image of his stallion Sir Henry, a full brother of Monsieur Tonson, and seven pages of text about Sir Henry, including his pedigree and racing experience. All attributes of a fine stallion considered, the writer concluded that Henry had "no superior." This endorsement was encouraging to a man who depended primarily upon earnings from the stud and an intermittent law practice to support a family and a busy but still young political career.[51]

Although the *Turf Register* was trying to help in every way, Peyton was unable to make use of the publicity because he was away from the farm so much during his first term in Congress. Yet his five-year-old Anvil with trainer Bob Wooding in the saddle won impressively at Hartsville in the fall races of 1834. They defeated horses entered by local turf regulars, and a correspondent reported that during the race Anvil and his trainer "went where and when they pleased."[52] Hoping to give a boost to local thoroughbred breeding and to earn stud fees for his program, Peyton stood Rattler at Murfreesboro for the 1835 season.[53]

Near the end of May of the same year, one of Peyton's fillies had run strong but came in second in a sweepstakes race for three-year-olds over the Nashville Race Course. At the fall races he entered another of his fillies, but she ran poorly, being distanced in the final heat.[54]

The poor showing by Peyton's fillies may have been a harbinger of other disappointments ahead, but the congressman was thinking politics. He had gone to Washington two years ago as a strong Jacksonian, yet he had become a leader in the opposition and, as such, one of the founders of the Whig Party in Tennessee. As the end of the year approached, he was confident that he was returning to the capital a much stronger congressman, better for the district and better for the nation.

WHIG CONGRESSMAN
DECEMBER 7, 1835–MARCH 3, 1837

Before the opening session of the Twenty-Fourth Congress on December 7, 1835, Balie's Tennessee colleagues James K. Polk and Cave Johnson believed they were close to having affairs of honor with him. Friends had alerted Polk to what they regarded as Peyton's intention to lure him into a duel, a warning that may have headed off a dangerous confrontation. Johnson's friends hoped if there were irreconcilable problems between the two, Cave would let the challenge come from Peyton. Advising that a challenge from him "deserves no notice," Laughlin, the vitriolic pro-Van Buren editor, described Peyton as "a bully, blackguard, and maniac."[1] No confrontations materialized, however.

More provocative antagonist than patient diplomat, Balie had criticized Speaker Polk harshly during a speech at Knoxville while on his way to Washington during late November 1835.[2] Although he did not intend his remarks to elicit a challenge, verbal assault was part of Balie's plan to harass Polk as the next election for Speaker of the House neared. His efforts and those of other friends of Bell were not enough, however, and Polk won the chair. Afterward, Peyton, Wise, and Bell continued to pepper the Speaker with acerbic criticism, but Bell kept a more civil tongue than his fiery collaborators.[3]

Peyton first spoke in Congress on the issue of slavery on December 18, 1835,[4] in connection with the right of petition then under debate. A group of abolitionists had petitioned Congress to affirm their rights to circulate antislavery tracts in slaveholding states.[5]

Taking the side of the slave owners, Balie contended that the petition contained "matter improper for legislation." Further, routine procedures to accept or reject the petition had not been followed. If Congress were to accept for consideration any petition that might be offered, the flood of documents would cover the tables of the hall "like the locusts of Egypt," he predicted. The petition should be rejected because "the House had no power whatever to interfere with the question [of slavery]," he argued.[6]

As the debate progressed, Peyton said that permitting persons from outside to violate the laws of a state that prohibited the circulation of anti-slavery materials had the effect of exonerating the perpetrators because they had not been physically within the state when the violation occurred. A person who committed crime at a distance against a state was just as subject to that state's laws as if he had committed the acts within its boundaries. The "sacred and inalienable" rights of thinking, writing, and sending the results through the mail should not be connected to "the efforts of a few fanatics to disturb the harmony and peace of the country," he concluded in a stinging slap at the abolitionists.[7] A month later, when the House took up the question of the abolition of slavery in the District of Columbia, Peyton emphasized that the Constitution did not invest Congress with the power to abolish slavery in the district or anywhere else.[8]

Soon after his slavery speech of December 18, Balie left the capital to join his wife and two children in North Carolina for Christmas. He returned to Washington in time to answer waiting correspondence and to review his thoughts about the upcoming campaign.[9]

How to marshal the loose confederation of the opposition, most of whom were then referring to themselves as Whigs, for the presidential, gubernatorial, and congressional campaigns of 1836 was uppermost in Balie's thoughts on January 1 of that year. Van Buren and his Jacksonian cohorts, then called Democrats, would make "a desperate push for the state" and put their strongest candidates in the field, he wrote to a friend in Smith County. He and John Bell had already been contacted "on the subject of taking the field, if it is indispensably necessary, to save the state." Although he did not feel qualified for it, he feared he would be forced to run for governor. "But in times like these," he confided, "you know that we belong to our country and not to ourselves."

As for the House seat he occupied, Balie hoped that if he did not seek it again, William B. Campbell[10] would run for it against the Democratic nominee, probably William Trousdale[11] of Sumner County. He believed Trousdale's sponsors, "the Van Buren warriors," would find Campbell invincible.[12]

Balie wanted his friends to know he was greatly pleased that Tennesseans had taken up the presidential cause of native son Hugh Lawson White. Warning that the Van Buren camp believed the voters of Tennessee would push the legislature to rescind its resolutions nominating White and instruct its U.S. senators to vote to expunge the Senate censure of Jackson, Peyton begged legislator Robert L. Caruthers to stand by White. "I am asked every day whether the Legislature of Tennessee will falter," he said, "and my answer is no, no sooner than the fixed stars will leave their places in the heavens." To keep Van Buren's Tennessee partisans at bay, Peyton wanted the legislature to "give some strong demonstration in favor of White" before adjourning.[13] That they did by endorsing White for president by a vote of 60 to 12 in the House and 23 to 2 in the Senate.[14]

Regularly browbeaten by the administration's newspaper, the *Washington Globe*, Peyton and other friends of White agreed that in the latter part of January they would organize their own Washington journal. It would counter the daily pro-administration rantings of the *Globe* while offering a medium to inform and advocate for presidential candidate White. Balie was one of eight men who committed to furnish capital to start the paper in the event they were unable to interest a single proprietor in the undertaking. The underwriters included Tennessee Congressmen James Standifer, Samuel Bunch, John Bell, John B. Forester, Luke Lea, and former Tennessee Congressmen William M. Inge and David W. Dickinson.[15] Perhaps because all of these were Tennesseans, the newspaper lacked the necessary broad base of support; it seems to have died aborning.

Although his speeches were often tinged with sarcasm and at times were downright belligerent, Balie enjoyed comic relief and contributed his part of it. When federal aid to navigation on rivers was restricted by law to the portion of the stream that lay below a designated port of entry, he proposed resolutions to instruct the Commerce Committee to investigate the "expediency" of moving the port of entry then at Nashville up the Cumberland River to the mouth of Laurel Creek in Kentucky, near the river's headwaters. Living twenty-seven miles upstream from Nashville, Peyton explained that his object in offering the resolutions "was to extend the Constitution." As it then stood, he said, the Constitution "did not reach above Nashville." His "only wish was to live within the bounds of the Constitution," but at present he was living above it.

His true purposes were to qualify the stream for federal aid to navigation all the way up to the Laurel and to keep the river open to barge traffic from the coal mines of eastern Kentucky. His jocular approach was well received; the House resolved as he wished.[16] Although the administration ignored the resolutions, Peyton did not give up. When the appropriations bill was on the floor on June 29, he tried by amendment to establish the port of entry and obtain funds for improving navigation above Nashville. Satisfactory results eluded him, however.[17]

A bill to curtail "executive patronage," the president's constitutionally provided power of appointment, was brought to the House early in February by the administration with the intention of killing it, although it contained the principles upon which Jackson was swept into office in 1828. Restraining executive patronage had been a rallying cry for the opposition since Jackson's reelection in 1832, and

William Bowen Campbell

Peyton saw the present exercise as a diabolical political maneuver to bury the bill. It was indeed an effort to spare the administration's choice for president the restrictions it embodied.[18]

Peyton charged that such behavior indicated that the Jackson party was trying to abandon its earliest principles. Professing to support the measure but in reality sending it to its death was duplicitous behavior that he would not tolerate. The Jacksonian party to which he had belonged—"if that party still has an existence"—was fast "merging into *the* party," he charged. It was another example that he still held fast to Jacksonian principles and would speak no ill of the Old Hero while the party left them both behind.[19]

Balie insisted that he was ever a true Jackson man.

> Sir, I never saw the day when I would not for General Jackson, as a personal favor, meet any peril in a good cause, make any sacrifice save that of honor and independence; surrender any thing but those principles and that freedom which he would be the last man in the world to yield.[20]

Reflecting opposition views, Balie had contempt for Jackson's principal supporters in Congress and the cabinet. "His men . . . have not the force, the intellectual, the moral, or the executive qualities to carry on the business of this nation. They are a timid, skulking, sneaking lot," he wrote to his friend Campbell. Speaker Polk was still a target for Peyton's scorn: "Wise scared Polk nearly to death the other day. For a series of oppressions constantly followed up, Wise caught him by the arm out of the

House when it was not in session and with his finger in his eye almost, said, 'Sir, I pronounce you a petty tyrant. I mean it personal & protect dam[n] you, protect,' which he did almost in a trot."[21]

No duel ensued, but Peyton reported Jackson to be "foaming and raging like the sea" because Polk did not fight. "Does he mean to suffer that splinter of a Virginian to insult him in that manner? If he can't fight, he had better resign & go home," the president was quoted as saying.[22]

A primary concern of President Jackson with which Peyton concurred was amending the Constitution in a way that in most circumstances would preclude election of the president by the House of Representatives. The question was before a select committee of the House on February 15, 1836, and Balie proposed by resolution a series of constitutional amendments to solve it. He argued that the office of president should be won by whomever received the majority of the votes cast in an August election. In the event there was no majority, another election would be called in December, and if there was no majority a second time, the election would devolve upon the Congress, as was the existing constitutional provision.

He included other changes that affected the presidency. The president and vice president would hold six-year terms, and the president could not again hold that office. Opposed to the practice of rewarding congressmen by presidential appointment to cabinet or other office, Peyton had a plan to stop it dead in its tracks:

> No Senator or Representative shall, during the time for which he was elected, and the continuance in office of a President in whose term of service he shall have acted, be appointed to any office or employment, or hold or make any contract with or under the authority of the United States.[23]

Peyton offered a similar provision to block trading a vote for an appointment when the House was voting to elect the president. But his colleagues were not ready, and few were surprised when the House voted quickly to lay the proposals on the table, where they died.[24]

After suffering nearly three weeks from "a most violent attack produced by cold, terminating in pleurisy of the head," Balie was out of his sickbed on March 9. He returned to the House to face "the damnable shackles of the party" that made opposition to Van Buren so difficult. In the House the opposition had been unable "to get up any great question of general interest" because Speaker Polk had deftly managed to deny opposition leader John Bell opportunities to speak.[25]

"Bell has been more outrageously oppressed than any Representative of a free people ever was before," Peyton wrote to

Robert L. Caruthers on April 16. "God Almighty never intended that such a man as John Bell and such constituents as sustain him, should be trodden under foot in such a cause . . . now . . . you must be a Van Buren man or you are a dog and a traitor."[26]

Disappointed because he had been unable to affect the course of national policy and concerned by ongoing financial problems on his farm in Tennessee, Peyton was ready by the spring of 1836 to seek a candidate to succeed him in the next election. Like the president, he wanted to pick his successor, and he was certain of his choice: William B. Campbell. Reflecting on life in the Congress, he observed to Campbell, "This is a good schooling, but will not do as a business. You never will lament the time you spent if it is well invested as any man of your habits would do, & you can leave it when you will." He was convinced there would be no effective opposition to Campbell, whom he believed could clinch victory by campaigning for aid to navigation on the upper Cumberland River, the main waterway in each county of the district.[27]

Balie's interest in forgoing a third term in the Congress heightened with the birth of his second son, John Bell Peyton, named for his closest political ally, John Bell. The baby was born February 14, 1836, in his grandparents' home in North Carolina where his sister, brother, and mother were visiting while Balie was in Washington.[28] Celebrating the baby's healthy arrival, he asked Campbell about the name, wryly suggesting it might be seen as having political overtones. "Is that treason or is it not?" And answering himself he said, "I claim it as one of my revered rights to call my boy what I please. Is that nullification, or only states rights?"[29] He asked his brother Ran, "What will our Van Buren kin . . . say to that? An attack on General Jackson?"[30]

The introduction of party politics into a contested election for Congress for the Twelfth District of North Carolina between James Graham and David Newland raised Balie's ire[31] to the boiling point and inspired a marvelous oratorical display on March 26. As the House continued in session past midnight, Peyton's speech did not begin until 1:30 A.M. He was called to order several times both by the chair and by the House.[32] Enthralled by the speech, a correspondent of the Richmond (VA) *Whig* reported to his editor:

> For fifteen minutes he held the collar men themselves chained as by a spell, with tears involuntarily wrung from their iron-bound hearts, and seared eyelids. They forgot themselves in the fervor of his unsurpassed eloquence. . . . He broke the power of [Van Buren] the magician.[33]

Newland's attempt to overturn the election of Graham succeeded, but he failed to gain the seat for himself due in no small part to Peyton's

Hugh Lawson White

eloquence. The House set aside the North Carolina election and notified the governor of the state of the vacancy.[34]

Balie had cooled enough by March 29 to take a relatively light-hearted view of certain New York land speculators who sought a charter to lay out a city across the Potomac within the District of Columbia. Called Jackson City, the speculation reminded Peyton of a Georgian's reply to a question about the produc-tivity of his newly purchased land in West Tennessee. "It produced sixty bushels of frogs to the acre, and a sufficiency of alligators to fence in the premises," he responded. Peyton said that, not content with appropriating to their own use the military fame of Andrew Jackson, absentee owners were also "disposed to connect it with the bullfrog speculation" to enhance the value of their property. He opposed the use of the presi-dent's name in this and other such cases, but Jackson did not object. Old Hickory had laid the cornerstone for the city on January 11.[35]

Peyton backed Henry Wise as he tried artfully to win House support for an inquiry into the procedures surrounding the deposit of federal monies in selected banks and especially to investigate the role of Reuben M. Whitney[36] in controlling placement of the deposits. On April 4 both tried to bring the issue to debate, but administration backers blocked their every approach.[37] Peyton failed again on April 6 as the House voted down his proposal to make a bill regulating the deposits of federal money the special order of the day on a certain day in May.[38] It was a matter that involved the safety of "the whole treasure of the nation," he warned unavailingly.[39]

By early spring Tennesseans were rallying to the cause of Hugh L. White, and Balie was proud of his home state. "Thank God, while other states have fallen, she is still erect, *standing* in the *pass*, defending the *Constitution* and the *liberties* of the people," he wrote. "She is the *Sparta* of the *Republic*."[40]

The high-spirited Tennessean soon had an opportunity to stand at the pass himself. The administration's bill asking the secretary of the Treasury to communicate to the House the procedures followed in selecting banks for the deposit of "the public money of the United

States" was brought up for consideration on April 19. Henry Wise moved to amend it by changing it from a call for information to a call for an investigation of the whole matter of federal deposits by a select committee of the House with special attention to any part played by Reuben M. Whitney. Ready to go for the Treasury's jugular, Peyton followed Wise with a strong, taunting speech.

Attacking the bill as it existed before the amendments were proposed, Peyton said that it inadequately addressed the vital question of the integrity of "public functionaries" and the safety of the public "treasure." Wise was seeking to learn about Whitney's commissions and his relationships with the deposit banks, information that should be before the country, Peyton explained. Resistance by the administration to a congressional investigation was ridiculous because the party in power would, he correctly predicted, appoint the committee of inquiry and would thus certainly surround Whitney with sympathetic friends.[41]

The majority bill sponsored by Representative George Coke Dromgoole of Virginia applied to the Treasury Department "to furnish, at their discretion, upon honor, and not upon oath, such evidences of guilt as they may have upon record. . . . Does any gentleman suppose that, if there be fraud or corruption, the evidences of it will be found among the archives of the department?" Peyton asked. He and Wise wanted a congressional committee invested with power to subpoena persons and papers and examine persons under oath.[42]

Deposit banks were so clearly at Whitney's mercy that, "like a privateer," he could demand to be paid for depositing federal money with them and the sums in prospect were of such size that few banks could turn their backs on them. Everyone should know that by using his power, Whitney could not only affect "the commerce and currency of the country," but could also bring irresistible political pressure to bear upon men and communities. Peyton deeply resented those who argued that to question Whitney's integrity was to attack President Jackson.[43]

When Dromgoole responded by accusing Peyton of blocking consideration of a bill to regulate the deposits, the Tennessean replied that he had almost daily sought to win House approval to fix a date certain to take up the bill, only to have the party majority reject his effort. Dromgoole "honestly and innocently believes that I, and not he and his friends, have been trying to thwart the measure," Peyton noted in disbelief.

> This is . . . a plain case, as much so as that of the Indian. His companion had been shot, climbing a tree, by a white man. They had an investigation of the matter, and the Indian asked the white man "why he shot his friend." "I took him for a bear," was the reply. Says the Indian with a stern, inquiring look, "White man shoot an Indian up a tree, with red leggins on, for a bear?" "Yes." "Well, I'm done."

Echoing "I'm done," Peyton then yielded the floor. He had found Dromgoole's perspective incredible.[44]

Ever a cross between southerner and westerner, Peyton rose on May 7 to answer John Quincy Adams of Massachusetts when the New Englander declared that the administration's concern about Texas was only a front to conceal its plan to conquer the region and reestablish the practice of slavery that had been abolished by Mexico. Hearing Adams "with no less astonishment than deep mortification," Peyton thought it strange that his colleague had "introduced the subject of slavery into the discussion" of defense for "the helpless women and children of the Texan frontier." He suggested that Adams, who lived far from the south-western frontier, did not understand the "vivid feeling of Southern and Western men" that stemmed from their periodic confrontation with "hostile savages."[45]

During House consideration of the fortification bill in May, Peyton wrote to William B. Campbell confiding that he had learned that the "unassuming, unlettered mechanic" J. L. McKoin of Sumner County had defeated Jo. C. Guild in the militia election for brigadier general. It was a victory for the opposition, and Balie was happy to see Guild, his old compatriot, lose to a Whig.[46]

With politics on his mind, Peyton reviewed the letter that Hardy M. Cryer had received from Van Buren in response to an inquiry Balie had suggested twelve months prior. Not satisfied with the letter, he wrote to the vice president on May 19, 1836, for a direct answer to the question: "Whether you did or did not approve of the President's veto of the bill for the improvement of the Wabash River, dated December 6, 1832?" The Wabash provision was part of the broader act for "the improvement of certain harbors, and the navigation of certain rivers," and Peyton thought he had Van Buren trapped. If the vice president approved of the veto, Peyton could depict him as being against internal improve-ments. If he disapproved of the veto, he risked his special protected standing with the president. But Van Buren chose to avoid a direct answer and opened himself to charges of being spineless in matters involving Andrew Jackson.[47]

As the first session of the Twenty-Fourth Congress was nearing its end, Peyton actively participated in discussion of the frauds perpetrated by land speculators in acquiring and selling tracts owned by the Creek and Choctaw before they removed west of the Mississippi. Favoring investigation by a select committee of the House, Balie doubted the value of an inquiry conducted by the executive branch.[48]

Averring that investigating committees of the House had proved "utterly impotent" historically, Congressman Abijah Mann of New York said that about all the House could do was to call the president's attention to the possibility of fraudulent dealings in the Creek matter and ask him to make an inquiry. Peyton objected that Mann had advanced "a new doctrine that this House was powerless for the purpose of inquiring into public frauds and abuses." It had not backed away from such responsibility when the U.S. Bank and the president were at odds, he said.[49]

After several exchanges on the floor, Peyton charged that the Democratic Van Buren party had introduced party politics into the fraud investigation debate. But they, in turn, blamed Peyton "for first blowing the horn of party." The alleged horn blower seethed.[50]

Van Buren's allies wanted to forestall congressional inquiry, and Speaker Polk obliged by casting the tie-breaking vote that stopped the investigation. Sensing mischief afoot, Peyton explained, "We say . . . there are rogues in the woods. The gentleman [Abijah Mann] replies, 'Well, they are all friends, and it is a party question. Hands off; don't touch them.'"[51]

Holding forth at length, the Tennessee congressman accused the administration's House leadership of conducting public business in secrecy. The leaders fulfilled the president's requests for emergency national security funds by juggling the budget instead of having the commander in chief state the need openly so that Congress could support him, reflecting the unity of the country at a time of danger. Peyton claimed that the majority were beginning to govern in secrecy.[52]

Alluding to the secrecy-obsessed behavior of certain persons in the administration, the congressman indicted the vice president for taking "a deep, personal interest in one of these very transactions, under the dark cover of midnight." He accused the majority party of perpetrating secret deeds in the name of the president, "a man whom they have so many reasons to love and trust, a man who has no secrets, but is open and frank as day in all that he does."[53]

Three days later Congress adjourned, and Peyton turned southward to Tennessee. Eager to be at home for the presidential election campaign, he declined an invitation to a dinner given for Congressman Wise by the citizens of Accomack County, Virginia, on July 14. Assuring his hosts that there lived not a man in whose honor he would "with more pleasure break bread and take wine, than Henry A. Wise," Balie offered a personal testimonial: "I have known him long and intimately . . . he has been the same bold, frank, honest, talented patriot and friend in every situation of life."[54]

In his letter to the Virginians, Peyton again seized the opportunity to distinguish between the president and his administration. Although the administration was "most infamously corrupt in many of its departments," he emphasized that he believed the president to be "a pure man, and an incorruptible patriot." Jackson's only fault was his loyalty to others that translated into an inability to recognize their weaknesses and their cunning. "He is surrounded by a mercenary corps, who, to advance their own selfish views, hesitate not to influence and exasperate his feelings by foul calumnies against his most sincere and disinterested friends."[55]

He challenged the voters of Virginia to hold the line against Van Buren. Assuring them that Tennessee continued to stand tall in defense of "the ballot box, the Constitution and liberties of the people," he urged them to join forces with others in the South and the West to block the New Yorker. It was time to end "these days of venality, hypocrisy and corruption," he said.[56]

At home again, Peyton found that his brother Robert Holmes Peyton had departed on June 25 with the Second Regiment, First Brigade, Tennessee Mounted Militia for service in the Seminole War. Robert Holmes had volunteered for six months as a private in Capt. Jo. C. Guild's company, most of whom were from the Gallatin area.[57]

Even at home the demands of politics were unrelenting. Traveling throughout the midstate to fill speaking engagements, Peyton rarely scheduled time for the farm and his valuable stud of horses. On one occasion, however, more than one thousand Smith County friends held a public dinner and rally for him at Carthage on Saturday, August 20; they had come to hear him speak, and they were not disappointed.

> The address of Mr. Peyton was characteristic. How he melted his audi-ence into tears—then with inimitable ridicule he convulsed them with laughter, and anon, he would elicit shouts of indignation at the outrage attempted on the freedom of elections, after stating that the President of the United States, the head of a hundred thousand officeholders, was in the field, openly electioneering for Mr. Van Buren, he solemnly put the question to them, whether they would tamely surrender the elective franchise at the footstool of Executive power? A thousand voices responded, "Never! Never. . . . We will die first!"[58]

The crowd toasted Peyton repeatedly. A prepared toast saw him as "true to the Constitution and to his constituents; fraud and corruption in high places have not escaped his rebuke. He is the bold and talented advocate of our institutions in their purity. His constituents are proud to support and cheer him onward in his patriotic course." Impromptu toasts followed. J. H. Ray shouted, "Balie Peyton loves General Jackson, but he loves his country more." William Harvey wanted him reelected to Congress, and Rowland W. Newby presented him as "one of the brightest political ornaments of Tennessee—a firm and independent statesman." Hardy Boaz said, "He's all horse." To James H. Vaughan, Balie had "shown himself worthy his station, and manifestly the true and genuine supporter of the republican principles of Thomas Jefferson."[59]

Those who offered toasts with tributes to White or Bell (or both) often included Peyton. Peyton and Bell were "the political stars of the West; Peyton was "one of the brightest stars on the White flag." He was linked with Congressman Bell, Henry A. Wise of Virginia, and Francis W. Pickens of South Carolina; they were not "anarchists" as the *Washington Globe* had charged, but "patriots without fear and above reproach, scourging the corrupt minions of the party." With Bell and Wise, he was one of a "triumvirate of noble spirits, who have manfully battled for freedom of thought and independence of action, in defiance of party opposition and executive dictation."[60]

Unable to attend the Carthage event, John Bell wrote a strong endorsement of his friend to the committee on arrangements. He had seen Peyton in action during three important sessions of Congress. Bell wrote:

> I have witnessed not only repeated displays of wit and eloquence, but a devotion to principle, and a judgment so correct and prompt as never to fail him on the most unexpected and important emergencies. . . . Such rare qualities are of the highest value . . . to the country generally.[61]

Balie could not attend a public dinner given for White on August 31 at Knoxville, but sent his regrets in a long letter that included forthright criticisms of President Jackson. He repeated the charges he had made during his Carthage speech of August 20.[62]

The Bell dinner in Nashville on September 4 attracted fifteen hundred persons but made no converts for candidate White, supporters of Van Buren claimed. The political oratory, characterized by "slanders and abuse" especially from Peyton, turned some White men away from their candidate, the pro-Van Buren editor Samuel H. Laughlin wrote to James K. Polk:

> Peyton abused everybody without stint, in the most rude and vulgar terms. . . . Of Mr. Grundy he said he would as soon expect to find female virtue in a whorehouse . . . as to find political virtue in him. He abused Judge [George W.] Campbell rudely and vulgarly, and assailed you in terms of a blackguard and bully.[63]

Peyton entertained a crowd of five thousand at Lebanon, Tennessee, gathered on September 6 to honor John Bell. Following the honoree's speech of three and one-half hours, Peyton spoke with his "peculiar charm" to the pleasure of his nearly exhausted listeners.[64] One of those present reported that Balie told "some of the best anecdotes and bits of such you ever heard" and was "so interrupted by outbursts of applause and laughter that he was compelled frequently to stop until it was over."[65]

Jackson County friends of Peyton held a public dinner for him at Gainesboro on September 17, and the congressman, in response, "went beyond his accustomed felicitous efforts—soft as the thistle's downy plume, yet piercing as its thorn." The cheers of the audience filled the valley and "re-echoed from the mountains."[66]

Jackson County was Peyton country, and for those who had any doubt about his views of state and national politics, he had disclosed them at length in a letter accepting the invitation to Gainesboro. Stringently objecting to Jackson's determination to name his own successor, Peyton said the issue in the presidential election was power and where it resided. "Is the *sovereign* power in the *people* of this country, or is it in the high officers of the government? This is the true issue." A crisis exists, he said, "the ballot box is assailed; the citadel of your liberty is in danger."[67]

Peyton and Bell next journeyed to James K. Polk's native Maury County "right under the nose of Polk" where they upheld White of Tennessee against Jackson's New Yorker. Polk sensibly declined to meet with them to debate the issues because it was virtually impossible to overcome the emotion that the White speakers stirred in their audiences.[68]

Peyton's entertaining power as a political speaker became known throughout the state. As he canvassed for White, his upcoming appearance at Somerville in West Tennessee was hailed by the Memphis *Enquirer*, September 15, 1836. The editor advised his readers to make the trip to Somerville and "listen to the pungent wit, scorching sarcasm, irresistible humor, and powerful pathos of Balie Peyton."[69]

During the summer of 1836, Peyton did not escape barbs aimed by the president during his journey to and from the Hermitage. Jackson repeatedly assailed him for his stand on the appropriations bill for the Cherokee treaty, even though Peyton's friends reminded the Old Hero that Peyton had voted and spoken in favor of the measure. In Sumner County, Jackson told neighbors at Mrs. Saunders' that John Bell, Peyton's colleague, told twenty lies in one speech and that Peyton was a bigger liar than Bell. But charges and countercharges aside, the decision rested with those who would cast their ballots on Election Day.[70]

On November 8, 1836, the voters throughout the country[71] elected Martin Van Buren president of the United States. He received 761,549 votes; William Henry Harrison received 549,567; Hugh Lawson White 145,396; and Daniel Webster 41,287.[72] In Tennessee the results were quite different, however. Peyton and Bell were jubilant as White carried the state over Van Buren by a vote of 36,012 to 26,185.[73] Nationwide the opposition party with its multiple candidates failed to throw the election into the House. In Tennessee they had defeated the handpicked successor to the greatest Tennessean of them all, President Andrew Jackson, and the year before had elected one of their own, Newton Cannon, governor of the state. The twin election victories certified the strength of the new Whig Party in the Volunteer State.[74]

After the election, Jackson said that "nothing but falsehoods appear to be the weapons of our modern new born White Whigs of Tennessee," and that they, specifically including Peyton, "appear to have abandoned the truth . . . and do not wish to be held accountable." He deemed it his postpresidential responsibility to expose their falsehoods to "the moral part and truth-loving portion of the citizens of Tennessee."[75]

At the beginning of the second session of the Twenty-Fourth Congress,[76] the administration, though politically victorious, was still in a defensive posture vis-à-vis opposition in the House. Blocking a congressional investigation of alleged fraud in certain departments of government, the executive branch upheld the character of its cabinet members and, above all, invoked the integrity of the president.

When the Congress received President Jackson's annual message on December 15, 1836, Peyton assailed the paragraph that endorsed "the ability and integrity" with which the various departments had been conducted. The president said it had been his aim "to enforce in all of them a vigilant and faithful discharge of the public business," and he believed that there was "no just cause of complaint . . . at the manner in which they have fulfilled the objects of their creation."[77]

Balie denied the president wrote that paragraph and charged that high-level officials had "fraudulently smuggled it into his message to evade scrutiny into their conduct." They had taken advantage of Jackson's poor health and his preoccupation with living long enough to return to his beloved Hermitage in the spring. "His thoughts were with his heart, 'and that was far away,' dwelling upon other and . . . holier meditations than writing eulogies upon public functionaries, whose conduct he was in no situation to examine," Peyton declared.[78]

"Now . . . I wish . . . to strip the Jackson mantle off these gentlemen, and let them stand up for themselves," he said. "They have abused their trust and abused the confidence of the President. . . . They shrink from responsibility [and] hold up General Jackson's character as their shield."[79]

Representative Wise had offered the only practical approach to discovering the truth about allegations of official misconduct, and Peyton endorsed it wholeheartedly. It was an investigation by a select committee of the House with the power to subpoena persons and papers. Balie compared an investigation of this kind with the kangaroo court style of trial and acquittal of Whitney staged by President Jackson at Jonesborough, Tennessee, in July 1836. Whitney answered predetermined questions that skillfully avoided the "true issues which involve his guilt or innocence," and sitting as judge, President Jackson pronounced him innocent. The prosecuting attorney, one John Kennedy, prosecuted "so handsomely" that he was rewarded with a federal appointment.[80]

Peyton's speech of December 15 attracted national attention. A Washington correspondent of the Baltimore *Patriot* thought it especially noteworthy.

> Short as it was, it was in point of sarcasm, energy, and nature's genuine eloquence, the best thing Peyton ever did except perhaps his speech during the famous all night sitting on the North Carolina contested election case at the last session. . . .

> Of that rising young man's oratory, emotion is the great characteristic. . . . The flash of passion is on his cheek—the beam of genuine feeling brightens his eye—the strokes of emphasis by arm and hand are strong and hearty—the sounds of his voice are the true notes of sensibility.[81]

The New York *Courier and Enquirer* praised both the speech and the speechmaker. When, during debate, Louisiana Congressman Eleazar W. Ripley charged Tennesseans with ingratitude toward General Jackson, Peyton "rose and burst forth in a torrent of eloquence rarely, very rarely, heard on that floor."

> Ingratitude of the Tennesseans! When General Jackson crossed the mountains with his knapsack on his back, and his rifle in his hand, did not the people of Tennessee take him to their bosom? Trace his career to fame, and you will behold every field of his glory, covered with the mouldering bones of Tennesseans.[82]

Peyton's speech was mocked by the editor of the Van Buren newspaper in Nashville, who said that Peyton was a clown who questioned the honor of General Jackson. The people of Tennessee would not "suffer the great and venerable man whom they have always delighted to honor . . . to be thus traduced with impunity by a mere boy of yesterday."[83]

No matter how hostile the criticism or how angry the debate, the American public could look forward to hearing from Peyton for a long time to come. At the moment, however, the personal sacrifices required by life as an elected official were weighing heavily upon him.

Evaluating his political future, Peyton believed he could not run for Congress more than once more, "if that." He expected that either Bell or himself would be pressured to run for governor to arouse enough opposition to the Van Buren forces to secure Grundy's defeat for reelection to the U.S. Senate. Confiding to William B. Campbell that he did not feel himself qualified to be governor, Peyton declared that he would not stand by and see the state lost to Van Buren "without a vigorous effort in any way that may become necessary." He much preferred to retire from public life, "at least for several years," unless he was required to sacrifice his "private interests . . . [and] decided inclination."[84]

Balie needed to attend to the farm and his horse business that he had neglected at great personal expense. As a congressman he had discovered that political demands preempted his days at home and left him little time to devote to business. Looking ahead, he predicted the disintegration of Van Buren's party and admitted he would like to be in Congress when it occurred. "I would like it," he wrote to Campbell, "but it will be out of the question for me. No young man without [a] fortune, and who has three children, should remain in Congress *more than four years.*" He begged Campbell to try it that long.[85]

Peyton was not the only public servant who suffered financially because his office usurped the time that he needed to earn additional livelihood. He did not have a legacy of the size left to James K. Polk by his father and grandfather, but even that did not last forever as the future president had exhausted it by 1842. Less than a year before he was elected president, Polk had trouble raising fifty dollars. Cave Johnson was struggling to make ends meet. He hoped the district would not nominate him for reelection to Congress in 1843 because he could not support a wife and three children on his government paycheck in a job that so often kept him away from home.[86]

Balie would have delighted in hosting the visit of John S. Skinner, founder and editor of the *American Turf Register*,[87] to Station Camp Creek in the spring of 1836, but Congress was in session and he could only entrust the chore to his brother Ran. Having received from Skinner "under his own roof, at his own board all the courtesy and kindness which a generous and hospitable man could bestow," Peyton urged Ran to serve him in any way that he could. "You will find him a high-minded and accomplished gentleman. No man [in Washington, D.C.] is more generally known or more universally beloved than Mr. Skinner."[88] Skinner once had said of Balie, "He is in his own spirit and character exemplary of what is best and most excellent in men."[89]

Later Ran took some of his horses to the spring races at Natchez where he picked up a forfeit of one thousand dollars in a match race in which his entry was Miss Blevins. While in Natchez, he and William J. Minor of that city made a match for five thousand dollars per side to race at Nashville in the fall of 1838. Ran nominated a Bertrand colt out of an Eclipse mare; Minor named Linnett's Own Sister, by Leviathan, dam by Marshal Ney, then a year old.[90]

The *American Turf Register* in its June issue noted that a two-year-old chestnut colt by Leviathan, dam by Archy, bred by Balie Peyton at the Station Camp Creek stud, had been sold for two thousand dollars. It was an indication that Peyton was reducing the "overstocked" condition at his stud, a determination he had announced in February in the same magazine.[91] As much as he wanted to race his thoroughbreds, he had not been able to prepare any of them for competition. At the Gallatin races on September 13, 1836, Balie paid forfeit for his entry, the chestnut colt Tom Benton, in a sweepstakes for three-year-olds.[92]

As the time approached for him to leave his horses and return to Washington, Balie wondered what the next few months held in store. What should he expect from the Van Buren men in Congress after his own lively participation in White's bid for the presidency? What would be his role in the Treasury hearings? Would he stand for reelection? Peyton returned to the capital to face the political uncertainty and changes that awaited him.

CHAPTER 4

TEMPEST IN THE HOUSE
1837

The first three months of 1837, Peyton's last in the U.S. House of Representatives, were some of his stormiest. At the center of the tempest was the proposed congressional investigation of one Reuben M. Whitney and his relationship with the Treasury Department. It appeared to offer a compelling opportunity to display the southern Whigs' "revulsion against corrupt party influences" and to raise questions about the administration's handling of public monies.[1]

On January 3, Congressman James Garland of Virginia presented resolutions asking the secretary of the Treasury to communicate to the House the status of public deposits in the several deposit banks for the past four years. Members offered amendments seeking to identify the Treasury Department's "agent or attorney" who corresponded or communicated with the banks in order to determine his compensation and by whom it was paid.

Sensing that the administration was repeating earlier failed efforts by Congressman George C. Dromgoole to whitewash the activities of the department by asking it to report on itself, Peyton proposed an amendment to refer the matter to a select committee, "with power to send for persons and papers." The secretary of the Treasury should be brought before the committee to answer questions that could then be properly asked of him. "Any other course," he said, would be "trifling with the dignity" of the Congress.[2]

The main question was about Whitney, Peyton continued. Was he a private citizen and the agent of the banks, or was he employed by the Treasury? If he was not on the Treasury payroll, why was his name in letters "as large as the sign of a livery stable" prominently posted within the front door of the department? If he was a private citizen, "What is he doing with a sign?"[3]

Peyton acknowledged that Whitney represented himself as being the agent of "some of the most respectable deposit banks," and manager of their interests in general. But it was his respectability and not that of the banks that was in question. To Peyton, Whitney was "a great traitor, a great liar and a great rogue." He had admitted being a traitor to his country during the War of 1812, a House committee had convicted him of perjury in 1832, and he had since been going about as "a sort of general, federal rogue, employed by a . . . [group of banks] to steal by the year for them," Peyton charged. Whitney had further enjoyed the protection of the secretary of the Treasury, "his friend, his daily associate, his bosom crony," who boldly denied that Reuben had any connection with the department.[4]

It was clear to Peyton that the agency which Whitney claimed, plus his intimate relationship with the secretary, made it possible for him to exercise significant control over the flow of deposits. His behavior indicated that banks failing to retain him as their agent fared poorly in terms of public deposits. As an agent for the banks instead of an employee of the Treasury, he was not required to give an accounting of the deposits in the banks he represented, and he was free to conduct his agency virtually at will. Peyton asked, "Is it not granting him a letter of marque and reprisal upon the banks, which he may plunder at pleasure?"[5]

Adding to a growing suspicion of Whitney's activities were allegations that he had given advance information to speculators regarding Jackson's specie circular of July 11, 1836, and that he had been an active participant in the resulting speculations. Nevertheless, as a resigned director of the national bank, he had earned the president's loyalty by sharing his knowledge of that institution's inner workings with him during the bank fight.[6]

Back in Tennessee, editor S. H. Laughlin of the Nashville *Union* busied himself trying to identify candidates who could help the Democrats return to power in the state. He cultivated the animosity toward Balie Peyton that his camp had developed during Van Buren's unsuccessful campaign in Tennessee. Peyton had been White's street fighter there, and the Democrats attempted to discredit him with accusations of all sorts. Their goal: replace him in Congress with one of their own in the election of 1837. Their admitted problem: finding a candidate who could beat him.[7]

On January 11, President Jackson reported to Andrew Jackson Donelson, then in Nashville, that Peyton and Wise were repeating in the current House session "all the electioneering speeches of Judge White and themselves." He believed there was no way to "deal with such scamps . . . but by holding them up to the people in their true colors."[8]

As the Van Buren men cast about for a candidate to run against Peyton, they hoped for an "anti" vote, a determination by the voters that they no longer wanted the incumbent. Chiding Balie for turning against Jackson, the Nashville *Union* editor confidently predicted: "The people of . . . Mr. Peyton's district will no longer submit to misrepresentation. They will choose men who will truly represent their feelings."[9]

Peyton never missed a chance to make a case against the Van Buren succession, especially when he could invoke Whig fear of unrestrained executive power. Invited to participate in a Whig rally and consolidation meeting in New York City, he sent his regrets because of the press of business before the Congress, but encouraged his fellow Whigs to look ahead to the next election.

> What coward will fly from the standard of liberty, because of one reverse? Shall we, can we, *dare* we give up our principles? Shall we ratify the *appointment* of the *successor*, and *anoint* him, too, as our Legislative Ruler? No, sir, no! . . . For what do we contend? The right of suffrage! The freedom of elections! The preservation of sovereign power in the hands of the people.[10]

On January 4, when the House appointed the select committee of nine members that Balie sought to investigate Whitney and the Treasury, he and Wise received appointment to two of the three seats reserved for the minority party. There was little chance that they could materially influence the final committee report, but they were prepared to exploit every opportunity that might arise.[11]

Representative James Garland, a Democrat of Virginia, was chairman of the committee, and he and his confreres chose Balie to prepare the written interrogatories to which Whitney would make written answers. Appearing before the committee on January 12, 13, 14, and 25, Whitney declined to respond to certain questions that he said were inquisitorial or personal rather than of a public character.[12] On January 25, about to engage in one of the most acrimonious political confrontations of his young public life, Peyton asked if, while secretary of the Treasury, R. B. Taney had encouraged Whitney's application for the agency he later obtained, or "did he positively refuse to receive or countenance you in that capacity?" Whitney wrote his answer and reviewed it briefly before handing it to the committee chair for reading aloud. He refused to answer, he wrote, because Peyton had asserted positively and publicly that Taney had not received him or countenanced him in his interest for the agency. As an accused party, Whitney continued, he was not a proper witness. "I think, in justice, that the individual who has made the allegations should be called to produce his proof."[13]

The response was a return to the contents of a card Whitney had published in the *Globe* on January 5 that challenged Peyton to prove Taney would not recommend him as an agent for the deposit banks.[14] First claiming that Wise, Peyton's "Siamese companion," had lied about him on the floor of the House, Whitney's card challenged Peyton to "adduce a single particle of proof" to sustain the allegation about Taney. Whitney also asserted that if Wise made the statement without proof, he was a calumniator and a liar. Both Peyton and Wise made their accusations "while shielded by constitutional privilege," he said.[15]

Why had Balie allowed the "card" to go unanswered? He probably understood that this adversary was but a puppet, "put forward to exasperate him into an unseemly exhibition of violence, and that he restrained himself until the man's insolence culminated in a face-to-face insult."[16]

When its unanswered challenge appeared as justification for Whitney to decline answering a committee interrogatory, Balie could ignore it no longer. His face was flushed with anger when he jumped to his feet and addressed Garland: "Mr. Chairman, I wish you to distinctly inform the witness that he is not to insult me here!" Standing between Whitney and Peyton, Wise[17] spoke up, "Mr. Chairman, the *d——d* insolence of this witness is insufferable, and has been borne long enough."

In a rage, Peyton stood before Whitney.

> You talk about my shielding myself behind my constitutional privileges to protect me from your insults in my presence, and, you d——d thief and robber, if you dare to insult me here or elsewhere, to my face, I will put you to death on the spot.[18]

No sooner had the chairman restored order than Whitney rose and began to ask for the protection of the committee. Angrily leaving his chair, Peyton called him a "d——d scoundrel" and demanded that he restrict himself to answering the interrogatories in writing. Standing just to the rear of Peyton, Wise saw Whitney put his right hand into his pants pocket.

> I expected him to draw a deadly weapon on my friend. . . . If he had drawn his . . . weapon . . . , it should never have done its execution. I considered my friend in imminent danger and stood prepared to . . . prevent his life from being taken by a villain.[19]

Seeing Whitney's threatening position, Peyton thrust his hand in his bosom, but Wise clasped the lapels of his excited colleague's coat. After the Virginian cautioned that the witness's blood "was not worth spilling" and that he was not worthy of notice, Peyton countered that he would notice "any d———d dog" who insulted him face-to-face. Whitney had been staring at him contemptuously throughout the questioning, and Wise said he had framed defiant glances as if he were "anxious to insult us by his looks."[20]

After the chairman sent Whitney from the room, Peyton apologized to the committee for "having been transported by such provocation to lose the momentary command" of his temper. The committee then unanimously adopted resolutions rejecting Whitney's response since it did not reply to the question and was disrespectful to a committee member. When the chair recalled the witness and advised him of the committee's action, he apologized and the hearing resumed. With Peyton posing the questions in writing and Whitney answering in that manner, the committee received its answer to the last of its interrogatories late the next day, January 26.[21]

Whitney recounted his experience before the committee in a letter that appeared in the administration organ of January 30 and challenged the House to decide whether it could tolerate the treatment he had received at the hands of Peyton and Wise.[22] On the next day he sent a letter to the Garland committee protesting that the summons served for "his papers" was too broad. In addition, he tried to explain that he was in Canada during the War of 1812 because to have returned to the States would have placed an unbearable financial burden upon him. He said he swore to obey the laws of the empire because it was a condition for his being permitted to stay.[23]

Following the matter closely from the White House, President Jackson wrote to his nephew in Tennessee that the reason for Peyton's "rude conduct" was that Whitney had proved the congressman to be a liar. Peyton and Wise were in a "disgraceful situation," Jackson observed with satisfaction.[24]

On January 17, prior to the Whitney-Peyton-Wise confrontation, the House passed Wise's resolutions introduced December 13 and appointed a select committee, chaired by him, to investigate the administration of several departments within the government. When the committee later began an inquiry into the Treasury Department, Wise called Reuben M. Whitney as one of the first witnesses. Responding by letter, Whitney cited the threats made on his life when he was before the Garland committee and declared that he would not answer the summons until the House "shall have redressed the wrongs" that he had experienced and until "full protection" was extended to him "from future insult and violence."[25]

A few days later, Peyton had mixed emotions when the House ordered the arrest of Whitney so that he could be brought before the bar to face charges of contempt of Congress. On February 13, the sergeant at arms reported to the Speaker that he had Whitney in custody and was awaiting further instructions.[26] At that time Garland's select committee had not completed its investigation, but the hostile exchanges during the committee meeting of January 25 were known throughout the country to anyone who followed the deliberations of Congress.

Brought into the hall before the leadership had set up procedures for dealing with him, Whitney declared that he had not meant to be in contempt and would gladly go before the committee if its members would agree to have no arms in the room.[27] It was a clever statement meant to build on exaggerated reports—deliberately circulated—that both Peyton and Wise were armed when he appeared before the Garland committee and had meant to kill him. Supported by the administration, Whitney was well prepared to turn his hearing on contempt charges into an investigation of Peyton and Wise.

After a wide-ranging discussion of how to deal with the contempt charges before them, the members appointed a committee of five to question Whitney and other witnesses. The House granted the committee of five and the defendant the right to summon and examine witnesses from members of the House and from outside, and permitted Whitney to be represented by counsel.[28]

Early on the first day, February 16, Peyton protested that the hearing on charges of contempt of Congress had been manipulated into a trial of Wise and himself. Was the proceeding "a bona fide investigation *or* a shameless fraud . . . aided and abetted by members of this House?" he asked.[29] The Baltimore *Patriot* and other friendly newspapers acknowledged that the hearing had turned into "the trial of Messrs. Peyton and Wise." The administration's behavior should cover certain "managers of the party with lasting disgrace," the editor of the *Patriot* wrote.[30] Even the editor of the hostile Nashville *Union* agreed that the two congressmen had been put on trial, but he said that they had brought the trouble on themselves.[31]

The first testimony came from members of the Garland select committee who had been present on the evening of January 25. They testified that there had been a fracas between Peyton and Whitney, that Peyton had spoken harshly to Whitney, and that Wise had joined in briefly. No blows were exchanged. They agreed that both Peyton and Wise had treated Whitney respectfully and courteously, except for the explosive moment of the confrontation. They noted that most of the interrogatories were put to the defendant after the fracas and that Peyton treated him courteously during that entire period as well.

Peyton's outrage at Whitney's oral statement to the committee was at least partially explained by the latter's violating committee rules that forbade a witness to speak when undergoing an examination by written interrogatories.[32]

Agreeing that Peyton and he were suddenly the accused, Wise demanded to know the identity of his accuser. He perceived he was on trial for he knew not what, accused by a person or persons unknown, with witnesses, accusers, and defenders all sitting as the jury. He firmly believed that the president had counseled certain members to get rid of Peyton and himself and that the movement to "kill them off" was well under way. Representative Samuel J. Gholson of Mississippi responded that Wise and Peyton had put themselves on trial, and he favored digging out all the facts so that the trial could be as fair as possible. He caustically denied that the opposition of the pair was of sufficient importance to the administration that it was necessary to have them killed off.[33]

Suddenly the contempt charges against Whitney were the farthest things from members' minds as they focused their attention on Peyton and Wise. Several select committeemen acknowledged that Whitney had scowled at Peyton more than once during the questioning, and all agreed that he had refused to answer several questions because of what he called their "inquisitorial" nature. Representative Ransom H. Gillet of New York minimized the affray. Insisting that Whitney's demeanor was "cool, collected and forbearing," he said he did not see Wise physically restrain Peyton nor did he see Whitney's provocative scowls. He did not think there was a real threat of violence in the confrontation and, agreeing with other witnesses, said that if Peyton had intended to use a gun, he had had plenty of time to bring it into play. Peyton and Wise were so calm after the event that Gillet had no fear of further trouble.[34]

The answers to interrogatories posed to R. B. Taney, former secretary of the Treasury and at the time chief justice of the U.S. Supreme Court, sustained Peyton's claim that Whitney had not enjoyed Taney's support as he sought to be agent for the deposit banks. Whitney had represented that in 1833 Taney was about to set up the position of agent and that he regarded him (Whitney) as the logical choice for the position. The former secretary stated that he had never recommended Whitney nor had he encouraged him to seek the agency. In fact, he said that he had no statutory authority to create such an office and that he did not know of the deposit banks having an agent during his tenure at Treasury.[35]

As the end of the session neared, the contempt hearing degenerated into a political dogfight. Whitney continued largely unscathed; Peyton and Wise were severely scratched. Anxious to deal with other issues, most of the House were ready to terminate the ordeal. On February 20, the members voted that it was "inexpedient" to proceed further against

Whitney on charges of contempt and ordered the Speaker to discharge him from custody.[36]

Extremely critical of Peyton ever since he had joined the opposition, the administration newspaper at Nashville had decided he was a good enemy to have.[37] But the *National Banner and* Nashville *Whig* defended him by emphasizing that Whitney was of "infamous character" and could not be believed on oath. The administration used the Whitney matter to head off any questioning of its operations by the Congress. In the process they sought to embarrass a young congressman who was more than a match for them.[38]

On Wednesday, March 4, Garland's select committee reported that it had found no violations of law or other improper acts in the relationship between the banks and their agent Whitney. The report concluded that the banks dealt directly with the Treasury Department and that their representative had no part in selecting the pet banks to receive government deposits.[39]

Peyton followed Garland with a minority report that claimed Whitney had used his influence with the administration to get secret information for the banks he represented. He again attacked Whitney's character and insisted that the majority of the House had bowed down to both the president and the agent.[40] His pleading had little effect. The Democrat-controlled House adopted the majority report.

"The farce is over," trumpeted the Baltimore *Patriot* on March 2. "The conduct of the majority party had been odious and . . . contemptible," but what could be expected of "such a crew of ignorant, disciplined, complying, unscrupulous, poor-spirited slaves of a superannuated despot." That party had identified "with Reuben M. Whitney," and to shield him, members "have sacrificed law and justice, and, I fear, *truth*," the editor contended.[41]

At the height of the Whitney hearings, Peyton discovered that the name of his four-year-old colt Livingston had been referred to in print as Col. Benton. With a twinkle in his eye, he wrote to the *Spirit of the Times* on February 15 objecting to the political embarrassment that such a change caused him. He cheerfully blamed the Democrats:

> My ch[estnut] Colt, 4 yrs. old next spring, by Crusader, dam Patty Puff by Pacolet, was named *Livingston*, and so recorded at his foaling. A Van Buren—Dick Johnson—Tom Benton Democrat expunged the name *Livingston* and substituted that of *Col. Benton* in its stead. Now, sir, I am opposed to *expunging*, and especially to the *Expunger*, and must insist that the original name—*Livingston*—be restored in your journal, written if you please, with a strong hand, and black lines across the *face* (a bad phiz—that—over which nature has drawn blacker lines than any which can be made with ink) of the said *Col. Benton*.[42]

One of Peyton's last acts in the Congress was to win passage of a bill to settle the claim of Tennessee Volunteers for interim pay between two active duty periods in 1813. They had been in the field from December 10, 1812, to April 1813 and from September to December 1813. Asked by Peyton to state the facts upon which a disbursement of funds would be calculated, President Jackson, who had been the troops' commanding general at that time, agreed that the troops were due pay for the April–September 1813 period, since they had been standing by as they had agreed when dismissed in April.[43]

When Jackson attacked Peyton and Wise in the early summer of 1837 for leaving the party, Hugh Lawson White came to their defense. They are two "who would not be dictated to in the discharge of their public duties by either [Jackson] or myself," he said.

> [They are] talented, well-informed, honest, bold, and men who fear-lessly discharged their whole duty, in defiance of all the calumnies of degraded and hired presses, the frowns of those who sat in high places, and even the statements of the Chief Magistrate himself, that they ought to be "Houstonized."[44]

During the Whitney political firestorm, Balie had not abandoned thoughts about his own political future. Confiding to a Smith County friend that it was not in his power to run for Congress again, he explained that "as a matter of necessity," he wished very much to retire, "at least a few years." His private affairs demanded it, but he left the door slightly ajar should he be called into the race for governor. Many of his friends were talking of him as a candidate for that office, he admitted, but if he should run, it would be "in a case of great necessity clearly made out." He was confident that William B. Campbell could easily win his seat in Congress.[45]

Eager to increase their power in Tennessee, many Whigs spoke of Bell as heir apparent to Grundy's seat in the Senate and favored "the flamboyant Peyton" to run for governor in the place of Newton Cannon, a colorless campaigner. But such was not to be. Any hopes that Balie might have entertained about becoming governor were dashed when his Whig friends John Bell, editor John Hall of the Nashville *Banner*, and soon-to-be U.S. Senator Ephraim H. Foster rushed to endorse the Democratic nominee Robert Armstrong.[46]

The *National Intelligencer* announced that it had been authorized to state that Peyton would not be a candidate for the next Congress. Noting the announcement, the Baltimore *Patriot* hoped he might reconsider and said that if he should not, "his absence from the next Congress will be a real loss . . . to the cause of free principles and good government." The newspaper applauded his public service and said that he was faithful and fearless, "a stream of many tides against corruption and its agents."[47]

After Congress adjourned, Balie began the long trip home. At Williamsborough, North Carolina, he accepted an invitation to a public dinner in his honor. In an impromptu, ringing speech, Balie pointed out the discrepancy between the promises and the actions of the Jackson administration. Listing various examples of maladministration by the Democrats, he was frequently interrupted by long bouts of cheering. He lamented that he had been a witness to the inauguration of Martin Van Buren, the first president in the history of this country to come into power "by the appointment of his predecessor."[48]

The speech attracted favorable comment as far away as Boston where a writer for the *Atlas* praised it and asserted that Peyton had done more than anyone else to open the eyes of the American public to the shabby behavior of the administration. He congratulated Balie for separating himself from the Jacksonian party "when he saw that everything which the people held dear was about to be swallowed in the vortex of Executive Power."[49]

A few days later Balie reached Maryville, Tennessee, where to a large crowd he "elucidated with ability the corruptions existing in some of the [federal] departments," convincing many that "the great political machinery had become somewhat lapsed." He said that political depravity existed in the administration to an alarming extent "from the captains of the cabinet down to the lowest menial in the Augean stables."[50]

Stopping at Athens, Tennessee, on April 20, Peyton made a speech that addressed another Whig principle: a protective tariff. The local editor held to the old view that such a tariff "extorted money from planters for the benefit of others," but Balie insisted that high duties and a tariff on certain imported articles were necessary to protect and encourage American manufacturers to produce such commodities as might be needed in wartime. Should the taxes thus generated cause government revenue to rise beyond prudent levels, the Treasury should return the surplus to the states. Federal surpluses should not be allowed to accumulate to the point that they become easy targets for speculators and political opportunists, he warned.[51]

Before completing his homeward journey, Peyton paused to make a speech at Madisonville, Tennessee, in which he eulogized his political friends and denounced Jackson-Van Buren Democrats. He praised White, Bell, and Wise while raising doubts about the ability of Polk and Grundy to be of continuing service to the state. A Democrat who was present dashed off a letter to Polk, warning that he believed Peyton's intent was to discredit him and Grundy so that the legislature could elect either Bell or himself to the U.S. Senate.[52]

Upon his arrival at Gallatin on April 25, Balie found that speculation about his political future was rife. Democrat William Trousdale believed

Nashville Whigs would prevail on Peyton to run against him for Congress, and the Nashville *Republican* endorsed Peyton for another term in Washington in preference to a possible gubernatorial campaign.[53] Jackson insiders believed that Tennessee Whigs, capitalizing on the earlier statewide White victory, were about to run Peyton for governor.[54] In East Tennessee, Jonesborough Whig leaders believed that the legislature would choose Peyton to succeed Grundy in the U.S. Senate.[55] Hailing Balie as possibly Tennessee's favorite son, the Jonesborough *Republican* sensed "a strong current of public opinion . . . in favor of his remaining in Congress."[56] The Philadelphia *Advertiser* stringently objected to Peyton's retirement from public life. "It's no time for master spirits of his caliber to think of leaving the ship when she is on the breakers, and when her only hope of salvation rests on such gallant spirits as Mr. Peyton and his compeers," the editor wrote.[57]

In a parting shot at Peyton, the Nashville *Union* tried to shame him by printing his strongly pro-Jackson speech of 1834 that defended the removal of the deposits from the national bank. It was the speech's "mawkish flattery . . . fawning sycophancy . . . and fulsome adulation" that nauseated "the Old Roman's stomach" and created in his breast a loathing and disgust for the congressman, the editor said.[58]

Although trying to focus on managing his farm and stud, Peyton did all that he could to help William B. Campbell gain his seat in Congress.[59] He had predicted many times that Campbell could be a sure winner, and the August elections justified his predictions. Campbell won over Trousdale by a vote of 4,426 to 2,689.

News of Campbell's victory was exhilarating to Peyton: "By the everlasting God it is glorious!" He hurriedly dispatched off a letter urging Campbell to find a way to support a national bank "of some sort," but not one that Van Buren might propose. He should love Henry Wise "like a brother," notwithstanding the Virginian was at times "rash" and "impetuous." Asserting that Wise's soul was as "big as the dome on the Capitol," Balie regarded him as "a noble fellow" lacking only "prudence and tact."[60]

Balie welcomed the election results, also, because the margins of the Whig victory strongly indicated that any Whig nominee would have emerged victorious. It effectively answered the Van Buren newspapers that "from one end of the Union to the other" had explained his decision to decline seeking reelection by saying he was "*afraid of being beat.*" He could not help appreciating a published evaluation of the congressman-elect as "a worthy successor to the patriot Peyton."[61]

Soon after the elections, Peyton set out for New Orleans to assess opportunities there for himself and his family. Brothers Holmes and Ran could manage the farm and attend the stud on a day-to-day basis, but Balie needed a situation to produce income for his family and to pay off farm-related debts. He was acutely aware that the fast-growing economy of New Orleans had been a gateway to financial success for several of his neighbors. Isaac Franklin and John Armfield had prospered as slave traders and Franklin alone as owner of Louisiana plantations. Gen. James Winchester's sons-in-law W. L. Robeson and James Breedlove had become wealthy from ventures as commission men, merchants, steamboat owners, and bankers. The port city offered easy access to Texas,[62] where Sam Houston had emerged as president of the new republic. Former Tennesseans were on every hand.

Although business in the city was reeling under the impact of the panic of 1837, there were positive signs on all sides. The first St. Charles Hotel had just opened to the public in the most imposing structure west of the Alleghenies. The parades and carnival that gave rise to the annual Mardi Gras made their first appearance, and the population was growing at such a rate that New Orleans would be the fourth largest city in the United States when the census of 1840 was reported.[63]

Recognizing the international character of the city and noting the recent reintroduction of thoroughbred racing and the presence of a newly organized jockey club, Balie did not need an extended visit to convince him that New Orleans was the place for him and his family. He returned to Gallatin, planning to move by early fall, but committed to promoting the Station Camp Creek stud from his new place of residence and by occasional return trips to Middle Tennessee.

Yet Balie could not avoid the temptation to lash out occasionally at political enemies. While on his excursion to New Orleans, he offered a portrait of President Jackson in the form of an essay for a newspaper at Reiney, Mississippi. He portrayed the Old Hero as having been driven away from his own basic principles during his second term of office by those who professed to be his friends but were in fact using him for their own selfish ends. Responding to Balie's criticism, the editor of the Jackson-Van Buren journal at Nashville called him a "political montebank" and said he would like to attempt a portrait of him, but his sudden changes of position and shape precluded it. He could be a monkey one day, a hyena the next day, and "something akin to a man" the next.[64]

Even as he prepared to move his family, Balie could not forget the early spring visit he had enjoyed with the famous thoroughbred stallion Priam near Richmond, Virginia. He had stopped while on his way home from the last session of Congress to see that celebrated animal, so recently arrived from England:

> [Priam] is full 16 hands high, fair measure . . . possessing the most *perfect symmetry* of parts. His presence commanding, his style and bearing strikingly grand. . . .
>
> He is a good bay, in a rich suit, with glossy mane, and tail of jet black. . . .
> He makes no display of muscle anywhere, but his muscle is of the hardest and firmest order, and most admirably adjusted.

Was Priam perfection? "No," he said, "[but] taking him all in all, I have never looked upon his like before, and never may again, unless he is destined to leave a son."[65]

Peyton had always appreciated superb thoroughbreds, but when he candidly examined his stud, he saw that there was work to be done. The stallion Anvil had stood the season, earning respectable fees, but the other breeding stock had done little to generate cash income. Probably the worst breeding news of all came from Portsmouth, Virginia, where Balie's Sir Henry Tonson died in August. He had been standing the season there.[66] There had not been time enough for his latest acquisitions, ten mares and two stallions, to produce revenues for him, but he listed them with their bloodlines in the *American Turf Register and Sporting Magazine* of September 1837.[67] Pushing to get some of his thoroughbreds in the hands of owners who would race them in exchange for some cash for his own pockets, Peyton sold Magnolia and a Rattler colt for two thousand dollars to horsemen in Vicksburg, Mississippi, while on his exploratory journey to New Orleans.[68]

Earlier Peyton had nominated his filly Pantanelli, "a paragon in beauty and finish," to run the two-mile heats in the Barry Sweepstake at the Gallatin Race Course to be run in the fall of 1840. She was one of twenty-three nominated for the event that carried an entry fee of $1,000 with a $150 forfeit. Promoting the event to the racing press, Balie wrote, "A more promising lot of colts, if we are to judge by their illustrious ancestry, have never been named for any stake, at least upon these waters. Large expectations are entertained." He said the entries represented the principal turfmen in Tennessee and adjacent states.[69]

An official timer in both Gallatin and Nashville races in September and October 1837, Balie paid forfeit for his three-year-old entry in the Congressional Stakes at Nashville. He made no entries at Gallatin, but took note that A. P. Youree's four-year-old colt, Balie Peyton, was distanced in the Club Purse race.[70]

Although most American thoroughbred races were over distances of one or two miles, Peyton had become interested in breeding four-mile stock. Although certain that such animals would come from imported English bloodlines, he had not decided whether the "*ancient* English importation or the *modern* importations" were best adapted to his purposes. Unwilling to delay until he had more information, Balie began "breeding from both, upon a scale which promises success, if it is to be attained, by no inconsiderable expense." In correspondence with the *Spirit of the Times*, he invited the comments of other breeders and won the editor's praise for being "one of Tennessee's most gifted and distinguished sons" and an "eloquent advocate" for the turf.[71]

After attending the Gallatin and Nashville fall races, Peyton moved his family to New Orleans during the latter part of October.[72] On September 5, 1837, the Nashville *Union* had taken cryptic notice of his departure: "'Honorable Balie Peyton of Tennessee has removed to New Orleans where he intends to practice law.' The above is from the New York *Express*, which paper does not inform us whether the *Honorable* gentleman intends to practice the *observance* or *violation* of law."

CHAPTER 5

NEW ORLEANS AND THE PEYTON STAKE AT NASHVILLE: 1838–1847

Eager for his wife, Anne, to see New Orleans, the city[1] he had chosen for their new home, Balie Peyton impatiently paced the deck of the steamboat that was bringing them and their three children from Nashville. The week-long trip via the Cumberland, Ohio, and Mississippi Rivers seemed an eternity to him. As the captain guided the craft out of the main current into the calm waters at dockside, Anne and the children looked out over the vibrant port city for the first time.

Once the boat was securely docked, they saw a horse-drawn carriage with an attendant holding high a placard on which "PEYTON" was crudely lettered. It was the transportation sent for their accommodation by James Waller Breedlove, prominent New Orleans businessman, steamboat owner, and son-in-law of the late Gen. James Winchester of Sumner County. Also awaiting them were the teamsters employed to pick up and deliver the barrels and crates that contained their home furnishings and other personal property.

During Balie's visit earlier in the year, he had rented second-floor office space on Magazine Street in a building next door to the Atchafalaya Bank, of which Breedlove was a principal owner.[2] Now the Peyton family settled into comfortable quarters at 223 Carondelet near the Breedloves' residence on the same street.[3] A few weeks later the Louisiana Supreme Court admitted Balie Peyton to the bar of that state.[4]

The excitement of setting up a law practice and moving without sponsor into high-level political circles in a strange city would have been adventure enough for most, but not for Peyton. Coveting his good reputation as a breeder and owner of thoroughbred horses, he stepped simultaneously into the New Orleans racing scene. Early in the spring of 1838, he became one of the six vice presidents of the New Orleans Jockey Club. He attended the spring races over the new Metairie Course and, with the other club officers, received the plaudits of local race enthusiasts for developing a course that reflected favorably on both the city and the state.[5]

Characterized by a correspondent of the *American Turf Register* as a "turfite" of unexcelled cleverness, Peyton was breeding mares to Rattler, Anvil, Priam, Leviathan, and Luzborough back in Tennessee. The offspring attracted widespread attention with offers as high as three thousand dollars each for some of the unborn. Describing several mares in detail, the correspondent justified a long report on them by observing that, by design, the owner was "breeding for the southern market."[6] Peyton was riding the high tide of enthusiasm for Tennessee-bred horses that had just reached New Orleans.[7]

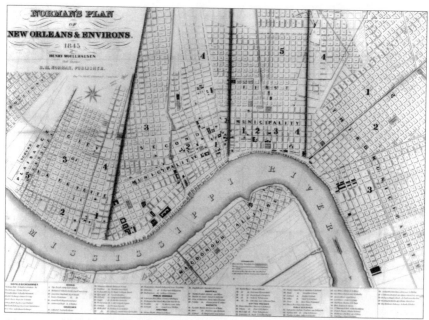

Map: New Orleans and Environs, 1845

Seeking further to improve the quality of his Tennessee stock, Balie took a New Orleans turfman, Dr. J. G. Chalmers, as a partner and purchased Black Maria, a much-admired brood mare. Even though "she was getting old, and [was] without foal," they paid the wealthy New Yorker John C. Stevens four thousand dollars for her and sent her to be bred to Imp. Luzborough. Negotiated in April 1838, the acquisition received favorable notice from editors of nationally circulated racing publications. One of them observed, "With Black Maria, Lady Burton, and Maria Shepherd in his stud, and his judgment in the selection of stallions, Mr. Peyton's colts ought to be nearly invincible."[8]

Emboldened by having Black Maria in his stables, Peyton opened "a stake to the world" and nominated her foals to run in a race for colts and fillies dropped in the spring of 1839.[9] Enthusiastic early response indicated that the stake would become one of the great events in American racing history. What prompted the young but veteran turfman to undertake such an ambitious promotion?

Peyton's challenge may have grown out of the "rivalry and difference of opinion between the 'friends' of [the outstanding sires] Glencoe and Luzborough." One explanation is that Black Maria had been scheduled by her former owner to go to Glencoe for breeding, but when Peyton purchased her, he sent her instead to Luzborough. The change in choice of stud so rankled one of the owners of Glencoe that he challenged with the progeny of Glencoe from Imp. Eliza by Rubens. According to the *Spirit of the Times*, "the proposition was accepted and subsequently converted into a sweepstake."[10]

A similar tale of Glencoe-Luzborough rivalry is set in a "friendly game of Boston" in Nashville where local players ridiculed Glencoe while enthusiastically praising Luzborough. The lone out-of-town guest, A. D. Hunt declined to accept the locals' offer to wager five thousand dollars on one of Luzborough's get against any one of Glencoe's that he might choose to run over the Nashville Course. When Hunt's father-in-law, James Jackson, learned of the proposal, he agreed to enter only the produce of Glencoe if the Nashvillians would open the contest to the entire racing world.[11]

Whatever the background, Peyton organized and promoted the race until enthusiastic anticipation of its running spread to England and Europe. The contest was scheduled to be held in 1843 over the Nashville Course in four-mile heats for a subscription of five thousand dollars each. Owners could nominate entries until the closing date of January 1, 1839. Concurrent with the announcement of the stake, Peyton had nominated also the get of another of his mares, Maria Shepherd by Imp. Priam, and James Kirkman of Nashville named the produce of Imp. Eliza by Imp. Glencoe.[12]

Fervently endorsing the stake, the editor of the *Spirit of the Times* agreed that Nashville was a convenient meeting place for "turfmen from the western, southern, and middle states." He predicted the event would draw as many as twenty subscribers and believed it would be worth five times the forfeit to an untried stallion "to have his get nominated in a stake of $100,000, four mile heats."[13]

Entries began to pour in. When the secretary of the Nashville Jockey Club accepted the last subscriber, he had a list of thirty nominees, which projected a purse of $150,000. The nominations included the produce of "the most distinguished brood mares in the Union, as well as the most fashionable stallions, both native and imported." In recognition of Peyton's success in attracting subscribers, the press gave it the name "the Peyton Stake." A New York racing editor adjudged it to be "by far, the most magnificent stake ever run for in this country or Europe."[14]

Surprised and gratified for the reception that the Peyton Stake was receiving, Balie could not ignore other breeding, trading, and racing matters in the four years before 1843. He anticipated good profits from the sale of Black Maria's produce, but he had to face expenses. To meet some of the stud's need for cash, he sold his half interest in the filly Catherine Barry by Imp. Leviathan out of Black Sophia by Top Gallant, later called Beeswing, to turfmen T. J. and M. Wells of Louisiana. The

Beeswing and her foal Newminster, 1863

late spring transaction brought Peyton fifteen hundred dollars and ultimately resulted in the racer being moved to New Orleans where in 1838
and 1839 she won fourteen thousand dollars for her new owners.[15]
Peyton's partner in Catherine Barry was Jo. C. Guild. The partners were
adversaries in political matters, yet brothers on the turf. Catherine Barry
won the Nashville sweepstakes for three-year-olds on May 7, defeating
the two other entries owned by Col. George Elliott and Andrew Jackson
Donelson.[16] In December 1838, Gallatin hotelkeeper Charles Lewis
purchased a bay filly by Sir Henry Tonson out of Lady Burton from
Peyton "at a high figure."[17] Attending the December 1838 races at the
Metairie Course, Balie relentlessly promoted his Tennessee stud to the
principal turfmen present.[18]

During 1838 Balie paid his brother Ran by giving him a partnership
interest in one or more of his horses, each to share in race winnings, stud
fees, and sales revenues. In a match race, two-mile heats, five thousand
dollars a side, Ran was ready with Blacklock but had to settle for twenty-five
hundred dollars forfeit from W. J. Minor when his filly, Thrush, was not
able to run on the first day of the Nashville races, September 29. Balie
and Ran were not so lucky when their only entry in the Gallatin races on
September 18, running for the Jockey Club purse of four hundred
dollars, lost to James Jackson's Exotic.[19]

Although Balie had been receiving generous attention in the racing
press, no one knew how he felt about the thoroughbred racer that bore
his name, Balie Peyton. He noticed that the turfman John Heth had
just purchased his namesake from another Virginian for the handsome
sum of eight thousand dollars. The *American Turf Register* recognized
the horse for a great race at Baltimore in May and predicted he would
rank at the head of the American turf by the fall races. He had already
posted the best American time for a four-mile heat.[20]

Peyton's own horses ran poorly in the few contests they entered in
1839. His chestnut colt by Sir Henry Tonson out of Lilac's dam was the
last to cross the finish line in the Nashville races on May 8.[21] In the fall
races at Gallatin, Balie was encouraged by the performance of his
Phantom by Gohanna out of Phantomia by English Phantom in
running second to Alex Youree's Osceola on September 23. The
winner clocked a time for four miles not previously equaled in
Tennessee.[22] In the autumn races at Nashville on October 7, Peyton's
three-year-old chestnut colt by Imp. Luzborough, dam by Oscar,
finished next to the last in a six-horse sweepstakes.[23]

Peyton was present on the same course four days later when
Osceola by Pacific, dam by O. H. Perry, won the first of three four-mile
heats. He and fellow Whig Lucious J. Polk[24] bought the horse before
the second heat started. After losing the second heat, Osceola won the

third and the race. Pocketing his winnings, Balie quickly sold his half interest in Osceola to Polk.[25]

Second place was the best Peyton could win at the Sumner County Fair horse show where his bay colt by Leviathan, dam by Magnolia, was runner-up to Jo. C. Guild's Wesley Malone by Leviathan, dam by Richard, who won the cup.[26] Looking for opportunities ahead, he nominated the produce of Black Maria to be dropped in 1840 for a large stake, two-mile heats, subscription two thousand dollars each, five hundred dollars forfeit, to be run at New Orleans in 1843 over the Metairie Course.[27]

But racing was even more disappointing for Balie the next year, 1840. His nomination for the Barry Sweepstake at Gallatin on September 14 did not run, but the winner was Flight by Imp. Leviathan, dam by Sir Charles, owned by his brother-in-law G. W. Parker. From the stake, named for Thomas Barry, another of Balie's brothers-in-law, Parker won eight thousand dollars, then a princely purse. In fact, it was nine hundred dollars more than "the Great Inauguration stake" at the opening of Jerome Park in New York twenty-six years later.[28] Balie's Tennessee could muster only fourth place in a sweepstakes for four-year-olds on September 15 at Gallatin.[29]

The also-ran performances of his horses may be explained by Peyton's emphasis in 1839 and 1840 upon servicing, selling, and buying good-blooded stock. He stood the stallions Anvil and Bellair at Gallatin in 1839 but sold Rattler for "a pretty tall figure."[30] As he promoted sales of his stock at the Nashville fall races of 1839 under the name of Balie Peyton and Company, he probably had reached a point that he had too many partners and wanted to reduce their number.[31] There was no question, however, that he needed sales proceeds to underwrite the Gallatin stud.

Breeder, turfman, and neighbor, Hardy Cryer had done his part to help the sale by endorsing Balie's stock in a letter that appeared June 15, 1839, in the *Spirit of the Times*. Cryer used only superlatives to describe Black Maria, the prize mare of the stud. She had produced Great Western, a Luzborough filly, "large and very strong," for the Peyton Stake to be paired with Hector, "a warrior king . . . large and likely," Balie's other nomination for the 1843 race. Hector was the produce of Maria Shepherd by Sir Archy and Imp. Priam. "If I were a sportsman," Cryer volunteered, "I would think that with entries such as your two . . . I should *need a large pocket* to hold the stakes they would win." He offered specifically favorable reports on the mares Bernice, Anna Maria, and Columbia and said that Maria Shepherd would go to Leviathan a few days hence.[32]

The thoroughbred Sir Henry Tonson

Offering twenty-nine horses for sale at the Nashville races, Peyton quickly disposed of fifteen and bought sole ownership of Black Maria for five thousand dollars. A company from Rutherford County bought the nine-year-old Anvil for an equal sum, and T. J. Munsford of Lebanon, Tennessee, purchased Maria Shepherd for three thousand dollars and Hector for two thousand dollars. Balie sold the other twelve at prices ranging from five hundred dollars to two thousand dollars each, mostly to purchasers from Tennessee, Louisiana, and Alabama.[33]

Soon after the fall races of 1839, Peyton sold the filly Great Western, his first nominee for the Peyton Stake, to Col. William Wynn of Virginia for three thousand dollars, but kept the promising thoroughbred to train at Station Camp.[34] He reacquired the filly prior to the Peyton Stake, however. Sales were on his mind when his brother Ran arrived in New Orleans about December 1, 1840, with a number of horses ostensibly to enter the city's early spring racing card. But Ran was really maneuvering to sell the stock for cash to reduce an indebtedness to Balie that he had incurred in 1836.

But selling thoroughbreds in Louisiana would not generate all the cash they needed. Before Ran brought the horses down the river, Balie placed a mortgage on his four-hundred-acre Station Camp Creek farm in Tennessee for fifteen thousand dollars to secure promissory notes he gave to Alexander Barrow[35] of New Orleans. This was necessary after Peyton applied for a series of cash advances that he used to infuse funds into his horse business. In addition to his home farm, the mortgage included an additional 240 acres of his Keefe place, twenty-six slaves, and all of his thoroughbred horses. It was a question of mortgaging or selling, and when his Kentucky political brother J. J. Crittenden[36] recommended the former course, he was relieved and later conceded that the loan enabled him to own the farm for the rest of his life.[37] To add to his equine woes, his Black Maria lost a colt foal in the spring, "a clean loss of $2,500."[38]

Misfortune haunted Peyton. Death claimed his prize acquisition Black Maria in early 1841 in what was an unexpected setback to his breeding plans as well as a major financial loss. The racing press expressed regrets at the untimely death of Black Maria, "a celebrated race mare," and acknowledged her passing was a great loss to her owner and to the turf.[39]

Later in the year, the purchase of three outstanding brood mares, Cora, Trifle, and Atalanta, added impressively to the lineup at his Station Camp stable.[40] Cora, "the own sister to the renowned Medoc," came to Peyton from John C. Stevens of New York City. Gov. Pierce M. Butler of South Carolina had joined Balie to visit Petersburg, Virginia, where they purchased Trifle by Sir Charles, dam by Cicero, and Atalanta by Industry, dam by Rattler, from Col. William Ransom Johnson and Capt. D. H. Branch.[41] Bred to Boston, Atalanta dropped a superb chestnut colt in the spring of 1842, and Balie named it "Cost Johnson," a compliment to his friend, the Honorable William Cost Johnson, a thoroughbred fancier of Maryland. About the same time Trifle produced a chestnut filly by the Kentucky stallion Eclipse, and Gov. Butler named her "Miss Peyton." Balie was so pleased with Trifle's filly that he returned the mare to Eclipse and she bore another filly, Gloriana, the next spring.[42] During the summer of 1842, Cora, considered "a flyer" before an injury forced her from the track when she was three years old, dropped a colt by Imp. Glencoe.[43] The next year Peyton bought a two-year-old chestnut filly by Imp. Leviathan, dam by Sir Charles, from his Gallatin brother-in-law, G. W. Parker.[44]

Peyton's own racehorses appeared infrequently at tracks during the years 1840–43, but his presence in New Orleans had resulted in other Tennessee turfmen, including his brother Ran, bringing or sending their horses to run on the local courses. Balie put aside his federal duties long enough to see his brother-in-law Barry's horse Celerity win the New Orleans Plate Race at the Metairie Course on January 12, 1841.[45] Unable to attend the spring races at Nashville, he celebrated nonetheless when his Harry Hill beat a strong field that included two of Leviathan's get and one each of John Dawson, Autocrat, Luzborough, Merman, and Count Badger. Harry Hill was a four-year-old by Cheateau Margaux out of Anna Maria.[46]

Running again at Nashville in the fall races, Harry Hill finished second to Gamma, William Giles Harding's[47] entry.[48] A chestnut colt by Imp. Leviathan, dam by Stockholder, jointly owned by Balie and Green Berry Williams, a local trainer of note, finished second in a sweepstakes for two-year-olds at the Gallatin fall races of 1842.[49] At the Nashville spring races of 1843, Peyton's entries ran poorly. A chestnut colt by Rattler out of Anna Maria finished fourth of seven in a sweepstakes for four-year-olds; his chestnut colt by Imp. Leviathan, dam by Stockholder, ran second and last in the two heats of a sweepstakes for three-year-olds.[50]

For all of the attendant activity, breeding, racing, and trading thoroughbreds did not generate the revenues that Peyton needed. Owning the Station Camp Creek farm was an emotional roller coaster for him. It was the place where his parents had settled in the West prior to 1800, and he had received it as their legacy to him. Yet it had been a burden because of the difficulty of operating a stud and a farm on a profitable basis since his father's death. He loved the place and maintained it in good condition, even though it had been a costly undertaking for him. A correspondent of the *Spirit of the Times* had visited the farm in 1842.

> His [Peyton's] summer residence is one of the loveliest spots in the country, and perhaps one of the most desirable stock farms. It is highly improved, tastefully arranged, and enclosed with the best cedar fences. Few have been more unfortunate with their stock, and none more richly deserves the smiles of Fortune.[51]

Balie needed fortune to smile not only on himself but on his sister Evalina Anderson, both brothers, and brothers-in-law Parker and Barry, all of whom were in difficult financial circumstances. A visiting kinsman, then a student at the University of Nashville, thought all of them were "pretty well broke."[52]

Peyton's political friends had seemed always ready to make loans to him when his need was greatest. John J. Crittenden and Henry Clay had become sureties for five thousand dollars for him in 1841, but when they drew a draft on him at the due date in 1842, he could not pay it. To save Peyton further embarrassment, Crittenden took up the draft himself. Overwhelmed by the unexpected kindness of his friend, Balie wrote that he could better have stood a rebuke. Although unable to repay the debt at that time, he apologized to both creditors, assured them he was doing all he could, and later paid it in full.[53]

Before the draft was protested for nonpayment, Peyton had tried futilely to raise the money by selling part of his Tennessee farmland or by borrowing money in New Orleans. Peyton's inability to raise personal funds reflected an economic downturn that was felt throughout the country.[54]

As far as his interest in the turf was concerned, Peyton could not have been in New Orleans at a better time. Horse racing in the city had been revived in 1837 after an interlude of several years, and the jockey clubs needed knowledgeable leadership. By experience, Peyton was ideally suited to such duty, and in 1841 and 1842 he was a member of the executive committee of the Metairie Course and was a vice president of the New Orleans Jockey Club at the Louisiana Course in 1841.[55] He was one of five "presidents" for the latter course the next year.

Occasionally, Peyton attended races far from his usual courses at New Orleans, Nashville, and Gallatin. He checked out his fellow turfmen of the East by attending races over the Union Course in New York in 1842. Mingling with a huge turnout of spectators, he was an interested observer at every race. At the end of each day he hastened back to the Astor House, where he passed the evenings comparing notes with other breeders and racing sponsors. Good storyteller that he was, he usually managed to put in a few serious and inviting words about his Tennessee stud and the New Orleans racetracks. He was one of many who thought the Union Course crowd remarkably large, even as the talent on the track was obviously of low degree.[56] And at Station Camp Creek, he happened to have just what Eastern turfmen needed: well-pedigreed colts and fillies aplenty.

Throughout his visit to the East, Balie was besieged with questions about the Peyton Stake because it had inspired a level of interest among turfmen never before equaled in the Western world. The size of the purse, $150,000 if all subscribers entered, the central location of Nashville, the addition of several races to an already busy racing season there, and the quality of the horses nominated combined to assure the contest a prominent place in the history of American racing.

The Peyton Stake capitalized on the excitement implicit in a produce or futurity stake created by the uncertainty that attends each nomination. An owner could be certain that his nominee would be the produce of the sire and mare that he designated. Beyond that it was wait and see. The developing history of each newly dropped nominee attracted the careful attention not only of its owner and the owners of competing nominees, but also of the racing world at large.

By the summer of 1841, owners of nominees to the Peyton Stake had begun breaking and training their horses. At the same time they were seeking information about the prospective field, especially the name, color, and sex of each horse, and other intelligence of almost any kind. Although the race date was two years away, the first wagers had been placed, and "several gentlemen" had already opened "books" and were ready "to lay out their money on the race."[57] A "traveling correspondent" for the *American Turf Register* predicted that the great race would constitute "a new era in the annals of the turf, both in this country and Europe."[58]

A year later—only one year before the race—subscribers began to evaluate their situations, assessing their animal's chances, and comparing the odds with the hefty five-thousand-dollar subscription fee. The fee loomed large, not only because the deadline for paying it was fast approaching, but also because times were hard and money scarce. A deep financial recession gripped the nation. An unidentified Tennessee turfman reflected the opinions of most when he predicted that no more than four to six of the thirty nominated would come to the starting post because "$5,000 is a large sum to raise in these times, and truly an awful one to lose by any one of our racers, who are mostly planters." The leading racing newspaper agreed the fee was "a figure that will keep many from starting."[59]

Two months before the race, it was obvious that most nominees had dropped out, that no more than five horses would go to the starting post, and that consequently the anticipated purse of $150,000 had shrunk to approximately $35,000. Racing fans nonetheless lost little of their enthusiasm. With the Alabama Stake and the Trial Stake scheduled for the same week at Nashville, purses for the three events totaled $63,000. It was going to be an occasion to remember with more than one hundred horses expected to compete. Considering the number, breeding, and value of the horses, there was general agreement that no one had seen anything like them "on any turf or at any meeting in the United States."[60] Even at $35,000 the purse of the Peyton Stake was richer than any before it. Many years later a prominent eastern turfman rated it as "the largest sweepstakes event that was ever run in the world."[61]

Among the numerous nominees that were held out of the race by their owners who paid forfeit were Ran Peyton's colt Burckhard by Pacific out of Black Kitty Clover by Eclipse. Balie's nominee Hector out of Maria Shepherd by Sir Archy and Imp. Priam was no longer his, and the new owner withheld him.[62]

Employing his eternal optimism rather than the mature judgment he found so difficult to use in equine matters, Balie had poured time and money into training the Black Maria filly Great Western. He had failed in his effort to retain Green Berry Williams as his trainer for the stake, but brought Capt. John Belcher, a well-known Virginia trainer, to Station Camp Creek for the task in the spring of 1843.[63]

By October 1, Balie's funds were so low that he was forced to borrow $4,992 from the Planters Bank of Tennessee to pay the owner's subscription fee. He secured the obligation by placing a mortgage in the bank's favor on his 240-acre Keefe land and on the lives of twelve of his slaves.[64]

On the appointed day for the big race, a large gathering crowded the Nashville Course, although the track and grounds were in deep mud from heavy rains on the two previous days. However, on race day, there was sunshine, clear skies, and mild weather; it was a beautiful autumn day. Many women prepared to watch the race from their carriages parked in the infield, and others filled "the ladies' grandstand" to overflowing. Men visited the stables to see the horses, listened to last minute "tips," and hurried to place their bets.

Among the spectators were many from all parts of the United States, some visiting the West for the first time and most arriving by steamboat. The Peyton Stake attracted visitors to Nashville from afar as nothing before. For at least one reporter, attending the event was a once-in-a-lifetime opportunity. "Never, perhaps, in this country was there a contest of this kind which excited so much interest; and the same from first to last was animating in the highest degree," he wrote.[65]

Responding to the call of the bugle accompanied by an affirmative roar from the crowd, four horses went to the starting post. First came Alexander Barrow's chestnut colt, by Imp. Skylark, out of Lilac by Leviathan, ridden by John Ford. Next was Balie's Great Western with jockey Monkey Simon in the saddle, followed by Thomas Kirkman's Glumdalditch, a chestnut filly by Imp. Glencoe out of Giantess by Imp. Leviathan with jockey F. P. Palmer (alias Barney) riding. The last to the post was Herald, by English Plenipotentiary out of Imp. Delphine, by Whisker, owned by Col. Wade Hampton and ridden by jockey Sandy. The owners represented the states of Louisiana, Tennessee, Alabama, and South Carolina.

Although the occasion belonged to Balie, the winnings did not. Thomas Kirkman took the money home to Florence, Alabama, after his Glumdalditch (bred by the late James Jackson of the Forks of Cypress, Alabama, and trained for this race by Isaac Van Leer) won the stake and Great Western finished last. Kirkman stripped the name Glumdalditch from his filly while still in the winner's circle and gave her the name Peytona "in honor of the stake and the gentleman whose name it bore."[66]

Disappointed and nearly exhausted, Balie looked ahead to the races two days hence in which he had two horses entered. But victory eluded him again. He wondered if his thoroughbreds had been influenced by

Great Western's example when one finished seventh in a field of nine and the other finished last in a field of six.[67] Peyton's only victory at the races came in a preliminary sweepstakes for three-year-olds that had never won a race when his chestnut colt by Imp. Leviathan, dam by Stockholder, won both one-mile heats over the only other horse to run.[68]

The running of the Peyton Stake enhanced Balie's already large reputation as a turfman, but it further drained him financially. He emerged from the event with additional debt and no quick way to repay it, but the conjunctive realms of horse racing and the racehorse held Balie as their willing prisoner. On March 12, 1844, he entered the filly Ann Hays at the Eclipse Course in New Orleans, best three of five, one-mile heats, and saw her finish second. By Imp. Leviathan, dam by Pacific, Ann Hays was a three-year-old owned by J. G. Skegog of Sumner County, Tennessee, who had left the filly with Peyton to train and trade. After her good showing, Lin Cock, a local turfman who a few weeks later became proprietor of the Central Course at Memphis, purchased her. She rewarded Cock by winning races over the Metairie Course on March 21 and 23.[69] During the spring of 1844, Balie was the first subscriber to the Grymes Stake to be run at New Orleans in 1846 and nominated two entries, later adding a third.[70]

Always thinking of his stables at Station Camp Creek, he sent a favorite mare to be bred to the celebrated stallion Priam standing at the Belle Meade stud in 1844.[71] During that year and 1845, he was also busily engaged as president of the New Orleans Jockey Club, Metairie Course.[72]

But the unexpected often hounded him at the track. He was glad he did not see the June races in Nashville where his horse lost a flat track race of two heats after winning the first when, for reasons unknown, the jockey fell from the stirrups and left his mount without a rider to finish the second.[73] He and his friends were equally astounded on December 14 when his favored chestnut filly Tarantula by Imp. Belshazzar, dam by Stockholder, ran dead last in all four heats at the New Orleans Eclipse Course. Prior to this poor showing, Tarantula had turned in fine performances at Nashville and Natchez.[74] During the Nashville spring races of 1845, Balie's two entries were beaten decisively.[75]

Even as his own horses faltered, Peytona, winner of the 1843 Peyton Stake, kept the Peyton name before the racing world. She outran Blue Dick to win the Metairie Course four-mile post stake in her first race of 1845.[76] Next appearing at the Long Island, New York, racecourse on May 13, Peytona won over the highly regarded thoroughbred Fashion by taking the first two heats. The largest crowd that had ever gathered for a horse race in the United States witnessed her victory. Fashion avenged the loss over the Camden, New Jersey, track on May 28, but Peytona had been a noble advertisement for Peyton the turfman. Surely disappointed that she had lost the second match to Fashion, Balie did not disguise his pleasure that the winner of the Peyton Stake had become known as the horse to beat when discussion centered on the best thoroughbred racers in the land.[77]

Thoroughbred fanciers in New York City were reminded of Balie again on May 17 when Maria Peyton, a three-year-old chestnut filly, won a race at Long Island, New York. Owned by the eastern turfman R. Ten Broeck, Maria Peyton was by the thoroughbred stud Balie Peyton, dam by Tariff.[78]

At Nashville for the autumn races, Peyton's chestnut colt by Boston out of Atalanta won the St. Leger Stake for three-year-olds over a Leviathan colt and became the owner's third nominee for the Grymes Stake to be run in the spring of 1846 at New Orleans. The colt won the third two-mile heat in the fast time of 3 minutes, 50 seconds.[79] The good luck at Nashville did not hold out for the Memphis races where Balie's chestnut filly by Eclipse out of Trifle finished third of four horses in a sweepstake for three-year-olds.[80]

Disappointed but undaunted, Peyton took the filly downriver the next year. She fairly flew at Vicksburg where she won the two races she entered.[81] Coming into the Grymes Stake as Balie's only entry from three nominees, the filly caught the fancy of many in New Orleans. On the day of the race, April 6, she dashed their hopes by finishing back in the pack in the first two heats and being badly distanced in the final.[82]

Two days before the running of the Grymes Stake, Peyton and his fellow New Orleans turfmen honored his friend J. S. Skinner, racehorse enthusiast and editor of the *Farmers Library*, at a dinner in the St. Charles Hotel. Skinner was nearing the end of a long trip that he had taken throughout the southeastern states to observe the region's agriculture. He addressed the gathering before yielding the floor to Peyton, S. S. Prentiss, and others who entertained until a late hour.[83]

Peyton had been expected to enter some of his horses in the spring card of 1846 at the Metairie Course, but he did not.[84] Early in December 1847, he yielded to his undying love of horse races only long enough to accept election as second vice president of the Metairie Jockey Club.[85] Two months before he sold his forty-five-year-old slave Phil, a racehorse trainer on the Station Camp farm, to Gallatin turfmen Jo. C. Guild, L. B. Edwards, and Hugh Calgy for one thousand dollars. By agreement, Phil had been working for his new owners for five months before they purchased him.[86]

An unusually active political life and the cost of racing horses were militating against Peyton's traditional role at the track. The racing seasons of 1847 came and went, but he had no entries at Gallatin, Nashville, or New Orleans. It had been two years since he had a horse in a race.

LAW AND POLITICS
1837–1845

For the first two years in New Orleans, attorney Peyton engaged in private practice, although he devoted every spare moment to the promotion of thoroughbred racing in Louisiana and breeding in Tennessee. At first, he planned a law office in New Orleans with J. Shall Yerger, a former Nashvillian who had been associated earlier with Jo. C. Guild in practice before the Tennessee Supreme Court.[1] After assessing their situation, Yerger located at Vicksburg, a move they believed would strengthen their partnership. "This is a capital arrangement," Peyton chuckled. "Shall and I will take the *suckers going up or down*."[2]

Due in large part to the economic recession[3] that held New Orleans in its grip, his first client relationships in the city kept him busily engaged. He was so busy "attaching steamboats" for debts that he hardly had time "to be civil." As a result he had few opportunities to indulge his interests in music and the theater, but was "looking quite into the *purses of men*."[4] His reputation was sufficiently established in New Orleans by late autumn that a Houston, Texas, law firm listed him as a reference in repeated advertisements in the *Picayune*.[5]

Notwithstanding the physical and emotional pressures generated by practicing law and managing horses, Balie maintained a lively interest in Whig politics. During the 1830s, Whig Party politics in Louisiana involved a combination of National Republicans—those who opposed the local Democrats and those who opposed President Jackson. Within those groups were the sugar cane industry which needed a tariff to survive, advocates of internal improvements to navigate better the rivers and swamps, and export-import merchants who valued some form of national bank. Like their fellow Whigs elsewhere, they stood for an activist government at the national level.[6]

Peyton would not turn his back on the political activities of his former colleagues in the Congress, however. Concerned in mid-June 1838 that a duel was imminent between John Bell and Tennessee Congressman Hopkins Turney, he advised Henry Wise to do everything in his power to avert such a meeting. Bell should not accept a challenge from "Hop" because the challenger was "too *mean*, too *low* as a man," but he should be certain his refusal puts "the onus on him." Balie believed that Bell, although a good shot, "would be rather too slow in a duel." Should a shootout be unavoidable, he advised that Bell should provoke Turney "to an attack" rather than engage in a duel. Bell "would be Hell in a street fight," especially if armed with "those rifle barrel pistols of his which will kill a buffalo [at] 50 yards."[7]

Peyton had a "last resort" suggestion for tactics if other efforts failed and a duel appeared unavoidable.

> Will it not be the best policy . . . for Bell to pull *Polk's* nose on some pretext & get into a fight with him? Let him meet P. & say (taking him by the nose) this is for setting on me that infamous scoundrel Hop. Turney, who no gentleman can notice. I am accountable to *you*—I will never notice him. Bell would then be committed to not meet T., and P. would have to act.[8]

Earlier in the year, Balie had urged Congressman William B. Campbell to seek reelection to a second term from the Sixth Congressional District of Tennessee. The incumbent was in a position from which his enemies could not move him, Peyton said, but warned that should he not run for office, someone of the Van Buren crowd might win it. Democrat Jo. C. Guild appeared to be contemplating a campaign for Congress and, notwithstanding their friendship in matters other than politics, Balie wanted him defeated. He confided to Campbell, "I should like for you to settle up *old scores* with him interfering against you in your [prior] canvass with [William] Trousdale."[9]

Six months after Peyton moved to New Orleans, Nashville Democrats were giving him credit for a key leadership role in carrying the state for Whig Hugh Lawson White in 1836. Most young men had become convinced "that Peyton was the real debater and leader," the active Democrat and U.S. Supreme Court Justice John Catron wrote, "and most declare Peyton had been chiseled out of his place, and the

front rank, by adroit design." Catron inferred that Bell had taken over
the Whig Party in Tennessee and that Peyton would have been a better
choice by the Whigs.[10]

Following local practices to escape the annual summer visitation of
tropical fevers, Balie and his family usually returned to Tennessee for the
hot weather months.[11] In 1839, however, he did not leave the city until
the latter part of July because of a pending legal case.

The state had charged John Gibson, editor and publisher of the
True American, with criminal libel arising from his alleged attempt to
destroy the professional reputation of a New Orleans medical doctor.
Both sides agreed that the editor had printed in his newspaper the
account of a lawsuit involving Dr. J. Monroe Mackie that contained a
report of an illicit relationship that he inaugurated with a young immi-
grant woman of Scottish descent. The prosecutors maintained that the
editor's purpose in printing the court proceedings was to defame and
libel the doctor.[12]

After the prosecution presented its evidence, Peyton explained that
he and his fellow defense attorneys would depend on two points that
would establish the innocence of their client. The first was "the right to
speak and write and publish, secured to the defendant in common with
every other citizen by the Constitution." The second point was "the truth
of the publication complained of." Reading from the constitutions of
Louisiana, Mississippi, and Missouri, Peyton showed that in each state,
"the liberty of the press was not to be restricted." As for the truth of the
publication by the defendant, Peyton said that the defense would prove
the following:

> Doctor Mackie introduced himself to the hotel where the Scotch girl
> had been living—that she had been previously well behaved—that the
> keeper of the hotel believed his calls to be professional—that the girl
> was poor, fatherless and interesting—had a sister who watched over her
> with parental care. The doctor gained her confidence, betrayed and
> ruined her, induced her to leave the house where her sister lived—had
> her now living in that of a free woman of color, and had urged her to
> enter suit against her brother-in-law.[13]

Peyton said the behavior of Dr. Mackie was established in the earlier
lawsuit and was reported by the defendant, whose object was "a good and
laudable one." Gibson recognized that as a practicing physician, Dr. Mackie
had access to "the bedsides of our wives, sisters and daughters," and as a
responsible journalist who cared about the morals of the community, he
printed the exposure. Peyton argued that where there is truth, there is no
libel, but the attorney general responded that the truth of the libelous news
story was irrelevant in a criminal case.[14]

On the second day of the lawsuit, Peyton returned to his previous arguments. If the attorney general's arguments should prevail, they would sweep away "those landmarks that guide us to the fountains of liberty," he said. Freedom of speech, freedom of the press, and trial by jury are the essential components of liberty, and they have never been denied "except where that denial had its origin in tyranny and oppression," he postulated. As for the attorney general's position that the truth of the publication should not be considered, Peyton asked if any judge would dare "tell a jury . . . to bring in a verdict of guilty in a case like the present one, and withhold all evidence of the alleged libel at the same time?" It was ridiculous, he said, to convict a publisher of libel because the news he printed was of an unflattering nature. By that measure it would be libelous to report robberies, rapes, murders, or any other antisocial acts that reflected unfavorably on the character of the perpetrators.[15]

On the fourth day of the trial, which from its beginning had attracted overflowing crowds to the courtroom, the judge gave permission to extend the arguments. His ruling was based on the objection raised by Peyton and his associate Pierre Soulé to the attorney general's introduction of legal discussions based on the laws of Spain and France. Later in the course of the debate, the prosecution referred to a quotation by Peyton from the Declaration of Independence as "a humbug." The ill-chosen remark enabled the former Tennessean to call upon the patriotic sympathies of the jury. He responded that the Declaration constituted "the very life, soul and spirit of our independence."[16]

On July 12, the judge ruled in favor of the state by denying the admission of evidence to support the truth of the alleged libel, but ruled also that the jury was the sole judge of the law and the facts in matters of libel. Answering for the defense, Peyton said he did not fault the judge's decision on the question of evidence, but was gratified that he recognized the jury as sole judges of the law and facts of the case. The district attorney, reversing his prior position, insisted that the prosecution wanted to go into the evidence of the untruth of the publication and brought in the Scottish woman who had suffered at the doctor's hands and seated her in the witness box.

Peyton cautioned the prosecution against exploring evidence "if it were only for the immorality—perhaps the infamy which it might disclose on the part of the person now placed there" to testify. Soulé objected to the "contradictory course" pursued by the prosecution who suddenly wanted to present evidence for the state after the court had ruled that the defendant could not present evidence relating to the same question. Moments later the judge ruled that the court would hear no more evidence from either the prosecutors or the defense but invited final summations by both sides. The speeches were brief, the judge charged members of the jury, and they retired from the courtroom at 3:00 P.M. About an hour later the jury reported that it was unable to arrive at a verdict in the case. Freedom of the press had narrowly survived another challenge, and in the process Peyton and Soulé had added positively to their professional reputations.[17]

By early 1840, Myra Clark Gaines and her husband, Gen. Edmund P. Gaines, commandant of the Western Department of the U.S. Army, retained Peyton as one of their attorneys in litigation growing out of efforts to block her inheritance of much of the land on which the city of New Orleans was situated. Her father, Daniel Clark, left a will made in 1813 that designated Myra as the sole heir to his extensive estate. However, the executors of the Clark estate ignored it and probated a will, made in 1811, in which she received no such legacy, although it had been revoked by the will of later date. The executors of the 1811 will had already sold the Clark landholdings to a number of buyers who had, in turn, built a significant portion of the city upon their purchases.

Recognizing Charles Patterson of New Orleans as one of many who had bought real property from the executors, Peyton and his colleagues brought suit in federal district court to challenge his title to it. Patterson and the two executors of the 1811 will were defendants in the case. Their attorney argued that Patterson had lawfully purchased property from legally qualified executors implementing the provisions of the probated Clark will of 1811. Patterson himself denied any knowledge of the will of 1813. His counsel argued further that Daniel Clark was never married and consequently had no legitimate issue. If Myra were in fact his daughter, she was illegitimate, and Daniel Clark's mother, still living, would become the "forced heir" to the property.

Peyton's team contended that any sale under the terms of a revoked will was null and void. Establishing the existence of the will of 1813, they adduced "strong arguments" to show that the will of 1813 was kept out of sight by a defendant who "surreptitiously possessed himself of it." It was he who produced the will of 1811 and had it probated "to the exclusion of the last and legal instrument, thus depriving Mrs. Gaines of property of which she was the rightful owner."

Ruling in the Gaineses' favor, the panel of two judges ordered Patterson to convey and surrender possession of the real property in question to Mrs. Gaines before the first day of the next term of court. Even though Patterson was only one of many property holders who held title under conveyances made by the executors of the 1811 will, the judgment was a sobering warning to the others. It was generally agreed that the case was on its way to the U.S. Supreme Court. Should the district court's decision be sustained, it appeared that ultimately

Mrs. Gaines would be adjudged to be the true owner of all the properties sold by the executors.[18]

Although busily engaged in the courts, Balie was aware of the
increasing value of land along the southern reaches of the Mississippi.
Hoping to profit by a modest speculation in 1839, he and a partner,
Richard M. Carter, purchased a tract of 160 acres in Plaquemines Parish.
It was located on the river below New Orleans near the South Pass, and
Balie and Carter each held undivided one-half interests in the property.[19]

Earlier in the year, Peyton made a complicated collection of
$14,513.28 on a mortgage note endorsed to him by the previous holder.
The amount of the note when made in 1837 was $45,885.81, but subse-
quent payments had reduced it to $39,556.67, against which he applied
the payment of $12,973.36 principal and $1,539.92 interest. As a large
plantation situated in Ascension Parish on the Mississippi River and the
slaves thereon secured the note, Peyton's paid down balance was as good
as gold. He undoubtedly traded it to reduce his own near chronic
indebtedness.[20]

But Tennessee politics had a way of crowding itself into Balie's life.
During the latter weeks of 1839, he learned that his younger brother
Dr. Joseph Hopkins Peyton made his first public political speech to a
crowd of fellow Whigs at Gallatin. Professing unease upon finding that
he was the principal speaker for the occasion, Jo admitted that once
under way he proceeded confidently and, encouraged by the audience,
spoke for two and one-half hours. The response to his remarks was
favorable enough to encourage the development of a latent political
ambition. A career in medicine, for which he had been trained, would be
as nothing when compared to the excitement of the political arena.[21]

During the latter days of 1839, Jo Peyton visited New Orleans and
reported that Balie was "doing a fine business and will be able in a few
years to retire with an independence for himself and his little ones." It
was an excessively optimistic evaluation of his brother's financial condition volunteered, perhaps, to reinforce Balie's strained credit rating.
But the principal purpose of Jo's visit was to get Balie's blessing for a
political life of his own.[22] Within a year he was considering a run for the
state senate and asking Congressman Campbell to speak a good word for
him among their fellow Whigs.[23]

Balie was ready for a campaign. The presidential election year of
1840 provided him an opportunity to take the stump for the Whig Party
ticket with the possibility he would be rewarded with an appointment by
the president. He did not need the attendant prestige, but he could use
additional income for his financially treacherous horse business.

On January 4, New Orleans Whigs staged a rally at the St. Louis
Exchange and voted unanimously to endorse the Harrisburg convention

nomination of William Henry Harrison for president and John Tyler for
vice president. Following Attorney General Adolphe Mazureau, who spoke
in French for the Gallic population, Peyton delivered "one of the most
effective speeches" the *Daily Picayune*'s reporter had ever heard. The
newsman wrote, "He so admirably blended his facts with fanciful anecdotes
and western phrases that he completely carried the meeting with him."[24]

Four days later, Balie perfunctorily shook the hand of Andrew
Jackson, who had just arrived to participate in the annual observance of
the Battle of New Orleans on January 8, 1815.[25] Surrounded by well-
wishers who radiated "the finest feeling of the people," Jackson had little
opportunity and less desire to converse with Balie, although a few words
about racehorses always narrowed the political chasm between them.

Back at the Hermitage, Jackson thought that Balie had tried to
undermine his standing with the people of Louisiana. "The Whigs in
N. Orleans with Balie Peyton at their head could not smother this kind
feeling and generous glow of gratitude," he wrote to his political confi-
dant Francis P. Blair.[26]

Peyton returned to the stump on February 13 as one of four speakers
for a Whig meeting at the St. Charles Exchange. As was customary, he
received the crowd's approbation and applause.[27] New Orleanians had
learned to expect entertaining speeches by the former Tennessean, and
he rarely disappointed them.

By mid-April, Balie heard from the gubernatorial campaign then
underway in Tennessee. From the heart of his old congressional district
came word that the Whigs of Smith County were solidly behind their
party's ticket. A published letter from one of them declared that "old
Smith is fully in her senses. . . . She cannot, she will not forget . . . the
true teachings of [Balie] Peyton and [William B.] Campbell."[28] Balie
found comfort in the good and flattering news from home.

Early in May, New Orleans Whigs staged a daylong celebration in
observance of the anniversary of General Harrison's attack against the
besiegers of Fort Meigs during the War of 1812. Afterward, Peyton
accepted election by the Tippecanoe Club as a delegate to the Whigs'
upcoming Southwestern Convention at Nashville.[29]

During the following month, New Orleans Whigs conducted four
well-attended political meetings, the last two of which were addressed by
the popular Mississippi orator S. S. Prentiss. The final meeting featuring
the Mississippian was held June 26, and featured a dinner in his honor
at the Carrolton House at which Peyton presided. Balie introduced him
with tasteful brevity, a consideration that must have been appreciated by
all present as Prentiss spoke for nearly two hours.[30] The pair appeared
together several times during the campaign for Harrison and Tyler.
When on the same dais, each was inspired by the other's oratory to such

an extent that they usually turned the occasion into a magnificent display of forensic fireworks.

The difference between the Whigs and Democrats was never more clearly defined than in 1840. Offering to replace the do-nothing Democratic administration with a promise of political leadership that would reinvigorate a struggling national economy, the Whigs exploited the question of action versus inaction. Peyton and other Whig spokesmen blamed the lingering recession of 1837 on the Democrats and proposed to replace a do-nothing mentality in the White House with a do-something capability.[31]

Addressing a Harrison-Tyler rally on July 3, Peyton said that the future of the nation and the future of the Whig Party were inextricably intertwined. That meant the Whigs would save the nation, he explained. Local attorney Randall Hunt also spoke, and a reporter wrote of hearing "strains of thrilling eloquence and power" from both speakers.[32] Having professed its neutrality since early in the campaign for president, the *Daily Picayune* declared the Whig Party was ascendant in the city in its July 9 issue. "The Whig flag now waves in triumph over New Orleans," it proclaimed.

As the summer and the race heated up, Peyton stepped up his efforts in behalf of the Whig ticket. On July 25, he engaged the loyal Jacksonian and prominent politician Henry S. Foote[33] of Mississippi "in the way of a friendly political discussion" at a barbecue in Cowan Springs, Warren County, Mississippi.[34] The debate may have been "friendly," but it was one of the several times that Foote recalled meeting the "sturdy" Peyton in the "fierce political strife" of the presidential contest.[35]

By August 17, Balie was in Nashville for the Southwestern Convention, which attracted a larger turnout than the Whig National Convention in May. On the next day he spoke to the assembled delegates, although his presence was overshadowed by the appearance of Henry Clay of Kentucky, the Whigs' national idol.[36] A friendly local newspaper commented that Balie spoke "in a masterly manner," although it reported none of his text.[37]

A few days later at Murfreesboro, Tennessee, Balie answered Felix Grundy, who had made a speech for Van Buren. Having previously indicated that he could not remain to

Henry Clay

hear other speakers and debate issues, Grundy started for his carriage at
the conclusion of his remarks. "I hope," said Peyton, "Mr. Grundy will
stay and hear me," but Grundy made no response and continued toward
his carriage. Raising his voice, the Whig champion opened with a
humorous anecdote that was later reprinted in New Orleans as a sample
of his electioneering rhetoric.

> I hope Mr. Grundy will not be like the lame captain . . . [who] went out
> to fight Indians, and came upon them unexpectedly. "Boys," said he,
> "there they are—they are very numerous—my own opinion is they'll
> whip us, but," said he, "fight hard—retreat in good order—as I am a
> little lame, I'll go now," and away he went.

The crowd sent up a shout that "rent the air and shook the hills."
After asking the other Van Buren men to ignore the example of their
lame leader and instead remain to hear him, Balie settled into an
address that a Whig newspaper reported as being "replete with sound
argument, impassioned eloquence, rich humor, and biting sarcasm."[38]

Before his speech at Murfreesboro, Peyton stirred the political pot
then boiling in the governor's race vigorously enough to attract Andrew
Jackson's unfavorable attention. The stirring was designed to dilute the
contents of the pot that were feeding Governor Polk's reelection bid.
Balie had asked a Middle Tennessee crowd if there were any present who
knew anything about a letter from Jackson to Polk certifying that the
latter's conduct in an earlier verbal exchange with Congressman Henry
Wise was entirely appropriate and approved by the president. About a
dozen voices responded that they had heard Governor Polk read such a
letter in a public address at Shelbyville. Peyton's question resulted in
Jackson's testy denial that he had written such a letter. He conceded
nonetheless that the sentiments in the alleged letter were entirely true.
The letter was an issue because Polk's opponents charged that he had
solicited it to quell rumors that he had not stood up to Wise when the
Virginian called him face-to-face "a damnable little petty tyrant."[39]

During the latter part of September, Peyton spoke to a large Whig
"festival" at Lebanon where, after a drunk had disrupted John Bell's
speech, the crowd had become quite restive. It was more at ease by the
time Bell finished his speech, and when Peyton approached the
speaker's stand with an easy smile and confident stride, he relaxed
tensions further by casually shouting, "Boys!! How are you?"

William B. Campbell's sister was present and afterward described the
scene:

> Then such a thunder of applause you never heard. . . . He took up the
> principles professed by General Jackson at the time he came into office

and showed from each one how far the present administration had deviated. . . . He seemed to be all feeling—all life—all nerve. . . . We listened to him until sundown . . . when . . . the people cried out, "Balie come to the courthouse and speak all night." The cry was so general that it was agreed to adjourn to the courthouse & after tea the speaking was resumed.[40]

A group of Sumner County Whigs, most of whom were from the southern part of the county, staged a dinner at Beech Camp Ground on October 13 to honor Peyton, Campbell, and Bell. Enjoying the occasion immensely, Peyton would not let the crowd forget that their leaders first had invited Polk and Grundy to attend and debate two of the honorees.[41] Peyton hurried back to New Orleans in time to cast his vote in the November election.

When he learned that Tennessee had given a solid majority to Harrison and Tyler, he celebrated, certain that his speeches in the state had contributed to the Whig victory. His greatest thrill came a few days later on November 17 when the *Daily Picayune* announced it had received enough election returns to declare the Harrison-Tyler ticket elected.[42]

President William Henry Harrison later told his grandson Benjamin Harrison that Balie Peyton elected him to the presidency, specifically referring to Balie's 1840 campaign speeches in his behalf in states where the race was closely contested.[43] Defeating the old Van Buren crowd nationwide, and especially in Tennessee and Louisiana, represented the fulfillment of some of Balie's fondest political dreams. It also put him in line for serious recognition for his effective work for the president-elect.

The new year, 1841, opened with Peyton harboring great expectations in politics and the law. The Whigs had returned to power in Washington, a presidential patronage appointment for himself was likely, and brother Joseph Hopkins was running for a seat in the Tennessee senate. His law practice was attracting favorable attention, and the *Myra Gaines* v. *Patterson* lawsuit that he had participated in winning in the U.S. District Court was on its way to the U.S. Supreme Court.

Balie ultimately received a presidential appointment as attorney of the United States for the Eastern District of Louisiana, but it did not come easily. First, the majority of the Louisiana congressional delegation preferred the New Orleans lawyer R. H. Chinn, leaving Peyton almost totally dependent on the president-elect. In addition to working through the state's congressmen, Chinn made a strong application to the Kentucky Whig leader J. J. Crittenden to whom he identified himself as a "Clay" Whig and Peyton as "one of the old Jackson crowd who are now good Whigs." Acknowledging Peyton as his only "formidable competition" for the office, Chinn hoped Crittenden would "procure" the appointment for him.[44]

Competition did not disturb Peyton, but the death of President Harrison on April 4, thirty days after inauguration, raised serious doubts about the appointment. Although the vice president had "urged his nomination" upon the president "as a cabinet officer," Balie wondered how Tyler would react to receiving the presidential mantle so unexpectedly. Would he wipe the slate clean and start the appointment process anew?[45]

The uncertainty of the moment caused Peyton's Tennessee congressional friends and Senator Alexander Barrow of Louisiana to make strong representations in his behalf to Tyler. Henry Wise conducted an overzealous pursuit of the appointment for Peyton, obtained a pledge from the president, and then "unfortunately spoke of it." Learning that Wise had embarrassed the cabinet by his remarks, Peyton observed dryly, "[He] had better have slept."[46]

Nonetheless, John Tyler would not let Balie's loyal work for the Whig presidential ticket go unrewarded, and on April 17, 1841, he appointed him U.S. attorney for the Eastern District of Louisiana. Peyton took the oath of office at New Orleans before J. W. Kurley, an associate justice of the U.S. Supreme Court, on April 29.[47] Among the rank and file in Louisiana, the appointment gave general satisfaction.[48]

There were details yet to be settled. Peyton sought clarification about the fees and emoluments of the position, and he asked whether he had the right to charge for office rent, then an annual expense of six hundred dollars. Was there a ceiling on his annual earnings and, if so, at what level? He stated frankly that he needed all that he was entitled to receive but wanted to start his record keeping "right" and make no changes afterward.[49]

Despite his appointment as district attorney, summertime political gossip in the capital about cabinet appointments frequently included the mention of Peyton's name. Cave Johnson reported to Polk that a Tyler cabinet "more talked of than thought of" would have Peyton as attorney general.[50] But there was good reason for the speculation: President Tyler was beginning to think of him for a larger responsibility.[51]

Soon after Balie began to represent the United States in the courts of the Eastern District, the president offered him a cabinet appointment as secretary of war. Flattered by the offer, Peyton declined, perhaps because he was not qualified for its duties either by training or by experience. More likely, he did not accept it because he was still in the horse-breeding and racing business and needed the flexibility and relative freedom to travel that the U.S. District Attorney's office provided.[52]

Although holding the office of district attorney did not preclude his continuing such private practice as time allowed, Peyton quickly exited the Myra Gaines case, or at least the courtroom in which it was being heard. He had appeared in U.S. District Court on May 7 to defend Myra

against certain counterclaims made by the defense, and he was reading
from a pamphlet that discussed a similar litigation in another court when
the judge stopped him. Unless Peyton told him what he intended to
prove, the judge would not permit him to continue reading. Then he
stated emphatically that should the attorney fail to cooperate, he would
hold him "amenable for a contempt of court and a violation of all the
rules of practice."[53]

The judge's threat brought color to Balie's face and fire to his eyes.
Admitting that he might have been guilty of an error, he insisted that
"before no other tribunal" would his action be construed as a contempt
of court. A newsman recorded his statement that if "the right of offering
evidence were denied him—if a bit and bradoon were to be placed in his
mouth—he would at once withdraw from the defense of the case." At
that point, he "took up his hat, bid good-day to his fair client and the
jury, and left the court."[54] Apparently prepared, Mrs. Gaines then
undertook her own defense, and at the end of the trial the jury ruled in
her favor. Her previous overzealous participation in the complicated
lawsuits arising out of her claim had resulted in other of her lawyers
leaving the case, and that probably had more to do with Balie's departure than the judge's stern admonitions.[55]

After this incident, Peyton seems to have been further involved in the
Gaines case because in 1848, S. P. Andrews, then an attorney for Myra
Gaines, advised her that when a recent U.S. Supreme Court ruling had
come down in her favor, "the high honor of the great legal triumph"
should be shared by Balie Peyton, Richard Chinn, and John R. Grymes
of the New Orleans bar and Gen. Walter Jones, Francis Key, and
Reverdy Johnson, Washington lawyers.[56]

One of his first trials as U.S. District Attorney was tailor-made for the
flamboyant prosecutor. The case was against a young sea captain who was
believed to have been consorting with pirates. The government had
lodged three charges against ship captain D. F. DePutron: committing
perjury for having represented at the Customs House that he was a citizen
of the United States when he was not, violating federal law that prohibited
engaging in the African slave trade, and aiding and corresponding with
pirates. Heard initially in recorder's court, the trial attracted public attention that filled the courtroom from the day it opened.

DePutron came into the courtroom accompanied by his next in
command, Osborne Abbott and Manuel Domingo, all unrestrained, and
by four crewmen in handcuffs. Prepared to testify against them were
witnesses Capt. W. B. G. Taylor, U.S. Navy boarding officer for the patrol
boat *Izard*, and John Thompson, a former member of DePutron's crew.

Captain Taylor and Thompson testified that DePutron had fitted
out the schooner *Independence* as a slaver, although the first mate told

the boarding office that it was used for pleasure excursions. But Taylor found incriminating paraphernalia aboard the vessel. It included a pirate flag with skull and crossbones in white against a field of dark blue, steel armor and helmet, an oversize Bowie knife, two guns, ten pairs of pistols, a keg of powder, nine dirks, a pair of double-barreled pistols, a map of the coast, and a variety of weapon-related items including bullet molds. There was even a copy of a volume called *The Pirate's Own Book!*

When taken into custody without resistance, DePutron had on his person a dirk, a Bowie knife, and a pair of loaded pistols. He told Captain Taylor that he regarded the *Independence* as a supply ship to a slaver. As for flags, he hung out the French flag whenever an inbound sail appeared and, when along the coast of Africa, hoisted the pirate flag to frighten away intruders. At other times, he displayed the American flag and pennant.

Among DePutron's personal papers were letters and documents that proved he was born in England, was then twenty-four years old, and had been at sea since a child. They also revealed that he had a brother, John DePutron, who lived in New Orleans. The brother's situation immediately attracted Peyton's attention because Thompson testified that while he worked aboard the *Independence* for a period of five or six weeks, the crew was aware that DePutron was awaiting the arrival of a topsail schooner and had them signal every vessel coming in sight from the eastward. Peyton wondered whether the expected schooner was owned and commanded by DePutron's brother, John.[57]

On the second day of the examination, the four crewmen made statements to the court. Serious examination of each produced nothing incriminating, and the court discharged them. DePutron, Abbott, and Manuel Domingo were remanded for further examination.[58]

Subsequent testimony elicited no new evidence, and final arguments occupied the last day of the trial, July 6. Peyton dropped the charge of piracy, admitting that they had not uncovered sufficient evidence to uphold it. Committing perjury and operating in the slave trade in whatever capacity were clearly against the law, and he insisted that both charges be sustained. In "an elaborate and able speech," defense attorney C. K. Johnson argued that so much contradictory evidence was in the record that no sense could be made of it. He petitioned for dismissal of all charges against the defendants.[59]

Peyton closed for the government in a speech that lasted two hours. One local newspaper reported it as "most ingenious and searching"; another said it was "able, argumentative, and occasionally interspersed with rich humor." He turned the defense plea of contradictory evidence against DePutron and, taking up a copy of the defendant's will, read his statement that he was born on the island of Madeira. Even DePutron's attorney had admitted the authenticity of the will, he said.

A quick exchange ensued, during which Johnson denied he had made such a statement. Peyton insisted that he had done so clearly and after further accusation and denial, Peyton asked angrily, "Do you assert that I misrepresent you?"

Johnson responded, "If you persist in putting words in my mouth which I utterly disclaim, then you do certainly misrepresent—." Seething because of the implied reflection on his integrity, Balie struck Johnson in the face. Persons sitting nearby separated the two men, and police quickly restored order. Deeply embarrassed by the outbreak in his court, the recorder remonstrated with both attorneys. After Peyton apologized and Johnson testily responded that the fracas had been of his adversary's making, the recorder called the court to order and ordered the defense to proceed. Agreeing with the defense that Abbott and Domingo should be discharged, Peyton concluded his remaining remarks as if nothing had happened.

With calm restored within the bar, the recorder announced his decision. He discharged Abbott and Domingo, but finding the evidence sufficient to inculpate DePutron in the two charges, he remanded the captain to trial in the U.S. District Court. He set bail at twenty thousand dollars.[60] Peyton prevailed in the trial but, by striking Johnson, he had shown again that he could not always control his own temper.

Early in the year, John G. Chalmers, Peyton's partner in more than one thoroughbred acquisition, had swindled him out of fifteen thousand dollars in a scheme that also cost several other "honorable citizens of New Orleans." As soon as he had completed his deceit, Chalmers left for Texas. Balie pursued him as far as the Red River "but in vain." He overtook two or three slaves and some baggage abandoned by the swindler before returning with the prizes to New Orleans.[61]

As a result of Chalmers's chicanery, Balie brought a lawsuit against him. In partial satisfaction of the judgment awarded, Sheriff L. A. Ducros executed a "deed of sale" to him on October 5, 1841, for certain Kentucky coal lands, two runaway slaves, and a one-third interest in the two-year-old brown filly Great Western that the pair had purchased from Colonel Wynne before the horse ever left the Station Camp farm. Peyton paid into the court $950 for the assets conveyed. Acquiring Chalmers's ownership in the thoroughbred was of obvious interest to Balie, but the lands conveyed seemed to have serious profit potential. He received "one undivided third part of five thousand three hundred forty-eight acres" in Wayne and Pulaski Counties, Kentucky, along the great south fork of the Cumberland River. Elaborating on the mining potential of the lands, the language of the deed was exciting.

> These tracts of land contain immense quantities of coal and extend from a short distance above the commencement of the coal region on this stream to the head of navigation on the Jumps and include all the coal on this river with the exception of one tract of fifteen hundred acres belonging to the heirs of John Smith, deceased.[62]

Peyton seems to have disposed of the newly acquired coal lands soon after receiving them, if they truly existed and were not a product of the swindler's imagination. He never registered his deeds to them in the counties of Wayne and Pulaski where they were located. No records of the properties are known to exist beyond the office of the Register of Conveyances, Parish of Orleans, New Orleans, Louisiana.[63]

Prior to his suit against Chalmers, Balie purchased three slaves for the sum of $620 "paid cash." They were identified in the deed of sale as "a Negro man named Adam, a Negro woman named Chloe and her son Caleb (a cripple)."[64] Later in the year, Peyton purchased a twelve-year-old slave boy named Jack from one Harvey Beach of New Orleans for the consideration of $950 cash. Jack was to live with the Peytons as their house servant.[65]

During the second week of January 1842, Peyton took up the DePutron prosecution again, this time in U.S. District Court where three indictments against the sea captain were pending. One charged him with "false swearing" under the provisions of an act of Congress "to provide for the enrollment and licensing of vessels for the coasting trade"; a second charged him with corresponding with and supplying a pirate; and the last with fitting out a vessel for the purpose of engaging in the slave trade.

On January 12, Peyton placed DePutron on trial to face the first indictment. By the final morning of the four-day trial, the defense seemed to have gutted the government's proof. Although he agreed with Peyton that the jury was the sole judge of the law and testimony in the case, the presiding judge usually upheld the many objections by the defense to the evidence presented by the government. At that stage, the audience in the courtroom expected acquittal, but Peyton made a dramatic closing speech and held the jury's attention by alluding repeatedly to the pirate-like character of the defendant. Charging that DePutron intended to enter the African slave trade in violation of the laws of the United States, he asserted that the evidence in the case showed that he was by profession a pirate, "ever ready to redden the waves of the sea with the blood of his fellow man." He cautioned the jury of the grave danger that would be risked by setting such a person loose on society.[66]

After receiving the judge's charge and deliberating the matter for about twenty minutes, the jury returned with a verdict of guilty.[67] The force of Peyton's rhetoric had enabled him to win again, but defense attorney C. K. Johnson persisted.

Within the next four days, the rest of the district attorney's case fell apart. He failed to get a conviction on the charge of fitting out a vessel for engaging in the slave trade, the judge granted a new trial on the perjury conviction, and Peyton agreed he would not prosecute the remaining charge. In fact, he decided that DePutron had been in prison long enough, if only for seven months, and believed further litigation would be of doubtful value. A few weeks later the judge set the defendant free. Suggesting that Balie had elevated DePutron beyond the level of his accomplishments, a New Orleans newspaper referred to the captain as the "magnificently magnified pirate."[68]

On April 21, District Attorney Peyton was back in federal court with a case that originated when two men, the defendants, "had feloniously and piratically . . . stolen and carried away from Melchisedeck Dechase, on the high seas," Spanish and Mexican dollars and doubloons amounting to $11,527 and certain other personal property. The thieves allegedly put Dechase adrift in an open boat somewhere in the West Indies.

After twenty-four hours, the jury was unable to reach a verdict, although the evidence was strong. The *Daily Picayune* reported nine of the jurymen favored a guilty verdict and three were for acquittal.[69] Peyton called for a new trial on May 26; the government again failed to sustain the piracy charge, but the jury found the defendants guilty of larceny.[70]

Although convictions on charges of piracy were difficult to obtain, plenty of other litigation occupied the attorney general. Peyton prosecuted more than one case that involved white-collar crime. He was distressed when he discovered that John M. Breedlove, a Customs House bond clerk, had been one of the principals in "the abstraction" of federal notes from the Customs House on July 26, 1841. A total of $99,915 was removed on that date. Eleven months later, John tardily but voluntarily confessed his participation in the theft.[71] Balie seems at first to have recused himself from the case, probably as a gesture of friendship to James Waller Breedlove, a kinsman of John's who had so readily assisted the Peytons in locating a suitable residence and office when they moved to New Orleans. Another lawyer acted for the district attorney.[72]

By the following summer, Peyton took charge of the Customs House case, his friendship with the Breedlove family notwithstanding.[73] Using "legal ability and ingenuity of a high order," he convicted John M. Breedlove after a trial that lasted several months. The judge sentenced him to a ten-year term in the penitentiary, but in March 1847, President Polk commuted the sentence and set Breedlove free.[74]

Balie prosecuted a case referred to in the local press as "the U.S. vs. Jesse Hoyt, the defaulter," and won a judgment in favor of the government in the amount of $220,837.86 on May 8, 1843. Hoyt, described by the *Daily Picayune* as a "rogue," had made a bond of $200,000 and had as sureties a judge, two lawyers, and three local businessmen. The newspaper's editor doubted the sureties would suffer: "We should suppose from their known reputation for shrewdness, that if they are able to respond to the call which the government will now make upon them, they must have managed ere this to have secured themselves."[75]

One of Peyton's most notable courtroom successes was his prosecution of the case of the *United States* v. *the Bank of the United States of Pennsylvania*, a privately owned bank.[76] At issue was the disposition of certain bank assets located in Louisiana in the amount of approximately $1.5 million that had been seized by the United States. The principal legal question was whether the Louisiana Commercial Court had authority with the consent of both parties to appoint receivers to take possession of and administer the holdings in question. Seeking to retain as much control of its fiscal affairs as possible, the defendant U.S. Bank of Pennsylvania questioned the Commercial Court's ruling in favor of the government and appealed it to the Louisiana Supreme Court. Peyton and the national government claimed that the bank owed the money to Louisiana persons and corporations and that the Louisianians had a good and proper claim to it. On appeal the bank repudiated the debt, objected to the Commercial Court setting the rate of interest to be paid on it at 6 percent, and denied the capacity of the receivers to sue.

The unanimous opinion of the Supreme Court delivered May 22, 1843, sustained the Commercial Court on all points raised except the interest rate, which it raised to 10 percent, the amount originally sought by the plaintiffs. It was a bruising blow to the defendant bank, but a time for celebration by Peyton and attorneys John R. Grymes and Thomas Slidell who had been associated with him to represent the local persons and corporations whose money was at stake.

A New Orleans editor hailed the successful ending of the complex lawsuit. "No cause has been decided by our courts for many years which excited so much interest," he wrote. "It involved a very large amount of money, and presented many questions of law which have been considered as unsettled in our courts."[77]

Following delivery of the Supreme Court's ruling, Peyton and his two attorney colleagues adjourned to the new restaurant on St. Louis Street operated by former New Yorker Antoine Alciatore. Crowded with other lawyers and merchants, Antoine's was just as overheated as the courtroom, but the crowd was jovial and many congratulated Peyton's team for winning an important, complicated lawsuit.

Not everyone was happy with the outcome of the litigation, however. Senator Richard Henry Bayard, a Delaware Whig, uttered "certain dubious expressions" about Balie in connection with the case. The "expressions" were insulting, and when he learned of them, Balie forced the senator to "retract and file his retraction in the office of the solicitor of the treasury." He then retaliated with a sizzling dismissal of Bayard as "a poor cuckold . . . of not much force."[78]

Although the bank case had further enhanced Peyton's standing as an attorney, it had not provided commensurate financial rewards for him. At first, on December 5, 1843, four fellow members of the New Orleans bar joined in a statement to the court that he would be "well entitled" to a commission of 2.5 percent on the amount actually collected. They referred specifically to the case as tried in the Commercial Court of New Orleans and in the Louisiana Supreme Court.[79] But after a delay of several months, during which time Peyton delivered additional professional services to "agents of the government," the office of the Solicitor of the U.S. Treasury refused to pay the fee he claimed for trying the case. The solicitor instead took the position that Balie was entitled to 5 percent of the amount realized by the government, but that such amount could not yet be determined. It could be calculated only after settlement of another lawsuit against the government filed in Philadelphia by the Pennsylvania bank.

When Balie tried to draft against the government for a partial payment of $2,000, the Treasury turned it down, although his fee for taking the case successfully to the Louisiana Supreme Court was approximately $10,625. Peyton was irate. He asked whether he should be deprived of his fee for monies already collected because of the prospective failure of the government in another suit brought in another state.[80]

A tragic riverboat collision on the early morning of March 1 brought Balie into a lawsuit that lasted most of the rest of the year. The northbound steamboat *Buckeye* and the southbound *DeSoto* collided at a point in the Mississippi River called "Old River," killing five passengers on the *Buckeye*. On April 9, the federal grand jury indicted the pilot of the *Buckeye*, Robert E. Klady, charging him with manslaughter due to his "misconduct, negligence or inattention" at the time of the collision. The *Daily Picayune* believed it was the first time that criminal charges had been brought against a pilot in any similar American maritime disaster.[81] The professional embarrassment caused by the accident and the trial was the only punishment Klady received. In court, Peyton could not sustain the broad charges of the indictment.

Later, another Mississippi River pilot faced similar charges. J. C. Wingard was pilot of the *DeSoto* when she collided with the *Luda*, resulting in the death of a passenger. Again, Peyton found it impossible to prove that negligence caused the accident.[82]

Beginning in 1841, Balie lived an important part of his political life in the rising career of his brother Jo, who on April 21 was married to Mary Elizabeth Hatton of Lebanon, sister of Whig Congressman-to-be Robert Hopkins Hatton. Following marriage, Jo put aside his medical practice, became the Whig nominee for state senator, and won the seat over the Democratic candidate. His success was due in no small part to Balie's favorable standing with Whigs in the district and to Congressman William B. Campbell's campaign counsel and open support. But the campaign trail was his own, and he made the most of it, appearing at militia musters regularly and taking the stump at every opportunity.[83]

Balie's shadow still fell so long over Middle Tennessee politics that Robert Armstrong[84] gave him credit for planning to have his brother-in-law Thomas R. Barry, who was always aligned with the Jackson-Van Buren Democrats, reelected to the state house of representatives in 1843 and Jo reelected to the senate. He told James K. Polk that Balie had "arranged" it while on a short visit to Gallatin in December 1842. He was wrong on all counts, however, because Jo had higher ambitions, and Barry resigned his seat before the election.[85]

When Campbell declined to seek reelection to Congress, Jo opted to run for the vacant seat. Following advice from Balie and Campbell, he carried out an active canvass. After receiving the Whig nomination, he aggressively turned on his Democratic Party rival, Daniel Smith Donelson, who lived nearby in Hendersonville, and won the office in the general election of 1843.[86] The victory sustained Armstrong's judgment that Balie's political clout, wherever and whenever applied, could not be ignored.

There were other family matters outside the realm of politics and Balie addressed them. He purchased a slave woman named Clarissa and her two young children for four hundred dollars in 1843 to keep ownership in the family when the Sumner County sheriff conducted a court ordered sale of certain properties of brother-in-law Thomas Barry. The sale was held to satisfy "sundry executions" from the circuit court and from a justice of the peace in favor of the Bank of Tennessee, one James Mays, and others.[87]

A year later, attesting to "the love and affection" he had for his sister Mrs. Thomas Barry, Balie sent Clarissa and her two children back home by placing them in trust to his brother Jo for her "sole use and benefit." He named Balie Jr. as successor trustee should Jo die or become incapacitated.[88]

Family aside, Peyton's attention always returned to the political arena. He was at his best helping a former congressional colleague in a major move as when he instigated the appointment of his Virginia friend Henry A. Wise as minister to Brazil. Was this an indication that Peyton valued such positions highly and would soon covet a ministry for himself?[89] The Senate confirmed the nomination of Wise early in February 1844.[90]

As a Whig holding a presidential appointment, Peyton could not avoid participating in the national election of 1844. He relished being in that position. In fact, the Democrats increased his enthusiasm for the canvass by nominating for president his former congressional nemesis and fellow Tennessean James K. Polk.

Daniel Smith Donelson

Approximately three thousand Louisiana Whigs gathered for the state convention in New Orleans on February 22–24, and Peyton was present but had no prominent speaking role. He was dealing with a busy court docket while eagerly awaiting the final selection of the party's national nominees.[91]

When the Whig National Convention nominated Henry Clay and Theodore Frelinghuysen on May 1, Balie was ready to take to the stump for them. Although his job as district attorney sharply curtailed the time he could spend outside the state, he knew he could be effective in Louisiana while his brother Jo made stump appearances in Tennessee.

Attending the "Great Whig Convention" in Nashville on August 21, Peyton and Prentiss made stem-winding speeches, but the presence of Henry Clay overshadowed all others. There were so many speeches throughout the city that Balie's and many others' were not reported in the press. Listening to what he thought was the greatest speech Prentiss had ever made, unsurpassed for eloquence and power, Balie was on the platform when he delivered it. Just as Prentiss closed, he fainted, presumably from the heat. Bending over "the great man's unconscious figure," Peyton smiled as he exclaimed, "Don't come to, Prentiss. Now is your time to die; this is the culmination of your fame!"[92] Prentiss survived.

Like many of his contemporaries, Peyton made business decisions based primarily on his short-term needs. He borrowed and spent freely. He entered partnerships that frequently ended in costly litigation or impromptu arrangements that were far from satisfactory. Many of his problems and opportunities alike were court related, but he had not yet mastered the art of trade and commerce.

Most of his business deals seemed to develop remarkable complications. In January 1844, Peyton filed a claim against the U.S. government to force it to pay him for his one-half undivided interest in a tract of land he had purchased in 1839 on the Mississippi River near the South Pass on which the government later built a lighthouse. His original partner, Richard M. Carter, had sold his one-half interest to the government without apprising Balie, even though earlier he had given Balie a power of attorney to sell the entire tract.[93] The partnership arrangement precluded the sale of a divided one-half the acreage. The United States and Balie had become partners who owned the entire tract, including the location of the lighthouse.

Unable to get relief from federal maritime agencies, he decided to make a claim to the Congress to instruct the secretary of the Treasury to purchase his interest in the land. The matter was debated annually in both House and Senate from 1845 through 1848, but Balie had enough political enemies in Congress during the Polk presidency to thwart any final action. The federal government and he were co-tenants, and neither could eject the other.[94] Many years later the Congress authorized a token settlement.

In the meantime, on May 22, 1845, Peyton pledged his interest in the property as security for a debt of seventy-five hundred dollars owed to H. R. W. Hill of New Orleans, a grandson-in-law of General Winchester. It is not clear how the debt was incurred, but most likely it was borrowed to pay off other obligations, some perhaps as the result of gambling losses at the races.[95]

Nearing the end of his term as district attorney, Balie's thoughts drifted back to Tennessee. What if he had sought a third term in Congress? Win or lose, what would it have meant for him and his family? Avoiding the tantalizing retrospective, he took comfort in his brother's election to Congress. He promised himself that he would correspond regularly with Jo, his personal representative in Washington.

FAMILY TRAGEDIES AND WAR
1844–1846

Joseph Peyton's career in Congress was a matter of both pride and ongoing concern to Balie. Emphasizing the value of effective oratory on the floor of the House, he congratulated Jo on January 28, 1844,[1] for his "mistletoe speech" of January 2 on the bill to refund the fine imposed on General Jackson by Judge Dominick Hall in New Orleans in 1815.

Asserting that the Democrats intended to divert the funds to revive the candidacy of former President Van Buren, Jo had spoken in a taunting metaphor:

> Mr. Van Buren was a mere political parasite, a branch of mistletoe, that owed its elevation, its growth—nay, its very existence, to the tall trunk of an aged hickory; but so soon as it was attempted to transplant it and force it to live upon its own resources, independent of hickory sap, it shrunk, and withered, and died; and you now found out that the only mode of reviving it again . . . is to call to its aid the strength and support and sustenance of the same old hickory.[2]

As this speech had been so favorably noticed, Balie counseled Jo that he should not rush to make another because he had much to lose.

> Keep up the same *tone* & *lofty* sentiment in all your future speeches. Be *bold* as *hell* & as cautious as *damnation*. Patriotic *madness* is excusable, & sometimes *necessary*, provided you always have method in your madness.[3]

In correspondence with Balie and William B. Campbell throughout 1844, Jo expressed concern for the welfare of the Whig Party at the national level. Outraged that their own President Tyler vetoed the first and second national bank bills passed on party line votes, the Whigs had read him out of the party.[4]

The young congressman was "more disposed to laugh at" the presidential aspirations of his Tennessee colleague in Congress, James K. Polk, but on election day the result was no laughing matter. Polk won the presidency over the greatest Whig of them all, Henry Clay of Kentucky. It was an agonizing surprise to Whigs everywhere.[5]

During the following winter, Jo acknowledged that Tennessee Whigs were dissatisfied with their party's course. He took comfort that even with their favorite son in the White House, Tennessee Democrats seemed equally dissatisfied with their party. Yet he and Balie wondered how that general dissatisfaction would affect the upcoming election.[6]

With the coming of summer, political enemies in the congressional district began to strike at Jo by circulating charges that Balie had offered protection to one Charles Lewis of Gallatin, the fleeing admitted killer of State Representative Isaac Goodall of Smith County. The report included charges that Balie had procured his discharge from jail, had harbored him in New Orleans, and had aided him in leaving the country. It was potentially a hot political issue because Goodall was a Democrat who had come into Gallatin in June 1844 to celebrate the election of President Polk when his Whig friend Lewis, then intoxicated, pressed a pistol to his chest and shot him down.[7]

Balie's true relationship with the killer was entirely at odds with the reports circulated in the district. It was true that both were Whigs, both were owners of racehorses, and Lewis had once purchased a thoroughbred from Peyton, but that was the extent of their relationship.

There had been no communications between them since the shooting until Lewis reached New Orleans on his way out of the country. Summoning Peyton to his room on the evening that he sailed for "one of the Spanish islands," Lewis offered his explanation of the killing. It was the first and only time that they met after the death of Goodall.

Wanting the widow of Isaac Goodall to share the experience of his brief visit with Lewis, Balie dispatched a letter to her. The killer had wept incessantly during the meeting, he wrote, interspersing sobs with assurances that the killing had been an accident and he had not intended to do it. Balie hoped it would be "some consolation . . . to know that her husband was not the victim of assassination."[8]

Lewis returned to the States in the latter part of 1844 and was arrested and incarcerated at Clinton, Louisiana. Soon he obtained his release without Balie's aid or knowledge, and made his way back to New Orleans.

There he consciously avoided Balie because he feared that Balie was aware that he had threatened violence against Jo Peyton and Capt. Young Douglass over political issues.[9]

Balie shared the surprise of others when Lewis appeared in Tennessee, voluntarily surrendered himself to the sheriff of Sumner County on December 13, 1845, and demanded trial. Entering a strong plea to dismiss the indictment for murder with malice and aforethought, Lewis's attorneys successfully contended that there was no prior contemplation of the act, and that it did not fit the statutory requirement for second degree murder or manslaughter.

President James Knox Polk

They emphasized the long-standing personal friendship between the two men, urging it as the reason Goodall did not resist the killer pressing his pistol against his body. It was a highly regrettable accident, they said. After hearing the arguments for both sides, the court ruled the killing to be excusable homicide and released the defendant, acquitted of all charges.[10]

Regardless of having his name smeared by his brother's enemies, Balie was excited by the progress Jo was making in Congress. On June 5, Jo spoke at length on the general appropriations bill in the House, and a week later tangled with most of the New York State congressional delegates in an exchange of "cards" in the *Globe* and the *National Intelligencer*. He had followed his brother's example by making himself known to his colleagues within a single two-year term.[11]

When friends staged a rally for Jo near Gallatin on July 26, 1844, to kick off his reelection campaign, Balie noted the event with pleasure.[12] On the following September 15, he was further gratified when Jo substituted for John Bell at a Lebanon political gathering and spoke for two hours.[13] His greatest satisfaction was learning in November that his brother won reelection to a second term in Congress.

Balie had to face political problems of his own. After the end of his four-year term as district attorney in 1845, he was not the choice of the new Democratic administration in Washington to succeed himself. Even Andrew Jackson, who believed that retaining "good *Whigs*" in office would be desirable, suggested to President Polk that "our quondam friend Bailey Peyton will not be retained."[14] Balie expected

Joseph Hopkins Peyton

nothing else as he had worked successfully with others to prevent Polk from winning the vote in Tennessee.

Consequently, he devoted much of his time to building up the law practice that he had neglected in favor of his federal responsibilities. His was a general practice that included a variety of cases. Few, however, provided as much public entertainment as a lawsuit against landlord Jeremiah Kinneally and his sister in which one of the tenants, a baker named William Roy, struck the woman when she tried to stop him from dismantling part of the building as he loaded out his equipment for another location. A phrenologist and lecturer on astronomy, Roy had just immigrated to America from Scotland and taken up the new trade. Peyton rebuked him for his attachment to the practice of phrenology and denounced him for removing parts of the rented building and striking Miss Kinneally when she remonstrated with him about it. The *Daily Picayune*'s reporter wrote of Balie:

> With regard to mesmerism, he told him, that when next he took a subject in hand—more particularly, should the subject happen to be a lady—he should be less violent in his "reverse passes" than he was with Miss Kinneally. If his clairvoyant faculty enabled him already to see the decision of the Court in this case, he had not a doubt, he said, but that he was aware of its being in favor of his (Mr. P's) client, Kinneally.

The court so ruled.[15]

Notwithstanding his busy career in politics, the law, and the financial hazards of thoroughbred breeding when he lived 450 miles from the stud, Balie and his family enjoyed living in New Orleans. All around their adopted hometown were the usual signs of urban growth: busy commerce, congested traffic, and new construction.[16]

The Peytons found it entertaining to observe the daily arrival and departure of travelers, especially when their numbers included visitors from the Nashville-Gallatin area. Often they welcomed Tennesseans who had migrated to the booming city, attracted by opportunities there and in nearby Texas. When not receiving visitors, Balie liked to attend periodic theatrical productions and on occasion joined in hosting a dinner to pay tribute to a star performer. The Shakespearean actor William C. Macready was one such honoree.[17]

The scenes changed quickly in the Crescent City but never fast enough to force the head of the household out of the public eye. It was a different kind of frontier, but frontier it was. Where was it all leading? Living in New Orleans, Balie and Anne constantly sensed something akin to the excitement of riding a Tennessee thoroughbred for the first time.

The Peyton children experienced "life shaped by their family's social and economic standing" further enriched by the diversity of peoples and cultures of the city. The first public schools opened in their municipality during the early 1840s, but their parents sent them to private schools and otherwise followed the practice of middle-class families in other communities, all the time "enhancing the notion of the ideal child."[18] Usually a nurse or nanny, assuming much of the mother's role, was part of the family. Nonetheless, Anne devoted herself to her husband and children. Though often absent for business and political reasons, Balie was a loving father. In 1840, the birth of the Peytons' second daughter Anne (called Nan or Nanny) underlined her parents' commitment to family life.

Five years later with little warning, death shattered the good life of the Peyton family. On January 13, 1845, Balie's wife, Anne Smith Peyton, died unexpectedly at their home at 83 Dauphine Street.[19] Invited friends of the family attended the funeral of the forty-three-year-old mother at the Peyton residence and burial in the Firemen's Cemetery late in the afternoon of the next day.[20] Balie, Emily, Balie Jr., John Bell, and Nanny struggled with their sorrow.

The Peyton children, whose ages varied from five to thirteen, faced an uncertain future. Emotionally distraught, Balie wanted them with him, but he knew they needed the love and guidance that might better be provided in a home where a mother was present. For the moment he kept them with him in school[21] in New Orleans, but when the heat of summer came, he delivered all four to Tennessee for the season and entrusted them to the care of his sister, Mrs. Thomas Barry, at Gallatin.

The autumn of 1845 brought further sorrow to the family. Just after election to a second term in Congress, Balie's beloved brother Jo was stricken ill and died on November 12, leaving his wife and two children.[22] At that time Balie was still in Tennessee after attending the Nashville fall races. He remained for several days with his family at the Barry home near the Station Camp Creek farm to assist in planning for Joseph's widow and children.

As if there had not been enough recent tragedy in Balie's family, his brother Ran committed suicide by shooting himself the following July. Ran had been on-site manager of the farm, including the breeding operation, and was the only one of the brothers who truly shared Balie's enthusiasm for the world of horses.[23]

To overcome the grief he felt as he had experienced the deaths of his wife and two brothers during a period of nineteen months, Balie immersed himself in his law practice and Whig Party politics. But the political environment was changing rapidly.

Campaign rhetoric had exaggerated Balie's well-known opposition to Polk into a "conspiracy against the life and character of the candidate" in 1844. Allegations that Peyton and unnamed associates were conspiring against Polk's life and character were first made in two letters addressed to the editor of the New York *Evening Post* and signed by a supposed citizen of Rutherford County, Tennessee. Balie denied the charges categorically and said that the story was "a fabrication from the beginning to the end."[24]

As bitter as their political rivalry had been, Peyton and Polk declared a personal truce in the autumn of 1845. Governor Pierce M. Butler of South Carolina, one of Peyton's partners in a thoroughbred racehorse, opened the way by asking a friend in the cabinet if the president would receive Balie, should he call to "pay his respects." It was represented to the president that Balie said that he had never had any "personal difficulty or misunderstanding with the President, that in politics he had differed with him, that in the political discussions in Tennessee he had used strong language towards him, but not stronger than was usual towards political opponents in that state."[25]

Agreeing that Peyton had stated their relationship accurately, Polk said that for several years the pair had no "personal intercourse . . . in consequence of the violence of party feeling which had separated them." He declared that he entertained no "personal unkind feeling towards Mr. Peyton," and promised that should he call, he would "receive and treat him courteously and respectfully."[26]

During the stressful year of 1845, Peyton adjusted to the fact that the Tennessee neighbor whom he so respected as a turfman, military hero, and Unionist had died on June 8 at his home, the Hermitage. Although he had split with President Jackson over political issues and was a key player in organizing an opposition party, Balie insisted that he had always held strongly to the principles that the Old Hero had espoused during his first term in the White House. He identified with the self-reliant frontier spirit of Jacksonian democracy, but could not accept low tariffs, the political spoils system, and "pet banks" as the alternative to a truly national bank. He could not accept in any way Jackson's attempt to name his own successor to the presidency. Balie would not miss butting political heads with Old Hickory, but indeed he would miss the chance occasions he had treasured when the two could discuss their attachment to horses and horse racing.

Balie Peyton in Mexican War uniform

When thinking of "the general," he had to acknowledge the desirability of a military command record for anyone with serious political aspirations. Was it time for him to have a battlefield experience? The next year provided that opportunity.

Although opposed by Whigs in the North, war with Mexico was regarded by most in New Orleans as unavoidable, even desirable. Notwithstanding the responsibility he properly felt for his four children who were then with him, Balie was among the first to volunteer for military service. On May 12, 1846, the day before Congress declared war, he "announced himself a candidate for the Rio Grande" during a spirited public rally at the Commercial Exchange.[27]

On or about May 24, Peyton sent his children, Nan, Emily, Balie Jr., and John Bell Peyton, to Nashville on the steamboat *Talleyrand*. By prearrangement, his sister, Mrs. Thomas Barry, took them into her care at Gallatin until he, the eternal optimist, should return from Mexico, supposedly in six months.[28]

Offering himself as a private in the ranks, Balie became a captain literally overnight and on May 13 was enlisting volunteers at a lively rate for a company to be called the Taylor Guards. Public excitement was at a high level. The editor of the *Daily Picayune* observed that the men of his company "follow a leader whom any corps might be proud to accompany to the field," and predicted that "Mr. Peyton will be required in a more imposing command than that of captain."

Before the end of the day, Maj. Gen. Edmund P. Gaines concurred and addressed Balie as "Col. Balie Peyton," authorizing him to raise the Fifth Regiment of ten companies of six-month volunteers.[29] The press applauded his promotion. The *Daily Delta* offered its opinion: "Under no more gallant spirit can a soldier serve than Mr. Peyton."[30] Claiming him as a native son and a former citizen, the Nashville *Republican Banner* saluted him as "that gallant Peyton."[31]

Colonel Peyton mustered his regiment into the service of the United States on May 22, and "the ladies of New Orleans" made the occasion a memorable one by delivering a hand-sewn regimental flag to him.[32] Presented by Mrs. Mary E. H. Gwin, wife of Sumner County-born William McKendree Gwin who was then the Polk-appointed commissioner to oversee construction of the Customs House at New Orleans,[33] the flag came with her assurance that victory would "perch upon it" when the regiment met the enemy.

On May 24, the *Galveston* steamed out of New Orleans with 420 men from five companies of Peyton's regiment aboard. Just over twenty-four hours later Colonel Peyton, his staff, and the remaining five companies left the city on board the steamer *Alabama*.[34] They were a part of the brigade of Louisiana Volunteers commanded by Gen. Persifor F. Smith.[35]

Peyton and his regiment had hardly left the city when Secretary of War William L. Marcy began to question General Gaines's decision to make requisitions for volunteers prior to receiving authorization from Washington. He was concerned also that Gaines had enlisted soldiers for a period of six months whereas he expected enlistments to be for twelve months or the duration of the war.[36] The confusion resulted in Marcy relieving Gaines of command of the Western Division and ordering him to Washington. After questioning and exoneration by his superiors, Gaines assumed command of the U.S. Army Eastern Department with headquarters in New York City.[37]

While Marcy was trying to evaluate General Gaines's call upon governors of the southern states for volunteers, Peyton and his regiment had reached the seat of war and were encamped near Burita.[38] Learning that his friend William B. Campbell was at the head of a Tennessee regiment that had passed through New Orleans headed toward Brazos Island, Peyton estimated that he had had time to reach the island and sent a letter by messenger, inviting him to "come up" to Burita. He was anxious to know if Campbell had any news of his children from whom he had heard nothing since seeing them off on the *Talleyrand*.[39]

Peyton expected his regiment would be a part of Gen. Zachary Taylor's army that he believed was preparing to march into the interior of Mexico.[40] But on July 21, General Taylor relayed orders from the War Department that directed the regiments of Louisiana Volunteers commanded by Colonels Peyton and Edward Featherstone and the battalion from Alabama under Lieut. Col. Philip H. Raiford to return home and disband. They would receive transportation to New Orleans and there be mustered out of service.[41]

The secretary of war ruled that Peyton's and Featherstone's regiments and the Alabama battalion were "not in service under any existing law" because there was no statutory authority to enlist six-month volunteers. Although invited to reenlist for twelve months or the duration of the war, nearly all chose to return home. They had responded to General Gaines's urgent appeal, had reached the Rio Grande, and were returning home satisfied that they had done their duty even if the War Department and its top general officers could not agree on the suitability of their term of enlistment.[42]

The administration's treatment of the six-month volunteers drew stern criticism in New Orleans. On August 2, the editor of the *Daily Picayune* voiced the feelings of most when he explained that there were very few reenlistments because the volunteers had been the victims of "the supercilious insolence of an incompetent Secretary of War [and] the hesitating policy of a weak, scheming and vacillating Administration." The secretary had taken two months to decide whether the Peyton and Featherstone regiments were "in the service or not," even though they were at the ready on the Rio Grande and had been among the first to arrive.

Whigs in Tennessee rejected the administration's decision. Disgusted, the Nashville *Republican Banner* observed, "Thus are the interests of the country sacrificed—the spirit of the volunteers crushed; and all to serve the dishonest purposes of party." The editor thought Peyton's leadership in the Whigs' successful effort to block President Polk from winning his own state on election day was central to having his regiment rejected. It was, he wrote, "shameless partisanship . . . narrow policy . . . utter disregard for the interests of the people."[43]

As Peyton's regiment prepared to return home, he put no pressure on anyone to reenlist but let them know that he was not going home. Instead, he joined the staff of General Taylor as a volunteer aide-de-camp.[44] He remained with Taylor's headquarters until transferring to the staff of Brig. Gen. W. J. Worth in a similar responsibility shortly before the American assault on Monterrey. His decision to stay in Mexico was widely applauded, even by the Nashville *Union*, a chronically severe critic of his political life.[45]

Zachary Taylor

Actually, Peyton was mustered out of service with his regiment on August 19, although he had been on leave with General Taylor in an unpaid capacity since August 1.[46] For his brief service as regimental commander, he later received a bounty land grant of 160 acres under the congressional bounty act of March 3, 1855.[47]

Peyton was present with Worth's Second Division of regular army soldiers when General Taylor's army arrived outside the walls of Monterrey on the morning of September 19. After conducting reconnaissance throughout the day, Taylor prepared to challenge the enemy force deployed to defend Monterrey, although it was twice the size of his own. On September 20 he detached Worth's division to flank the city and take the Saltillo Road, the route over which supplies and reinforcements would reach the defenders. Late in the day, Worth engaged the Mexican troops and continued in bitterly contested battle with them throughout the next three days and nights.[48]

On the day after the battle, September 25, Peyton wrote of Worth's operations:

> The division . . . was ever successful . . . putting to rout the enemy's cavalry on the plains, driving his infantry through the chaparral and from the housetops, scaling immense heights, capturing guns and storming fortresses . . . deemed impregnable. . . . And, best of all, these brilliant exploits were performed with the loss of fourteen killed and fifty-six wounded.

Praising the performances of both regular and volunteer soldiers that on September 24 resulted in the capitulation of the Mexican Army before them, Peyton referred to Colonel Hays's Texas Rangers with great respect.

> The 1st Regiment of Texas mounted riflemen, commanded by . . . Col. J. C. [Jack] Hays . . . has fully sustained its former reputation. . . . On the morning of the 21st, Col. Hays, with several companies of his mounted riflemen, were thrown forward to open the ball, which he did most beautifully.[49]

Ever alert to boost the reputation of his fellow Whigs, Peyton praised the bravery and effectiveness of the First Regiment of Tennessee Volunteers. Although not in Worth's division, the regiment included many from Peyton's old congressional district and the commander was his long-standing political brother Col. William B. Campbell.

> The 1st Regiment of Tennessee Volunteers . . . suffered more severely, perhaps, than any other . . . during the siege, having had twenty-seven killed on the field, and seventy-seven wounded, some of them mortally, and many of them seriously, and this out of a force of only 379 men. . . . [It] was the first regiment which stormed the fort . . . and unfurled the stars and stripes upon its walls.

Peyton gave the Mexican Army credit for making a brave stand and commended Gen. Pedro de Ampudia for the conciliatory assurances that he gave after capitulating to the American forces. Ampudia's assertion that Gen. Santa Anna "was disposed to peace" led Balie to believe that the Battle of Monterrey might be the last battle of the war.[50]

During the battle, Balie had been at Worth's side. On one occasion, the general sent him to take a message to General Taylor at the other end of the city. A sympathetic writer later recalled the episode: "Mounted on a thoroughbred . . . Peyton, though continually under fire . . . performed the trip at a dead run and in safety. . . . With modesty and true sportsmanship he always credited the success of his trip to his horse." He admitted the animal "was a little skittish . . . at first, somewhat like the fellow's hog, between a wild and a shy."[51]

Peyton believed that General Worth had "immortalized himself" in storming Monterrey. He applauded the general's "judicious conduct & noble & gallant bearing" and noted that he had not shied from danger but was ever close to "the music of balls from escapets to cannon, including grape, canister & the whole orchestra of martial music."[52]

General Worth returned the compliment: "To Col. Peyton, Louisiana Volunteers, who did him the honor to tender his very acceptable services as aide-de-camp, he feels under especial obligations to him for his valuable counsel and splendid exhibition of courage."[53]

Worth was pleased to use Peyton as a political conduit to Washington, sending his "warmest regards" to Senator Crittenden along with his expressed hope that the senator would become the next president of the United States. Sarcastically addressing what he must have believed was the general's raging vanity, Balie wrote to Crittenden that Worth had not "fully made up his mind as to whether or not he will accept the office of secretary of war, which he considers as having been tendered to him in advance." To be interested in the appointment, Worth would want to see "improvement" by Crittenden

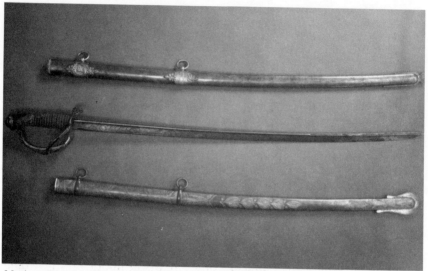

Mexican War sword and scabbards of Col. Balie Peyton

"in one particular & that is on the point of dignity, & distance." The general meant "to sustain all the pomp & circumstance of office himself, & cannot think of running under a chief who is not up to the mark in the article of dignity. . . . All in all, he is the high combed cock of the army, head & shoulders above the crowd."[54]

Subsequently, the Louisiana legislature tendered "special thanks" to Peyton, six other officers, and all of the Louisiana Volunteers.[55] Traditionally opposed to Peyton and other Whigs in general, the Democratic Nashville *Union* congratulated him for his conduct at Monterrey, noting that it gladly put aside politics during wartime.[56]

A group of New Orleans friends honored Peyton by presenting him a beautiful sword, the blade of which was decorated with oak leaf clusters, stands of arms, and other patriotic symbols. It bore the inscription, "Presented to Col. Balie Peyton, 5th Regiment Louis[a] Volun[r] National Guards by his friends of New Orleans. His country required his services. His deeds will add glory to her arms."[57]

Although he received no military encomiums from President Polk and his cabinet, Peyton chuckled when they agreed that he exercised significant political control over General Taylor. The president wrote of the cabinet's perception of Taylor and Peyton on November 14, 1846:

> The cabinet . . . agreed that he [General Taylor] was unfit for the chief command . . . that he was a bitter political partisan and had no sympathies with the administration, and that he had been recently

controlled, particularly on the expedition to Monterrey, by Balie Peyton, Mr. [George W.] Kendall, editor of the *Picayune* at New Orleans, and asst. adjutant General [William Wallace Smith] Bliss, who were cunning and shrewd men of more talents than himself, and had controlled him for political purposes.[58]

Unable to work out all of his combative energies against the Mexican Army, Balie was ready for a vigorous defense of General Taylor when Brig. Gen. Thomas Marshall of Kentucky censured "old Zack" for what he regarded as bad generalship or culpable neglect. In a face-to-face discussion of Marshall's allegations, "the language finally became so warm" on October 11 that Peyton slapped him in the face. A scuffle followed, but the contenders were quickly separated, and friends of both men expected that a duel was imminent.[59]

Newspapers at New Orleans and Nashville reported that Peyton and Marshall had agreed to meet the next morning and settle their differences by force of arms.[60] But like other affairs of honor in which Balie involved himself, this one was settled amicably without a shot being fired.[61] When he learned that he had misunderstood the statement by Marshall that prompted his explosion, he immediately tendered an apology through Gen. Albert S. Johnston, which the Kentuckian accepted.[62]

Returning to New Orleans from Brazos de Santiago, Peyton reached Galveston on October 23 on the steamship *McKim* in company with Gen. Albert S. Johnston, Kendall of the *Picayune,* and "a large number of discharged volunteers."[63] He arrived in New Orleans a few days later to an informal but enthusiastic dockside welcome. Earlier he had confided to Senator Crittenden that, if the war continued, he might return to the battlefield but said, "If I do, it will be with a command so organized that President Polk cannot disband it, or remove me from office."[64]

Peyton received another challenge, but this one did not become an affair of honor. On November 1, Col. Jefferson Davis[65] of Mississippi wrote to Balie from New Orleans alleging that his published letter describing the Battle of Monterrey was "inaccurate" and did "much injustice to the Miss. Regt." He asked Peyton "to remove the impression created by this statement, bearing as it now does the sanction of your name."[66]

Responding by letter on November 3, Balie let Davis know that he was not dealing with an opponent likely to concede:

> I regret that you did not more particularly point out the inaccuracy & injustice to which you allude & thereby enable me to amend the one & rectify the other. Nothing surely could be further from my wish or intention than to do injustice to the Miss. Regt.

Peyton admitted that he had commended the assault by the Tennessee Regiment, which was beyond his own powers to observe, but explained that his account was based on information supplied by its commander, Col. William B. Campbell. He assured Davis of Campbell's integrity.[67]

Eager to brief Colonel Campbell further on the controversy, Peyton first discussed Davis with S. S. Prentiss,[68] who knew him well. They agreed that the Mississippian "only wished to make a little Locofoco capital at home for Mississippi consumption."[69]

Confident that he was ingratiating himself with his fellow Mississippians, Davis persisted. On November 14, he wrote Peyton again. Dwelling on the agreed fact that Peyton was not present to observe the First Tennessee in its assault, Davis only wanted Peyton to disclaim any knowledge of the Tennesseans' role in the battle.[70]

But Peyton had left the city before receiving Davis's letter of November 14. Anxious to see his children, Peyton traveled by steamboat, arrived at Nashville on November 15, and took lodging at the City Hotel. "Troops of friends" double-timed to see him, but after a brief visit he proceeded directly to Gallatin to be with his family.[71]

Before leaving Nashville, he received an invitation from "a large circle of . . . old friends and acquaintances" to a public dinner honoring him and "the valiant men" with whom he had shared American arms. John Bell and Ephraim H. Foster[72] and seventy-two others signed the invitation that spelled out a tribute to Peyton. On November 25, Balie declined the invitation, explaining that he must hasten back to New Orleans where his law practice required immediate attention.[73]

Balie was gratified to find his children well. He was especially pleased to see the three older ones completely at ease on horseback. Although she always begged to ride with Emily, six-year-old Nan was not ready for a horse of her own. But after mulling it over, her father decided to make arrangements to have a pony for her for Christmas.

Attending to other personal matters while in Sumner County, Balie signed a bill of sale for a slave identified as "my boy Anthony about eighteen years of age of a light mulatto complexion" to Albert T. Burnley, a political friend of New Orleans. The purchaser paid eight hundred dollars for Anthony, who accompanied Balie on his return to New Orleans.[74]

Before he returned to New Orleans, he addressed a large crowd of Sumner Countians assembled in Gallatin at the courthouse on November 21. Peyton was responding to citizens of neighboring Davidson County who had proposed to erect a suitable monument in Nashville to the brave Tennessee volunteers who fell at Monterrey.

Called to chair the meeting, Judge John J. White presented resolutions to approve the erection of the monument, to solicit funds throughout Sumner County in support of the undertaking, to express admiration for the conduct of Gen. Zachary Taylor, and to pay tribute to the First Regiment Tennessee Volunteers.

Before asking for adoption of the resolutions, Judge White announced the presence of Peyton, and the crowd called loudly for him to tell them about his experiences at Monterrey.[75] Balie described the battle at length. He again complimented Col. Campbell's Tennessee regiment and "pronounced a glowing . . . eulogy upon the conduct of the Army, both regular and volunteers . . . and spoke with much feeling of the brave men who had fallen in the battle, who . . . deserved the noblest monument that could be erected to their memory."[76]

At the conclusion of Peyton's moving speech, the assembled citizens voted unanimously to adopt the monument resolutions.[77] Although disappointed a few weeks later when Davidson County support for the project waned, Sumner subscribers decided to erect it in Gallatin. After selecting a site in the city cemetery, they designed the monument with a box-shaped base that on each side exhibited a limestone panel on which were inscribed the names of the fifty-five Sumner County soldiers who died in battle or from disease contracted while in Mexico from 1846 through 1848. The base supported an obelisk that produced an overall height of twenty-eight feet.[78]

Upon his return to Louisiana, Peyton was outraged to discover that Col. Davis had taken his battle complaint to the public by writing in newspapers and making speeches. His speech of November 10 at Vicksburg was particularly galling.[79] Balie wrote to Campbell: "His speech is egotistical, illiberal, vindictive, & impudent. His letter is less offensive, but he there makes a direct issue with you as to the facts. He is a low and cunning demagogue . . . but has no taste for fighting you."[80]

Always ready to volunteer advice for a friend who might be challenged to fight, Peyton had counsel for Campbell: "If you find a difficulty with him unavoidable, put him on the offensive. Meet him, get into a conversation, fly into a rage, & run over him. If he calls on you, take him with a rifle, or dragoon saber & cut off his head." But cooling the heat of the reckless advice he had just written, Balie advised restraint. "Be prudent, keep out of it if you can," he said.[81]

Campbell was willing to let it be a war of words.[82] But Balie wanted Campbell to "notice Col. Davis" and "make him look very ridiculous." Perhaps he believed Davis was trying to slip into the Taylor camp: "Davis is a cunning, ambitious man," he wrote. "He has the sagacity enough to see that Polk & his party are gone to the devil & that Gen. Taylor will be the next president."[83]

Always proud of the kinds of enemies he attracted, Peyton was glad to add Jefferson Davis to the list. At times he seemed to enjoy his adversaries even more than his friends. Thinking of his enemies stimulated him, and he used his intellect and sharp tongue to respond.

But how was this belligerence going to help him adjust to civilian life and reestablish his law practice? This time Balie needed friends, and even more he needed clients. He had been away from the city and his law office for nearly seven months.

TAYLOR FOR PRESIDENT
1847–1849

Having "recommenced the practice of law" in New Orleans early in December 1846,[1] Peyton began to lay plans for his political future then threatened by the ascendancy of the Democrats in Washington. Writing Colonel Campbell in Mexico, he reported on the welfare of Mrs. Campbell before assessing the colonel's opportunity to be elected governor of Tennessee. Election would be easy; he needed only to permit his name to be offered. Believing that he could be elected without leaving the army or his home, Balie urged him to make his plans known.[2]

Campbell's heroism on the battlefield had elevated him to such a commanding position in the state that his political opponents feared they could not stop him. Peyton explained:

> The locofocos are so much alarmed at your name, that they have introduced the name of Col. [S. R.] Anderson[3] as their candidate. But that is all humbug. [Aaron V.] Brown[4] is their man for re-election, & no mistake. They will endeavor to sow the seeds of discord in your Regt. so as to stop your glorious career, but you must talk to the boys & appeal to the officers, to scout the [Democrat] "monster party" from your ranks.

Predicting that Gen. Zachary Taylor would emerge from the war as the Whig candidate for president, Peyton wanted Campbell to be ready to join the Taylor movement: "Be very careful . . . & caution your Whig

friends, also, to say nothing which can be tortured into any disparage-
ment to Gen'l Taylor. For if he lives, & no disaster befalls him, he is
bound to be the next President."[5] But for all of Peyton's encouragement
and counsel, Colonel Campbell chose to stand aside from the 1847
governor's race in Tennessee. Neill S. Brown returned the office to Whig
control, however, before the Democrats took it back in 1849.

Even though he faced a holiday season separated from his children,
only the tragic death of his seven-year-old daughter Nan could have interrupted Balie's political fixation. And it did. Learning she had died from
injuries sustained when thrown from the back of a pony he had provided
as a Christmas gift, he felt as if someone had driven a knife into his heart.
When he left her and the other children in Tennessee after his visit
following the Battle of Monterrey, he had arranged for the pony to be
delivered to his sister's farm during Nan's holiday from school in Nashville.
The supposedly gentle animal arrived as scheduled, but on one of her first
rides, it threw the child from the saddle. Before she could recover, a flying
hoof of the excited pony struck a severe blow to her head. She died a few
moments later. For her father the tragedy was compounded by his inability
to reach Gallatin from New Orleans in time for the funeral.[6]

Trying to put Nan's death behind him, Balie looked beyond the
multiple tragedies his family had experienced to plan a leading role for
himself in a presidential campaign for General Taylor. He could always
lose himself in politics. To preempt the general's favor, he promoted a
mass meeting in New Orleans for a public tribute to the Louisiana hero.
Recruiting dignitaries that included "that noble little gamecock S. S.
Prentiss," Mayor A. D. Crossman, Lieutenant Governor T. Landry,
Speaker of the House Preston W. Farrar, Judge Henry Adams Bullard,
Recorder Joshua Baldwin, and the French-speaking local Gallic leader
Bernard Marigny, Peyton assembled a large crowd on February 17 at the
Exchange on St. Charles Street.[7]

Heeding calls from the audience, Peyton spoke first. For more than
one hour, he held the crowd spellbound with a dramatic story of the
assault on Monterrey. Prentiss spoke for another hour, and other
speakers followed. When the last had finished, those assembled adopted
resolutions praising General Taylor and the officers and men of his
command for their "fortitude, enterprise, discipline, and gallant
bearing." Trying to shield Taylor from critics who objected to his permitting the Mexican Army to withdraw instead of suffering destruction at
his hands, Balie made certain the last paragraph of the resolutions was
carefully phrased. Referring to Taylor and his men, it stated:

> The lustre of their achievements can only be equalled by their generous
> and noble forbearance in victory toward a vanquished and submissive

foe, and their disposition uniformly evinced to spare an unnecessary effusion of blood and mitigate the horrors of war.[8]

A month later Peyton was one of the principals who arranged a meeting for March 30, 1847, to celebrate General Taylor's victory at the Battle of Buena Vista. When he called the meeting to order, the "thousands" gathered at the new Commercial Exchange cheered every mention of the general's name. For Peyton it was an occasion awash in patriotism but ultimately designed to promote Taylor as a Whig candidate for president. He did not make one of his typical extended speeches but introduced the several speakers "in a most felicitous manner."[9] Earlier in the day, Balie had spoken to and toasted with the members of the local New England Society as they honored their guest, Col. Caleb Cushing, a former Massachusetts congressman,[10] who later addressed the Taylor rally.[11]

Confident that Taylor would be the Whig nominee, Balie devoted most of 1847 to promoting the general for president and rebuilding his own law practice. When the members of the New Orleans bar organized the New Orleans Law Association in May 1847, they elected him one of two vice presidents, an indication of the high esteem in which they and others held him.[12] To relieve himself of the burden of managing from a long distance, he turned over the supervision of the farm and stud in Tennessee to his brother-in-law Thomas Barry, who practiced law and was a good turfman. On March 22, 1847, Barry received Balie's power of attorney that gave him broad authorization to buy, sell, and mortgage properties.[13]

Scanning the national political horizon for signs of Taylor's strength, Peyton was delighted when the Native American Party, in convention at Philadelphia in September 1847, threw its support to Taylor for president and Henry Dearborn of Massachusetts for vice president. Peyton noted carefully that there were no points of view or "platforms" to reconcile; Taylor was a great American hero chosen for his heroism.[14] The convention action by the Native American Party boosted the potential candidate's stock, although he was not a member of that party. To Balie it was an indication that the general's friends could rally the public to vote for Taylor as a military hero.

During the summer Peyton and Judah P. Benjamin[15] spoke at a Whig rally at Baton Rouge, General Taylor's hometown, where a cross section of citizens found it easy to flock to his colors. Peyton, Benjamin, and other Whig workers followed the hometown rally by holding several "rough and ready" meetings across the state.[16]

As a Taylor candidacy became increasingly popular with his fellow Louisianians, many began to believe that he could be above partisanship, "president of all the people."[17] Although that sentiment was noble enough, Peyton knew General Taylor could not expect to be the nominee of a political party and yet somehow free of the party. It was an issue that Peyton postponed discussing with him until after he completed his military command duties.

Throughout 1847, Peyton observed American troops departing for or arriving from Mexico. On July 10, Balie offered congratulations and welcome to Col. William Trousdale of Gallatin who had just reached the city by steamship from Vera Cruz. Although the two were political opposites—one Whig, the other Democrat—both of their fathers were among the first settlers in Davidson and Sumner Counties, North Carolina, and both sons had been neighbors and members of the bar at Gallatin.[18] The appearance of three additional regiments of Tennessee volunteers in New Orleans on their way to Mexico provided Balie an opportunity to greet many of them and say a good word for General Taylor.[19]

As New Orleans prepared a grand reception for Taylor, Peyton worked tirelessly to promote it. He hoped the success of the occasion would open the way for him to play a larger part with the presidential aspirant. Upon the general's arrival in the city on December 1 and during the visit that ended on December 5,[20] Balie confirmed that he was in good standing with him.

Learning from Taylor that he had written letters to Senator Crittenden of Kentucky and Col. Jeff Davis of Mississippi "to define his position more clearly on . . . the future conduct of the Mexican War," Peyton sensed at once that the clarifications, even though briefly stated, carried the potential for political trouble. To avoid the consequences of the Wilmot Proviso, the general had proposed to establish a boundary line between Mexico and the United States following the Rio Grande upstream until it intersected the latitude of 36°30' and thence west with that latitude to the Pacific Ocean. He would withdraw the army to this line but would hold the Mexican seaports now in possession of U.S. forces.[21]

There was no reason for Taylor to stake out this or any other position so far in advance of the election, Peyton told him. "Will it not be better," Balie asked, "after we know whom we are fighting, after they have selected their commander, exhibited their plan of campaign, and formed a line from which they cannot retreat?" Taylor's proposal for the boundary line would be just another of the "conflicting opinions not only between Whigs and Democrats, but between officers of the army and amongst Gen. Taylor's own friends" on that question, Peyton reasoned. "Is it not inexpedient . . . to take *one* line against the *field*, as the racing men say?" He vigorously objected to raising the issue of withdrawing the army to any line before peace was made.[22]

Although Taylor's lack of experience in politics was dangerous to him and his backers, Peyton believed that the problem was manageable. Assured that Taylor would receive him attentively at any time or place, he was ready to undertake perhaps the most arduous political campaign of his lifetime.

Receipt on December 30 of resolutions adopted by the Alabama legislature in honor of "the gallant old veteran" enabled Peyton to include them along with a new year's greeting to General Taylor at Baton Rouge. Acknowledging to the sender, Alabama Governor Reuben Chapman, that the resolutions honoring the general were done in a "handsome manner," he assured him that their subject was "the most honest, patriotic and disinterested of men."[23]

Promoting Taylor became a virtual obsession with Peyton in 1848. Giving his dreams full rein, he could see himself at best as a cabinet member and/or a close political advisor to the president. At worst he could be the holder of some other desirable presidential appointment. Already Whigs in the capital were frequently speaking of him as a possible choice for secretary of war.[24]

Yet there was one especially vexing question: How to get the general nominated with the necessary breadth of support that usually comes with party nomination? As neither Democrats nor Whigs seemed ready to embrace Taylor as a presidential candidate, Balie lingered over the thought of an antiparty campaign. He was hard-pressed to believe that a person could be elected president in opposition to the political parties of the country. But still—and forever—a Whig at heart, Balie began to entertain the possibility of enlisting aid for the war hero from among those who cared not about party but about the dedication and ability that he had demonstrated in the Mexican War. With that base of support secured, he and Taylor insiders would then package the candidate in such a way that the Whig Party would find him extremely attractive. Perhaps Taylor could be enough of a Whig to satisfy the party but at the same time honor his desire to be the president of the United States, not the president of a party and its followers. After all, suspicion of party was a basic Whig characteristic.[25]

The interim would be awkward for Peyton, who was known as a fire-breathing party man. It would be no less difficult for the candidate who vigorously eschewed party politics. It was easy to imagine that, should Balie take a prominent lead in the nonpartisan effort, he would be reminded of his own past as a party loyalist without peer, that his four-year federal appointment in New Orleans would be waved in his face, and that even Whig associates of old would question his sagacity. Nonetheless, Peyton was ready to go ahead with the appeal to those who cared not for party. At the same time, he was ready at the earliest opportunity to maneuver Taylor into position to receive the Whig nomination. Ignoring his own dangerous position, he wrote cheerfully to Crittenden, "Every thing seems to be going well for Taylor."[26]

Going along with those who believed that "the great mass of the people" wanted "the choice of a President . . . made irrespective of party considerations," he signed a call for Taylor supporters to meet in New Orleans on January 22, elect delegates, and make arrangements for a state convention.[27] A large number responded and after choosing the prominent local businessman Maunsel White to be president of the evening, they watched with approval as he appointed Peyton to chair a committee to draft resolutions "expressive of the sense of the meeting."[28]

When Peyton presented resolutions endorsing Taylor, the crowd shouted down a man who tried to voice his opposition and called Balie to the speaker's stand. Alluding to the mention of "platform" in the resolutions, he said it contained more references to the character and public service of the general than to his position on matters of public policy. It was "the platform on which Zachary Taylor stood before the American people," and it was broad enough for all parties, he insisted. "It was the platform he had always occupied." When Peyton said, "He would not be the President of a party—he would be President of the United States," the crowd cheered wildly. Lapsing into a question-and-answer dialogue with himself, Peyton continued: "Did they appreciate him? They did. Did they admire his gallant acts? They did. Would they support him? They would." And they did. The resolutions passed with a resounding "Aye" vote.[29]

Balie's leadership in the Taylor meeting of January 22 prompted a scathing article on the editorial page of the New Orleans *Daily Delta* that raised questions about his motives in the upcoming presidential election. Showing sarcastic contempt for Peyton, the writer reminded his readers that Balie "had sprung from somewhere in the pine swamps of Tennessee" and had been elected to Congress as an ardent Jacksonian but changed two years later to the Whig Party. He charged that although Balie decried political appointments, he had been "a *placeman*," holding a lucrative appointment by President Tyler for four years. After the War Department disbanded the regiment he had raised for the Mexican War, Balie remained with Taylor's command and since had purged himself of party and "taken to patriotism and General Taylor."[30]

Stung by the article, Peyton encountered the editor of the *Daily Delta* on Chartres Street two days later and assaulted him, but passersby restrained both men before serious damage was done. A. Walker, the editor, printed his version of the attack under the heading, "Cowardly Assault," and alleged that Peyton was "heavily armed" and had been lying in wait for him.[31] The editor of the Louisiana *Courier* also denounced the attack on Walker.[32]

Peyton answered in a paid advertisement in the *Daily Picayune*. He said Walker's account of their meeting was "as destitute of truth" as his article "a few days before, was of decency."

> It is true that when I met him on Chartres Street, I boxed his jaws soundly, and expressed my opinion to him, in no doubtful terms, of his veracity and courage. . . . His only defense was a reiterated apology— though, as I learn, he became more valiant after I left him.[33]

Walker responded in a *Picayune* advertisement by threatening to "clearly establish [Peyton's] dastardly character" by publishing "evidence" in his possession, but which he had "pledged not to parade before the public, unless it is rendered indispensable." He warned that should there be anyone in the city who "credits" a word of Peyton's statement, "He is certainly ignorant of the reputation of this man."[34]

After venting his wrath on the editor, Balie faced a more difficult issue. How was he going to promote the nonpartisan Taylor to traditionally partisan voters? The pro-Taylor Whig editor of the Plaquemine *Ibervillian* reminded him that not everyone wanted Taylor to run an antiparty campaign. He regarded Taylor as a Whig, and the *Ibervillian* would support him as such.[35]

The rebuke at Plaquemine raised questions elsewhere. The New Orleans *Bee* now saw Taylor as an avowed Whig, and the Louisiana *Courier* alleged that Peyton, "the Taylor orator *par excellence*," had conspired with other Whigs to conceal the fact of the general's commitment to Whiggism. They had attempted by artifice "to dazzle the senses of Southern Democrats and insult the judgment of the entire American people." The *Courier* believed that Peyton and those like him had placed the general "in an essentially false and dishonorable position."[36]

On February 22, as planned, those who favored Taylor convened in New Orleans to nominate electors to vote for him in the approaching campaign. Although the delegates debated minor points at length, there was virtually no mention of political parties but a steady focus on marshaling the strength of those present to support Zachary Taylor. They chose electors for each of the six districts of the state and adjourned amidst cheers for the general.[37]

Three weeks later the Louisiana Whig Convention selected delegates to its upcoming national convention at Philadelphia. Peyton was not among the delegates chosen because many local political activists believed he had become too much Taylor and too little Whig. His strategy was to keep himself at a discreet distance from party regulars while trying to persuade Taylor to accept the Whig Party as his ticket to the White House.[38]

The general was slow to move toward the Whigs. As late as April 22, he said he would accept the nomination of either party but would not be a pledged candidate of either.[39] But when Clay announced that he would contest the nomination with him, the situation changed. Peyton led a committee from New Orleans to Baton Rouge, where they urged the general to embrace Whig principles enough to bring him into that party's favor.[40]

Taylor accommodated the committee by acknowledging that he was a Whig, "but not an ultra Whig." He copied and signed a statement drafted by Logan Hunton, James Love, and Peyton in the form of a letter to his brother-in-law, Capt. J. S. Allison, that set forth the principles upon which he could base a campaign. About party, he reiterated, "If elected I will not be the mere President of a party. I would endeavor to act independent of party domination. I should feel bound to administer the Government untrammelled by party schemes." Taylor said he would use the veto power only in extraordinary circumstances. He would respect the will of the people as expressed by their elected representatives to Congress in matters of the tariff, currency, better highways, and other internal improvements such as aids to navigation for the nation's rivers, lakes, and harbors.[41]

Phrased as it was, Taylor's statement opened the way for Whigs to accept him. He abandoned his original notion of running as an independent and instead would run as a moderate Whig, trying all the while to minimize partisanship.[42] A key reason that the Whigs accepted Taylor without a platform was that they had erroneously predicted that "economic disaster" would follow "reestablishment of the subtreasury and the lowering of the tariff of 1846."[43]

A former Whig member of the Tennessee congressional delegation who had been in the House from 1837 to 1841, and who had been in the city since 1843, became editor of the New Orleans *Evening National* in May 1848. Balie stopped in at the editorial office and congratulated the new editor, John Wesley Crockett, his cousin Martha Hamilton's husband and son of the noted Tennessee frontiersman and congressman David Crockett.[44] Operating as a commission merchant in the city for the preceding five years, John Crockett, unlike Peyton, had avoided roles in politics and public life and, as a result, they had seen little of each other. The new editor could not have been surprised when his "cousin" solicited his assistance in the Taylor campaign.

Although he was not a delegate to the upcoming Whig National Convention, Balie sent by the Kentucky Whig Congressman Garnett Duncan a "statement" that Taylor had written to him on May 20 in which he took a clear stand in favor of Whig principles. It was a masterly stroke. The general's supporters at the convention used it to forestall attacks on their candidate and to show that he had always been a Whig in principle.[45]

Peyton eagerly awaited the results of the party conventions. On May 22 at Baltimore, the Democratic National Convention nominated Gen. Lewis Cass for president and Gen. William O. Butler for vice president. A few days later the Whig Convention at Philadelphia chose General Taylor to head its ticket with Millard Fillmore for vice president.[46] Few had worked more effectively than Peyton to bring Taylor into line for the nomination.[47]

Prior to the Whig convention, representatives of organized labor met at Philadelphia and nominated their own presidential ticket. They chose Gerritt Smith of New York for president and William S. Waitt of Illinois for vice president. More threatening to the Taylor candidacy was the nomination of Martin Van Buren by both the Barnburners, who had defected from the Democrats and were in convention at Utica, New York, and the new Free Soil Party, organized at Buffalo, New York, in opposition to slavery.[48]

The selection of a Louisiana citizen as a nominee for president meant it was time to celebrate in New Orleans. Balie was ready. On June 24 between seven thousand and ten thousand local Taylor men and Whigs in general, bolstered by a large turnout from Lafayette, crowded onto Canal Street[49] to ratify the nomination of Zachary Taylor. Thirty minutes before the speeches began, a cannon near the levee sounded the signal for lighting the downtown area. Rockets whizzed into the sky and myriad lanterns, torches, and lamps dissipated the darkness of the evening.[50]

After the first speech, William DeBuys, the presiding officer, appointed a committee on resolutions, one of whom was Peyton. Before excusing the committee, he asked Balie to read a communication he brought from General Taylor. That simple act was a public acknowledgment that Balie was a Taylor "insider," and the crowd stirred anxiously. For his part, Balie was eager to put down rumors that the general had repudiated the conduct of the Louisiana delegation at the national convention and had decided to turn his back on the Whigs and run as an independent.

> I rise . . . to read a communication authorized to be published by Gen. Taylor in relation to a subject which has caused some little misunderstanding in the city. In company with several friends, I have been up to Baton Rouge, and we found "the old man" as calm as he always is upon the eve of a great battle, more solicitous for his friends than for himself.[51]

"Enthusiastic and prolonged cheering" greeted Peyton's remarks,[52] and after a moment of breathless silence, he read the prepared statement:

> The undersigned whose names are affixed . . . make this publication at the special instance and request of Gen. Zachary Taylor himself. From sundry articles which have appeared in several of the public journals of

the city of New Orleans, Gen. Taylor is given to understand that persons claiming to speak for him have produced the impression that he is not satisfied with what Judge [Lafayette] Saunders, and the other members of the Louisiana delegation to the National Whig Convention who acted with him, saw fit to say and do in that body in his (Gen. Taylor's) behalf; and that he repudiates such acts and sayings.

We are authorized by Gen. Taylor to say that the course of the Louisiana delegation in the Whig Convention, lately assembled at Philadelphia, meets with his entire, full, and unequivocal approbation.

That he not only never doubted, but never intimated a doubt that his honor and reputation were safe in their hands.

                        Balie Peyton, Logan Hunton, A. C. Bullitt[53]

The audience was ecstatic. Cheers rang out up and down Canal Street. Taylor's colors were flying high. A few speeches later, including a masterful presentation by S. S. Prentiss, the crowd roared its approval of Taylor's nomination and resolved to assist him in the campaign ahead. They promised a "speedy and harmonizing organization of our friends, and a bold and candid appeal to the patriotism of our countrymen."[54]

The ratification meeting placed Louisiana firmly behind General Taylor and dispelled growing doubts outside the state that he was about to break away from the Whig Party. Peyton's mission to Baton Rouge made those happy circumstances possible. He had saved the general from potentially damaging representations made by other of his friends but based upon his own remarks.

Outside Louisiana, editors and politicians gave Peyton credit for controlling the candidate. The Richmond *Enquirer* said that "General Taylor had surrendered to Peyton & Co."[55] President Polk regarded Taylor as "the political puppet" of Peyton and George W. Kendall, publisher of the *Picayune*.[56] The Charleston (S.C.) *News* recognized Peyton's importance to Taylor but believed that the general wanted to avoid a party contest.[57]

When General Taylor finally put the nonpartisan issue to rest by officially accepting the Whig nomination on July 15, Peyton breathed easily for the first time in several months.[58] The nominee continued to be silent on most issues, however, giving Cass supporters opportunities aplenty to attack him.

With Taylor firmly established as the Whig nominee, Balie began a busy round of speaking engagements for him in the state. A large, approving crowd met Peyton and Benjamin at Baton Rouge on July 8 to cheer the Whig nomination of the city's favorite son. Of that occasion a *Picayune* correspondent noted, "Persuasion from the stump, kindly offered, turns away wrath and disarms the egotism of mere political partisanship."[59] Balie and Duncan Kenner of the Taylor camp addressed a rally at Bayou Goula where the hostile editor of the Louisiana *Courier* gave them a bad review. He dismissed the former with the comment: "We are told Mr. Peyton exhausted his stock of anecdotes relative to Old Zack, with which every man and boy in the Union is already familiar, and which are not very well adapted to make a strong impression by being repeated for the five hundredth time."[60]

Peyton and other Taylor advocates promoted the candidate by holding him up as a man of experience and heroism. They dwelt on his positive personal qualities and illustrated his self-control by telling war stories about his conduct while under enemy fire. Carefully avoiding the question of "platform" or plan of action, neither of which Taylor wanted to advance, Peyton became a ready target for the opposition. When asked what the candidate believed or proposed to do, Peyton and the other spokesmen were "as silent as a spike in a barn door."[61]

While the campaign was under way, Balie and many fellow Whigs north and south worried about the influence that they believed Henry Clay would try to wield over Taylor, should Clay be elected to the Senate and Taylor to the White House. The great Whig senior statesman "with his energy and vigor of character impelled by a morbid state of feeling . . . will play hell and break things . . . and unless the old general obeyed his order in all things, he would make war upon him, too," Peyton wrote to Crittenden, who had just been elected governor of Kentucky. Every Whig in Washington expected Clay "to kick up a row as sure as he comes."[62] Peyton was probably aware that Clay regarded him as one of the "hot heads who had grouped themselves around Taylor" to protect him and themselves from the old-line Clay organization.[63]

Thinking of the presidential canvass beyond the bounds of the three states he knew best (Louisiana, Tennessee, and Kentucky), Peyton was concerned about the candidacy of former President Martin Van Buren and asked Crittenden about its effect on the election. "Will his running not throw the election into the House? And if so, will he not be the dangerous man? And if he is elected, will not . . . the [election] shake the pillars and test the cement which binds these states together?"[64]

For the moment, however, Balie had little time to think about the campaign except in terms of Louisiana. He appeared with Prentiss and Benjamin at Clinton to endorse ratification of the nominations of the National Whig Convention. A week later, sharing the platform with Prentiss at Plaquemine, he tried to discredit Cass with southern voters by charging that he was antislavery and a strong supporter of the Wilmot Proviso. Peyton quoted the candidate as saying that he owned no slaves and that he "detested slavery."[65]

On September 4, Peyton was one of six participants in an eight-hour Whig-Democrat debate at Baton Rouge that he described as "a sort of Shakers dog fight." The New Orleans *Daily Delta* reported it as "an Eight Hours Cannonade between the Great Guns of Whiggery and Democracy," but the *Crescent* regarded the event as "the grand 'model' debate of the campaign." Whether shoot-out or model debate, the structure limited each speaker's time to about sixty minutes, hardly enough for some to warm to their themes. The format virtually precluded the determination of victor and vanquished. With Balie were Whigs Prentiss and Benjamin. The Democrats were L. J. Sigur, Col. Isaac T. Preston, and J. C. Larue.[66]

The next day Peyton spoke to a crowd of two thousand at Clinton, Louisiana, but was unable to persuade the Democrats to send someone to engage him in debate.[67] Colonel Preston, scheduled to speak to a meeting of Democrats later in the day, declined Peyton's invitation to join him in debate on the platform.[68]

Having traversed the state "from east to west" during the summer months,[69] Peyton began to look to Tennessee as an appropriate ground for autumn stumping. Before the end of September, he accepted an invitation from the Nashville Rough and Ready Club to speak to the citizens of Davidson County on Saturday, October 14, and a similar invitation to speak at Memphis on October 23.[70] The Davidson County appointment provided an opportunity for Balie to see Emily, then in boarding school at the Nashville Female Academy, and to visit the farm.[71]

Eager to share his enthusiasm for General Taylor, Peyton spoke to a large crowd assembled on Broadway in downtown Nashville. He declared that he was still "a Jackson man," a friend and neighbor who believed in the integrity and leadership ability of the Old Hero. He had come home to Middle Tennessee in the cause of another man with essentially the same traits of character, a hero who would do without fail what he thought best for the country. A local Whig editor reported he had never heard a speech "calculated to do more good for the cause of old Rough and Ready." He wished that Peyton could speak in every county of the state.[72]

The Nashville pro-Cass press hooted at Peyton for asserting that he was still a Jackson man. There could be no greater difference between two men than Jackson's open proclamation of his views and principles and Taylor's refusal to make pledges or discuss courses of action he might follow.[73]

Although it was too late in the campaign to undertake an extensive speaking schedule in Tennessee, Peyton made stump speeches at Murfreesboro, Gallatin, and Lebanon before leaving for Memphis. Typically speaking for about three hours, he was warmly received and unchallenged except at his hometown of Gallatin where, on October 15, his companion of old, the Democrat Jo. C. Guild, met him in debate. Both acknowledged their long-standing friendship and conducted themselves in a gracious manner. After Peyton had established that General Cass's "conversion to Southern institutions was hypocritical and for the avowed purpose of getting the nomination of his party," Guild countered with a question: "Do you think, Col. Peyton, that General Taylor would veto a bill containing the Wilmot Proviso?" When Balie responded that he did not know what the general would do in those circumstances, Guild pounded

Emily Turner Peyton

his point home. He could not imagine his friend, "a distinguished Southerner," could support a candidate "about whose opinions on the most vital questions he knew nothing."[74] But Peyton was following the campaign plan: avoid taking positions on specific issues.

Debating at Murfreesboro on October 16, Peyton recalled his appearance there in 1836 when he advocated the election of Hugh Lawson White to the presidency. This time he began "with his soft, mellow voice filling the whole room" and advanced to a loud denunciation of the Democratic nominee whom he predicted would fail his party as had Van Buren in his single term. In answering the Cass speaker's criticism of Taylor, Peyton's remarks were "scathing and withering . . . yet just," a correspondent reported. As was his custom, he excoriated "the slanders and slanderers" of General Taylor and "called upon the good men of all parties" to unite with him in exposing them.[75]

At Lebanon, a reporter for the local *Packet* wrote that he had "never listened to a more able, interesting, and eloquent speech" than Balie delivered at the new courthouse on October 17. Beginning by recalling scenes from his boyhood school days at nearby Hickory Ridge "to the great amusement and merriment of his hearers," the former congressman moved on to a comparison of the platforms of the three presidential candidates. Admitting that Taylor had deliberately avoided the usual pandemonium about platform, Balie said that his integrity, cool courage, and unalloyed patriotism made up a better platform than any compilation of political promises, the usual platform contents.[76]

Back at the Station Camp farm on October 22, Peyton assessed the status of the presidential contest in five states for Governor Crittenden of Kentucky. "Tennessee is safe for Gen'l Taylor or much so as old Kentucky, but by a small majority, say from 2,000 to 5,000," he wrote. "Louisiana I consider safe beyond all question." The prospects in Pennsylvania appeared good, but he feared that the Whig members of Congress who had gone over to Van Buren would "play the devil in Ohio." Betting on the outcome of the election was widespread, Peyton confided. "Our friends will bet high, bleed at every pore if the old man is beaten."[77]

On October 23, Peyton boarded the stage to Memphis where he concluded his Tennessee tour on Saturday night, October 28, with a speech on Court Square. Although he had postponed his appearance five days from the original date, he spoke before "one of the largest assemblages ever congregated" in the city. His wide-ranging speech was "a brilliant effort," a Memphis editor wrote, "entertaining his friends and worrying his enemies." As he spoke his "charm and power . . . seemed to increase," contributing to the writer's conclusion that "it was one of the very best, most forcible, effective and powerful efforts" that he had listened to during the canvass.

But the evening was not without its challenges. When he had spoken about an hour and a half, a "goodly number of 'Democrats'" began to chant the name of a speaker they had brought in to respond to Balie. The chanting "broke out into a pretty general tumult and disorder among them" as they tried to drive the speaker from the stands.

The troublemakers soon discovered they faced a formidable adversary. Peyton told them that General Jackson had failed to force him from the platform, and he "hardly thought a pack of scrubs and curs would do it." The longer they continued their noisy conduct, the longer he spoke. After four hours on the stand, he concluded by saying that he had talked twice as long as he would have done if he had been treated with decency. He said that he wanted to show them that he "could both resent and defy their ill-bred insolence."[78]

The opposing speaker spoke an hour and a half, and Peyton remained for a thirty-minute rejoinder. There were still six hundred persons present when he concluded his remarks at one o'clock on Sunday morning. A few days later, Whigs in Memphis claimed that the speaking had "infused a fresh, glorious, and enthusiastic feeling and spirit amongst the friends of General Taylor."[79]

In New Orleans again by November 1, Balie predicted Taylor would carry Tennessee. "Every body, black and white, are in favor of the Old Man," he bragged. Still in good voice, he was one of six speakers to address a Whig-Taylor rally of six thousand persons gathered on Judge Joachim Bermudez's plantation on Gentilly Road near the city. It was the last big home political event for the presidential nominee prior to the election.[80]

For Taylor and Peyton victory was at hand. On November 7, voters nationwide elected Zachary Taylor president and Millard Fillmore vice president. The results were doubly sweet to Balie. Louisiana gave Taylor 54.6 per cent of its vote, and Tennessee had also voted for Taylor by a majority of 6,286 votes, a much better showing than Clay's margin of only 113 votes over Polk four years earlier.[81] The election of Taylor was a dramatic recovery by a party rocked by Clay's defeat at the hands of Polk in 1844. The victory had been boosted by Van Buren's 291,263 popular votes that he attracted principally from the Democrats. It was the Whigs' second and final chance to have one of their own occupy the White House.[82]

Although Peyton, Crittenden, and others had warned the president-elect that Henry Clay would be a dangerous political friend, a casual act of courtesy by Taylor seemed to have been a reckless invitation to listen to the Whig sage's counsel. Learning that Clay was planning to spend part of the winter in New Orleans and having received an invitation from him to visit at Ashland when en route to the inauguration, Taylor reciprocated by inviting Clay to spend a week with him at Baton Rouge. If that should not be convenient, he offered to see Clay during his stay in New Orleans.[83]

Taylor's friends feared that such a visit would open the door for Clay to inject his dominating political presence into the president-elect's circle of closest advisors. They also worried that such an association might open the way to an intraparty clash of old Whigs versus new Whigs who wanted to broaden the party's base. Before the offer of hospitality could be retracted, Clay arrived at Baton Rouge by river in early January and found the president-elect putting Peyton and Albert T. Burnley[84] aboard the same boat bound for New Orleans. He greeted Clay briefly, but with Peyton present, "no invitation to stop was extended." Balie and his allies had succeeded in protecting Taylor from the political craftiness of the senior of all Whigs.[85] Boxed out of the inner circle, Clay told his Kentucky friends that if he were successful in his bid to be elected to the U.S. Senate, he would not interfere with the administration but would maintain his independence.[86]

Even as Balie maneuvered to consolidate his own strong position with the president-elect, President Polk made an announcement that excited the entire country. There was gold in California! Verifying the earlier reported discovery of gold near the Sacramento River, the president explained that it existed in large quantities and was of high quality. The statement, included in his final message to Congress, launched the California gold rush and gave urgent impetus to the westward movement.

What should Peyton do? The exciting news came after he had completed plans to accompany Taylor to Washington for the inauguration, and he accepted the timing as a signal that he should continue at the general's side. Wherever the journey took them, he would find plenty of gold talk and young men making plans to cross to California. As much as he needed money for his family and farm, he first wanted a good appointment from the new president. He hoped that such a job might serve both his needs: funds and challenging adventure that would distract his mind from the untimely deaths of his wife and daughter.

The Taylor entourage set out along a route to the capital that began at Baton Rouge and continued by riverboat to Vicksburg, Memphis, Nashville, and Louisville. There would be an overland deviation to Frankfort, capital of Kentucky, before resuming river travel on the Ohio to Madison, Indiana; Cincinnati, Ohio; and Wheeling, West Virginia, from whence they would travel by rail to Washington.[87]

Balie and his daughter Emily, at home in New Orleans between terms at a Nashville girls' school, joined Taylor's retinue aboard the steamboat *Tennessee* at Vicksburg on February 2 and followed at his side all the way to the District of Columbia. Others in the traveling party included Maj. R. S. Garnett and Dr. Charles McCormick, an army surgeon; A. C. Bullitt, editor of the New Orleans *Picayune*; Judah P. Benjamin; and several other Louisiana political figures.[88]

An enthusiastic crowd greeted General Taylor and his retinue when they reached Nashville on February 7.[89] The onset of cholera and an epidemic of smallpox in the city prevented the attendance of many citizens from surrounding counties, but those present made an impressive demonstration in his honor. Mexican War veterans waved flags and campaign hats, and city and state dignitaries conferred official greetings and honors upon him. Greeting the president-elect at Peyton's invitation, William B. Campbell observed that Taylor made "a very favorable impression on all who saw him."[90] On February 9, a sizeable local crowd heard General Taylor respond to a warm welcome from Whig Governor Neill S. Brown. Peyton did not make a speech but arranged for key Tennessee politicians to have a private moment with Taylor.

Nashville followers speculated unendingly about the makeup of Taylor's cabinet, but they could get little information from those who escorted him. By that time Peyton was thinking of an appointment as a foreign minister, preferably to Brazil or Mexico, and those close to him believed Taylor would honor his wishes.[91]

After a busy day and two festive evenings, General Taylor and his party boarded the steamboat *Daniel Boone* and resumed their journey.[92] Louisville was the next stop. That night, Balie was one of several speakers who addressed a large dinner audience gathered to pay tribute to the president-elect.[93]

The stop at Louisville could not be made without acknowledging Kentucky's greatest Whig, Henry Clay. Yet Balie could not forget the "unbecoming" attitude he had displayed after Taylor's nomination and election. Clay, he believed, was likely to make war upon both Taylor and the party.[94]

Steaming upriver toward Wheeling, the boat carrying the Peytons and the presidential party encountered ice floes that on February 19 blocked their passage. They debarked into horse-drawn sleighs that whisked them over deep snow the remaining distance to Wheeling, from whence they traveled by train to Washington.[95] They reached the nation's capital after nightfall on February 23. The president's suite then included fifteen persons: Colonel Peyton and daughter Emily; Maj. R. S. Garnett, U.S. Army; Col. J. T. Van Allen of New York; Judge Benjamin Winchester of Louisiana; Judah P. Benjamin; A. C. Bullitt of New Orleans; Dr. McCormick and lady, U.S. Army; Col. James Taylor of New York and daughter; Howard Christy and lady of Kentucky; and a Miss Johnston and a Miss Wickliffe of Kentucky.[96]

Soon after their arrival, President and Mrs. Polk entertained the president-elect, his fellow Louisiana travelers, and a few special guests at dinner.[97] Peyton must have been glad that three years before he and Polk had agreed to forget the bitter political rhetoric that had locked them into adversarial relationships. Dinner conversation was pleasant, and voices were raised noticeably only when speculating about the extent of gold deposits in California.

Peyton and Emily sat near members of the cabinet at the inauguration ceremonies on March 5. Balie did not intend to let Taylor lose sight of him! He knew he had not been forgotten when, a few days later, he and A. C. Bullitt were guests of President and Mrs. Taylor at one of their first White House dinners. In addition to Peyton and Bullitt, there were about thirty other guests, including the members of the cabinet, the heads of the war and navy "bureaus," Senators Daniel Webster, Thomas Hart Benton, and Thomas Corwin, and members of the president's staff and household.[98]

Enjoying the victory politics that came with the beginning of a Whig administration, Peyton remained in the city several weeks. He consulted with the secretary of the Treasury, seeking an appointment for Samuel Strong of New York City who was then an active member of that state's Whig general committee. He did not mention that Strong was the president's son-in-law but pointed out that he was formerly employed in the New York Customs House and would like to be employed there again. Assuring the secretary that Strong was well qualified by prior experience,

Balie said, "He can do more, and does do more, in politics than any other 20 men. . . . He is sober, true and effective." All the secretary needed to do was to intimate or write to the collector of customs on the subject, and the job would be Strong's. Such a result would "gratify two such good men and true," Balie said in oblique reference to the Taylor-Strong relationship.[99]

By the middle of May, the president had privately offered Peyton appointment as minister plenipotentiary to Chile;[100] he had accepted it, and he left for New Orleans in order to prepare to leave the country later in the year. Although there was no official announcement, many political friends knew that he had agreed to accept a foreign assignment, and at least one believed that he had left with the commission in his pocket.[101] The offer was patronage of a modest order for the political services he had rendered the new president, yet he accepted it gracefully.

MINISTER TO CHILE
1849–1851

When the administration announced in June that the president had appointed Peyton envoy extraordinary and minister plenipotentiary to Chile, the news was generally well received. Balie's partisan enemies of old were not pleased, however. Calling him "an empty swaggerer," a New York *Post* editorial bitterly recalled his confrontation with Reuben M. Whitney during congressional hearings a dozen years before. Feigning comfort in the existence of a language barrier that could protect all concerned, the writer concluded, "He is now sent to bluster at Chile but as he can say nothing the Chileans will understand, he is not likely to do any harm there."[1]

Ignoring his political critics of yesteryear, Peyton prepared to leave the country. One detail of his departure involved the sale of a ten-year-old slave boy named Henry to Mrs. Elmira Cosner of New Orleans for $380.[2]

After spending the remainder of the summer in New Orleans, Peyton went up to his Tennessee farm, visited sisters Sarah Barry and Rebecca Parker, and arranged for sons John Bell and Balie Jr. to attend school in Alexandria, Virginia, during his foreign assignment. Emily would accompany him to Chile as his personal secretary.[3]

Checking his stables carefully, Balie discussed plans for the horses with his brother Holmes and brother-in-law Thomas Barry, who would be in charge during his absence. He made a point of greeting the thirty-four slaves on his Station Camp Creek farm. The older men and women were productive farm workers who, without their knowledge, had served him well as security for debts more than once.[4]

Upon receipt of official notification that the president had appointed him to duty in Chile, Peyton sent an official letter of acceptance to Secretary of State John M. Clayton on July 20. A few days later he left Gallatin for Washington, where he stopped briefly before setting out to join President Taylor and his traveling party on a swing through Pennsylvania, New York State, Massachusetts, New York City, and Philadelphia. He reached the presidential entourage at Niagara Falls on September 4 and traveled with its members for the rest of the journey.[5]

Peyton was back in Washington in mid-September[6] to confer with the secretary of state. He found the U.S. conducting negotiations that led to the Clayton-Bulwer Treaty with Great Britain relative to an Isthmian canal and limiting British presence in Central America to British Honduras and the Mosquito coasts. The treaty and the need for a cooling off period for anti-U.S. sentiment caused by the war with Mexico prompted the State Department to adopt a policy of maintaining the *status quo ante* in Central and South America. Little excitement seemed in prospect for U.S. ministers assigned to governments in the region.

Discussing a minister's personal conduct as a representative of the United States, the secretary referred to Balie's predecessor as having been unable to control his temper, but the advice was appropriate for Balie as well. The president, he said, was confident that Balie would not permit himself to be led into that kind of error "under any circumstances."[7]

Learning from his predecessor, Seth Barton, that the legation's library had only one volume dealing with international law, Peyton asked the secretary to permit him to purchase nine additional books on that subject. Declining permission for the outlay, the secretary instructed him to make an inventory of the legation library upon his arrival in Chile and send it to Washington for evaluation. The response did not satisfy Balie, and he continued to seek the books, which he regarded as "indispensably necessary to the representative of the United States at Chile."[8]

After further briefing, Peyton went to New York City to set out for South America. He chose a sea route to Chile by which he and Emily could transfer to the steamship *Falcon* at Havana with the expectation of reaching the city of Panama on the west coast of the isthmus by October 27. There they planned to board the British mail steamer for Valparaiso, Chile. When the *Falcon* was late reaching Havana, the

Peytons took the steamship *Ohio* for New Orleans where unfinished personal business matters begged for Balie's attention even until the last minute.[9]

Just before their departure from New Orleans for Chile, Peyton wrote a pensive letter[10] to his friend Campbell. His first thoughts turned to his "old home and friends" to whom he apologized because he had spent so little time with them on his last visit. When he wrote of politics, he admitted worrying about the future of the Whig Party.

> The sun of Buena Vista does not shine on the Whig Party of late. The elections everywhere indicate a great cooling of the enthusiasm which brought "Old Zack" into power. It does seem to me that the Whigs are incapable of maintaining power. . . . Even this city [New Orleans] has just gone horse, foot and dragoons for the Democrats & it is more than probable that the Legislature & Governor will go likewise . . . one short year after Gen'l Taylor carried the state by nearly 3,000 votes.[11]

A party that wins the White House can find it has swapped one set of problems for another, Balie ventured. The coveted control of federal employment resulted in President Taylor's awarding patronage and spoils that "produced consternation and outrage."

> Patronage is a dangerous element of power, a two edged sword which cuts both ways. Although the cabinet is composed of good men . . . , I do not think that they have well managed the patronage with which Gen'l Taylor . . . has entrusted them. Jackson was the only man I ever saw who knew how to use patronage & he entrusted it to nobody.

Distressed that his old congressional district lately had elected a Democrat, Peyton blamed local Whig leadership. Unable to accept a weaker role for the Whig Party in Tennessee, he thought he might abandon public affairs altogether. "Politics is a miserable calling," he confided. "When I return, Campbell, I shall settle down on my old farm where I was born."[12]

On November 13, Peyton, in robust health and excellent spirits, and Emily, who was then eighteen years old, embarked from New Orleans on the steamship *Alabama*. Ten days later they arrived at Chagres, an Atlantic port town on the isthmus of Panama. At once they began the tedious crossing to the Pacific by navigating the Chagres River to near its source and taking mules the rest of the way through the mountains to the west coast city of Panama. After a slow passage upriver, they had to wait for mules to return from the coast before they could complete the crossing. The combined delays resulted in their failing by one day to connect with the monthly British mail ship they intended to take for Chile. They waited in the port city until its next departure, December 27.[13]

While at Panama, Balie attended a dinner given in his honor at the American Hotel by local businessmen. The situation was made to order for him, and he entertained the crowd with his usual charm and wit.

> Mr. Peyton was frequently interrupted by the cheering of his countrymen. His remarks, especially advisory to his emigrating fellow citizens, were excellently well adapted to the occasion, and met with a response in the bosom of every man present.[14]

The high point of their stay was a combination of two social events in which they joined the elite of Panama for a concert party and, on the next evening, a ball, both given by the governor. There, as elsewhere, the chief subjects for conversation were the California gold rush, the high prices that speculators were receiving for steamer tickets, stories of lost baggage and robberies experienced during the crossing from Chagres, and the Americanization of the city of Panama.[15]

Leaving Panama on the next monthly British mail ship, the Peytons disembarked at Valparaiso, the crown jewel of Chile, on January 25, 1850. They reached the capital city of Santiago by stagecoach on February 5.[16]

Scanning the environment of the two largest cities in Chile, Peyton saw that the principal buildings in Valparaiso reflected European architectural design but the appearance of Santiago was somewhat primitive. Its low adobe structures with barred windows and secluded patios dominated the scene, most totally devoid of other ornamentation. Soon after, but unrelated to Peyton's arrival, a building boom took shape in Santiago characterized by the construction of large, lavish residences. Public and commercial buildings followed, and the appearance of the capital city was transformed within a few years.[17]

When he arrived in Santiago, there were only seven hundred Americans in all of Chile, but sixteen hundred French and about two thousand British. The nation's orientation was decidedly European, especially influenced by Great Britain and France, whose governments and business houses furnished financial assistance, trade, and training in diplomacy and the arts. Chile looked to the United States for engineering and the application of science. Economic development was hobbled by a literacy rate of only 13.5 percent as late as 1854.[18]

Chile had an agricultural economy with little manufacturing, but there were numerous flour mills. The country enjoyed rich mineral resources, and mining employed a sizeable number of men. Interior transportation was by animal-drawn carts, wagons, and stagecoaches, but an American entrepreneur-engineer, William Wheelwright of Massachusetts, was in the final stages of completing a fifty-one-mile railroad from Caldera to Copiapó. He had just begun work on a rail line to connect Valparaiso and Santiago. Due to the long, narrow dimensions of the country and its twenty-eight-hundred-mile Pacific coastline, much of her transportation was furnished by coastal shipping, both by sail and by steam.[19]

Catholicism was the state religion in Chile; there was virtually no tolerance of the Protestant faith. The church had always been an important element in the nation's political power structure and since 1831 had increased its influence, encouraged by the conservative governments of that period.[20]

Peyton had arrived in a country that achieved its independence only thirty-two years before. Its government had operated within the forms of nineteenth-century constitutionalism but not always with the spirit of democratic republicanism. The stability of the Chilean government was unusual among its neighbor states and won it recognition as "the honorable exception in South America."[21]

It was probably a good thing that Balie was unaware of high-level Chilean perceptions of the quality of U.S. diplomatic envoys in general. Manuel Carvallo, Chilean minister in Washington, had commented on the selection of U.S. Foreign Service representatives in a dispatch nearly three years before.

> Here the legations . . . are [usually] conferred not on persons meritorious for their talent, education, judgment or manners, but to public demagogues who win elections, or friends of the President or [cabinet] ministers. Diplomacy here is not a career, as it is in other nations. A doctor without patients, a lawyer without clients, a trader who has gone bankrupt—these get named as often as members of the Congress.[22]

Out of town at his summer residence when Peyton reached Santiago, President Manuel Bulnes formally received him on February 16. Escorted by high-ranking Chilean officials to Moneda Palace, the presidential palace in what had once been the royal mint, the American minister presented his credentials. Assuring the Chileans of "the continued friendship and undiminished regard" of the people of the United States, Peyton paid tribute to their "heroic struggle for independence" and congratulated them for their "deliverance from colonial dependence." He commented on the revolutionary heritage of both countries.

> The revolution of Chile was, in many respects, a counterpart of the
> North American revolution; the history of the one is, in the main,
> the history of the other; alike they fought, suffered, and triumphed.
> The free institutions which they erected upon the ruins of monarchy
> are, in theory, the same.

The American minister said that the stability of Chilean institutions,
the respect citizens show for the law, and the government's "mainte-
nance of national credit" were a combination that the United States
found admirable. "Chile is a brilliant star in the galaxy of republican
states. . . . An elder republic may be justly proud of a young sister who
has, by her example, reflected so much honor on the cause of free
government," he said.

Current developments in California indicated that the two countries
were destined to become more closely related, Peyton predicted, "united
by the ties of social intercourse and the golden bonds of commerce."
Chile's interests in the wide field of commercial enterprise now opening
on the California coast was second only to that of the United States, he
acknowledged.

Peyton declared that the increased trade between Chile and the
United States could redound to the benefit of both nations. It could be
the basis of achieving the "fervent desire" of the U.S. government "to
improve and strengthen the relations of friendship," which existed
between them.[23]

At the moment he was unaware that Chilean flour mills, taking
advantage of an overproduction of local wheat, threatened to
dominate the flour market in California, outcompeting U.S. mills, which
had to transport their product additional thousands of miles around the
Horn to market.[24] Nor did he expect that by 1852 Peruvian flour mills
would be feeding California because they enjoyed the short haul.[25]

Balie's remarks prompted the Chilean president to respond warmly.
He hoped that Chile would continue to deserve the "honorable opinion"
of the government and people of the United States, which he saw as "the
worthy model of liberty and civilization." He was pleased by the prospect
that the commerce of the two countries could be conducted on "the
broad basis of a common interest."[26]

President Bulnes, a Conservative, whose second and final five-year term
as president was nearing its end, had succeeded his uncle, Gen. Joaquin
Prieto, who had also served two terms (1831–1841). During that same
twenty-year period, Chile had prospered.[27]

Balie was pleased by the reception he and Emily received in
Santiago during their first month in residence. "Myself and daughter
have been . . . treated with every mark of respect, by the authorities and
citizens since our arrival at this place," he reported to Secretary Clayton.[28]

The warmth of their reception further belied the true feelings of most Chileans toward the United States. Peyton soon learned that the Mexican War had made many of them suspicious of American intentions. After all, numerous public figures in the United States had spoken openly of annexing all of Mexico and more. Where would the expansion-minded gringos stop?

The national pride of Chile suffered even more when many of her young men, among the first to reach the California gold fields in 1849, encountered discrimination and violence from the Americans. The California legislature created additional ill will in 1850 by passing what was popularly called the Foreign Miners Tax Act. Only native or naturalized citizens of the United States could mine without a license; it required all foreigners to have a license that could be acquired for twenty dollars per month.[29] There was further hurt when most Chilean forty-niners failed in their efforts in the mines. That disappointment stoked further anti-American sentiment at home, even though Americans failed in comparable numbers.[30]

Taking up the duties of his office, Peyton discovered that the records and papers of the legation were "scattered" and in "great confusion." His predecessor had left papers and bookcases in the care of an "American businessman" in Santiago, had taken some papers with him to his next assignment at Rio de Janeiro, had put some in Peyton's care in New York, and had entrusted others to the U.S. consul at Valparaiso. When he could find a building that would both house the legation and serve as his residence,[31] Balie planned to collect and secure the records there.

If there was anything that the minister needed more than books on international law, it was a secretary for the legation. When Congress elevated the office to a full ministry, it had neglected to include funds for a secretary. After a brief delay, the secretary of state arranged to fund the position and the president appointed one B. Rowan Hardin to the office. Hardin failed to appear, however, and the minister was irate. He assigned Emily the duty of acting secretary of the legation before dashing off a letter to Senator John Bell to ask his intervention with the president and the secretary of state. Balie wanted a secretary at once and desperately needed one who could speak and translate Spanish because neither he nor Emily was fluent in that language. He had asked for a man for the position because males customarily served the State Department in such roles and because South Americans expected to deal with male secretaries.[32]

Balie first learned that Jesse B. Holman was the president's next choice for secretary of the legation when he read an account in the *National Intelligencer* of June 29, 1850. In his first dispatch to the new

Secretary of State Daniel Webster, Balie asked him to expedite the secretary's trip to Chile as his services were badly needed at the legation.[33]

Holman reached Santiago on January 5, 1851, almost a year after Peyton and daughter had arrived in Chile. Peyton received him cordially, but he was not the Spanish-language scholar that Balie had sought.[34]

Emily Peyton gladly stepped aside from her position as acting secretary of the legation but continued to work as her father's private secretary. She was not paid for her work for the legation until the latter 1850s, when Senator John Bell of Tennessee was able to get her claim of $1,822.22 approved and paid.[35]

Holman's attention to detail caused Balie to examine the expenses of the legation and of his own livelihood. To live in a style comparable to other foreign diplomats in Chile, Peyton estimated that his expenses would exceed the provision made by the department. He could live on a minister's salary of nine thousand dollars per year only by observing strict economy. Long a patron of the performing arts, he defended spending as much as three hundred dollars for a box in the theater as "altogether necessary."[36]

Peyton was not to have Holman's services much longer, however. An illness that beset the secretary early in 1852 kept him from work much of the year, and on May 14, 1853, poor health forced his resignation.[37]

Sent to Santiago with instructions to negotiate a new treaty of commerce with Chile,[38] Peyton introduced the subject in early conversations with Andrés Bello,[39] senior official at the foreign ministry. The treaty signed at Santiago on September 1, 1833, still regulated commercial relations between the two countries, but Chile had announced plans to exercise her option to terminate it.[40] Favorably disposed to negotiating a new treaty, Bello said he would be glad to have further discussions with the American minister. As they were then in the middle of the withering heat of summer, Peyton correctly surmised that the host government would do little about the treaty until autumn.[41]

Soon after Balie's first meetings with him, Bello was replaced as negotiator by the foreign minister José Joaquin Pérez, who during the latter part of April was replaced by the new foreign minister Antonio Varas.[42] Peyton and Varas then promised to swap documentary evidence of their authorities to act for their respective governments as the former made it clear that the United States would insist on equal treatment and unqualified reciprocity and would not agree to most favored nation status or accept special treatment for either party. Privately, Balie doubted that domestic political considerations would permit the foreign minister to engage in treaty negotiations in the near future. Nonetheless, Varas predicted his congress soon would pass an act equalizing the fees charged to U.S. ships in Chilean ports with those charged Chilean ships in their own waters. He hoped such action would prompt the United States to make a similar concession to Chilean ships in American ports.[43]

President Bulnes surprised Peyton by suddenly returning to Andrés Bello to negotiate the treaty for Chile. At that time Bello was still in a position in the foreign ministry second only to the minister. Balie found himself dealing with Bello on treaty matters and with Varas on current relations between the two countries.[44]

In their first formal meeting, Bello suggested a treaty provision to create a joint commission, made up of citizens, one-half from each nation, to settle all claims between them. It would meet at the seat of government against whom claims were made, and in case of tie votes a "third party" should be called in to make the decision. If his remarkably cumbersome plan were not enough to slow the talks, he suggested that it was necessary first for the Chilean Congress to act to abolish discriminatory duties and fees then being charged to U.S. ships. He wanted also to hear Washington's reaction to his proposal for a claims commission before taking up further treaty provisions. Peyton suspected that rather than lowering charges to others, the Chileans might raise the fees charged their own ships as there was great pressure from wealthy landowners to turn to customs services for revenues.[45]

A month later, Bello proposed to amend the existing commercial treaty with the United States by redrafting the fifth article that governed embargo, the practice of detaining foreign vessels in port in time of national emergency. Professing to model the draft after a suggestion made by France, Bello sought a more favorable treatment for the detaining power. In essence, it would pay shipowners and crews considerably less as indemnification against losses incurred because they were detained.[46]

Peyton was shaken when news of the unexpected death of President Taylor reached him sometime in September 1850. After the initial shock, he recalled his close relationship with Taylor during the period when the general was making his decision to run for president. He was proud to have maneuvered the general into the Whig Party. By letter to Governor Crittenden, he shared his "sorrow at the death of our noble and patriotic friend."[47]

After notifying the Chilean government of Taylor's death, he presided over a memorial gathering of local American citizens, who adopted resolutions of sympathy and respect for the late president. He advised all concerned that Millard Fillmore had succeeded to the presidency.[48]

Nearly six months had passed when Peyton received the State Department's response to Bello's two principal suggestions for the new treaty. In both instances the United States found the provisions unacceptable, but Balie was able to deliver that disappointing message along with much more favorable news. He presented copies of President Fillmore's proclamation "suspending discriminating duties upon Chilean vessels and their cargoes in the ports of the United States." The proclamation put an end to Chilean complaints about maritime reciprocity. Seizing on those positive developments, he promised Bello he would soon deliver a proposed outline for the treaty.[49]

On February 22, 1851, Peyton sent his thirty-eight-page draft of the treaty to Bello and the State Department. He expected the Chileans would accept the provisions relative to commerce and navigation because of their interest in exploiting the California market. On the other hand, he would have great difficulty in obtaining concessions in religious matters such as "the baptism and education of Protestant children of foreigners and the intermarriage of Protestants with the Catholics of the country or with other foreigners." He blamed the priesthood, among whose number were many of the leading members of congress, for the nearly universal intolerance of other religions in Chile. Although he believed the time "propitious" to challenge the church, he asked for instructions as to which of the religious issues were negotiable and which he should defend to the end.[50]

Four months later, Chile still had made no significant response to the proposed treaty. Realizing that treaty proposals dealing with the church would forestall negotiations indefinitely, Peyton pointed out that England had decided to forgo a treaty in preference to yielding on the religious questions. The national elections in June that had diverted the Chilean government's attention from the treaty coupled with a lingering illness that had settled upon Bello left negotiations in limbo for several months.[51]

By the end of August, Bello submitted Peyton's draft treaty to the Chilean president and congress without ever having discussed his government's concerns about it with the American. The strategy was to make it a target that politicians could fire upon with abandon. It was a clever way to distract national attention from internal problems and to focus it on the United States, the young North American bully, especially at a time when revolution was being discussed openly in Chile.[52]

A year later, Chile continued to ignore its promise to negotiate provisions of the treaty. "This government," Peyton wrote to the secretary of state on August 13, 1852, "manifests no disposition to proceed in this matter of the new treaty and have not even so much as noticed the proposal which I have submitted."[53] Facing the strange combination of Chilean indifference and hostility, Peyton relied on his original instructions: the United States would conduct its relationships with Chile without a treaty should it be impossible to obtain an agreement that affords adequate protection to her interests.[54]

The responsibilities of his office occupied Balie's time but he maintained a lively interest in Whig politics back home. He was elated to learn that his comrade of old in Tennessee politics, William B. Campbell, had received the Whig nomination for governor.[55] Balie wrote to him of the "pride" and "exultation" he felt on hearing the news. Other politicians could not obtain "this distinction," but Campbell "could not . . . avoid it," he noted.[56]

Always eager to receive mail from home, Balie was shocked when he opened a letter bearing the news that his brother Robert Holmes Peyton had been killed in an altercation with their sixty-four-year-old neighbor, John McElwrath. Robert Holmes had gone to McElwrath's place on October 7, 1851, to retrieve a buggy that the latter had borrowed from his sister but had refused to return. McElwrath told Robert that he could have the buggy only if he took it by force. Undeterred by the threat, Robert began untying the shafts. McElwrath pushed him back and drew a knife from his waistband. Peyton attempted to disarm his attacker by striking him with his walking cane, but it broke and McElwrath drove his knife into the younger man's chest, inflicting a wound from which he died moments later.[57]

While at school in Virginia, Balie Peyton Jr. learned of his uncle's death and was so disturbed that he came home. He sought out McElwrath, found him in town, cursed him roundly, "and would have shot him publicly" had not the killer "made off and shut himself up in a room." Balie Jr. took out his anger on one of McElwrath's servants by beating him severely because he had "acted very impudently" to his aunt, Sarah Peyton Barry, owner of the carriage in dispute. Strongly persuaded by his Uncle Thomas Barry, Balie Jr. returned to school.[58]

Saddened by his brother's senseless death at the hands of a neighbor, Balie was grateful that Balie Jr. had not compounded the violence by killing McElwrath. The courts would deal with the killer, and Balie, as an attorney, would accept the verdict.[59]

Although Balie's horses were far away, a high-ranking secretary of the host government introduced him to Chilean racing by accompanying him to see a race between some of the most famous horses of the country.

Regarded as "a kind of Napoleon among the racing men of Chile," the secretary brought Peyton to see one of his own racehorses run and win the featured race.[60]

When the American minister remarked that he was not greatly impressed with the racing power displayed that day by the best Chilean horses, the proud secretary countered by asking if he thought there were any better racehorses in the United States. Trying to be diplomatic in his response, Peyton explained that the American race-horse was larger and stronger, could carry more weight, and was faster. His explanation sent blood coursing to the face of the secretary who, confident that Peyton was talking beyond his ability to perform, challenged him to produce an American horse for "ten thousand a side, owners to ride."

Balie accepted the challenge but not before recognizing that he would be handicapped by being sixty pounds heavier than the secretary. The date of the race was set sufficiently far ahead to allow Peyton to bring two "great, strong race horses" from his stable on Station Camp Creek. There would even be time for him to lose weight, but he did not choose to diet. He had great confidence in American thoroughbreds for the reasons he had stated, but he had confidence also in his ability to ride.

The proposed match attracted little attention until the Tennessee thoroughbreds arrived a few months later. Then it became "the excitement of the day, and the sporting event of the nation." Confident that their proven horseman would win over the heavier American rider on a mount brought from great distance, Chileans were enchanted with the prospect of winning their eagerly placed bets. The foreign colony bet almost unanimously on Peyton's horse, encouraged by the British whose confidence was based on the fact that the American thoroughbred had descended from blooded English stock.

On race day, a carnival atmosphere pervaded the vast crowd assembled in Santiago. It was an occasion for Chilean horsemanship to reinforce national pride and to bring financial rewards for those who bet on the secretary and his horse.

At race time the jockeys and horses seemed ready for the four-mile race. Peyton, "dressed in a closely fitted jockey suit" and looking "the perfection of developed manhood and grace," was up on a strong son of Imp. Leviathan. The secretary, "dressed in the style of his country," was mounted on a gray horse locally known for "both speed and bottom." Like the other racehorses of Chile, he was undersized by North American standards and had never competed against a thoroughbred.

Breaking clean at the first start, the two horses ran side by side for about three-quarters of a mile. Peyton exerted a "strong, steady pull" on his mount from the beginning, but the secretary had to push his horse

WALLACE'S MONTHLY.

VOL. I.	FEBRUARY, 1876.	No. 5.

Entered, according to Act of Congress, in the year 1876, by JOHN H. WALLACE, in the Office of the Librarian of Congress, at Washington.

TERMS, THREE DOLLARS PER ANNUM.   **SINGLE NUMBER, 30 CENTS.**

AN INTERNATIONAL HORSE-RACE.

[Drawn and engraved expressly for WALLACE'S MONTHLY.]

Balie wins race in Chile, recalled many years later in Wallace's Monthly

to stay alongside. The "great, raking stride of the Leviathan" wore heavily on his smaller competitor, and when Peyton let his horse "extend himself" until he was in "a full running gait," the small gray fell hopelessly behind.

> As soon as the secretary saw Mr. Peyton looking [back] at him he dropped all diplomatic courtesy, and rising in his stirrups and shaking his fist at him fiercely, he shouted at the top of his voice, "You can go to hell!" Mr. Peyton galloped on the two remaining miles. The foreigners and sailors cheered. . . . The Chileans were . . . speechless.[61]

Sometime later Balie was delighted to learn that far from the track in Santiago, his racing colors, carried by the sorrel filly Aversion, had claimed a three-heat victory over two other thoroughbreds during the spring races at the Walnut Race Course at Nashville.[62] The results confirmed to him that his horses at home were receiving attention and training. The event also caused him to speculate on just how much he could accomplish if the governments of the United States and Chile would give him the attention that he, as minister, deserved.

ANXIOUS TIMES
1850–1853

Peyton arrived in Chile when political tensions were rapidly rising to a point of crisis, the first time that had happened since 1830. The Conservatives had governed during those twenty years without serious opposition from the Liberals, but they now faced a sobering challenge from a new generation that feared the Conservative candidate Manuel Montt for his authoritarian proclivities. This situation was unknown in Washington where the State Department continued to regard Chile as a government of stability.

Although on arrival Peyton paid tribute to Chile's efforts to maintain freedom for its people under a government chosen at free elections, he soon learned that the Conservative Party controlled election results. Adroitly administered by the president and the provincial governors, its power came from a coalition of businessmen, wealthy landowners, and the church. The Liberal Party, drawing on the same constituencies for its younger membership, was virtually no different in matters of policy. To Balie, there was little to choose between the parties.

Heretofore the president, "acting with promptness and decision," had avoided bloodshed and preserved the "public tranquility," but there was apprehension in the country that the ruling party might encounter armed resistance before the elections scheduled for the summer of 1851. Peyton dutifully reported this to Washington.[1]

The remaining months of 1850 and the first three of 1851 passed without violent internal conflict. When the earth began trembling on April 12, 1851, it was not revolt but an earthquake, the first Balie had experienced. Aftershocks continued for a week.[2]

Following the earthquake, Peyton had another new experience; his first taste of revolution came on the morning of April 20. Awakened by the sound of musketry and cannon fire, he rushed from his quarters to warn an American family that lived nearby. Then mounting one of his saddle horses, he rode at a gallop to the scene of the action. There two regiments of the regular army had revolted under the leadership of Col. Pedro Urriola and were attempting to take the artillery barracks near the plaza. He described the event:

> [The rebels] filed from the plaza through Main Street . . . and formed on the Cañada, a street . . . where they built a temporary breastwork in front of the barracks of the artillery battalion and attempted to reduce it, but the besieged served the cannon through the windows with effect. . . . The building was at length fired by the assailants with a view to dislodge the defending forces, but the flames were rapidly extinguished. About this time, the artillery was advanced from the barracks into the streets where it was taken by the insurgents. But their leader, Col. Urriola, having fallen mortally wounded, they surrendered.[3]

Informed that about two hundred regulars and rebels had died in the revolt, the president immediately declared martial law and created a military tribunal to try the offenders. Peyton expected to see widespread "summary punishment by shooting," but, nonetheless, he congratulated the president for suppressing "the outbreak."

Committed to standing "aloof" from the politics of the country, Peyton was under no illusion about the reasons for political opposition there.

> I do not doubt but what there exist great abuses in the mode of conducting elections by the executive of this country, and that the system is essentially vicious and tyrannical, as it is understood that the Governors, or Intendants, of the provinces are in the habit of depriving the people of the elective franchise by threats and intimidation . . . in some instances . . . corporal punishment and imprisonment.[4]

The president of Chile enjoyed Peyton's support only because the minister could see no prospect of significant changes in national policies should an opposition government be elected. Asserting that none of the candidates had "the moral courage, or influence, to withstand the power of the priesthood in accomplishing those reforms which are most needed," he concluded that peace and internal stability could be maintained best by the incumbent administration.[5]

When he returned from the short-lived uprising, Balie saw that it had overflowed into his parlor. There, with his wife and children surrounding him, was Col. D. Justo Arteaga, a regular army officer who had been "deprived" of his command several months prior "in consequence of his supposed connection with the [political] opposition." When Arteaga asked for asylum in the legation, Peyton promptly granted it. He reasoned that if he permitted Arteaga to be arrested, the colonel would be shot, and "his execution would be the signal for a sanguinary civil war, marked by the most inveterate feelings of revenge."[6]

At once Foreign Minister Varas objected to asylum for Arteaga, but Peyton delayed any action in the matter by asking the State Department for instructions. In the meantime, he worked out an arrangement through the good offices of the Brazilian minister to permit Arteaga and his family to leave the country without interference. Soon afterward he granted asylum to another insurgent, Santiago Herrera, and arranged for his passage out of the country around June 21.[7]

Peyton regarded Chile as "treading on the brink of the precipice . . . one false step may . . . plunge her into the abyss of anarchy and civil war." Five months prior to the April 20 outbreak in Santiago, the government had put down a minor uprising in a neighboring province and declared martial law in the area. Elsewhere federal authorities "broke up" political clubs and muzzled the press. The situation was rendered even more dangerous by the presence in the south of a large portion of the regular army under the command of Gen. José María de la Cruz, who had warned the government not to execute the insurgents. As many as could escape their abortive attempt to reduce the artillery barracks in Santiago fled to join Cruz, a close friend of Colonel Urriola, who had been killed before the barracks.[8] Although Cruz, a national military hero, was not pleased with the government, he first resisted revolution as the answer to the country's political problems.[9]

Sensing insurgency, the government moved against those opposition members of congress "compromised" in the attempt of April 20 and "banished" several and initiated proceedings against others. Some fled the country. "A great many arrests, commitments, and other summary proceedings" had occurred, Balie reported, "embracing all classes except the clergy."[10] Even after the incumbent Conservative Party and its presidential nominee Manuel Montt[11] won the national election, Peyton expected civil disturbances to break out at any time.[12]

Revolution was not to be denied. Eleven days before the inauguration on September 18, the regular forces stationed at La Serena in northern Chile, for which Coquimbo was the principal port, revolted. Backed by a large majority of the local citizens, the rebels overthrew the regularly constituted civil and military authorities in that province with very little bloodshed. They made many arrests, seized "the public money and other public properties," and often attempted to force wealthy citizens to make loans to them. The new president faced the most serious crisis in twenty years of Conservative rule.[13]

While government attention was focused on La Serena and Coquimbo, Peyton reported major unrest elsewhere:

> A similar revolt occurred at Concepción and Talcahuano, the most important city and port in the South. . . . The Custom House, forts, arms, munitions, public money and other property, including a steamer . . . belonging to the government of Chile were seized, and all of officers, civil and military, arrested and deposed, and others appointed in their stead by the insurgents.[14]

The armed militia, "a well organized and efficient body of men, more numerous by far than the regular army," led the revolt in the South, Peyton related. Prior to the outbreak, General Cruz was relieved of his regular command and from his office as governor of the province of Concepción. His troops, very much attached to him, were ordered to the frontier "ostensibly to keep the [native] Indians in check but really . . . to remove the troops beyond the reach of political influences."[15]

Congress responded to the rebellion by conferring "extraordinary powers" upon the president, who immediately declared all the provinces from Coquimbo to Concepción under martial law or state of siege. Although General Cruz had retired to his farm in the South and had thus far avoided joining the revolutionary party, its leaders claimed to have his support. It was not long before his popularity with soldiers and citizens alike propelled him into leadership of the opposition military forces.[16]

The uprisings notwithstanding, the government observed the nation's anniversary of independence and the inauguration of the new president on September 18. Attempting to atone for the weather-curtailed celebration of the prior year and eager to show public support for the new president, the government ordered the annual white-washing and the patriotic decoration of residences and business houses throughout Santiago. With the help of officers from the Naval Astronomical Expedition, Peyton decorated the legation by installing eye-catching transparencies over the two street-side windows. "In one of the windows the Chilean, and in the other the American coat of arms was represented, with flags of the two nations blended, and the words 'Libertad' and 'Union' inscribed," Navy Lt. J. M. Gilliss[17] recorded. The navy men had erected a large star on the facade of their observatory on the castellated crag of Mount Lucia above the city. Visible from anywhere in Santiago, it was brilliantly illuminated at dusk.

Invited to meet "the public authorities and foreign ministers in the Senate chamber" at ten o'clock on September 18, Peyton and the four U.S. Navy officers, all dressed in appropriate ceremonial regalia, rode in a carriage to the appointed place. There they joined a large gathering of military officers, "a considerable proportion of church dignitaries," ministers of the cabinet, municipal authorities, and members of the university. Marshals quickly formed the entire assemblage into a procession that passed through the streets to the cathedral where priests conducted a high mass to inaugurate the president. The streets were lined by soldiers and crowds of citizens, but there were no displays of enthusiasm, just "passive curiosity."[18]

Following the inauguration mass, Peyton and the American officers went directly to the palace and greeted President Montt and his family. They adjourned with Montt and the French ambassador to make a ceremonial visit to the School of Arts two miles away. Winding their way home unescorted for the first time that day, the Americans stopped for a hasty dinner and then drove their carriage about the city to view the illuminations. Military bands, strategically spaced, offered early evening concerts, but the crowds on the streets deserted the musicians early, fearing that the revolutionists might attempt to seize the occasion for their own purposes.[19]

Soon after the inaugural holiday, Peyton reported to the State Department that Chile was "in imminent danger of a violent revolution." The situation was so threatening that he escorted his daughter Emily from Santiago to Valparaiso, where she took passage to the United States, arriving in New Orleans by steamship on November 4. As of September 24, 1851, Balie reported that to the best of his knowledge there had been "no seizure of the ships or other property of the citizens of the United States."[20]

A few days later word reached Peyton that ships of the British Navy were denying U.S. ships egress from the port of Coquimbo because Chilean revolutionaries had seized a privately owned steamship belonging to a British citizen. Undaunted by the government's approval of a British blockade of the port, he fired off a warning to the British chargé d'affaires that "any attempt on the part of Her Majesty's armed vessels to detain or capture vessels of the United States in the port of Coquimbo will be considered an aggression not justified by international law." Soon afterward the British Navy lifted its blockade of U.S. ships and Chile closed the ports of Coquimbo and Talcahuano.[21]

Although assessing and reporting the unsettled conditions of the country kept Peyton busy, he took time to follow up on his sons' education. He had written to them to enroll in a school located farther north than Alexandria, Virginia, but the letter reached them after they were already settled into the academic routine at Benjamin Hallowell's. Having encountered the barriers thrown up by his own inability to speak Spanish and French, Balie was anxious for his sons "to pay great attention" to instruction in those languages. He provided access to sufficient funds for his sons, even enough for them to pay the bill for shirts and other clothing that he ordered for himself from a clothier in Philadelphia.[22]

The situation in Chile further deteriorated during the last three months of 1851. "Ports [were] closed, commerce suspended, martial law proclaimed, prisons crowded . . . all social intercourse broken up," Peyton wrote on November 20. On the day before, regular army forces led by General Bulnes confronted General Cruz and the rebels at Monte Urra in the South. Heavy fighting ensued with both sides claiming victory.

There was little contact between the armies until December 8, when the concluding battle of the campaign was fought near the confluence of the Maule and Loncomilla Rivers. Approximately eighteen hundred soldiers died in the ferocious encounter. There was no clear victor on the field, and again, each side claimed victory.[23] Peyton observed sardonically, "Such another victory would . . . well nigh annihilate both armies."[24]

The bloody clashes of November 19 and December 8 unexpectedly paved the way for the cessation of hostilities. On December 23, Peyton advised the State Department that a treaty of peace had been signed by General Bulnes for the government and General Cruz[25] for the revolutionaries. Bulnes agreed to seek a general amnesty to all who participated in the uprisings. Peyton hoped the amnesty included several transient Americans who had joined the rebellion when General Cruz assumed its leadership. On Christmas Day, Balie issued a statement to the government and people of Chile "congratulating them upon the restoration of peace."[26]

The participation in the revolution of about seventy-five Americans who had stopped on their way home from the California gold rush provided the government of Chile another opportunity to embarrass the United States. The former forty-niners had formed two companies and joined General Cruz in the province of Concepción, and it was not clear that the amnesty agreement covered them. The issue quickly found its way to Peyton's desk via the consul at Talcahuano, Samuel E. Eckel.[27]

> Apparently, Consul Eckel had grave doubts about the rights of the American interlopers. Peyton pointed out that if the terms of the treaty provided amnesty for all who participated against the government, it would become the duty of all official representatives of the United States to insist upon a faithful compliance with it.[28]

A month later Eckel reported to Peyton that the Americans who had surrendered with the rebels were free and he had seen several of them at Talcahuano. They had not been "molested" and apparently were in no jeopardy for their brief participation against the government.[29]

Peyton had expected a general roundup of the "misguided" American citizens who participated in "the late revolution." Complaining that the Chilean administration nourished "the most bitter and unaccountable feelings . . . against the people and government of the United States," Peyton alleged that it was determined "to have an American victim." And he was just as determined to prevent it.[30]

As Peyton pushed Foreign Minister Varas for official assurance that the Americans had been included in the amnesty,[31] an uprising led by inmates in the Chilean convict colony near the Straits of Magellan resulted in the deaths of several persons, including the governor. With virtually no navy of its own to challenge the escaped prisoners on the high seas, Chile petitioned Peyton and the British minister for aid from their navies. The American minister replied regretfully that there was not a ship of Commander McCauley's Pacific fleet in Chilean waters or otherwise available.[32] The British, with a large fleet in the area, responded at once and hunted down most of the rebels.[33]

The difference between the relative readiness of the American and British fleets in the area was exemplified by Admiral McCauley's refusal to go to the assistance of the Americans who had joined General Cruz's rebels and by the willing cooperation extended to Peyton by Rear Admiral Fairfax Moresby of the British Navy. "The admiral has manifested a very friendly and accommodating spirit," Balie wrote of his assistance during the various uprisings.[34]

Monitoring and reporting the attempted revolution was only one activity that engaged Balie's attention. Among the minister's principal duties were the protection of the rights of individual U.S. citizens in Chile and the protection of ships and seamen operating under the Stars and Stripes. There were other duties: trying to persuade an embezzler living in Chile to repay the embezzled funds to a citizen victim in New Hampshire;[35] delivering commissions of newly appointed consuls to the ministry of foreign affairs;[36] revising downward at least one consul's excessively high schedule of charges for consular services and standardizing practices among the four American consuls in Chile;[37] pursuing old ships' claims such as that of the barque *Pantheon*;[38] and dealing with current maritime problems such as those of the American schooner *Henry L. King*.[39]

A persistent issue involved the apparent impressment of two Chilean and one French seamen from the U.S. whaling ship *Addison* in 1851. Thomas H. Lawrence, master of the whaler, complained that Chilean Navy officers boarded his ship while in harbor at Valparaiso and forcibly removed the three crewmen to a Chilean Navy vessel on its way to sea. The Chileans claimed that the seamen sought their aid to escape an abusive master and that their assistance was a humanitarian act. Whether it was truly impressment, the situation touched a sensitive nerve in U.S. maritime history.[40]

As soon as he learned of the incident, Peyton filed a strong protest with the Chilean foreign minister. Simultaneously, he asked the State Department for instructions, observing that it was possible "the affair may be made to assume a grave and very important aspect."[41]

In a conference with Peyton, Secretary Holman, and Lt. Archibald McRae[42] of the U.S. Navy, who was acting as the minister's military attaché, Foreign Minister Varas insisted that his government had acted properly and was not "impressing" but answering the call of Chilean seamen who claimed mistreatment at the hands of their master. He said the government would release the French sailor unless he had voluntarily entered into a contract to serve in the Chilean Navy. Apologizing for the "irregular or informal" manner in which they had removed the seamen from the *Addison*, Varas would not admit any liability for damages to the whaler owners or its crew.[43]

Varas was accomplished at evading issues by delaying official responses to them, but Peyton would not accept his postponement-into-oblivion tactics. On April 29, 1852, Varas officially responded to the *Addison* matter in a statement of forty-three handwritten pages. The government's position was unchanged from previous informal representations to Peyton, except in this instance the foreign minister was critical of what he regarded as Peyton's magnification of an inconsequential event into an issue that threatened the good relations between the two countries.[44]

Peyton replied by demanding that Varas supply documentation to the lengthy position paper he submitted on the *Addison*.[45] On July 29, Varas sent a "sheaf" of papers to the U.S. legation that purported to furnish the proof Peyton requested.[46] The submission apparently answered the questions that most vexed Balie. Two months later he asked for further instructions on the *Addison* case and recommended that, all things considered, the United States should attempt to settle the matter by demanding and enforcing the immediate discharge of the French seaman from the service of Chile.[47] At that juncture, he marked the *Addison* case off his list of principal concerns.

Throughout his tenure, Peyton repeatedly made the case to the State Department for an increased U.S. naval presence in Chilean waters. He believed that a frequent showing of the flag would contribute mightily to protecting the interests of American citizens and to indicating that the United States attached importance to its relationships with its South American neighbor.[48]

Two-way communications with the fleet commander Charles S. McCauley were so unsatisfactory that Peyton accused the officer not only of neglecting his calls for aid, but of the "extraordinary conduct" of withdrawing all U.S. Navy ships from the Chilean coast at an inappropriate time. On January 13, 1852, he begged McCauley to return to Chile as soon as possible.[49] The minister obviously had no authority to issue orders to the navy commander; all that Peyton could do was beseech and threaten. He was so unsuccessful with McCauley that he turned to the British Pacific fleet commander for aid when insurgents, in an act of piracy, seized a U.S. merchant ship near the Straits of Magellan and chased another.[50]

Peyton's unsatisfactory relations with Commodore McCauley ended abruptly in September 1852 when the captain was relieved of his command. When McCauley came into Valparaiso to transfer command to his successor, Capt. Bladen Dulaney, he and Peyton ended what had become a mutually frustrating relationship by recognizing that communication difficulties had precluded their working together as closely as the latter had desired. Insisting that the navy had a role to play in supporting diplomacy at the local level, Peyton was encouraged to learn that orders from Washington to enforce Peyton's demands for the release of a U.S. citizen awaited Dulaney's arrival at Valparaiso.[51]

Balie devoted a significant amount of his time in Santiago to dealing with issues involving U.S. merchant ships. He represented shipwrecked seamen and the owners of their ships; he appealed quarantines; warned shipmasters away from ports where danger from insurrectionists lurked; pressed claims for the owners of vessels that had been embargoed or otherwise detained in Chilean ports; and won an agreement from Chile for the U.S. Navy to anchor a store ship at Valparaiso in lieu of maintaining a separate storehouse on shore.[52]

Since reaching Valparaiso on a British mail ship operated under contract with the Chilean government, Peyton had coveted that oceangoing enterprise for the United States. Learning that the contract was about to be rebid, Balie raised the question with Washington.[53] The State Department had just negotiated the Clayton-Bulwer Treaty with Great Britain, however, and was not interested in challenging British mail contracts in South America.

The wheels of justice turned slowly in Chile, especially when a U.S. citizen was enmeshed by them. On September 24, 1851, Peyton informed the State Department that Samuel Thompson had just been acquitted of murder charges and released after being held in "close confinement" at Concepción for fourteen months. He was discharged from custody into the care of the U.S. consul at Talcahuano and the commander of the USS *St. Mary's*, then in port there, who made personal application to authorities.[54] It was a victory of sorts for Peyton.

Another case involving a U.S. citizen grew out of a dockside brawl on August 22, 1852, when a Chilean died of multiple stab wounds. A U.S.

merchant seaman, William N. Stewart, the only North American in the melee, was arrested and charged with murder.[55]

Peyton and William Duer,[56] U.S. consul at Valparaiso, undertook to defend Stewart, but the judge stalled in ways that suggested that Stewart was being set up for conviction and execution.[57]

Peyton and Duer applied relentless pressure that resulted in the court's acquitting Stewart of the charge of murder, but the government held him in prison pending further charges. Peyton persistently entreated the State Department for stronger measures to win freedom for the seaman,[58] and President Fillmore finally intervened.

Peyton delivered the message on December 8: "If . . . the government of Chile should permit the accused to be deprived of his life or liberty . . . the government of the United States however anxious it may be to cultivate the most friendly relations with Chile, will consider such conduct a gross outrage." The president's message was heard and a few days later the judge set Stewart free.[59]

As he had not often prevailed in his encounters with the Chilean government, Peyton must have spent more than a few hours evaluating his situation in the foreign service. Not only had the Chilean authorities seemed to delight in delaying negotiations on almost any issue, his own government had been slow to act because of the long time required for communications to pass through the mail between Washington and Santiago. Sometimes the lapse was six to eight months.[60] The United States Navy was of little help in protecting the lives and property of American citizens in Chile because it could intercede only on direct orders from Washington. And for much of his tenure, Balie had been without the services of a secretary at the legation who was fluent in Spanish. In addition to these restraints, Balie sensed a calculated effort by the church and state in Chile to discredit the United States and especially its citizens living and/or working in their country.

Peyton insisted repeatedly that the Chilean government did not treat the United States and its citizens with the same consideration they showed to the British and French. By the spring of 1852, he was "convinced that no claim, however just, presented by our citizens or government," would be allowed by Chile.

> It is not for me to prescribe a remedy . . . but the sooner the proper remedy is applied the better for all concerned, as any extraordinary patience and forbearance on the part of our government will be . . . viewed in the light of a concession . . . and tend to invite further aggression, not only on the part of Chile but of all the other states of South America, where our mariners and commerce are continually exposed to wrong and depredation.[61]

Peyton had been unable to make any headway on a new commercial treaty between the two countries and had been unable to resolve numerous claims made by U.S. citizens against Chile. Most claims that he sought to perfect were not settled until August 7, 1892, when a convention between the two countries was signed at Santiago.[62]

The American minister had become weary of conducting fruitless diplomatic discussions with Foreign Minister Varas:

> It has been my consistent endeavor to cultivate amicable relations with the authorities here, no easy matter owing to the peculiar temperament of the minister, who . . . is not familiar with the conventional rules of society, nor the courtesies of diplomatic intercourse. . . . I have borne with the minister's peculiarities and am disposed to do so as long as the same may be done consistently with the respect which is due to my official station as the representative of the United States at this capital.[63]

Before leaving the legation, he wrote to Secretary of State Marcy, "I have seen and suffered enough in my late experience and intercourse with this government to prepare me for any aggression, however gross it may be, on American rights and American citizens."[64] He later confided to a friend, "I was so much disgusted with those semi-barbarians in that 'one horse republic' that I fear I manifested it in a very unambassadorial manner."[65] Also, he had stored in the back of his mind repeated entreaties from his sisters and other family at home seeking his return to Tennessee.[66]

The new year, 1853, had begun with Balie learning that his sister Evalina Anderson had died at home in Sumner County. The wife of Dr. E. R. Anderson, she had seen little of her brother since he was first elected to Congress.[67] Aware that he had absented himself from his family more than he had ever planned, Balie felt especially vulnerable when he contemplated the deaths of his wife, daughter, three brothers, and sister within the last seven years.

Balie Peyton was ready to leave his post; he had had enough. Not only had his relations with the Chilean foreign minister been unpleasant, the U.S. government had tried his patience by its slow responses. His situation had not been made easier by three different American presidents and four different secretaries of state holding their respective offices during the four years of his appointment.[68] He was certain, also, that the recently inaugurated Democratic President Franklin Pierce would not reappoint him.[69]

Earlier he had sent word to President Fillmore through unofficial sources that he wanted to be recalled; he confirmed the request to the new Secretary of State W. L. Marcy on April 30. At the same time his colleague William Duer asked to be replaced as consul at Valparaiso. On July 15, Marcy sent a dispatch to Peyton advising him that Samuel Medary had been appointed minister in his place and was expected to leave for Chile by the middle of August. Two weeks later the president named Thomas E. Massey as secretary of the legation.[70]

The impending departure of Peyton and Duer was "greatly regretted among the Americans" in Chile. Both were highly regarded, and their appointments were believed by many to have been the most popular made thus far to their respective offices. American nationals widely appreciated Peyton for his candor and good humor.[71]

Although Balie believed he had failed to win the respect due the United States from Chile, two important Chilean historians later evaluated him favorably. Acknowledging that he had represented U.S. interests vigorously, Diego Barros Arana wrote that his "discreet and respectful conduct tended to make people forget . . . the procedures of some of his predecessors."[72] All in all he "left agreeable memories in Chile," Agustin Edwards concluded.[73]

An American student of diplomatic and commercial relations between the United States and Chile, writing seventy-five years later, commended Peyton's performance:

> All things considered, Peyton ranks as an efficient agent at his post. He was sent there at a trying time and had to face a number of situations requiring a high degree of tact, executive ability, forcefulness and self-control, and he measured up well to the occasion in practically every instance.[74]

By August 1, Balie had moved to Valparaiso to welcome the new envoy and, if possible, to leave on the ship that brought him. Although he had read a newspaper report stating his replacement had sailed and would reach Valparaiso on the American steamer *Uncle Sam*, the new minister was not on board when the ship docked August 2. Peyton was bewildered. Due to the slowness of the mails, he was unaware that the president's first appointee had resigned the office soon after accepting it.[75] Slow communications with Washington had plagued him to the end.

Having waited beyond the end of his appointed term, he wrote the secretary of state that he was embarking for California on a sailing ship, that he had advised the foreign minister that Reuben Wood, the new American consul at Valparaiso, would be in charge of the legation until the next minister arrived, and that no official business of consequence was pending. His final act was to transmit the complaints of the masters of several American merchant vessels who reported "violent and oppressive" conduct by Peruvian authorities at the Chincha Islands, a cluster of small islands located in the Pacific Ocean off the west coast of Central Peru. Admiral Moresby had substantially confirmed the masters' statements to Peyton as he had been "on the spot soon after the occurrences." Balie's last recommendation to the secretary of state was to send an armed navy vessel to the islands where the improper activities had occurred.[76] Little did he imagine that the president would not have a replacement for him until the latter part of the next year.[77]

Ready to return to the United States, Peyton was eager to reach California and sample its gold-fueled prosperity. He hoped to find opportunities in the gold boom to retire the debt that seemed always to be hanging over the Station Camp Creek farm.

CHAPTER 11

CALIFORNIA
1853–1855

Peyton looked back in contemplation from the deck of the clipper ship *Mischief* as it sailed out of the harbor of Valparaiso on September 23, 1853, headed north to San Francisco. He did not yet know that Emily had safely completed her earlier trip home to Tennessee, and he wondered about her well-being. During the idle days at sea, he must have thought about the others of his family. How were Balie Jr. and John Bell faring at school in Virginia? Were his three sisters in good health? And what about the farm, the slaves, the horses, and the land itself? He had the treasured memories of beautiful Anne, his only wife, who had succumbed to a fatal illness nearly a decade ago. And young Nan—he could never escape the tragedy of the accident that took her life.

Then surely his thoughts turned to himself. Why was he on the way to California? Was he trying to run away from the haunting reality that Anne and Nan were no longer with him? Was it a driving loneliness that caused him to volunteer for the Mexican War, to seek the later appointment to Chile, and that now prompted his bid to be a factor in the life of the fast-developing state of California?

Balie needed a friend and partner and found one in another attorney and former congressman, William Duer, the American consul at Valparaiso with whom he had developed good rapport. Both were ready to leave the Foreign Service, and they had agreed that California held opportunities for both. Now on board with him were Duer and his family, all bound for San Francisco, where the two attorneys planned to open a law office. Overcoming frequently adverse sailing conditions, the *Mischief* brought them and their fellow passengers into San Francisco Bay on November 9.[1]

The harbor was lined with docks from which piers stretched out to accommodate the arrival and departure of ships of all sizes. Peyton looked out over a city that had risen phoenix-like from six major fires that swept its complex of hastily built wood and canvas structures between 1848 and 1851. The last had gutted the entire business district. He saw new commercial and government buildings of brick or stone, designed to be as fireproof as such materials could make them. Prominent among the others was the recently completed Montgomery Block, the largest building in the city for the next ten years, built by businessman Henry W. Halleck. Notable on the skyline was the handsome Jenny Lind Theater, then in use as a city hall and courthouse.[2]

Peyton and the Duers came ashore into a city with a population of about forty thousand people that six years before had been a Mexican town of two thousand. It had drawn its residents principally from the eastern states, but significant numbers of Chinese, Australians, South Americans, and Europeans had come, too. There were days when a storekeeper heard eight different languages spoken by his customers. All had come for the riches, and their faith in achieving their goal was still strong. The new partners noted that the preponderance of the population was male. They noticed also the hurried pace of its citizens. Everyone was in the race for gold and the wealth it represented, although no small number stopped to spend some of their newfound riches in the numerous gambling halls and bordellos.[3] Reporting on the kaleidoscopic changes that were occurring in California almost every twenty-four hours, twelve San Francisco newspapers published daily editions; there were also six weeklies and two tri-weeklies.[4]

A few days after landing, Peyton took up residence in the Oriental Hotel, and he and Duer opened their law office nearby.[5] Friends from the East stopped in to welcome their neighbors of old. A Tennessee acquaintance reported seeing Peyton in his law office and ventured of his practice that he could realize a "handsome fortune" if he convinces San Francisco that he is "'quibble quick and paper bullets of the brain' skilled."[6]

Confident that by application to the practice of law he could prosper and accumulate the funds needed to operate his Tennessee farm and stud free of debt, Balie was not timid about letting others know of his wide and considerable experience as an attorney. But try as he might, he could not relegate himself to his law office and the courtroom. Life in San Francisco was too spirited for him to close his eyes to what was happening outside.

Peyton could not take a passive role in public affairs, and he believed that if he were to have a future in state politics, it would be as a recognized leader of the Whig Party. Assured that his ability as an orator was obvious to anyone who heard him, he was ready to be a principal speaker for the party. The language barrier in Chile had quieted his public voice for three years, and he was more than ready to return to the rostrum. By midsummer he and his fellow California Whigs were in high spirits, aided in no small part by a serious split in the dominant state Democratic Party.[7] As time for the state convention approached, the editor of the *Daily Alta California* believed there had never been a time in the West when the Whigs "were so sanguine of success."[8]

Balie was a delegate to the two-day state convention at Sacramento in July 1854. There he accepted election to the party's state central committee and undertook active duty on the convention's resolutions committee.[9] His appearance in California had whetted Whig appetites as far away as New York City where there was speculation he would run for a seat in the U.S. Senate. The New York *Express* noted, "We have a rumor here that the Whigs of California will probably elect Mr. [William McKendree] Gwin's successor, and that Balie Peyton, formerly member of congress from Tennessee, will be the man."[10]

Although selection of the best choice to carry the party banner in the senatorial campaign would not come up until the next year, the convention agenda assured a busy time for the delegates. They directed most of their attention to nominating two candidates for as many seats in Congress and to approving a statement of policy drafted by Peyton and the six other members of the committee on resolutions.

Establishing Whig goals for California, the statement gave priority to the most desired internal improvement of them all: a transcontinental railroad. The project should be "the paramount duty" of the national government, justified not only by the uses of commerce but also by its role in the national defense. Trumpeting the Whigs' traditional anticorruption, clean government theme used against the Democrats the year before, the document called for "a revolution in public affairs" to restore the integrity of their state government. The remaining policy declaration held that federal territories had unfettered rights to form a new state constitution when there is population enough to qualify, that the national government should complete the survey of public lands to end the vexatious delays of the Land Commission, that government should protect inviolate the property of all classes, and that the party was committed to securing a homestead for "every actual settler" on the public lands. Enthusiastic about the

future of the party in California and the nation, Balie joined his fellow
partisans in a "shout" to their Atlantic Coast brethren: "Union of the
Whigs for the sake of the Union."[11]

After the convention adjourned its official deliberations, the Whigs
held a public meeting in front of the Orleans Hotel on July 26 to ratify
the nominations just made. Described with fellow party leader E. D.
Baker by an opposition newspaper as one of "the guns let off on the
occasion," Peyton took careful aim at the Kansas-Nebraska bill passed
by the House and Senate and signed by the president near the end of
May, and hit it as "the veriest humbug ever concocted to cheat and
spoliate the South." It was conceived, he said, by "a demagoguish democrat [Senator Stephen A. Douglas] to create sectional issues, and
advance his own political prospects." During the convention, he had
successfully defeated efforts by fellow Tennessean Henry A. Crabb to
endorse the bill in the state party platform. Could Peyton sense that the
controversy around the act would speed the dissolution of the Whigs as
a national party?[12]

Asserting that the Constitution of the United States considered slaves
to be legal property, Peyton argued that federal territories should be
open to a settler and his property of whatever kind. Then at such time
as the territory should become a state, the settlers would choose that it
be free or slave.[13]

Although generally defending the South on the slavery question,
Balie tried to distance himself and California Whigs from the issue.
Noting that California had been a free state from the day its constitution
was adopted, he asked, "What have we, in California, to do with this
question?" In partial answer, he said the matter was one about which
"gentlemen might honestly differ . . . not a test of Whiggery or Whig
principles."[14] In short, he would ignore the question of slavery in
California politics.

Challenging the sympathetic Whig crowd gathered in front of the
Orleans Hotel to fight the party's battles, he said that he had come
before them "fat and grain-fed" but that he had "enlisted for the war . . .
a soldier in the cause to the end." He was ready to make the rounds of
the campaign barbecues and "would be proud to go into any of the
gulches when invited to eat of such a banquet with the poorest or
proudest of . . . voters."[15]

Peyton reminded his listeners that the Whig Party had challenged
Andrew Jackson's support of Martin Van Buren for president in 1836,
and that the Whigs had "overcome the Old Hero" in Tennessee.
He told of several humorous election campaign incidents, "which
excited unbound merriment and applause." Promoting the Whig
Party, Peyton arrived in the gold country "with all his peculiar,

captivating, and impressive powers as a popular speaker in full and vigorous exercise."[16]

But neither Peyton nor the nation could escape the impact of the Kansas-Nebraska legislation. The act effectively repealed the Missouri Compromise of 1820 as both of the new territories it created, Kansas and Nebraska, were located above latitude 36° 30'. It provided further that the settlers of each could, by "popular sovereignty," decide for themselves about slavery. Public reaction was very negative from both the anti- and proslavery forces.

The most frightening impact of the act was that it set off a series of events that further cast the issue of slavery in a sectional context and slowly but surely narrowed the middle ground where a workable compromise might be negotiated. Before the bill was signed into law, opponents of slavery gathered at Ripon, Wisconsin, and on February 25 recommended formation of a new Republican Party. The new party movement spread quickly to Michigan, Ohio, Indiana, and Vermont as Whigs, Free Soilers, and antislavery Democrats joined in large numbers.

Although opposed to abolishing slavery, Peyton had no positive suggestions for dealing with the practice. As a slave owner, he professed a sense of responsibility mixed with frustration. He equated freeing his slaves to abandoning them. A correspondent for the *Republican Banner and* Nashville *Whig* paraphrased his remarks:

> The only property he owned was about fifty Negroes and a tract of land, the support of which had brought him in debt; and if any man could tell him how he could possibly rid himself of them he would be glad to know it. He had been laboring all his life to support these Negroes, and he never would forsake them so long as he could not better their condition.[17]

Within the limits of existing statutes, Peyton wanted fair treatment for slaves who had violated the law. Discussing a reported slave uprising in Tennessee, he had told John Bell that he was opposed to lynching. He insisted that if a slave was guilty of any violation of the law, there were adequate criminal statutes and procedures to prosecute him within the legal system.[18]

As the time approached for the municipal elections in San Francisco, Whig political strategists persuaded the party to refrain from nominating candidates. They had recognized a strong sentiment among the voters for a reform ticket that did not represent the major parties. As a result, Balie allied himself with the Citizens Reform Ticket sponsored by the Know-Nothings. It included twenty-seven Whigs, nine Democrats, and nine Know-Nothings. In California, the Know-Nothings had grown out of the nonpartisan politics that had been promoted by leading businessmen in San Francisco since 1851. Tactically, they drew on the practices of secret nativist societies that had appeared around the country. By failing to accomplish needed reform in California, they later lost credibility with the voters. By 1857, they had faded almost out of sight.[19]

At a San Francisco rally for reform nominees on September 4, Peyton addressed "an eager crowd" on a section of Montgomery Street blocked off between Merchant and Clay Streets. Emphasizing the need for reform in the administration of the city's affairs, he claimed that such a change could be brought about by good men who would address their responsibilities conscientiously. Better city government would be provided not by a certain political doctrine but by qualified public servants who would work at their jobs.[20]

Did the rally help the reform candidates? Yes, but not as much as they had been helped by the obvious need for reform in the city government. They swept the election.[21]

Soon after the September election, sobering news from Tennessee reached Balie. His sister Rebecca Parker was dead at the age of forty-eight. She had been married to G. W. Parker for twenty-four years and was the third of his sisters to die.

Although stunned by the sadness he felt, Peyton suddenly realized that he had been in San Francisco for twelve months; it had been a memorable year. The cityscape was changing all around him. New, impressive-looking banks, theaters, hotels, and shops lined the downtown streets; virtually all were built of brick or stone. One of the most impressive structures was the three-story Customs House and another was the American Theater, both of brick. Outside the central business district, acres of wooden cottages on narrow lots replaced the tents and shacks of previous years. Development continued along the waterfront and stevedores loaded and unloaded cargoes, interrupted only for a day of celebration to recognize the second record-setting arrival of that most famous of the early clipper ships, the *Flying Cloud*. The sleek sailing vessel arrived after traveling around the Horn from New York City to San Francisco in eighty-nine days and equaled its own record for ships powered only by sail set on August 31, 1851.[22]

Appearances notwithstanding, by the end of 1854 the five-year growth of the city began to slow markedly. Gold production dwindled as the richest placers had run out and a serious depression set in. Some estimated that as many as one-third of the city's one thousand shops and storehouses stood vacant. Widespread loan defaults closed most of the major financial houses. Trade was sluggish. Fluctuations in the local economy reminded Peyton of New Orleans, but many other features of the city were comparable: the busy port, the mixture of race and cultures, and a certain sense of adventure that overhung each day.[23]

During the spring of 1855, Balie thought seriously about seeking public office. He had developed a good reputation in San Francisco as a lawyer and considered himself a viable candidate for city attorney. After the Whigs and most local groups opposed to the Democrats came into the Know-Nothing camp, he accepted their nomination for that office when tendered on May 25. He and the others nominated to run against the Democratic ticket for city offices promoted themselves as "the People's nominees."

On May 28, the voters chose Peyton for city attorney by the narrow margin of 51 votes of 11,525 cast. Only the marshal's race was closer; three votes separated victor and vanquished in that contest. But the Democrats prevailed, electing the mayor and enough other offices to return to power in the city. The election was generally regarded as a "test struggle" between the native and the foreign-born citizens, the Democrats representing the latter and the Know-Nothings or "People's nominees" the former.[24]

For a few weeks, it appeared that the fifty-one-vote margin would not stand because of challenges that demanded the Eighth Ward ballot box be thrown out due to irregularities. Then questions were raised about which of two charters governed the elections, the existing city charter or the charter passed by the last legislature for the next municipal government about to be formed by merging the county and city into one. The resolution of these matters was favorable to Balie, and he immediately undertook the duties of his new office.[25]

Although busily engaged in San Francisco, Balie was never comfortable about being away from his sons as they grew into young manhood. Balie Jr. had chosen to continue his studies beyond the courses offered at Hallowell's school by drawing on funds his father had made available for the sons' education when he went to Chile in 1849. He used part of the money to travel to Germany, where he studied at the Berlin and Heidelberg Universities. He returned to the Station Camp Creek farmstead in 1858 and enrolled at the Cumberland University Law School in nearby Lebanon, Tennessee. His brother John Bell did not elect to study abroad but came home to farm and study law. Both were graduated from the Cumberland Law School in 1859.[26]

By the end of the year 1855, the Whig Party in California had virtually disbanded, and most of its members had joined the Know-Nothings. That meant Peyton would parade locally under the banners of the Know-Nothings, or the Americans, as they soon became known. He was recognized as one of the most articulate spokesmen in the succession, and he was pleased to do whatever he could to limit the effectiveness of the Democrats. Although he had participated in California politics as Whig, Know-Nothing, and American within the space of two years, he held to his long-time views of Jacksonian nationalism and the indivisibility of the Union. Peyton thought the present Democrats were too little like Jackson, too much like the Van Buren crowd that succeeded him, and too likely to exacerbate divisive issues that were abroad in the land.

A well-attended party gathering at Sacramento on June 25, 1855, provided a bully pulpit for Balie. There he and his fellow speakers Wilson D. Flint, David S. Terry, former Mississippi Governor Henry S. Foote, and E. C. Marshall launched the state campaign of the no-longer-secret Know-Nothings, then calling themselves the Americans. Addressing the practice of secrecy, a popular objection to the Know-Nothings, Peyton announced that the organization would be secret no more. "Fellow Whigs, fellow Democrats, the Americans are unmasked tonight . . . the guyascutus is loose."[27]

Peyton was suggesting that this fierce imaginary animal was the creation of those who feared it or something even worse had been hidden behind the previous Know-Nothing practices of secrecy. The abolition of secrecy had loosed it for the public to see. "You have heard one principle stated correctly; it has been objected that our organization is a secret one; that objection exists no longer," he declared.[28]

Peyton took the campaign trail that led to further speeches for American Party nominees at Diamond Springs, Placerville, and mining towns throughout the northern part of the state. Between stops travel was laborious. In the towns accommodations were primitive. But despite the obstacles, he and other party leaders "were clearly working up enthusiasm prior to the meeting of their nominating convention" on August 7 at Sacramento.[29] But his enthusiasm as well as his travel-worn body seem to have been exhausted by convention time. He was uncharacteristically quiet during the session, yet he resumed an active political life three weeks later after a period of rest.

On Saturday night, September 1, 1855, Balie was one of four speakers who addressed a "considerable force" of adherents to the American Party at a mass meeting in San Francisco. His discourse was twice disrupted by the passage of fire-fighting equipment and personnel through the crowd assembled to hear him on Sansome Street opposite the American Theater. The first intrusion scattered those present in all directions, but they soon reassembled. Not long after he resumed speaking, the fire-fighting units returned, making their way noisily through the crowd. This time Balie bestowed "a few severe remarks upon the cause of the interruption" to his listeners' great pleasure and warm applause.[30]

On the rostrum again three nights later before an attentive and enthusiastic crowd in front of the American Saloon on Montgomery Street, Peyton apologized for the harsh language that he had used when responding to the interruptions by the firemen during his previous speech. He paid tribute to them as a "popular and deserving body." Turning to the business at hand, he castigated Democrats, denounced corruption in government, and held high the banner of reform.[31]

A surge of reform support carried the American ticket in California state elections to a commanding victory on September 5. The party won majorities in both houses of the legislature.[32] Balie and his political cohorts celebrated.

During the summer-long campaign, Peyton had few chances to indulge his appetite for the theater. Perhaps he saw *Midsummer Night's Dream*, playing at the American Theater in June or one of the plays at the Metropolitan, *The Countess and the Serf* or *The Hunchback*. Surely the engaging single man stopped in at some of the numerous cotillion parties and ballroom dances that were advertised regularly in the newspapers. His relaxed manner and entertaining conversation made him welcome at social events public or private.[33]

Events outside California did not escape his attention, however. He followed reports from "Bleeding Kansas," regularly noting that the territory was virtually in a state of civil war. First the pro- and then the antislavery forces seemed to have the upper hand politically, but repeated violent conflicts suggested no one was in control. By comparison, California was a peaceful paradise.

One of the postcampaign ceremonial duties that befell Peyton was the honor of welcoming Governor-elect J. Neely Johnson to San Francisco on his first visit since election as the American Party candidate. Arriving by steamboat from Sacramento, Johnson greeted a crowd at the wharf and then proceeded by carriage directly to the Oriental Hotel where Peyton and a large body of citizens awaited him.

Fulfilling that "most agreeable duty," Peyton welcomed Johnson in the name of the citizens of San Francisco and congratulated him as "the successful champion of the American Party." Moving quickly from celebration to predicting the governor's future, Balie asserted, "In your election, sir, a great work is begun—a mighty stride has been made towards reform. California has been redeemed. . . . She will . . . shine as one of the brightest stars of the American constellation."

He saw other opportunities for the governor. In one specific area Johnson could expect "the same brawny arms and strong hands" that elected him to "lay down the rails, and turn loose the iron horse upon the Pacific road." There were cheers from the large gathering when

Balie envisioned "the clank of his hoof on the plains, and his neighing in the mountain passes, and . . . [his] dashing into our great city, with the fire streaming from his nostrils."[34]

The American Party's control of both the legislative and the executive branches of government in California and Peyton's popularity as a party spokesman combined to raise speculation in 1855 that he might be elected to the U.S. Senate. The names of Henry A. Crabb, E. C. Marshall, and his friend Henry S. Foote were also in circulation as possible candidates.[35]

Although the American Party controlled the legislature, the margin was thin. To be comfortably in control, Peyton believed the Americans needed the support of certain Democratic legislators who were known to favor reform measures. If the Americans should elect one of their Democratic friends to the U.S. Senate, Peyton insisted that the result would be dependable support from enough other Democratic legislators that his party would be able to pass its legislative program. Declaring publicly that he favored giving allies their due, he asked that his name be withdrawn from consideration for the nomination. He also wanted to block the senatorial ambitions of Crabb, his fellow former Tennessean, who was "in no way qualified for the office." Regarding Crabb as an "irascible fanatic" with "extreme pro-slavery proclivities," Peyton recognized nonetheless that he would attract some votes and was "quite formidable" as a "young man and old Californian . . . [like] a large majority of the legislature."[36]

To Peyton's great pleasure, Crabb withdrew his name from consideration for the Senate. Foote received the nomination, although he had been ready at any time to withdraw in favor of Balie. The American Party's efforts came to naught when the legislature could not agree on the election of a senator and left the seat unoccupied until 1857.[37] The most disappointed candidate was the Democrat, William McKendree Gwin, who had held the seat since it was created in 1850, but who had to wait two years to muster enough votes to reclaim it.

The results were both vindicating and disappointing to Peyton. Although he and Senator Gwin were in opposing political camps, they maintained good personal relations throughout Balie's time on the West Coast. More than once they reminisced about their times in Washington during the Jackson presidency and shared memories of life in New Orleans in the 1840s.

If Democrats were to have the Senate seat, Balie much preferred the Jackson-tutored Gwin over the Tammany-trained David C. Broderick, whose candidacy for the Senate had deadlocked the legislature. When Broderick was elected two years later and brokered the other seat to Gwin in exchange for control of federal patronage,

Peyton was pleased that Gwin was in office again. He expected that Senator Gwin would "checkmate Broderick and save us from his shoulder striking, ballot box-stuffing appointments." And, in fact, that was precisely what happened.[38]

Following predecessors who had served single one-year terms, Peyton found the records of the city attorney's office in disarray. Nonetheless, he took up the variety of legal issues that one might expect to find in the municipal government of a boomtown scarcely five years old. They ranged from writing opinions on conflicting city ordinances[39] to defending the city's title to certain waterfront properties claimed by others. On a regular basis, he fielded questions about the administration of local government and worked to see that ordinances and regulations were properly drawn and uniformly interpreted. His duties did not include investigating crimes and prosecuting criminals.

The waterfront properties question, usually referred to as the city slip properties, involved a significant amount of money and promised to require Peyton's full-time attention. From its beginnings, the city had reserved certain waterfront properties for later development of the harbor and docks. In the rush to build the city, private developers had filled in significant acreages that adjoined the city's lots, an act that raised questions about values and titles to much of the land. The state legislature contributed to the confusion by periodically reconsidering a bill introduced in 1853 that would have authorized the sale of additional "water lots" for a distance of six hundred feet into the bay beyond existing boundary lines.[40]

Sometime before September 1, 1855, the council authorized Peyton to retain two other attorneys to deal exclusively with the waterfront properties issues. Their special attention was unavailing, however, as the courts ruled against the city and in favor of the claimants. Six months later, the council directed him to hire the firm of Holliday, Saunders and Carey to assist in recovering other properties, the rights to which would soon expire.[41]

Balie represented the city in litigation about renewing the bonds of the funded debt and prevailed when the Twelfth District Court ordered that the commissioners give new bonds subject to the approval of the Common Council. The court concurred with Peyton's position that by law the council had the exclusive right to judge the sufficiency of the bonds. At the same time in the Superior Court, Balie commenced action on behalf of the city to recover possession of five pieces of downtown real estate that had been appropriated by others.[42]

As he faced the multiple responsibilities of his office, Peyton decided that one term was enough. But before the year ended, he, the mayor, and the surveyor general laid off the city and county into districts as prescribed in the consolidation act. On-site surveys later confirmed their work.[43]

While he was city attorney, Peyton was appointed in a private role to act as receiver for the banking house of Sanders and Benham when it suspended business on November 5, 1855.[44] On December 1, he published a report of the condition of the bank, which showed its liabilities exceeded its assets by $66,784.29, a sizeable amount for the time.[45]

The emotion and excitement that often attend litigation did not replace the thrills of a horse race in Peyton's life. He lamented the lack of thoroughbred racing in San Francisco. For a moment in December 1854, the prospects appeared to be changing. "A grand match race . . . for $6,000 . . . over the Pioneer Course" was announced, and he was elated. The promoters chose him to be a judge of the race, one of the few contests between thoroughbred horses that had been run in California. It is doubtful that there was a more experienced turfman on the scene. Although the race attracted about two thousand spectators, the new state was not yet ready to support that kind of horse race. The popularity of trotting races forced thoroughbreds to wait a few years before establishing a sure place for themselves on West Coast racecourses.[46]

Peyton conceded there was little he could do to advance thoroughbred racing in San Francisco; he understood that there was no way to promote a futurity there comparable to the Peyton Stake. But if Balie wanted to think of that grand old occasion, all he needed was a trip to the track to visit jockey John S. Dunn who, like himself, had strayed from his eastern moorings. Formerly, Dunn had been the trainer of the celebrated mare Peytona, winner of the 1843 Peyton Stake.[47] There was no limit to the amount of horse talk they could exchange or to the size of the dreams they could dream about the future of thoroughbreds in California.

Even before assuming office as city attorney, Balie and any who read the local press knew that public resentment was building against city council members. Except for protection of themselves and their premises, most residents of San Francisco wanted to be free of interference by government, especially local government. But they were not willing for government officials to be free of interference by the electorate. In 1854, when a member of the council, Henry Meiggs, left by ship with several hundred thousands in gold that he had amassed by forging city warrants, public resentment turned to anger. Other council persons immediately came under fire for failure to detect the forger and prevent the crime. Shocked by the success of Meiggs's forgeries and escape, citizens feared that other officials might be engaged in acts similarly destructive of the public interest. The discovery of "extravagance, favoritism in the award of city contracts, and close connections with gamblers and other underworld figures" magnified their fears.[48]

Many leading businessmen spoke up in the same reform spirit that elected Balie to city office; however, leadership of the movement to clean up city politics early fell into the hands of James King, editor of the *Evening Bulletin*, a widely read local daily. The zeal with which King undertook the task promised his own premature death and the sudden, dangerous rise of the Vigilance Committee of 1856. As an attorney, sworn to uphold and defend the law, Peyton could see trouble ahead.[49] And being who he was, he secretly relished the prospect.

GOLD RUSH POLITICS
1855–1859

Elected city attorney on the reform ticket, Peyton shared many of the reformist views of editor James King. Although his office did not directly involve him with criminal prosecution, Peyton was concerned about the growing public indignation at what citizens perceived as a breakdown in law enforcement and judicial indifference to cases of serious criminal conduct. No stranger to violence, Peyton understood that some of King's printed allegations carried the potential for violent responses.

In crusading editorials King attacked corruption wherever he discovered it, but two of his favorite targets were the police and the courts. He charged that the police were not arresting known lawbreakers and the courts were refusing to convict those brought to trial. He directed some of his heaviest blasts at the well-entrenched forces of gambling and prostitution, in his opinion the principal sources of the city's troubles.[1]

People were at fault, not the institutions of free government, King said. He delighted in publishing their names alongside their deeds. Employing extremely provocative terms, he denounced both Charles Cora, a local gambler then in jail, who had shot and killed a U.S. marshal six months before, and James P. Casey, editor of the rival newspaper the *Sunday Times*. Previously, he had exposed Casey for winning a seat on the city council by stuffing several hundred premarked ballots into the ballot box of a precinct where he served as an election inspector. If that were not complaint enough, King alleged that Casey, a former New Yorker, was a convicted criminal who had served a term in Sing Sing. In a rage, Casey immediately denied the accusations. When King announced he would produce documentary evidence to prove them, Casey "threatened to shoot him on sight." Refusing to be intimidated, King replied that he would be leaving his office at the usual time on the following afternoon.

On the next afternoon at the promised hour, King left the *Bulletin* and started on foot down Montgomery Street when Casey confronted him. Ordering King to draw and defend himself, Casey raised his own weapon and fired a single shot into his antagonist's chest. After a few hesitant steps into a nearby shop, King collapsed. Police arrested Casey at the scene of the shooting and rushed him to the county jail. From his cell, he listened nervously while the sheriff successfully withstood the demands of a mob that had gathered to lynch him.[2]

Public excitement was at fever pitch. Many openly called for reactivating the Vigilance Committee of 1851. Most saw the shooting as a death knell to reform unless they acted quickly. Early the following morning, business leaders organized the Vigilance Committee of 1856, and within forty-eight hours, twenty-five hundred members enrolled. Without opposition, the committee then took Cora and Casey from the county jail and locked them in its own rooms.

A core committee of forty-one headed by William T. Coleman, who had chaired the Vigilance Committee of 1851, furnished direction for the new group. The avowed purpose of the organization was to take law enforcement and the courts into its own hands. Some who opposed the Vigilance organized a much smaller group called Law and Order to uphold the existing law enforcement officers and judges. Governor John Neely Johnson asked the Vigilance to free Casey and let the local courts try him for attempted murder; the leaders declined, however, saying that Casey and his friends controlled city government and that there could be no fair trial under those circumstances.

Six days after the bullet entered his chest, James King died. On May 22, the day of his funeral, members of the Vigilance Committee acted quickly. They removed Casey and Charles Cora from their cells and hanged both the same afternoon, even as King's funeral procession wound its way through the city.[3]

Setting up headquarters and jail in a rented building, the Vigilance Committee fortified it with sandbags stacked high. At once it was known by the not-so-threatening name of Fort Gunnybags, but serious business was conducted inside. For two weeks leaders of the committee looked into corrupt practices in the conduct of elections and in the general operations of government. They decided that in major criminal practices not involving murder, the best protection for the public was banishment. By June 9 they had ordered eight persons to leave the state or face summary justice. The example prompted a number of other suspects to leave voluntarily.[4]

Fearing that no man who spoke his mind could be any more secure than James King, citizens rushed to join the Vigilance.[5] The organization quickly grew to approximately five thousand, about five times the size of Law and Order. From the outset both were infiltrated by hoodlums and unscrupulous political operatives, many of whom had perpetrated the abuses that had given rise to the new extralegal organizations. Although numerous prominent business and civic leaders were members of the Vigilance, several representing the same sections of the community were members of Law and Order.

Peyton enrolled in neither group, but he understood the origins of the Vigilance and noticed among its leaders a number of old Whigs. He sensed no desire on their part to exercise control any longer than might be required to sensitize city officials to concerns shared by the majority of citizens. Yet the presence of an opposition force, although comparatively small in number, posed a potential for violent conflict between the two. Recognizing the need for conciliation, Balie began to think of himself as a peacemaker or conciliator between Vigilance and Law and Order.[6]

Unable to stop the larger committee with their own smaller numbers, Law and Order appealed to Governor Johnson to issue an order requiring the Vigilance to disband. Johnson responded on June 3 by proclaiming San Francisco to be in a state of insurrection. On the next day, Militia Gen. William T. Sherman, a banker who was also head of the Law and Order group, circulated orders calling for the enrollment of militia, and Peyton and his colleagues in conciliation rushed messages back and forth between Sherman and the Vigilance, trying to work out a peaceable settlement.

Governor Johnson came down to San Francisco from Sacramento by steamboat to discuss the situation on June 7, and representatives of Law and Order met him in the early evening at the wharf. After consulting with them, he went uptown later that night to meet a deputation from Vigilance accompanied by Peyton. Soon afterward other conciliators joined Balie and sought an interview with the governor.[7]

Speaking for the conciliators,[8] Col. J. B. Crockett said he and his group had no connection with the Vigilance Committee but were "actuated" by a desire to avoid mass bloodshed. He and his associates had visited the headquarters of Vigilance and, although he could not speak for the committee, he felt authorized to state that they would try to avoid any further confrontation with any other public groups. He said that it was his considered opinion that the Vigilance Committee "would in a few days voluntarily disband."⁹ Reflecting the views of Peyton and the other conciliators, Crockett expressed hope that the governor would "pursue a conciliatory course and not precipitate a crisis that would involve the city and state in a civil war."¹⁰ In reply, the governor said that he, too, wanted to avoid bloodshed, but if there should be a "collision," the fault would rest on the shoulders of those who "disregarded the authority of the state."¹¹

During another conference the same night attended by General Sherman, the conciliators, and advisors to the governor, Gen. John F. Wool of the U.S. Army reversed himself and declared to the militia general that he had no authority to issue federal arms to a state militia without direct orders from the president. When Wool seemed reluctant to put his decision in writing to Sherman, Peyton intervened. "General Wool," he said, "I think General Sherman has a right to a written answer from you, for he is surely compromised." Wool then produced a copy of a letter to the governor that denied he had promised to make arms available on the governor's request and was otherwise evasive. Sherman immediately took the letter to the governor and resigned his office rather than command an unarmed force for an administration that he believed was under the influence of advisors inclined to violence.¹²

What would be the next step in reconciling opposing forces in the state and returning the control of government to the electorate? Commanding only an unarmed militia, the governor was powerless to act, but Peyton shared Crockett's confidence that the leaders of the Vigilance Committee would disband it before the end of the summer. He conceived a strategy that called for encouraging public gratitude for the good things the Vigilance had done while lobbying quietly in the background for responsible citizen participation in government. He wanted the Vigilance to pass from the scene just as quickly as the group had come upon it.

Peyton looked for a chance to gain the committee's confidence. His first opportunity came when he was chosen unanimously to chair a meeting of "citizens not connected with the Vigilance Committee" on June 12. Superior Court Judge D. O. Shattuck, selected the night before, had resigned earlier in the day because of pressing judicial business.¹³

Addressing the crowd assembled in John Middleton's Auction Rooms on the corner of Montgomery and California Streets, Balie explained that the Vigilance Committee had not meant to ignore the Constitution and the laws, but to punish those who sought to subvert them. How else could they deal with ballot box stuffers, shoulder strikers, and assassins? He recalled past elections in certain wards when hoodlums rushed honest election officials, destroyed their tally lists, and drove them away. They had even held the mayor at bay "by an array of revolvers and

Bowie knives." Peyton did not want bloodshed, but hoped the people would rally around the Vigilance, and "stand up firmly in defence of their [own] rights and liberties."[14]

The assembled citizens adopted a series of resolutions that endorsed the Vigilance, asked the governor to withdraw his proclamation of June 3, and called for calm in the community. They scheduled a mass meeting for Saturday, June 14, for public review of the resolutions just adopted.[15]

When the crowd assembled on Saturday, the committee in charge of arrangements announced it had nominated Peyton to be president of the day and principal speaker. By

General William T. Sherman

voice vote, the ten thousand[16] or more present registered their thunderous approval, and the president appeared on a balcony of the Oriental Hotel.[17]

Asserting that the rise of the Vigilance Committee had been timely in the political life of the city, Peyton declared that its intervention made it possible to hold elections free from fraud. The Vigilance had put a damper on ruffianism. "They have accomplished more in a few days than the laws (such laws and such officers of the law as we have had in power) could accomplish in so many years—the restoration of the people to the right of free voting, free thinking and free speaking," he said. Praising the committee for what it had done, he was careful to explain that it was not to take the place of government but to make it possible for representative government to govern.[18]

Likening the Vigilance to "the monster-exterminating Hercules," Peyton recalled that the hero of old had strangled two snakes while he was yet a child in his cradle. The committee in its infancy had strangled two felons, "who richly deserved it for their crimes." The most difficult labor of Hercules was to capture and rid the country of "certain harpies with claws of iron and bills of brass." He had done it, and the Vigilance likewise had "rid the country of the same brazen-faced sort of birds." There were more to go and the people knew who they were, he insisted.[19]

Peyton showed the crowd a ballot box with false bottom and sliding side that had been used to facilitate stuffing desirable ballots and discarding others.

I ask you . . . has there been in San Francisco for the past several years any government which emanated from a free expression of the popular will? [Cries of no! no!] The men who have made the laws and executed them . . . have acted under a fraudulent power of attorney not received from you but from those who have worked together to overthrow the popular will. . . . What kind of government could be built on stuffed ballot boxes?[20]

He said that some elected officials had been literally stuffed into office. Again he held up the infamous ballot box for all to see, then pointed to it and suggested that it spoke eloquently of fraud.

Here is the orator of the day! [Applause.] . . . It is a great machine. It will elevate the meanest scoundrel in the country to the highest office in the state! [Applause.] It ought to be sent to Washington and deposited in the archives! [Repeated applause.][21]

By a loud voice vote, the crowd passed resolutions brought from the Thursday night meeting to endorse the Vigilance. At that point, Peyton feared his oratory might have given the committee new momentum when he really meant to be showing that it had completed its work. After banker William Sharon proposed a resolution to demand the immediate resignation of city and county officials, most of the judges, and those members of the state senate holding over to the next term, Peyton realized he was about to lose control of the meeting. He announced his opposition to the proposal and, hearing a motion to adjourn, put the question, which carried, and completed the evening's agenda.[22]

Fortunately for Peyton and all concerned, the leaders of the Vigilance had already determined to discontinue operations. They would not join William Sharon's call for the resignation of city officials because they had no plans to interfere with the impending merger of city and county governments. There was already a transitional Board of Supervisors in place to assist in implementing the Consolidation Act of 1855, which reduced the two governments into one. Voters would elect officeholders under the new consolidated authority at the general election in November 1856. Those officials whose resignations were required by the act had resigned effective July 1.[23]

Peyton had hoped that the committee would disband without further displays of violence. But that was not to be. Those of the committee who wanted last-minute drama charged, tried, and convicted Philander Brace, a minor political operative, with two murders that had taken place the previous year. Soon afterward, on July 24, one Joseph Hetherington shot and killed Dr. Andrew Randall in the lobby of the St. Nicholas Hotel in a dispute over an unpaid debt. As police were taking Hetherington to jail, Vigilance men seized their prisoner. They charged, tried, and convicted him of murder. On July 29, "to assuage the more excited members of the general committee who wanted blood," men designated by the executive committee hanged Brace and Hetherington.[24]

After the hangings the leadership began to close out the committee's activities. On August 18, Peyton joined thousands who turned out to view the final parade of Vigilance military units following which the organization voluntarily disbanded. He was grateful that a dangerous chapter in the life of San Francisco had come to a close. Three months later Governor Johnson revoked the insurrection proclamation of June 30.[25]

Balie's daughter Emily had joined him in San Francisco during the rule of the Vigilance Committee ostensibly to work as his private secretary but more likely to persuade him to return to the Station Camp Creek farm and his family. She left San Francisco after a few months with a promise that he would follow her as soon as he could pay off his California debts.[26]

What did the Vigilance Committee experience mean to Peyton? Although he was not swept into high political office by the role he played in avoiding a violent confrontation between the committee and the governor of California, his many public appearances and consultations with both sides of the controversy had elevated his reputation significantly. By the time the committee disbanded, San Franciscans recognized him as an unexcelled public speaker and as a person who could keep his wits when most of those around him were about to lose theirs. Politically, he remained a classical Whig who had adapted to the Know-Nothings and American Party when the party of his first choice faltered in California. He proudly held to his belief in the union of states and the representative form of government that sustained it. But what was ahead? Would the public call on him to assume some kind of new civic responsibility?

Balie had already chosen the assignment he wanted. His task: preserve the American Party in California and carry the state in the presidential election for the nominees of its national convention, former President Millard Fillmore and Andrew J. Donelson. It was a difficult undertaking. Fillmore and Donelson were later the choice, also, of the national convention of the fast-fading Whig Party. A surviving group of Know-Nothings from the Northeast had convened to nominate a ticket of John C. Fremont of California and W. F. Johnston of Pennsylvania, overlapping the new Republican Party ticket of John C. Fremont and William L. Dayton of New Jersey. James Buchanan of Pennsylvania and John C. Breckinridge of Kentucky carried the banner of the Democrats.

The Americans and the old Whigs supported the Compromise of 1850 but opposed the Kansas-Nebraska Act, even as the Democrats favored both and construction of a transcontinental railroad. The new Republican Party

Andrew Jackson Donelson

advocated the admission of Kansas as a free state and supported the construction of a transcontinental railroad. The Know-Nothings wanted slavery banned in all federal territories.

Abolitionist themes at the Republican convention caused Peyton to agree with American Party leaders that the new "black Republicans" posed a threat to all the older parties. As early as May 5, 1856, Balie had complained to Senator John Bell that "the damned Black Republicans are about to break up the American Party" in California, but he was prepared for a vigorous canvass. He was more than comfortable with Donelson, his old Tennessee neighbor, as the vice presidential candidate. Committed to the Old Hero when they had arrived in Washington more than two decades before, both later left Jackson's party because they claimed it had been hijacked by politicians who were steering it away from his main purpose: preserving the union.[27]

Even before the Vigilance Committee disbanded, Peyton, Foote, and W. W. Stow, another American Party stalwart, addressed the American Party State Convention at Sacramento August 1, on behalf of the Fillmore-Donelson ticket. A week later Peyton, Foote, and Duer were the speakers featured at the American Party ratification meeting, which drew an interested audience on the Plaza in San Francisco.[28]

Canvassing the northern part of the state for the American ticket, Peyton used his expansive sense of humor to win the confidence of the crowds and then demolished the opposition, party by party, man by man. Greeted by an excited throng of American Party supporters at Michigan Bar on August 15,[29] he spoke at length during a rally at Folsom on the next evening. Examining the candidates, Peyton could find little to recommend the front-running Democratic nominee James Buchanan. He lashed out at the Democratic platform, which he saw as a gallows for the unfortunate Buchanan and at the same time one of the most "ingenious contrivances to cheat the people ever invented." The platform was made up of "slippery elm, blackjack, dogwood, and a sprig of shillalah thrown in," he said.[30]

There was more. Andrew Jackson had thought Buchanan "deficient in moral courage" and did not attach much value to him, Peyton said, adding, "He is a well meaning fat, old fogy gentleman . . . without a great controlling mind . . . easily controlled by others."[31]

The Democrats had no claim on California, Peyton contended. Their convention had adopted a railroad resolution, "a sort of cow catcher, intended to pick up California" but they had put it on the back of the train instead of the front. They also claimed to favor "opening a communication between the two sides of the continent," but he understood they were referring to a spiritual communication, not the telegraph.[32]

Next taking up Fremont, Balie predicted he would not be a serious contender in the contest because he was purely a sectional candidate. He said Fremont was "a sprightly explorer," but was not qualified to be president. Balie might vote for him for express-rider across the Rockies unless Kit Carson were his opponent. He joked that once Fremont had shown his manhood by eating a horse, but "still Kit Carson was ahead of him," as he had eaten six mules. Certain that Fillmore would carry California by a large margin, Balie said that he was clearly the best candidate of the three, the only one with prior experience as president.[33]

Accompanied by fellow party man Henry A. Crabb, whose political reliability he continued to doubt, Peyton concluded his swing through the northern mining towns by the end of August. The Sacramento *Daily Union* reported him "delighted with the prospects of Fillmore in the interior of the state" and "sanguine of his carrying California." He radiated confidence during his appearance at a "grand jollification and Fillmore rally" held in San Francisco on August 30.[34]

When the American Party held its state convention there on September 2, 3, and 4, Peyton was one of a half dozen leaders who kept the crowd's spirits high. Nominated to head the list of electors for the Fillmore-Donelson ticket for the state at large, Peyton[35] was elected by acclamation, "the cheering all the while being intense." He vowed that he was committed to national victory for the ticket for both personal reasons and matters of principle. He had been a personal friend of Fillmore since they entered the Congress together in 1832, and he had served on committees with him and loved him. Above all, he said, the candidate was a Union man in every respect.[36]

Peyton told the delegates that he had a special place in his heart for Andrew Jackson Donelson. They were raised together and had grown up under the watchful eye of Old Hickory. His first speech at the bar was made in a case where Donelson represented the other side. But their pasts aside, Balie was proud to find him on the Union ticket.[37]

Donelson shared his Uncle Andrew's devotion to the Union. "Every nullifier and every abolitionist in the United States is opposed to Fillmore and Donelson because they are the Union candidates," Peyton contended. "It is the duty of the American Party to guard the Union against the aggressions of [such] demagogues."[38]

Taking a political cause to the voters by word of mouth was still the most effective technique available in 1856. That meant speeches by party leaders to crowds wherever they might be gathered, even in the interior mining towns. All understood that most who attended came to be entertained, but many were seriously interested in campaign issues, especially those that affected them directly.

Soon after the convention, Balie and fellow elector R. N. Wood set out to take the American ticket to the voters in the mining counties from Calaveras to Butte. Often meeting speakers for the Democratic ticket and, less frequently, Republican Party orators, Peyton and Wood made the case for Fillmore and Donelson on a daily basis for the next month.[39] Sometimes riding in horse-drawn coaches but most of the time on horseback, Balie and his colleague traveled through the mining country as far north as Oroville in Butte County.

On October 1, Balie represented the American Party ticket at Camp Seco, a few miles west of San Andreas in Calaveras County, and a correspondent of the San Francisco *Daily Herald*, a Buchanan organ, reported the event. "Col. Peyton arose and addressed the meeting in a respectful manner, and with his usual tact and ability, made the best he could of a bad cause," he wrote. "The Colonel thinks Mr. Fillmore is perhaps the only man left in the republic who can restore quiet to the country—that, if elected, he will have the slavery question settled in the Supreme Court, and that will be the last of it."[40]

A typical exchange occurred on the plaza in Placerville on October 9 when Democrats, Milton S. Latham, and a certain Colonel Henley met Peyton and Wood in free debate before the largest crowd ever assembled in the mountains.[41] A correspondent for the *Daily Alta California* reported the humorous aspects of the event.

> The orators spoke alternately, and the debate was kept up with much spirit until a late hour. Both parties were highly gratified . . . each having achieved a great triumph in its own estimation. . . . all persons felt gloriously good, and a few of the more ardent got gloriously tight on the strength of their prospects.[42]

As election day drew near, Peyton seemed to be putting more emphasis on goodwill and good humor than on discrediting the opposition. At a Fillmore rally in San Francisco on October 30, a reporter wrote that Balie had "made one of his characteristic speeches, which not only enchained the crowd, but put everybody in a good humor with himself, his opponents, and . . . all the world."[43]

Physically worn by the rigors of the canvass, Balie hoped that the late nomination of the Fillmore-Donelson ticket by the Whig Party at its national convention on September 17 would provide the extra support needed to win the White House. But the prospective boost did not materialize.

Any hopes that Peyton had of going to Washington after the election to cast California's electoral vote were dashed by the victory of the Democratic ticket in California. Buchanan and Breckinridge won the state over the Americans by a majority of fifteen thousand votes. The Republicans with Fremont ran a weak third.[44] Throughout the rest of the country, Buchanan and the Democrats prevailed in a contest that was fought openly along sectional lines: North versus South, antislavery versus proslavery. In a postelection jab at the supposed antiquity of the leaders of the American Party, the San Joaquin *Republican* recommended that Peyton, Foote, and Henry A. Crabb "be carefully boxed up" and sent to an Eastern geologist "as specimens of California fossils."[45]

After the election, Peyton returned to his law practice with the goal of working himself out of debt and accumulating funds to return to his farm in Tennessee. Since serving as city attorney, Peyton had mixed politics with private practice in the law firm of Peyton, Duer, Lake and Rose at 137 Montgomery.[46] He was able to stay free of politics during the first half of 1857, but again was drawn inexorably into the activities of the American Party as the time for that party's state convention in Sacramento approached.

Hoping to revitalize a party that was rapidly losing members in the wake of the national election, Peyton successfully opposed a proposal to form a coalition between the American and Republican Parties.[47] When delegates to the 1857 state convention met as scheduled on July 29 at Sacramento, he had already circulated a strong letter advising against nominating a slate of state officers.[48] He feared a losing ticket would be the death knell for them in California. But determined to field a ticket,[49] the delegates nominated candidates for all open state offices. They subsequently lost every one of the contests.[50]

From the time of his arrival in the city, Peyton's stature as an attorney had contributed much to his popularity. One of his first lawsuits reported in the California press was tried in the Recorder's Court and involved his role as defense attorney for Hezekiah H. Bateman,[51] charged with assault with a deadly weapon. The charge had arisen from an attempt by Batemen to avenge an insult that Frank Soule had passed against his wife in the columns of Soule's newspaper. After warning the publisher that he was armed and ready to confront him, Bateman gave him time to arm. Later in the day the two men, accompanied by friends, walked past each other on the street twice before a third party fired shots in their midst on the next pass. Batemen returned fire harmlessly, and no one was wounded.

Appearing before the recorder, Bateman admitted that he had intended to assault Soule, but Peyton and his associate in the case, E. D. Baker, emphasized the provocation and the judge dismissed the charges. He fined Bateman three hundred dollars for seeking revenge on a populous street and thereby putting the lives of innocent citizens in jeopardy.[52]

Unwilling to accept the verdict of the Recorder's Court, the district attorney appeared before the grand jury and secured two indictments against Bateman for assault with intent to kill. When the case went to trial before a jury in the Court of Sessions on August 24, Peyton and Baker again represented Bateman and entered a plea of not guilty. On the day before, the grand jury had returned an indictment against William Newell for assault with a deadly weapon upon Bateman in the June 30 shooting spree.[53]

The defense attorneys first proposed to read Soule's provocative newspaper article into the record, but the judge ruled against them. Peyton then presented convincing evidence that William Newell fired first and that he fired at Bateman. He also presented testimony from the same eyewitness that Bateman did not fire at Soule but fired at Newell.[54] After the final arguments, the judge charged the jury. Within five minutes the jury returned an unqualified verdict of acquittal.[55]

Entering the muddled California land title picture, Peyton helped win temporary relief for squatters in Suisun County who were charged with resisting a survey of unconfirmed private land by the surveyor general of California. Brought by the U.S. District Attorney in federal court, the case attracted special attention in real estate and banking circles.[56]

Occupying land claimed by A. A. Ritchie that was originally a Spanish grant, the squatters blocked the surveyors because the question of title to the tract was simultaneously at issue before the U.S. Supreme Court. That meant the claimant did not have confirmed ownership, and they feared he was trying to further his claim by having it surveyed. If they acquiesced in the survey, they feared it might be interpreted that they were waiving claims Peyton believed they held under the Pre-emption Act of March 3, 1853. He and the court agreed that the squatters were secure in their premises on Ritchie's claim until the Supreme Court should issue a confirmed private land title to him or someone else.[57]

By his handling of the case, Peyton soon became known as "champion of the squatters," not only for Suisun County but also for Contra Costa, where similar situations existed.[58] He wrote a long explanation of the complex legal issues in the case for the San Francisco *Daily Alta California*, which printed the letter on July 9 and again on July 15, 1854. The squatters' litigation inspired the editor of the Nashville *Daily Gazette* to suggest, "The best title in San Francisco is said to have 'a shanty and yourself in it with a revolver. If the title needs confirmation, blow somebody's brains out.'"[59]

Balie Peyton neglected but never abandoned his interest in the performing arts, first cultivated in New Orleans. San Francisco had become a good theater town by the mid-1850s, and from time to time, he was in the audience at the Adelphi and Metropolitan Theaters, at the opera, and at the Lyceum. Periodically, he joined others in tendering a complimentary benefit to an actress or actor who soon would be leaving the city. It was a generous way of saying good-bye, as actor Joseph A. Mengis found on December 17, 1855. In another instance, Balie initiated benefits for actress Julia Dean Hayne and actor Charles Wheatleigh in 1856. A year later he was one of the sponsors of a benefit for the departing Shakespearean actress Sarah Stark.[60]

Balie's prominence led others to call upon him to assist in many good causes. In 1858, he became a member of the California Advisory Committee for the Ladies' Mount Vernon Association, a national group just chartered and authorized to purchase President George Washington's home Mount Vernon, his tomb, and two hundred acres of surrounding land for preservation as a historic shrine. Peyton's responsibility was to help raise money in California for the undertaking, and he and his colleagues set about it on February 24, 1859.[61]

Disappointed that thoroughbred horse racing was slow to make its way to California, Peyton had talked it up but had little to show for his effort. Finally in the autumn of 1858, there was public acknowledgment of efforts to encourage better breeding practices, and the *Daily Alta California* predicted that the state could have fine horses comparable to the best anywhere.[62] In one of the first reported thoroughbred races in San Francisco, a horse owned by former Tennessean W. W. Gift won handily on October 30, 1859.[63] Peyton was at the race, but the belated advent of racing on the coast was too late to affect his plans for returning to Tennessee.

Notwithstanding his public prominence, Balie left few traces of his social life in California. He enjoyed receptions and parties and the company of women, but no woman ever took Anne's place with him. A jaunty social newspaper in San Francisco raised a question about Peyton and "a January and May pair," who produced a daughter named for the former Know-Nothing city attorney. The editor of the *Ubiquitous*, formerly the *Phoenix*, observed that "there could hardly be a neater summary of an eternal triangle, squared by the addition of a fourth party" than this.

"Where's old Harris? Horned. Where's Mrs. Harris? Diddled.

"Who's father to Peytona? That's not so soon unriddled."[64]

In earlier times anyone who cast doubt on Balie's character would have felt his wrath at once, but in this instance he seems to have ignored the tease.

Perhaps Peyton achieved his highest social recognition on May 2, 1859, when he was elected president of the Pacific Club, an exclusive San Francisco men's organization. He enjoyed the club's facilities that included a restaurant; rooms for wine and smoking, billiards, and reading; and a number of furnished great rooms.[65] Meeting friends there, Balie kept up with local happenings and discussed issues of the day.

Aware that the circumstances of his Tennessee family had changed during his long absence, he purchased a flour mill close by his farm through arrangements made by his brother-in-law Barry on April 2, 1859.[66] Located near the intersection of the Nashville Pike and Station Camp Creek and adjoining John T. Baber's farm, the mill used water power except at dry times of the year when a steam engine was employed. Peyton acquired the property in partnership with Richard A. Chapman, expecting him to oversee the operation. The arrangement soon proved unsatisfactory, and on January 1, 1861, Peyton bought his partner's interest.[67]

As pleased as he was to be heading the Pacific Club and as optimistic as he was about the future of California, Peyton was increasingly concerned about the future of the country. And he was terminally homesick. His sons had just finished law school, and he wanted to be their partner in practice. Emily had visited him in San Francisco, but he had not seen his sons or his remaining two sisters for nearly ten years. Talk of secession and war heightened his concerns about his family and his slaves, horses, mill, and farm in Tennessee.[68]

Holding tightly to the belief that all political issues could be resolved within the framework of the Constitution and the existing government, Peyton recognized that during 1858 and 1859, the often intertwined questions of slavery and states' rights had become principal factors in reducing virtually all issues to sectional considerations. He noted that Republicans were appearing in increasing number in both houses of Congress, but none represented the South. At the same time, many southern political leaders intensified their open discussion of secession.

The Southern Commercial Convention had just demanded the repeal of all federal and state laws that in any way prohibited or interfered with the African slave trade.

Although he agreed that each state had the right to decide the question of slavery within its boundaries, he believed that no state had a right to secede because it would fracture the Union. Could he have a part in mustering forces to forestall it? Had he waited too long? Could he play a part in reconciliation, if not between the sections, at least between his border state friends and neighbors whose loyalties seemed split between North and South, irrespective of family or long associations?

Uncertain as to how he would fit into the unfolding drama, Balie knew he needed to be in Tennessee. He was convinced that he would be able to do nothing for his extended family or the Union he loved if he remained in California.

By November 1, 1859, Peyton had closed his law office in San Francisco and booked passage to New York by steamships and the isthmus crossing. On Saturday, November 5, he was on board the *Golden Age* as she steamed out of the bay through the Golden Gate and turned southward toward Panama. A colorful political figure and "a leading lawyer of San Francisco," Balie Peyton was "homeward bound," the *Daily Alta California* noted on November 2, 1859.

He was at sea when news of John Brown's October 16 attack on the arsenal at Harpers Ferry reached San Francisco. He first heard the report several days later when the *Golden Age* arrived at Panama.[69] Would he reach home before sectional differences became irreconcilable? The question tormented him.

HOME AGAIN
1859–1861

Completing the journey from San Francisco to Nashville via the isthmus and New York, Peyton was anxious to promote an alternative to the sectional political forces that he believed were pushing the country ever closer to civil war. He arrived in New York on November 27 on the steamship *Baltic*;[1] but before he left the city, he visited the office of the *Spirit of the Times* to reestablish old connections in the turf world. Welcoming one whose name had appeared many times in the columns of his newspaper, the editor wrote, "The Hon. Balie Peyton . . . honored us with a call on Tuesday last [November 29]. He is one of the right kind of turfmen, and Tennessee will rejoice at his return to his old home."[2]

En route to Gallatin from New York, Balie stopped to see a relative, Jesse E. Peyton, who lived in Haddonfield, New Jersey. There he learned from "Cousin" Jesse that well-wishers in nearby Philadelphia wanted to honor him at a public dinner a few weeks hence. Ostensibly it was to celebrate his return to the eastern states, but Jesse, Balie, and most of the prospective hosts determined to use the occasion to advance the formation of their mutual dream: "a conservative, national union opposition party." Some were following the lead taken earlier in the fall by the Philadelphia *North American* when it called for Tennessean John Bell to be a Union presidential candidate. Ever an unflinching Unionist, Balie told his cousin that he "would as soon think of slapping his mother in the face as think of breaking up the union of states."[3]

Jesse had visited Nashville in October. Finding that his cousin's departure from California had been delayed, he consulted with John Bell about the prospects for a new party, but Bell was reluctant. After discussing the matter at length, Bell promised that once Balie and Jesse had an opportunity to confer, he would go along with whatever they thought best.[4]

After Balie left the Northeast for Tennessee, a Union meeting in Philadelphia on December 7 attracted an "enormous" turnout and paved the way for a similar meeting that drew a massive crowd in New York City on December 19. As a pro-Union newspaper editor looked without avail for Union meetings in the slave states,[5] Peyton's Pennsylvania friends wanted to honor him as a means of opening a dialogue with the South that could lead to joint political action. He was ready to forgo the dialogue and proceed at the earliest possible moment to organize the proposed party because it could be the means of heading off violent internal strife, but he would wait.[6]

Upon arrival at Nashville, Peyton let the editor of the *Republican Banner* know that he needed the newspaper's help to persuade Bell to become a candidate for president. He delivered the message in person, and on the next day the editor printed flattering notice of his return.[7] The political success of his visit to the newspaper office became clear when, in its edition of January 5, 1860, the *Republican Banner* declared that John Bell should be the opposition candidate for president.

Two days after his conversation with the Nashville editor, Balie wrote to Bell suggesting that they go together to Philadelphia and throw all their "weight & strength fearlessly and boldly" into the effort. "The times are auspicious. Pennsylvania is the state & Philadelphia the city in which to set the ball in motion," he wrote. "I look to you as the man upon whom the great rally is to be made . . . some of the leading men of the city are well disposed toward you & only require . . . a stirring, rousing speech or two . . . to show their hands."[8]

Peyton was disappointed, however, when Bell seemingly backed away from his promise to Jesse and professed no enthusiasm for the campaign. Undeterred by Bell's lack of interest, Balie prepared to attend the Philadelphia meeting without him. He promised to use the occasion to take the "most decided ground against all mere sectional parties, North and South."[9]

Before the end of December, he received the letter of invitation that he expected, signed by eighteen Philadelphians.[10] It attested to the high regard in which members of the host committee held the honoree and expressed the goodwill they entertained for residents of the South.[11]

Regretting recent "partisan" attempts to alienate the people of the South from their fellow citizens in the North, the Philadelphians called for "the reciprocal interchange of . . . friendly sentiments." Union-loving Pennsylvanians were eager to exchange assurances of friendship with Peyton because he had "faithfully represented a state which, under circumstances of severe trial . . . maintained and proclaimed its attachment to the Union."[12] Unionists but not abolitionists, the hosts were trying also to crush a rising antislavery sentiment that threatened to sweep the city.[13]

Pleased that Cousin Jesse had been a key promoter of the event, Peyton accepted the invitation on December 28 and expressed his gratitude for its kind tribute to him. He believed that zealots from both sections were advocating points of view that were irreconcilable, and he agreed with the editor of the Philadelphia *North American* who wrote, "The present excitement and ill feeling between the two sections is owing in a great degree to the constant and reciprocated efforts of ultra party leaders of both sections to propagate extreme and unfounded views of the policy of each other on the exciting subject of slavery."[14]

Although Bell assured the Philadelphia committee by letter that he greatly desired to have a part in honoring his longtime friend Peyton, he explained that business obligations prevented his attendance. As for the tensions threatening the Union, he said he had faith in the judgment of the mass of the people of the entire country, and he trusted its responsible exercise would find for all interests a middle ground in the Constitution and the Union.[15]

Wasting no time, Peyton packed his valise, hurried northward by rail, and was in the nation's capital on January 5. That evening he visited Tennessee Congressman Robert Hopkins Hatton, brother of Joseph Hopkins Peyton's widow, and they talked family and politics until a late hour. He wanted to be sure the Fifth District representative, recently elected as an American Party candidate, understood what he was about to do at Philadelphia. Hatton did comprehend the importance of his position and hastened to reaffirm his commitment to the Union. After two days in Washington, Balie left for Philadelphia and Haddonfield, where he visited in the home of Cousin Jesse until the day of the Peyton dinner.[16]

Excitement was building at Philadelphia. By the time Balie reached the city "several hundreds" had signed the subscription list to the dinner, and the host committee had selected the Academy of Music as the only hall in the city "large enough to accommodate the company expected."[17] The hosts sent invitations to numerous political leaders opposed to the Buchanan administration, most of whom were Whigs, former Whigs, Americans, and a few Democrats. Several attended, including Senator J. J. Crittenden of Kentucky; Congressmen Horace

Maynard and T. A. R. Nelson of Tennessee; Senator Anthony Kennedy of
Maryland; Senator J. P. Comegys and Congressman George Fisher of
Delaware; Congressmen Thomas Corwin of Ohio, J. A. Gilmer of North
Carolina, and W. M. Dunn of Indiana; and J. P. Verree, Henry M. Fuller,
J. H. Campbell, S. S. Blair, and John Covode of Pennsylvania.[18]

Guests occupied all of the 378 places set for dinner, and just before
the ceremonies began, the dress circle and galleries were thrown open
and "at once filled with [additional hundreds of] ladies and gentlemen,
representing the wealth . . . beauty, and intellect" of the city. It was a
grand occasion.[19]

Peyton addressed the dinner guests after they had toasted him with
nine hearty cheers, the last "a tiger of colossal proportions." Recognizing
that the purpose of the gathering was "higher and nobler" than an
expression of personal regard for himself, he accepted the honor as a
compliment to Tennessee and the South.[20]

Recalling the issues that earlier had menaced the Union, Peyton
applauded those who had withstood the forces of disunion. He mentioned
President Thomas Jefferson and Senators Henry Clay and Daniel Webster
but did not mention President Jackson. Asking if there existed a
party in the country "whose principles and practices tend to uphold
the Constitution and . . . perpetuate our glorious Union," he answered in
the negative. "The Democrats have a party," he continued, "[and] the
Republicans have a party; but where, in the name of God, is the party of
the Constitution?" He elaborated, "It is time—high time—that the people
should arise from their slumbers in the resistless majesty of their strength,
and hurl from power all sectional men, trample under foot all sectional
issues, and inaugurate such a party."[21]

Peyton indicted the Democratic Party, in power for the prior six
years, for failure to halt the drift toward national crisis. The party was
corrupt and had become divided. "Now, I think these democratic
gentlemen, before . . . claiming a right to the monopoly of government
offices, should at least show some little harmony amongst themselves—
some cohesiveness aside from 'the cohesive power of public plunder' of
which Mr. Calhoun spoke," he said.

Assuring the crowd that his criticism of the Democratic Party was
directed at its leaders, he said he was convinced that patriotism and devotion to the Union animated the party's rank and file. Focusing their
personal ambitions on the White House had caused the party's most
ambitious leaders to become politically cross-eyed, he chided. "No one
could tell where they were going."[22]

Although the Republican Party offered itself as an alternative to the
Democrats, the choice between the two posed a false dilemma, Balie
contended. Each represented opposite sides of a sectional issue: the

status of slavery in the territories. And each had turned its back on any possible compromise. The nation should not destroy itself over this issue, he argued.[23]

Interrupted repeatedly by prolonged outbursts of applause and lusty cheering, he declared, "Come what may, I am for the Union. I wish to live in it, and, if necessary, fight in it, and die in it. Dissolve the Union? What flag would we fight under? . . . Our strength is in the Union."[24]

What to do? Peyton offered the proposition that he had come to make. It was time to organize a Union Party.

> It is only necessary for you . . . to inaugurate this great movement, and the hearts of conservative men everywhere will respond. . . . We want a national man, an honest man, a tried man. Place him upon the Constitution; let the Union be his platform; let the people be the great convention which shall bring him forward; and we will rescue, redeem, and disenthrall our country from the hands of these sectionalists.[25]

Senator J. J. Crittenden, who had been generally considered the choice to be the new party's candidate until he adamantly refused the honor, followed Peyton to the lectern. Blasting the sectionalism of the two major parties, he insisted that the only hope for peace and harmony would be found in a new party with a truly national view.[26] Crittenden took time out to pay tribute to Peyton, "the intelligent friend and true patriot . . . deservedly honored at this meeting. . . . I have known him long and well, and have held many a consultation with him in this same great cause."[27]

After Crittenden, other speakers from North Carolina, Louisiana, and Pennsylvania held the audience until Tennesseans T. A. R. Nelson and Horace Maynard made remarks that closed out the evening at an hour so late that many had already departed. Nelson's remarks reflected the unity that had prevailed throughout the evening, but Maynard threatened it by charging that by their "agitation of the slavery problem," northern men had sowed "a crop of hatred which will reap bitter fruit." In response, the presiding officer proclaimed his firm disagreement and assured the few remaining in the hall that they could go home confident that the Union "is eternal and indestructible."[28]

The unity of the meeting so inspired the editor of the *Daily Evening Bulletin* that a few days later he warned of the commercial consequences of disunion. He connected the manufacture of ornamental ironwork by a Philadelphia firm for the new Tennessee State Capitol with preserving the Union. Asserting that the supply contract created "a mutual interest, . . . a bond of union too strong to be severed by mere politicians," he said that the interruption of commerce by political strife could deny the skilled work of local artisans to distant parts of the land where such services were not available.[29]

On the Monday following the dinner, Balie, Jesse, and Marcellus Munday of Philadelphia met and outlined the core principles of the Constitutional Union Party. Simply put, the principles were "the Union, the Constitution, and the enforcement of the laws." At Balie's insistence, Jesse agreed to visit the South to "see the prominent men of the Whig Party" and to solicit them to become delegates to the convention of the Constitutional Union Party scheduled the following May in Baltimore.[30] Balie pushed hard for the convention to be held in Philadelphia but was overruled.[31]

Expressions of goodwill from the Peyton dinner meeting were echoed by the governor and legislature of New York who invited the legislatures of Tennessee and Kentucky to pay them a friendly visit, and a Philadelphia newspaper urged the state of Pennsylvania to do the same. Such invitations, given the times, were not "idle ceremony" but recognition that "the Union of states rests on mutual kindness and good feelings," the editor wrote.[32]

Although the visit to New York did not materialize, the legislatures of Kentucky and Tennessee met at Louisville on January 24 in a support-the-Union banquet. Both sets of legislators then traveled to Columbus, Ohio, for a similar gathering hosted by the governor and legislature of Ohio and attended, in addition, by the governors of Indiana, Ohio, Kentucky, and the lieutenant governor[33] of Tennessee, and the city councils of Louisville and Memphis. The travelers were received warmly during stops at Cincinnati and Dayton en route to the state capital.[34]

Arriving in Nashville from Philadelphia, Balie saw nothing but busy times ahead. A few weeks before, he had announced that he, Balie Jr., and John Bell Peyton would practice law together in Sumner and surrounding counties from an office in Gallatin, but he could not escape the magnetic attraction of politics for the Union. Immediately ahead were county, state, and national conventions, interspersed with countless consultations and frequent speeches. He would spend little time at the office of "Peyton and Sons, Attorneys at Law."[35]

He would have even less time to devote to the farm, which during his ten-year absence had suffered from the lack of care that a resident owner typically would have provided. Thomas Barry and Emily had done what they could, but the farm was far from self-sustaining. Broomsedge had engulfed one of his large fields, and when, in the spring of 1860, Balie examined the costs of the lime and other "stuffs" recommended to kill it, he jested that "hiring a dentist to draw the sedge out by the roots would be cheaper."[36]

Although farm problems were vexing, Balie observed with pleasure that support for Bell was growing in Tennessee. A chorus of endorsements for Bell and the Union Party sounded from the weekly press all

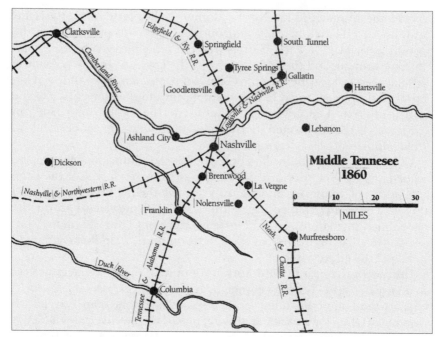

Map: Middle Tennessee

over the state.[37] Outside the state, several other conservative newspapers followed the Tennessee lead. Among them were the Baltimore *American*, the Baltimore *Patriot*, the Cincinnati *Gazette*, the New Orleans *Bee*, the New Orleans *Bulletin*, the Philadelphia *Enquirer*, and the Boston *Courier*.[38]

A group of state legislators, none of whom would associate themselves with the Democratic or Republican Party, caucused, declared Bell to be their choice for the party's presidential nomination, and asked for the calling of Union conventions at the county, state, and national levels. Peyton quickly emerged as a favorite for elector at large from Tennessee.[39]

A Bell meeting at Gallatin on February 6 was "quite a large one," but opponents of Peyton explained the attendance as being supplied "to a large extent" by "the Democracy and the old personal friends of Col. Peyton, who had a very natural and commendable curiosity to see how he looked and spoke after an absence of so many years from his old homestead."[40] The gathering was in part a welcome home for Peyton, but the principal reason that a broad spectrum of citizens attended was their concern about the drift toward civil war.

The state Union convention at Nashville on February 22 nominated Bell for president by unanimous vote and chose Peyton and Nathaniel G. Taylor of Jefferson County to be state electors at large for the presidential ticket. The chair sent Peyton and two others to deliver news of the convention's action to the nominee, who returned with them to address the assembled delegates.[41]

Bell accepted the nomination in a brief speech, but those who followed had much to say. A reporter said the delegates received Peyton's remarks "with applause, repeated and prolonged," but did not report the contents of this or other convention orations. At some point in the procedure, the assembly elected Balie, Andrew Jackson Donelson, and Gustavus A. Henry, later a Confederate senator from Tennessee, delegates to the national convention that would formally organize the Constitutional Union Party.[42]

The state Union convention declared its intent was to represent all Tennesseans who were alarmed by the prospect of a divided nation, irrespective of their traditional political allegiance. The new party wanted to unite with all men everywhere to maintain the Union, and it strongly condemned the continued "agitation" of the slavery question.[43]

Peyton perceived the convention as "one of the largest and most enthusiastic that ever convened in this state; and . . . marked by the most perfect unanimity of sentiment." He was so pleased by the convention proceedings that in reply to a previous invitation, he immediately accepted membership on the national executive committee of the new party.[44]

Balie's active participation in the Constitutional Union Party did not please the Democratic newspaper in his hometown. Although the editor admitted that "our people have always had a great liking for Balie Peyton, the man," he lamented his falling under the influence of John Bell. Bell "first misled him into the bogs . . . from which he has never been able to extricate himself, but keeps on blundering after the same *ignis fatuus* which has proved so deceptive to his ambition." Had Peyton remained a Jacksonian Democrat, his political stature would have been enhanced far beyond its present levels, the editor insisted.[45]

Even though they supported his defection from the Jacksonian crowd, many of Balie's friends believed he had fallen short of developing his personal potential. His long-standing colleague Virginia Governor Henry Wise recalled to Tennessee Congressman Robert Hatton that he had heard Peyton make "the most eloquent and effective speech that ever was made in Congress." But he said the brilliant orator had limited himself by failing to read representative literature. "If Peyton had only ever read anything, he would have made one of the greatest men that ever figured in [the history] of this country. As it is he has few superiors," Wise conceded on April 23, 1860.[46]

News of the death of his sister Angelina Belle Peyton Eberly in Indianola, Texas, on March 15 reached Balie a few days later. Deeply saddened, he remembered her in the words used by Jim Bowie and other Texas frontiersmen to describe her. Bowie had referred to her in 1835 as "that grandest of American women in this country," and others agreed that she was "not only . . . a devoted patriot, but . . . one of the handsomest and most queenly women ever born in the valley of the Mississippi." The oldest of four sisters, Angelina had fled to Texas in 1821 with her first husband, Jonathan C. Peyton, when she was twenty-three years old. He died within a few years, leaving her with two children, a son, Alexander, who died in 1843 in the Texas Archives War[47] and a daughter who died in childbirth in October 1850. Angelina had married Capt. Jacob Eberly in 1836, and he died soon after her son's death.[48] She remained in Texas where she had a large landed estate.

Tennessee Unionists were not surprised when Peyton's new party breathed the breath of life for the first time in Baltimore on May 10, 1860, nor when the Sumner Countian represented Tennessee on the committee to set the agenda. Meeting in the old Presbyterian Church at the corner of Fayette and North Streets, the delegates organized the Constitutional Union Party and nominated John Bell for president on the second ballot. Sam Houston, the charismatic former governor of Tennessee and Texas, was second on the first ballot, but his voters switched to Bell on the next roll call. They then nominated Edward Everett of Massachusetts for vice president.

Following Balie's concept as expressed to Bell the previous December, the delegates bypassed the usual platform and instead adopted a brief statement that made no mention of slavery but called for the recognition of "no political principle other than the Constitution . . . the union of the States, and the enforcement of the laws." With no serious platform debate, harmony reigned throughout the meeting and the delegates remained focused on preserving representative government within the Union.[49] Peyton may have been recommending that Bell follow the course successfully pursued by Gen. Zachary Taylor who was elected president without a traditional platform, but this time candidates faced issues that threatened the survival of the nation.

Peyton's personal Unionism seemed deliberately to avoid the question of slavery. Certainly, neither he nor the new party offered a plan to deal with it then or at any future time. Although he did not favor its extension to the West, he was opposed to abolition. His absence for ten years, while in Chile and California, probably precluded his fully understanding the sharp political division that had developed east of the Rockies during that period. He surely did not sense that "out of common Americanism . . . divergent nationalisms . . . had developed."[50]

Prior to the Union Party's convention, the Democratic Party had split over the question of slavery in the territories. Before the rupture,

Tennessee Democrats in convention had declared Andrew Johnson their choice for nomination for president. But when delegates to the National Democratic Convention convened in Charleston, South Carolina, in April, they failed to agree on a candidate. Reconvening in Baltimore on June 18, they nominated Stephen A. Douglas, but nearly all southern and border state delegates walked out. The defectors met again on June 28 and nominated John C. Breckinridge for president, a move that confirmed the schism. In the meantime, Abraham Lincoln had become the new Republican Party's nominee, chosen in national convention at Chicago. His party platform prohibited slavery in the territories but would not interfere with it in the states.

Peyton saw the nomination of Lincoln by a purely sectional party as a threat to slavery and the Union. But he failed to show how his new party could protect the interests of southern voters from the antislavery Republicans. Although the Constitutional Unionists appealed to reason and caution, they offered nothing to a people in crisis. The Constitution and the Union were yet in place, but just calling for their preservation would not solve the problems facing the nation. The new party offered no specific proposals to address the moral and economic problems inherent in slavery as practiced in the United States.

Although Peyton had campaigned in two or more states during the presidential races of Harrison and Taylor, he restricted his postconvention appearances for Bell to Tennessee. The decision to limit his campaign travel may have been at least partly occasioned by a growing likelihood, recognized by Bell leaders, that Lincoln would be elected. But as he prepared to canvass the state, Balie showed nothing but enthusiasm and confidence.[51]

The Breckinridge or Southern Democrats constituted the biggest challenge to a Constitutional Union victory in the state, and Balie focused on them and their ticket. Before the end of the summer, he had agreed to assist the Bell-Everett campaign by appearing in a series of debates with his opposite number, Landon C. Haynes, the Breckinridge ticket's candidate for state elector. They published a schedule of fifty-one appointments, the first of which was on August 30 at Winchester and the last on November 2 in Chattanooga.[52]

Prior to taking up the Haynes-Peyton schedule, Balie made speeches for Bell at Gallatin, Lawrenceburg, Pulaski, Cornersville, and Columbia, and appeared briefly in communities along his route of travel.[53] Outlining a history of the "slavery agitation," Peyton insisted that the question before the voters was Union or disunion—"not so much who shall be the President of the United States, as whether we *shall have* a United States." He repeatedly blamed the Breckinridge Democrats for the "corrupt and distracted condition" of the country. At Columbia he held his audience for more than three hours in what his older friends said was "the greatest speech of his life."[54]

Opening the debate series at Winchester, Peyton turned his humor and sarcasm upon Haynes's portrayal of Breckinridge. His wit won the audience, even as it undercut the serious remarks of both speakers. Peyton was always prepared to provide for those in the crowd who came primarily for entertainment.[55]

Peyton and Haynes satisfied their own partisan presses. The Nashville *Republican Banner*, committed to Bell and Everett, always reported that Peyton triumphed over whomever the opposing speaker might be. The Nashville *Daily Union*, dedicated to the Breckinridge-Lane ticket, was blind to Peyton's successes and reported that Haynes had won every time they debated. From Pulaski, where William H. Polk had joined them to speak for the Douglas ticket, the partisan *Republican Banner* reported on September 5 that Balie had come down on his opponents "with a fierce energy . . . making them visibly wince and abandon their ill-considered charges." His speech elicited "a ringing chorus of shouts such as old Giles [County] has not heard in many a long year."

The largest public turnout for Peyton and Haynes was at Memphis on September 11. When Balie arrived by train, Bell supporters paraded him through the city. Later in the day he, Haynes, and William H. Polk spoke to a large crowd. The latter two made the first statements that were mutually hostile, growing out of the party split. When Col. W. D. Ferguson, a veteran of two wars, a Unionist, and a member of the crowd, prompted Polk to ask Haynes what he would do if Lincoln were elected, a reporter paraphrased Haynes's intemperate response.

> He would await the first overt act of aggression upon the rights of the South; and then he would summon him (Colonel Ferguson) and go to Washington and hang Lincoln; and if he (Colonel Ferguson) refused to go, he would hang him and all like him with grapevines.

The crowd called for Colonel Ferguson to take the stand to answer Haynes, but Peyton begged the colonel to stand fast and "leave Mr. Haynes to *me*." At first greatly excited, the crowd became quiet when Peyton began to speak with tears streaming from his eyes. A reporter for the Memphis *Enquirer* wrote: "Those who witnessed it will never forget it . . . the day when the spirit of disunion was so pointedly rebuked, not only by our able elector, but by the thousands who heard him and his glowing eloquence."[56]

Another local newspaper, hostile to the Constitutional Union Party, reported Peyton's speech with considerably less enthusiasm but admitted that he had spoken with obvious effect.

> Col. Balie Peyton closed the discussion in behalf of Mr. Bell. His anecdotes, though covered with the cobwebs of antiquity, were revamped with great ingenuity. . . . We must do him the credit to say that his review of Mr. [William L.] Yancey's speech, delivered some weeks since in this city, was masterful, potent and irrefutable. He made a real Union speech.[57]

A week later Peyton and former Governor Neill S. Brown spoke for Bell to an audience of more than eight hundred, assembled on short notice, at the Davidson County Courthouse in Nashville. "The pure patriotism and political sincerity of [Gov. Brown] commands the admiration of his audience, and attracts and enchains their attention," an observer wrote. The same writer said of Peyton, "a masterly effort, solid and sensible, and rational, and abounding in lively anecdote, and earnest, heart warm appeals for the preservation of the Union."[58] But Randal McGavock, a Harvard student and future mayor of Nashville, reported a different view; in his opinion Peyton "was quite drunk."[59]

When Peyton and Haynes debated at Nashville, Breckinridge Democrats complained that Peyton had equated Union with Bell and disunion with Breckinridge. Balie charged that the Kentuckian was in the race to assure the election of Lincoln, which would estrange the eight cotton states and break up the Union.[60] Finding that these equations drew popular response, Peyton repeated them and enlarged his argument to hold that Breckinridge Democrats were responsible for the rise of the Republican Party.[61] He said that the southern Democrats were inviting their fellow citizens not to the ballot box, "but to prepare for the cartridge box." It was clear to Peyton that the men who nominated Breckinridge were "*open*, bold and RECKLESS DISUNIONISTS."[62] He declared that Breckinridge marched under a "traitor flag, beneath whose folds were found parading every disaffected spirit in the South."[63] McGavock was present again, and after hearing Peyton and Haynes, he gave both credit for "good speeches."[64]

Having fulfilled their scheduled appearances[65] in Middle and West Tennessee, Peyton and Haynes announced October 18 they would close the campaign with a sweep through East Tennessee, staging at least fifteen debates.[66] By that time both speakers were repeating previous charges and countercharges, with little or no new material.

Peyton embarrassed Haynes during their last appearance in Knoxville. After reading from the *National Intelligencer* to prove that Yancey was conservative and not for secession even if Lincoln should win, Haynes listened while Peyton took the same newspaper and, reading from the same editorial, proved the opposite. Haynes had "garbled" what was said, and Peyton had exposed "the gross and contemptible hypocrisy of such an attempt at deception." Local editor William G. Brownlow afterward asserted that "the Breckinridgers feel it yet, and will feel it until after the election is over, and long after that."[67]

On November 4, Abraham Lincoln received only 40 percent of the popular votes nationwide but won the race for president with a clear majority of the electoral votes, 180 to 123 for the other three candidates. Bell led the voting in Tennessee with 69,170 votes to 65,053 for Breckinridge and 11,394 for Douglas. Lincoln was not on the ballot.[68] The Bell-Everett ticket was able to win only two other states, Kentucky and Virginia.

Peyton, Bell, and their allies had failed to unite the country around their version of the Constitution and the Union primarily because all the other parties and candidates had claimed that they, too, supported the Constitution and the Union. There had never been a chance for a party that invoked high principles but offered no solutions.

As Lincoln reviewed prospective cabinet appointments, Thurlow Weed recommended that he consider Peyton, a proven southern Unionist, for secretary of war.[69] Lincoln did not accept Weed's suggestion, but if he had offered the appointment, Balie would surely have declined to accept it. He had done all that he possibly could to avert war; he was not going to administer it. Proud that he had been instrumental in carrying Tennessee for Bell, he was gratified that he had had a role in promoting the Constitutional Union Party even in defeat.

When the Electoral College of Tennessee met at the Capitol on December 5, the electors called Peyton to the chair and he dutifully recorded the electoral votes for president. All twelve of the Tennessee electors cast their votes for Bell for president and for his running mate, Edward Everett, for vice president.[70]

Peyton's hometown Union newspaper, the Gallatin *Courier and Enquirer*, praised him for "the great service" he performed in the presidential campaign. It was the "unbending energy with which Col. Peyton discharged his duties" that "won for him an abiding place in the affection of the Party."[71]

To determine the course of Tennessee in the crisis, Governor Isham G. Harris called a special session of the general assembly for January 7, 1861. A senator who drafted a resolution proposing that Tennessee join a Southern confederacy could not find enough support to bring the matter to a vote. Support materialized quickly for a more deliberate process, however. The house and senate called a referendum for February 9, at which time the voting public would determine whether a convention should be held on the question of secession. The ballots would give voters the choice of "convention" or "no convention," but would include a list of delegates identified as "Union" or "disunion." The delegate choices would be null and void if "no convention" received the majority of the votes cast.[72]

Exploring all options, the general assembly appointed twelve delegates to attend a "conference convention" called by certain border state leaders for Washington beginning February 7. In session until February 27, the convention adopted a number of recommendations for amending the Constitution, but none provided a satisfactory basis for agreement on the issues that separated the North and the South.[73]

Peyton worked stringently against having the proposed state convention, but was both disappointed and surprised by the outcome of the referendum. Sumner and Smith Counties, his district, voted in favor of the convention, but chose him and other Unionist delegates to represent them should the convention be called.[74] Statewide, voters rejected the convention by a substantial majority, but by a four-to-one ratio elected Unionist delegates. The voters could not have been more cautious.[75]

Even before Tennesseans went to the polls, Mississippi, Florida, Alabama, Georgia, and Louisiana had seceded, following South Carolina's example. On February 9, representatives of the seceded states concluded their meeting at Montgomery, Alabama, by forming a provisional government for the Confederate States of America and electing Balie's one-time quarrelsome correspondent, Jefferson Davis of Mississippi, president.

The anti-disunion vote in Tennessee encouraged Peyton and the other Unionists in his hometown to continue the fight. On April 1, a Gallatin Union meeting recommended Balie to be the party's nominee for governor at the state convention set for May 2. Willing to accept neither abolition nor secession, he responded with typical eloquence. His every word breathed "the spirit of lofty patriotism and deep devotion to the Union." The crowd's enthusiastic applause forced him to pause frequently. Smith County Unionists jumped on Peyton's bandwagon a few days later, but crucial developments distracted public attention. Soon Peyton and his son John Bell decided to join the local home guard movement "to secure our homes from invasion, come from what quarter it may." He and the original subscribers declared the guard's purpose was to maintain peace; "it is to be a peace army, if we may use the paradox."[76]

Balie shuddered when, on April 12, Confederate forces fired the first salvos of the Civil War at Fort Sumter in Charleston Harbor. Three days later President Lincoln declared the existence of a "state of insurrection" and called for seventy-five thousand volunteers. When the War Department established a quota of two regiments for Tennessee, Governor Harris issued his famous response: "Tennessee will not furnish a single man for purposes of coercion, but 50,000 if necessary for the defense of our rights and those of our Southern brothers." Public opinion in the state tilted toward secession. Within the next thirty days, Virginia, Arkansas, and North Carolina seceded.

With the opening of hostilities Balie Jr. left his law partners and enlisted in the Hickory Guards, a Nashville volunteer company of the Confederate Army. It was a decision made doubly difficult by his father's undying loyalty to the Union and by the hurt that both felt when they could not reconcile the issues that divided them. But when the time came for Balie Jr. to take up duties at Camp Trousdale, his father presented him the sword he had received for his own valorous service in the Mexican War.[77]

On April 18 Peyton, John Bell, Neill S. Brown, Cave Johnson, Andrew Ewing, and Return J. Meigs II issued a joint statement that called upon the people of Tennessee to guard their neutrality during the existing emergency. Agreeing that Governor Harris had properly refused Lincoln's request for troops, they expressed total disapproval of secession "both as a constitutional right, and as a remedy for existing evils." They found coercion equally unacceptable because it would "dissolve the Union forever and . . . dissolve it in the blood of our fellow citizens." Tennessee should avoid taking sides with either party because she had not wronged any other "state or citizen of this Union," they argued.[78]

Although their plea was heartfelt, these men did not favor neutrality under all circumstances. Should the Lincoln administration determine to overrun and subjugate the Southern states, they believed it would be the duty of Tennessee to resist by force of arms. Their appeal for neutrality had little effect in Tennessee, and within a few days most of the signers, including Peyton, agreed that the state should prepare to defend against an invasion by an army from whatever source. Peyton and his allies hoped it would yet be possible for Tennessee to work out a plan to prevent civil war by meeting in conference with the other slave-holding states that had not seceded, but it was too late.[79]

A deadly momentum was pushing Tennesseans closer to alignment with their Southern neighbors. Confederate Col. William B. Bate of Sumner County noted that Tennessee Unionist leaders were losing confidence in their cause and would soon join the Southern leadership. He said there was a good chance that Peyton, Campbell, John Bell, and Andrew and Edward Ewing would abandon their commitment to the Union and join the Confederacy.[80]

With secession fever rising in Tennessee, Balie's good friend and fellow Unionist Joseph Smith Fowler resigned as president of Howard Female Institute at Gallatin and moved with his family to Illinois. Fowler's decision to leave was based on the advice of the institute's board of trustees, who feared for his safety as tensions mounted.[81] Another good friend, the Tennessee state librarian Return J. Meigs II, left the state a few weeks later under heavy criticism for his pro-Union sentiment.[82]

On May 8, the Tennessee General Assembly voted to declare the state independent of the Union and authorized representatives "to enter a military league" with the Confederacy.[83] The action was predicated upon ratification by the voters in a statewide referendum to be held on June 8.

Peyton worked tirelessly to try to defeat secession in this second referendum. By that time he was certain that to vote for secession was to vote for war. None of his public appearances in this connection was more noteworthy than his speech to "an immense concourse of citizens, excited to fever heat" at the courthouse in Gallatin on the eve of the balloting. Although the crowd included a large majority of pro-secessionists, they listened attentively as he made "a manly and touching appeal for the preservation of the Union."[84]

Seventeen years later, Julius A. Trousdale, Gallatin attorney and son of Governor William Trousdale, recalled the event at which he had been present. Peyton had spoken with characteristic candor. An advocate of secession, Trousdale said that he and the others present could never "cease to admire his [Peyton's] . . . patriotism, and cool daring in remonstrating against the fatal step about to be taken . . . when the popular feeling was nearly solid against him."[85]

What turned out to be even more memorable was his prediction of the effects of war on Tennessee families. Many of the youngest and finest men would die or be maimed, he predicted, and families would be disrupted and the countryside ravaged. What would be the fate of the slaves? Citizens of all ages would be at the mercy of an occupying enemy army, he said, as he pictured with uncanny accuracy "the dire consequences that were about to follow."[86] Yet on the appointed day, the voters of Sumner County and the rest of the state cast their ballots overwhelmingly for separation and military affiliation with the Confederacy.[87] Call it what you will, Tennessee had seceded.

Almost lost in the rush of fast-moving events was a meeting of the state Constitutional Union Party on May 2 to select its nominees for governor. Assisted by Peyton's active support, William B. Campbell became the nominee. Balie, John Bell, Neill S. Brown, and John S. Brien communicated the news of his nomination to Campbell and persuaded him to accept it.[88] But the overwhelming vote in favor of secession cast in the referendum of June 8 caused Campbell to withdraw from the contest. On August 1, the incumbent Governor Harris won easily over his only opponent, William H. Polk, the late president's brother.

During the summer of 1861, Peyton could not avoid the buildup to war going on all around him. His son, Balie Jr., was at nearby Camp Trousdale, training with the Twentieth Tennessee Infantry Regiment, C.S.A. Nashville was astir as young men left for training camps, and the few factories and shops of the city began to convert their production to military supplies. Pro-Confederate sympathy throughout the area was at fever pitch, although many, like Balie, believed there was nothing ahead for the South but suffering and devastation.

Since returning from California, he had given himself to failed political efforts to save the Union, yet Balie had not totally ignored his depleted stud. He wanted to improve the bloodlines and to reestablish his reputation with turfmen throughout the country.

Within ninety days of his visit to the editor of the *Spirit of the Times* in November 1859, a list identifying six of his horses appeared conspicuously in that newspaper.[89] Of the lot only the chestnut filly Fanny McAlister, nearing her second birthday, merited special mention. "[She] in particular, is a most beautiful and bloodlike creature; her form is almost faultless, and she is as much bound to run as a young duck to swim," a correspondent noted. In addition to Fanny, Peyton listed two mature chestnut mares, one with foal by Third Boston; a four-year-old chestnut filly with foal by O'Meara; a two-year-old chestnut filly; and a chestnut colt, nine months old. A Kentucky visitor, reporting February 20 from Gallatin, said that Peyton owned "a four-year-old Third Boston . . . that looks flattering, a facsimile of Red Oak," then in training for the spring races.[90] The pedigrees of all were adequate, but not of the distinction that characterized Peyton's stud from 1830 to 1849.

Although he had only one thoroughbred in training for the season ahead, Peyton recognized that the local racing club and its facilities needed reorganizing and rehabilitating. After several morning gatherings at John H. Malone's store on the public square where lovers of the turf gathered daily to discuss horses, Peyton organized the Gallatin Jockey Club of Sumner County, Tennessee, and prepared the Albion Course for the spring races of 1860. Members immediately elected him president.[91]

When the spring races of the Gallatin Jockey Club opened on May 16, Peyton knew that he was glad to be home. Presiding over the opening, he saw many old friends. He never felt better than when he gave "a full and explicit charge" to the riders and trainers in the first race. A visiting turf reporter commented that he was a president "who thoroughly understands the responsibilities of his office."[92] He was also a president who concealed well his disappointment at having no horses ready to run. His personal finances were so depleted that he borrowed one thousand dollars from Emily to meet pressing obligations.[93]

An old friend and distinguished turfman-trainer Green Berry Williams added to Balie's welcome home to Gallatin when, on June 9, he claimed the name of Emily Peyton for his yearling chestnut filly by Lexington out of Sally Roper by Imp. Albion. E. E. Jones, senior editor of the *Spirit of the Times,* saw the yearling and said she was "a beauty."[94] Other horses carrying the Peyton name kept it before the racing world. At Augusta, Georgia, on May 1, the "hitherto invincible gray" gelding Bailie [*sic*] Peyton lost a nationally followed match race to R. A. Alston's chestnut colt Tom Puryear. Owned by A. C. Jones, this racing Bailie was the get of the original thoroughbred Balie Peyton.[95]

Eager to see his colors on the track, Peyton entered three horses for the 1861 Gallatin spring races.[96] But on the first day of racing, he ran only Fanny McAlister,[97] a good choice because she won "in a gallop" over a lone opponent. Balie was unusually pleased by her performance because she had run two one-mile heats over a track deep in mud from rain the morning before. One observer wrote of the winner, "Fannie [*sic*] is one of the most beautiful animals, and one of the fleetest ever raised in Tennessee."[98]

Balie did not send any other horses to the starting line, but he sent Fanny McAlister back for the last race of the season on May 25. The first one-mile heat of four was closely contested, but she won in one minute forty-five and one-half seconds, a time "old turfmen pronounce . . . the best ever made in Tennessee." But in succeeding heats she faded and finished a disappointing third.[99]

The Gallatin Jockey Club, at Peyton's insistence, finished its scheduled three days of racing on May 25, nearly a month after Memphis had postponed its racing season indefinitely and six weeks after Confederate units had fired upon Fort Sumter. Only eighteen days had passed since the Tennessee General Assembly authorized the governor to negotiate an alliance with the Confederacy. When would the horses run again?

Uncharacteristically thinking of protecting his assets, Balie quickly made an inventory of his fine horses. His son John Bell accompanied him "into the blue-grass pastures with a blank book and pencil, and carefully noted the color, sex, white stars, white feet, [height] and every peculiar mark of each of his blood stock as well as his work animals (most of which were thoroughbred)," so that they could "accurately describe any animal which might be stolen."[100]

As always, the farm and less frequently the flour mill cried for his attention. He spent the first few days of September looking for his millwright, a runaway slave whom he believed to be in adjoining Robertson or nearby Montgomery County. From the farm he frequently corresponded with friend Campbell, sharing their mutual concern about impending war and swapping family news from camp and home. Like Campbell, Peyton could see no way to repudiate his belief in the Union. "I have as yet seen no cause to change my views as to the course proper for me to pursue in these distressing times," he confided. "What the future may reveal the Lord only knows."[101]

A timely blessing for the Peytons was the marriage of Frances Elizabeth Trousdale of Gallatin and John Bell Peyton on October 8, 1861. Frances, later known to Balie as his "beloved Fanny," was a daughter of Governor William Trousdale. During the next fifteen years she and John had two sons and two daughters, the only grandchildren that Balie ever had.[102]

On December 25, Balie made a gift of a six-year-old slave girl to his daughter-in-law. He referred to the child as Cornelia Lee "of light complexion, the daughter of [his] slaves Eliza and Tony." The gift was for Frances's "sole and separate property" and did not separate Cornelia from her parents as the slave family, Balie, Emily, and the newlyweds all lived on the Station Camp Creek farm.[103]

Concerned that Balie Jr. was already an officer in the Confederate Army, his father hoped the marriage of John and Fanny would keep the new husband at home, free of military service. Balie knew that he had done his best to forestall the conflict; he never intended to have his sons participate in it. For the moment, he enjoyed sharing the newlyweds with the Trousdale family at Christmas.

CHAPTER 14

UNIONIST IN A REBEL STATE
1862–1865

Fulfillment of Peyton's prediction that the war would cause suffering and tragedy to strike families both North and South came in 1862. He knew that by January 1 the Confederate Army had stretched a thin defensive line through Bowling Green across southern Kentucky to meet any attempted overland invasion by the Union forces. And he knew that his son was somewhere in that line. He was also aware that to block ingress by waterways, the Confederates had built forts in northern Tennessee to command the two rivers that connected Tennessee to Kentucky as well as the Ohio River. Fort Henry guarded the Tennessee River and Fort Donelson overlooked the Cumberland. Peyton and most Middle Tennesseans believed they were secure—out of harm's way—but that false sense was shattered on January 19, when Union forces decisively defeated Confederate troops at the Battle of Mill Springs, about thirty miles southeast of Columbia, Kentucky, and forced them to withdraw from the field.

The first specific report from Mill Springs to reach Peyton found him at Gallatin. He was stunned. A telegram from Nashville newspaper editor George Baber advised that his son Balie Jr.[1] and Confederate Gen. Felix Zollicoffer, a former Nashville congressman and newspaper editor well known by the Peytons, had lost their lives in the battle.[2] Young Balie had fallen in an exchange of point-blank fire with elements of the Second Minnesota Regiment. A Union color-bearer pointed out

Balie Peyton Jr.

the Confederate lieutenant to a kneeling rifleman who "drew a bead upon him" and fired the fatal shot at a distance of "not more than fifteen feet" as Balie Jr. was firing his pistol into the ranks close before him.[3]

Peyton the father openly wept, recalling his son's farewell visit when both believed they were too manly to shed tears. He tried to understand, remembering the quick, almost reckless response he had made when the call for volunteers for the Mexican War was issued. Still finding it difficult to accept Balie Jr.'s decision to fight, he took consolation in learning that his son fell from a single shot fired in the heat of battle.[4] Young Balie had died for his beliefs, and his father sadly admired him for it.

After days of anxious waiting, Peyton gratefully accepted news contained in a telegraphic dispatch from Gen. Albert Sidney Johnston received in Nashville on February 1. The bodies of Balie Jr. and General Zollicoffer would arrive in the city the same day on the Bowling Green train. Orders originated by Union Gen. George H. Thomas, who had campaigned in the Mexican War with Balie Sr., facilitated the return. Gen. A. D. McCook sent a captured Confederate surgeon, Daniel B. Cliffe, to accompany the bodies to Munfordville, Kentucky, where they were transferred across the lines to the Confederate Army. Both had been embalmed and placed in metal caskets sent by Union Gen. Don Carlos Buell from Louisville. At first Balie Jr. had been buried with 114 other dead, but Surgeon Cliffe had the coffin disinterred and prepared for shipment to Nashville.[5]

Upon receipt of Johnston's dispatch, the Tennessee General Assembly interrupted its deliberations to make appropriate arrangements for "the reception and funeral" of the late Confederate officers. Both houses joined to pass resolutions of sympathy and praise. In tribute, the governor closed state offices in the city, and the mayor asked the business community to close for the rest of the day.

Governor Harris led a procession of state officials, including members of the legislature, to the Louisville and Nashville Railroad Depot to receive the fallen heroes. Joined by Balie Sr. and other members of both families, the procession retraced its steps to the Capitol and delivered the bodies of the two gallant soldiers to lie in state in the

Hall of the House of Representatives.[6] On the next day Balie, Emily, and John Bell stood in the Hall as long lines of sympathizers moved slowly past the caskets. John Bell noted that their father's sword had not been returned with the remains. He did not know that it had been picked up on the field of battle by a Union Army officer until forty-five years later when Capt. M. C. Tuttle of St. Paul, Minnesota, returned it to him.[7]

Throughout the city, citizens mourned the deaths of the brave soldiers. The mayor and city council passed resolutions of sympathy for both officers. Referring to "the brave and dauntless Lieut. Balie Peyton Jr.," they paid tribute to him and extended their sympathy to his father.[8]

A letter to Balie Sr. from Gen. A. D. McCook, who received Balie Jr.'s disinterred remains at Camp Wood, Kentucky, expressed a Union officer's tender concern:

> It was my painful duty, as commander of this camp, to receive the remains of your gallant son, who fell bravely leading his command at the battle of Mill Spring. I have no personal acquaintance with you, but I have often heard my father speak of you as one of his friends, and I, as a son of a friend, to the son of a friend, have had all possible attention paid to the remains.[9]

Telegram announcing the death of Balie Peyton Jr.

Further expressions of sympathy poured in on the father from every side, the vast majority coming from pro-Confederate friends. He probably speculated that if they could have curbed their desire to leave the Union, there might not have been this occasion for sharing his grief. When neighbors laid his son to rest in the family cemetery on the Station Camp Creek farm,[10] Balie was a more convinced Unionist than he had ever been. But what could one conservative Union man do to hasten an end to the conflict, especially when living in a Confederate state?

Friends were still offering condolences when Federal troops captured Forts Henry and Donelson on February 16 and took fifteen thousand prisoners, most at the latter installation. Confederate Gen. Albert Sidney Johnston quickly withdrew his troops from Kentucky, falling back all the way to Murfreesboro. When citizens learned there would be no defense of Nashville, panic set in. Many left the city for refuge farther south, but most remained to endure the fear, uncertainty, and periodic riots that prevailed until Federal troops marched off river transports onto the streets of Nashville on February 25.[11]

Peyton had rushed to his farm where he remained for several days. Like his Nashville friends, he recognized that the Confederate decision not to defend the city had saved it from the devastation that would have accompanied a military contest for possession of it. The fate of the farms surrounding the city, including his own, was yet to be determined.

Six days after Federal troops entered Nashville unopposed, President Lincoln appointed U.S. Senator Andrew Johnson of

General view of the City of Nashville, 1862

Greeneville to be military governor for Tennessee. A five-term congressman (1843–53), Johnson had served as elected governor of the state from 1853 to 1857 and U.S. senator since 1857. Peyton looked forward to conferring with him. He wanted to share his belief in "the hopelessness of the Southern cause and the propriety and necessity of Tennessee returning to her appropriate place in the Union at the earliest day possible."[12]

Johnson arrived in the city by train on March 11, but six weeks passed before Balie could have a serious conference with him. Then he went with local Unionists William B. Campbell, Jordan Stokes, William B. Stokes, and William H. Polk to discuss plans for restoring the state to the Union.[13] The result of the meeting was an agreement for the conferees to call a mass meeting on May 12 to discuss restoring the former relations that existed between Tennessee and the United States.[14]

Union loyalists gathered on the appointed date and, with William B. Campbell presiding, endorsed Governor Johnson and "the policy of his administration" since his arrival. The only other significant action taken that evening was Campbell's appointment of a Union Central Committee, all from Nashville. He passed the opportunity to appoint Peyton and himself, possibly because both were at home most of the time at Gallatin and Lebanon. More likely, the reason was that Campbell was uncertain what Johnson expected from the Central Committee.[15]

In June the governor asked Peyton to go to Washington, D.C., with William H. Polk to confer with the president on a plan to drive the rebels out of East Tennessee where they were in control.[16] While in the capital, Balie met with other Tennessee politicians to recommend nomination of a judge to succeed West H. Humphreys[17] as federal district judge for Tennessee. Impeached by the House, he had been removed by the U.S. Senate. Balie seconded the nomination of Connally F. Trigg who was later chosen for the appointment.[18]

An effort to cast doubt on Peyton's loyalty to the Union appeared in a letter published in the Atlanta *Intelligencer* early in July, purported to have been signed by a number of Tennesseans. It charged that his true allegiance was to the Confederate states and he was only parading as a Unionist. The editor of the Nashville *Daily Union* was confident Peyton would deny the accusations categorically because he was at that very moment in Washington City with a group of "other loyal Tennesseans on public business." The publication was probably the handiwork of Radical Unionists[19] who wanted to remove the Conservative Peyton from the governor's inner circle of advisors.[20]

Those who wanted to portray Peyton as a rebel had probably noticed that he had agreed in mid-June to seek the release of Jo. C. Guild,[21] a

Gallatin attorney, jurist, and vocal secession advocate who had been exiled to prison at Fort Mackinac, Michigan, on April 11 by Governor Johnson. Although Peyton and Guild were on different sides of the secession issue, they had been personal friends for more than forty years. The governor agreed to release Guild if he would take an oath of loyalty and post bond for his subsequent behavior. Guild agreed, and when he swore allegiance to the United States on August 1, Peyton and John S. Brien signed at Nashville as sureties on the required bond of ten thousand dollars.[22] He was not permitted to leave Fort Mackinac until September 25.[23] When he arrived in Nashville on October 8, Peyton met him and accompanied him to the governor's office where Johnson issued a final permit for the former exile to return to his home at Gallatin.[24]

During the latter part of 1862, all of 1863, and into the latter part of 1864, Peyton served his Sumner County neighbors repeatedly as their representative in issues involving them and the Union Army commander at Gallatin, the arrogant Gen. Eleazer A. Paine. Although he could make little headway with the general, Peyton found the governor much more receptive to his complaints. Paine's oppressive conduct was so severe that other Union generals began to have serious doubts about him. With Peyton's help, Gen. Lovell H. Rousseau collected sufficient evidence against Paine regarding the excesses he had committed against the citizenry; in 1864, Gen. Ulysses S. Grant evaluated the complaints and adjudged him "entirely unfit to command a post."[25]

The onset of war seemed to magnify Balie's financial difficulties. On October 24, 1862, he pledged his grain mill on Station Camp Creek to his neighbor John F. Cage to secure a debt of two thousand dollars that he owed him and was unable to pay.[26] He could do little productively on the farm. The presence of Union Army guards on the Louisville and Nashville Railroad along the northern reaches of the farm and the periodic challenges for control of the tracks by mounted Confederate raiders were interruptions enough to idle agricultural operations. As a result, he conducted little more than subsistence farming but occasionally had enough hay to attract visits from nearby Union foragers.

On November 9 and 10, Peyton swapped visits at Gallatin with Gen. Thomas L. Crittenden, son of his friend John J. Crittenden of Lexington, Kentucky. The general was in camp not far from Peyton's farm with a sizeable Federal force commanded by Gen. Thomas J. Wood en route to Murfreesboro. Eager to share his visits, Peyton wrote to General Crittenden's father, who had another son, Gen. George Bibb Crittenden, on active duty in the Confederate Army. "I had the pleasure of seeing your son Gen'l Thomas L. Crittenden as he passed through. . . . I visited him [at] camp twice, and he with Gen'l Wood rode over to Station Camp with me bringing along your little grandson and namesake, who at eight years old rides quite boldly and is the pet of the Army." Earlier, on April 8 and 9, Generals Wood and Thomas L. Crittenden led a division of Gen. Don Carlos Buell's Army of the Ohio at the bloody Battle of Shiloh.[27]

As was his inclination, Peyton gave personal considerations little or no attention when he was called to a public responsibility. Dispatched by the governor, he and Horace Maynard visited the nation's capital in May 1863 to seek the War Department's approval for their recruiting volunteer regiments in eastern states to partici- pate in an expedition to free the people of East Tennessee, still under

Andrew Johnson

rebel rule. The War Department granted immediate permission for recruiting, provided that the approval of the governor of any state solicited must first be granted. The governor of New York readily endorsed recruiting in his state, and Peyton and Maynard visited Harrisburg, the capital of Pennsylvania, to petition that state's governor for permission to recruit a brigade.[28]

After returning from the East, Balie discovered his favorable standing with Governor Johnson and other Nashville Unionists had led to their inviting him to attend the July 4 celebration in the state capital as a "distinguished guest."[29] Although honored by the invitation, he must have wondered just how strong were the bonds that bound him to the inner circle. Among many of that group, abolition had become more important than saving the Union, and he was not, nor had ever been, an abolitionist.

As the end of the year approached, Peyton saw attitudes among the Unionist leadership in Tennessee harden until it split into Radical and Conservative factions. Fighting a war to preserve the Union was not enough for those who would rule the occupied South with an iron hand while making ready to abolish slavery in the states. Governor Johnson, editor S. C. Mercer of the Nashville *Daily Union*, Gen. Alvan Gillem of East Tennessee, and Col. William B. Stokes emerged as leaders of the hard-line Radicals. Peyton, Campbell, and John Lellyett led the Conservatives who advocated a more compassionate administration of reconstruction, who objected to abolishing slavery, and who looked beyond the Republican Party for the next president.[30]

Although he gave politics continuing attention, Balie practiced law actively. At the beginning of the new year, 1864, he associated himself with the prominent attorney John S. Brien[31] of Nashville, a partnership that promised strong representation to clients in Middle Tennessee.[32] Litigation kept him busy. One particularly time-consuming case was his prosecution before a military commission of Confederate Army Pvt. Robert T. Gossett, charged with committing four separate murders, stealing, and attempting other murders in Robertson and Cheatham Counties.[33] Details are missing, but the commission convicted the soldier of murder, and he was hanged on July 8, 1864.[34]

In another trial before a military commission at Nashville, Peyton won freedom for a citizen who had been arrested and, without trial, sentenced by General Paine to be shot. His offense: devotion to the Confederacy. The offender, one Thompson of Sumner County, was placed in irons and held until the day set for his execution when friends informed Peyton of the situation. Faced with the shooting set for four o'clock that afternoon, Peyton induced General Rousseau at Nashville to countermand Paine's order and bring the prisoner to Nashville for trial. Acting as Thompson's attorney, Peyton defended him before a military commission in a three-week trial that exonerated him of any wrongdoing.[35] He continued until the end of hostilities to represent other local citizens in their relations with the military governor[36] and the occupying army.

Late summer brought a renewal of political maneuvering as parties, factions, and candidates worked out tickets for president and vice president. During August, Peyton traveled to Chicago to attend the Democratic Party Nominating Convention with a delegation led by William B. Campbell that included, in addition to himself, Jordan Stokes, John S. Brien, and William Lellyett. Checking into the Tremont House on August 26, the Tennesseans were among the earliest arrivals.[37]

In short order, the delegates chose a ticket of Gen. George B. McClellan for president and George H. Pendleton for vice president. But the conciliatory tone of the convention and the platform declaration in favor of immediate cessation of hostilities reassured Peyton. Although McClellan repudiated the peace plank as adopted, he tried to win support for peace by capitalizing on "Northern defeatism." However peace might be approached, the Democrats believed their ticket offered

Tennessee State Capitol during Civil War

a viable alternative to another four years of a Lincoln presidency. Peyton heartily concurred.[38]

As the Conservative Tennessee Unionists appeared to be defecting to the Democrats, their Radical brothers held a Union convention at Nashville to deal with the reduction in their ranks and to nominate a ticket of Lincoln and Andrew Johnson. Still in great numerical ascendancy, the Radicals adopted new requirements for suffrage that disenfranchised the peace-seeking Conservatives. The privilege of voting would be extended only to those who made an oath to "oppose all armistices or negotiations for peace with rebels" then in arms. To be eligible to vote, one had to disown the Democratic platform and candidate McClellan.[39]

At home from the Chicago convention, Peyton was momentarily slowed to inaction by the Radical stand to close the polls to McClellan voters. Still thoroughly committed to McClellan, he was dazed. His fellow delegate Jordan Stokes, unable to get Balie to move, wrote Campbell asking for help. Campbell must have delivered because by September 30, Peyton had agreed to run as an elector[40] for the McClellan ticket. Then on October 1, he addressed a meeting of McClellan supporters called by the local Constitutional Union Club.[41]

Warming to the McClellan gathering, Peyton predicted the election of Lincoln "would be the utter destruction of the only hope for the salvation of our bleeding country." On the other hand, he said the election of

McClellan would make possible a "permanent and glorious" peace and the Union "reestablished over every square foot of our great republic." McClellan's way was the humane way, he said, whereas Lincoln's was "subjugation and extermination."[42]

Peyton struck at what he saw as the Lincoln administration's use of excessive force during the occupation. Those from outside the state could not "appreciate or understand the atrocities and unrecorded crimes that had been committed by . . . heartless little despots" such as General Paine against the people of Tennessee, he declared. He did not believe there was an instance in history when a people had been "so trampled upon, so degraded, whose property had been so wantonly and rapaciously taken, [and] whose citizens had been so causelessly and hellishly murdered." He asked, "Is this the way to win back an erring people?"[43]

Referring to the governor as "Proclamation Johnson" for governing by loyalty oaths and proclamations, Peyton blamed him for the action of the Radical convention that required voters in the upcoming election "to swear they will not vote for McClellan before they can vote at all." As Johnson was a candidate for vice president on the Lincoln ticket, Peyton insisted he had no moral right to require voters to take loyalty oaths or sacrifice their right to vote. On this issue he found support from the *National Intelligencer* in Washington that agreed the oath was "over done."[44]

When the Tennessee McClellan electors further evaluated the governor's proclaimed requirements for voting, they drafted a protest to President Lincoln.[45] Acknowledging that there was a serious legal question about Tennessee's right to participate in the election, they were willing to leave that judgment to "competent authority." But if there was to be an election in the state, and if loyal men were entitled to vote, all loyal men should be permitted to vote, they petitioned, not just those aligned in support of the Lincoln-Johnson ticket. In order for all loyal men to enjoy the franchise freely, it would be necessary for the president to overrule the governor and order the military not to interfere in any way. They offered numerous objections to the governor's election oath as discriminatory against those loyal citizens who did not agree politically with him. All of the electors signed the petition, and one of them, John Lellyett, delivered it to the president on October 15 and asked for a reply to take back to Nashville.[46]

After reading the petition in Lellyett's presence, the president said that the document appeared to have been "concocted" with the help of "New York politicians." Assured by Lellyett that it was the work of Campbell, Peyton, and the other electors, Lincoln responded that he expected "to let the friends of George B. McClellan manage their side of this contest in their own way. And I will manage my side of it in my way." He did not put his answer in writing, but indicated that the McClellan electors would hear further from him.[47] The president had no intention of ruling in their favor.

Testing President Lincoln's expectation to let the Nashville friends of McClellan manage their side of the campaign "in their own way," the Conservatives organized a rally for the general on the evening of October 21 at the Davidson County Courthouse. They chose Peyton and Col. G. W. Ashburn of Georgia to speak to a crowd that included Union soldiers and government workers recruited in the North. After Ashburn had finished, Peyton took the platform amidst tumultuous applause. But before he could say more than a few words, shouts and loud footsteps on the stairway interrupted him. Pushing into the room, someone shouted, "Disperse you damned rebels and traitors!"[48]

> An armed band of soldiers burst suddenly into the room and with drawn bayonets and the most fiendish yells and oaths. . . . A scene of wild excitement ensued. The lights were extinguished, the crowd rushed pell-mell through the doors and out at the windows, and some even descended to the pavement below from the second story windows by the help of friends on the outside. The rest were rudely pushed down the stairs by the bayonet's point. The noise and confusion increased to the end, and, amid fierce shouts for Johnson and Lincoln by the intruders. Thus was a peaceful meeting of soldiers and citizens interrupted . . . broken up.[49]

Who had sent the armed soldiers in to break up the meeting? Most Conservative Unionists and McClellan men blamed it on Johnson, although an East Tennessee military unit claimed credit for initiating it. Blame or credit aside, the forceful suppression of free speech in a public political rally attracted attention outside the state. Indignant that the McClellan meeting had been broken up, the editor of the Louisville *Daily Journal* asked, "Is this Tory outrage to be regarded as the Concord of a new revolution?"[50]

Three days after the Peyton speech disturbance, Governor Johnson for the first time identified closely with the aspirations of African-Americans. Speaking to a large crowd, most of whom were still in bondage, he said he would be to them a "Moses," helping "to secure and perpetuate" their freedom. He also used the occasion to label the McClellan Conservative Unionists as rebels. Referring to the Peyton-McClellan meeting, he said, "We will not listen to their counsels. Nashville is no longer the place for them to hold their meetings. Let them gather their treasonable enclaves elsewhere."[51]

A day later Peyton and his fellow McClellan electors heard from the president. He would not sustain, modify, or revoke Johnson's plan but regarded the issue as one that should be settled at the state level. He advised the McClellan men, "Do as you please on your own account, peacefully and legally, and Governor Johnson will not molest you." As for his own part, Lincoln said that he would not interfere in the election in any way "except it be to give protection against violence."[52]

After reviewing the president's response, the electors reluctantly agreed to withdraw the McClellan-Pendleton ticket in Tennessee. They worked off a portion of their anger by drafting a letter, flavored with Peytonian sarcasm, to President Lincoln. Directing the president's attention to Johnson's election oath proclamation, the respondents blamed the president for failing to exercise adequate supervision of his subordinates. He was responsible for Johnson's acts because the authority of the military governor was derived directly from the president, they contended.[53]

The electors said the president's tolerance of "independent movements" such as had led to the suppression of Peyton's speech of the twenty-first was similar to the toleration of "independent movements" by governors in the South that had set off "the great rebellion." They remembered that Governor Harris's earlier movement for independence from the Union led to the same denial of civil rights that they were currently experiencing.[54]

The election in Tennessee on November 8 attracted such a low voter turnout that it was a farce. The vote in Shelby County showed Lincoln with 1,579 to 24 for McClellan. It was 1,317 to 25 for Lincoln in Nashville and 107 to 12 in Gallatin. Although the total vote is unknown, the electors cast their votes for Lincoln and Johnson, only to have Congress refuse to accept them because it regarded Tennessee as still in rebellion at the time of the election.[55] Nationwide Lincoln and Johnson won easily.

Governor Johnson's acts of blatant hostility to the McClellan Democratic ticket climaxed a growing split between him and Peyton. Step by step the governor had distanced himself from the former congressman by embracing Radical Republican policy, forcing his will on the occupied city of Nashville, and controlling elections in the state by requiring loyalty oaths of voters. Although Peyton at first had been one of his valued advisors, Johnson counseled with him less and less after mid-1863. The governor had become increasingly impatient and tended to rule by fiat.

The early months of 1864 had been tense times for Peyton, but as always his thoroughbreds offered diversion. Running in the first public competition since 1862, one of his horses won decisively over a Nashville entry at the Gallatin fall races. Looking ahead, Balie led the planning for a sweepstake for three-year-olds over the Albion Course at Gallatin to be run during the spring races of 1865. He and other local turfmen were determined to keep the "spirit of racing" alive in Sumner County.[56] But the war was not over.

Even before the election of Lincoln and Johnson, Peyton learned from press accounts that Gen. John Bell Hood had broken off contact with Sherman near Atlanta and was moving his Confederate forces northward toward Nashville. His entire army had crossed the Tennessee River by November 18, and on the afternoon of November 30, Hood reached Franklin to find the town defended by twenty-three thousand Union troops commanded by Gen. John M. Schofield. Deciding that he must immediately dislodge Schofield to clear his way to Nashville, Hood attacked the same day. He sent wave after wave against the Federals and took staggering losses, but after night fell, Schofield withdrew his troops to Nashville. Although he had lost five generals and several key field commanders, Hood followed and took up a position about three miles south of the Federal defense line that was anchored at Fort Negley.[57]

Closing his law office, Peyton retired to the Station Camp Creek farm where he wanted to be present to try to protect it if the Confederates should break through or around Nashville. When General Thomas attacked the rebel lines on December 15, Balie could hear the cannons clearly at the farm. It was the same the next day, but on December 17, the day was strangely quiet. Thomas had driven Hood out of his positions south of the city, and the Confederates were in full retreat.[58] Did Hood's defeat signal the beginning of the end for the Confederate Army in the Western Theater? Balie devoutly hoped that the fighting might soon stop.

The advent of the new year witnessed the dissolution of the partnership of Peyton and John S. Brien and the beginning of the partnership of Peyton and Philip Lindsley.[59] Occupying Balie's office at 44½ North Cherry Street, they practiced in both military and civil courts and were active in the collection of claims for eastern merchants.[60]

Entering the year 1865, Balie and many Nashvillians, both Union and Confederate, expected an early end to the war. They were not to be disappointed. Richmond fell on April 3, and General Lee surrendered to General Grant at Appomattox Courthouse, Virginia, on April 9. First seeing the news in print April 10 on the bulletin board of the *Dispatch* on Union Street, Peyton rushed back to his office before a tumultuous celebration developed in the downtown area. He would celebrate, too, but with anxious concern for the first years of peace.

Balie was uncertain about marching in the official Nashville victory parade. He was spared the decision on the morning of the event when news reached the city that President Lincoln had been assassinated. Military and city officials canceled the parade, and an attitude of jubilation abruptly turned into one of mourning. Balie attended a called meeting of the Nashville bar and joined his old friend Guild and the others present in drafting and signing resolutions of sympathy for the president's family and the nation.[61]

On the day of Lincoln's funeral, observed as a national day of mourning, Peyton took his place in the throngs that paraded through Nashville. The slow procession ended at a vacant field on Harding Pike where a speaker's stand had been erected. The ceremonies were concluded there with speeches by Governor Brownlow and General Rousseau, the latter of whom had become a close personal friend of Peyton's.[62]

The conclusion of the war suggested there would be changes in the political environment in Tennessee, but opinions differed on the nature of them. President Johnson's friend and advisor Sam Milligan[63] was confident that the legislature was "drifting under rebel influence." He attributed that development to the increasing power wielded by Peyton and Campbell and "their ilk" who, he observed caustically, had "suddenly grown great, and I predict will shape the legislation of the state."[64] Balie enjoyed Milligan's prediction that he would wield decisive power in formulating state legislation, but he resented the suggestion that it would be used to return control of the state exclusively to secessionists.

Summertime brought with it the approach of congressional elections. Anxious to try to moderate the policies of the Radical Unionists, Balie not so secretly yearned to go back to Congress. He wrote to William B. Campbell on June 23, asserting his preference for the former governor to be the candidate but taking care to tell him that he himself had been strongly solicited to run. In fact, Balie wrote, "If you decline the canvass, I will run and have my name at once announced, as candidates are multiplying and the time is short."[65]

John Lellyett seemed to think that Balie would not make a satisfactory candidate, and Jordan Stokes believed that in any event, Balie would not run. Another political friend, J. C. Golladay, tried to get Campbell to commit to running but begged him to clear the field for Peyton if he was not going to become a candidate.[66] Wasting no more time, Campbell decided to become a candidate about July 1 and sent a note to Gallatin notifying Peyton. Although disappointed that the former governor had not deferred to him, Balie professed to be pleased with the decision.[67]

Peyton was having a better time of it on the Nashville Race Course where horses belonging to him and General Rousseau were winning most of the races. Their bubble of success burst after they sought to disqualify a horse because he was called Unknown and had no pedigree. Voted down, Peyton and the general watched helplessly as Unknown beat their horses in the next race.[68]

Racing in Nashville returned to its traditional spring and fall pattern on October 16, 1865. Turf editors recognized the schedule as the beginning "of the revival" of racing in Tennessee and applauded the historic production of fine thoroughbreds in the state. Proud that the track once again provided a venue for the sport of kings, Peyton judged some of the October races. He was most rewarded, however, when his black filly Minnie Waters won the Laurence Stake in two heats on October 16.[69]

With the help of Balie and others, along with his own hard work and good reputation, Campbell was elected to Congress. Soon after he arrived in Washington, he received a letter from Peyton transmitting claims against the federal government in the amount of $2,299 sought by Mrs. Maggie A. Elliott, daughter of Balie's neighbor, the Unionist and old Whig William Franklin. The claims were "for forage and other articles taken by Col. [David R.] Haggard and General Paine for the public use" for which they issued no vouchers. Balie had no doubt that the 150 to 200 barrels of corn taken by Haggard was "applied to the public use." He was in doubt about General Paine who, "as you know, had a way of his own about such things, and whether he applied [them to] the public or his own use is more than Mrs. Elliott knows."[70]

Promising to supply evidence to support the claim, Balie asked for information about the form in which it should be presented. Begging Campbell to give his "early attention" to the matter, he said that General Rousseau, then in Washington, would render him "any service in his power."[71] Rousseau had resigned from the army and, as a Radical Republican, won a seat in the Congress in 1865. The fixation of his Radical colleagues on measures to punish the seceded states resulted in his abandoning their cause and becoming a proponent of moderation in dealing with the South and a supporter of President Johnson.[72] The Congressional Radicals would soon affect Peyton the same way.

The end of the war was just that. Military operations ended; fighting ceased. The federal government had no plans or strategies to restore the rebel states to their prewar places in the Union. There had been virtually no thought of providing for a constructive transition from slave to citizen. There was no movement toward aiding the South in economic reconstruction or lessening the economic impact of the termination of slavery on the region. The lack of planning led to the development of federal policies that grew out of the arrogance of victory and the "realization of newly-found power." Though "spent and exhausted," the South offered "stolid resistance to the unfriendly gestures of its assailants."[73]

Yet Lincoln and Johnson believed that the people of the North desired "to be magnanimous to the defeated South." On April 14, 1865, Lincoln had explicitly cautioned North and South to extinguish all resentments "if we expect harmony and Union." Johnson spoke for many Unionists when he said of the people of the former confederacy, "I do not want them to come back into this Union a degraded and debased people."[74] The conversion of these noble sentiments into practical policy was opposed effectively for more than a little while by Unionists who believed that the seceding states should be punished first, helped later. All seemed content to rest the future of the former slaves in the hands of missionaries and school teachers supported by northern philanthropy.

War had not solved problems. It had only provided a new period of peace in which victor and vanquished were left to address again the issues that they had faced at its beginning. The victors, however, held the power to impose their will.

RECONSTRUCTION—
TRY AS HE MIGHT
1866–1875

Although the Union had survived and was beginning its first full year of peace since 1860, Peyton could find little in the conduct of the federal government that bode well for the future. He was "not so much surprised as disgusted at the . . . state of affairs in Washington." Confiding to William B. Campbell on January 5, 1866, he wrote:

> In the worst days of the French revolution there were few worse men than [Thaddeus] Stevens and [Charles] Sumner. They are absolute despots in the two houses. . . . I am sure they would confiscate the land and other property of the South to pay the national debt. I have a hope [that] . . . before many years . . . the West will induce a union with the South so as to protect both sections—the great planting and agricultural interests—against unjust and partial legislation. But the South has a long, dreary night before it.[1]

While outraged by the actions of Stevens and Sumner in the Congress and smarting from the treatment he had received from the Radicals in Nashville, Peyton still believed in representative government. He demonstrated his faith by going before the voters of Sumner and Smith Counties in 1866 as a candidate for state senator. Inspired by the Conservative sweep of county general elections in March, he was severely disheartened soon afterward when that very result caused the Radical-controlled legislature to enact enforcement measures for the franchise law that prohibited rebels, former rebels, and rebel sympathizers from voting.[2]

Even though by midsummer Conservatives were discussing various possibilities of ousting Governor Brownlow and his administration,[3] Peyton clung to his course of seeking elective office as the best opportunity to exert influence on state government. If he lost the election, flagrant voter control by the Radicals would be exposed graphically. If he should win, he would then be in a position to be heard and possibly to influence the behavior of the legislature.

On July 23, 1866, Balie was grateful to learn that President Johnson had signed congressional resolutions restoring Tennessee to its former relation to the Union,[4] even though he knew the other former Confederate states were still at the mercy of the Radicals in Congress. Noting that the state's congressional delegation had taken their seats, he was reasonably confident that Senators Joseph Smith Fowler and David Patterson would support reconciliation in preference to punitive reconstruction measures. Balie was less sure of the stands that might be taken by the state's congressmen.

At the local level there was no hope for Conservative Unionist candidates. Balie experienced it firsthand. Radical control of voter registration was so complete by the autumn elections that he was one of only 108 voters permitted to register in his home county where, before 1862, about 3,000 votes were usually cast in local and state contests. There was no chance for a Conservative candidate, as tightly controlled voter registration throughout both Sumner and Smith Counties effectively disenfranchised most Conservatives.[5]

On November 4, Peyton lost to Hiram S. Patterson, a Smith County Radical, by slightly more than one hundred votes. The margin did not expose the Radicals' voter control as clearly as Peyton had hoped. He shrugged helplessly when the anti-Peyton editor of the Nashville *Daily Press and Times* chortled with glee as he announced Patterson's victory over "the heretofore invincible Peyton . . . the Copperhead candidate."[6]

Defeat at the hands of the Radicals only heightened Peyton's resolve to return to public office. As for the upcoming congressional elections of 1867, he believed that his friend the incumbent William B. Campbell could be reelected, probably without opposition. If Campbell were not going to run, Balie was ready to seek the office, trusting always that his candidacy would be "entirely agreeable" to the Conservatives of the district.[7]

Despite his optimism, Peyton well knew that any Conservative Unionist candidate would be at a great disadvantage because of the power of the Radicals. Looking beyond the state, Peyton presciently predicted that the Radicals would impeach the president "at this session or . . . the next" because "they want his office." Completing a quick commentary on the national scene, he suggested that General Grant would not stand by the president because they would hold out the White House to him as bait. "Oh," Peyton exclaimed, "for one term of Old Hickory!"[8]

During the latter part of March, the political situation at both national and state levels so distressed him that momentarily he lost interest in seeking public office. He complained to Campbell: "I am sincerely fearful that our free system of government is gone forever, and have no heart, nor hope, nor disposition to mingle in the sad and destructive current of events."[9]

"Parson" William Gannaway Brownlow

Warm weather and the June selection of a Conservative candidate for governor revived Balie's interest in winning nomination to Congress by what had by then become known as the Conservative Union Party. He had joined members of the party when they embraced the leadership of President Johnson and the Washington Conservatives who wished to implement the Lincoln-Johnson policy of leniency in reconstruction.[10] But he was not the only one of his political colleagues who aspired to represent the Fifth Congressional District in Washington.

A week before the Conservative Union District Nominating Convention, John Lellyett solicited Campbell's support for the nomination. Listing Judge Thomas N. Frazier, John S. Brien, William G. Brien, and himself as "willing" to run for Congress, Lellyett then reduced the list by elimination until only he remained. At that point he offered to withdraw in favor of Campbell, should the former governor seek the nomination. Dismissing Peyton as "hardly thought of here [Nashville]," Lellyett suggested that the former congressman had certain personal characteristics or other behavioral baggage that weighed heavily upon him. "If those who have a right to judge, think it wise to run Peyton, I am *not unwilling* to stand aside for him. I highly respect and love the noble heart of this man and deplore his disqualifications. If, however, he were sent to Washington, it would be the means of doing him harm and us no good."[11]

What were the "disqualifications" that Lellyett mentioned? Was Balie drinking alcohol excessively? Was he gambling recklessly? Either of these or a combination of the two might have been the answer. Political canvasses have frequently inspired the excessive consumption of alcohol by candidates and their supporters. And it is true that horse races not only afforded gamblers an opportunity to participate beyond their financial means, but made it unthinkable for owners not to bet on their own entries. Although there is almost no mention of Balie's shortcomings in preserved correspondence, William B. Campbell hinted in a letter about this time that all was not well with Balie. All of his friends in Middle Tennessee were prospering in the immediate postwar business climate, he said, "with the exception of Peyton."[12]

Peyton wanted to be a candidate, even though the general assembly had enfranchised African-American men on February 26 as a part of Governor Brownlow's plan to keep his regime in power. The right to vote was so well received that it virtually guaranteed African-Americans would cast their votes for Brownlow's Radicals.[13] But Peyton was not deterred.

Appearing at the Fifth District Convention held in Nashville, July 6, 1867, Balie received the nomination for Congress after a prearranged complimentary vote had nominated Judge Thomas N. Frazier of Nashville, who had declined to accept it.[14] At the age of sixty-four, a serious "disqualification" for Balie was poor health, so poor at that time he doubted he would be able to travel the district during the campaign. But he pledged to do all that he could to acquaint the voters with the overriding issue of the contest: "freedom and prosperity versus slavery and degradation with no hope of enfranchisement." His opponent was the Nashville attorney John S. Trimble, who had previously served in both houses of the Tennessee General Assembly.[15]

The action of the convention unleashed showers of praise upon the nominee, including this comment by the editor of the *Republican Banner*:

> The nomination of the Hon. Balie Peyton recalled as Gov. Foote remarked, the older and better days of the republic. Judge [John S.] Brien spoke in warm and feeling terms of his old companion and friend. So may we all, for there is not a purer nor better man in Tennessee. Generous and spirited, eloquent and consistent, he presents a brilliant contrast to his competitor.[16]

In a hastily assembled but largely attended public meeting at Gallatin on July 8, Peyton announced his acceptance of the nomination and declared his optimism about the contest. On the day before, two Nashville newspapers endorsed him. One editor observed, "He is at once earnest and humorous, brilliant and profound, capable of reaching every comprehension."[17] Another, describing Peyton as "a man of large experience and ability as a statesman," said that news of his nomination would be received "with a thrill of satisfaction throughout the district."[18]

Not all were thrilled by Peyton's nomination, and the editor of the *Daily Press and Times* predicted dire consequences for his candidacy.

> The nominee, who had some distinction in the ante-bellum political contests, is well known as a steadfast enemy of all Radical measures presented to the country. . . . He was badly beaten last year in his own district for state senator by Mr. [Hiram S.] Patterson and will be buried out of sight by Mr. [John] Trimble.[19]

On the day before the election, Peyton swore the candidate's oath of allegiance before a Radical justice of the peace at Gallatin.[20] But there was little prospect for success on the next day. The polls would be open in Gallatin, but all other polling precincts in the county would be closed. One by one the judges and clerks had resigned as the day of election approached, intimidated by threats of what might happen to them if they received the votes of former slave males, who were newly eligible to vote in Tennessee. Recognizing that the support of freedmen throughout the county was solidly behind Trimble, the Radicals set up additional voting places for them in Gallatin. A company of regular army soldiers guaranteed their safety going to and from the polls.[21]

When the votes were counted after the polls closed on August 1, Peyton was badly defeated. Districtwide totals showed Trimble had 9,357 votes, Balie had 3,163, and D. H. Mason had 480. The Radical Union Party had controlled the vote in Sumner County so successfully that Peyton ran third at home, receiving only 233 votes to Mason's 328 and Trimble's 625.[22] In normal times the loss would have been humiliating, but these were not normal times. It was the first occasion in American history that African-Americans had voted in large numbers. Radical candidates celebrated a landslide victory. Governor Brownlow was reelected; all Radical candidates for Congress and all but three Radical candidates for the general assembly were elected as well.[23]

Drained both physically and emotionally by the futile campaign, Balie was ill-prepared to receive news of the death of his long-time political ally William B. Campbell on August 19. Cherishing the mutual respect that existed between them for more than three decades, he rushed to the Campbell home in Lebanon twenty miles away to be at the side of the grief-stricken family.[24] He truly shared their pain.

In 1868, the strength of the Radical Union Party was so great in Sumner County that its leaders began to challenge certain rulings by Judge Thomas Barry and soon turned against him, although they had applauded the even-handed justice he had previously dispensed. The fact that Peyton was his brother-in-law did not help him in his relationships with them. Serving as chancellor of the Seventh Division and judge of the Circuit Court of Sumner County, he had been appointed by

Governor Brownlow only "until his successor should be chosen and qualified." Such an appointment left the door open to a special election and, responding to pleas from Sumner Radicals, the governor called an election for March 28. With control of the election machinery in their hands, the Radicals were certain they could replace Barry with the man of their own choosing: James F. Lauck, a Kentuckian, former colonel in the Union Army, and chairman of the Sumner Republican Union Party.[25]

Peyton moved quickly to enlist support for Judge Barry. It came readily from Conservative Unionists and former Confederate soldiers and sympathizers, but a well-attended mass meeting of "the loyal people of Sumner county" held at Gallatin on March 10 endorsed Lauck.[26]

The campaign was fiercely contested, and as it neared the end, both sides predicted violence at the polls and each prepared its own defenses. On election day the Radicals produced a legally constituted "metropolitan police force" of eighty "colored men" under the command of a white captain and a sergeant. The force had been created by deputizing the officers and men of the local company of Governor Brownlow's new state guard. To thwart the designs of the metropolitans, Peyton and other friends of Barry persuaded the mayor of Gallatin to muster special police volunteers. Identified by a badge prepared for the occasion, each furnished his own arms. The exact number was never recorded, but it was believed to have been in excess of three hundred.[27]

During the day, the local regular army detachment twice intervened to prevent a confrontation between the two partisan police forces. Throughout the night, army patrols moved through the streets and violence was averted.[28]

When votes were counted, Lauck appeared to be the winner. Employing Jo. C. Guild as his attorney, Barry filed for an injunction to prohibit Lauck from taking office because large numbers of voters had been denied an opportunity to vote and the ballots of others had been thrown out. Challenging the validity of the election, Guild appealed the lawsuit all the way to the state supreme court. On March 12, 1869, the court ruled that no valid election had been held and that, as a result, Barry was still in office.[29] Guild had consulted frequently with Peyton on the legal steps taken in Barry's behalf.

Like many Tennesseans who had opposed much of Andrew Johnson's behavior as military governor, Peyton had realigned with Johnson when the Radicals turned against him.[30] At the same time, most of his staunchest supporters during the war moved into the Radicals' camp because they thought he was not penalizing the rebel states sufficiently. In their new roles as Johnson advocates, Peyton and most Conservative Unionists became Democrats. Eager to cement his new political relationship, Balie was present as convener and temporary chair when county representatives of "the Democracy of Tennessee" gathered at the state capitol on June 9. His was a strong voice in the Democrats' endorsement of Johnson as the party nominee in the upcoming presidential election.[31]

During the late summer of 1868, there was public movement toward moderation and respect for the law and away from confrontation and violence. By September 19, Peyton had taken a seat on a countywide joint committee that he had helped organize. It included representatives of both political parties dedicated to holding free and open elections and bringing an end to the intimidation, threats, and power plays that had surrounded recent balloting. The membership of the committee was evenly divided between representatives of the two parties: the Republican Union Party (Radicals) and the Democrats (Conservatives).[32]

Ready for an election free of governmental restraint, voters throughout the county welcomed the committee. Peyton appealed for voters' peaceful cooperation on election day and asked Governor Brownlow to abort any plans he might have for sending state militia to patrol the precincts.[33] At the last minute, the governor appointed the Nashville town marshal to be commissioner of registration for Sumner County, a move that focused renewed attention on voter eligibility. On election day, the commissioner's clumsy handling of registration certificates was suspect in the eyes of most and resulted in a number of eligible voters losing their right to vote. The Radical William F. Prosser[34] carried the day in Sumner County for Congress, and the Democrat Horatio Seymour outpolled General Grant for president 490 to 470. Locals grumbled loudly about Brownlow's commissioner of registration, although it was generally accepted that his bungling efforts had little or no effect on the relative totals polled in the county.[35]

The beginning of the end of Radical control in Tennessee came in 1869 with the resignation of Governor Brownlow to take a seat in the U.S. Senate. As the Democrats began to line up candidates for state and local elections, the Hartsville *Vidette* proposed Peyton as a candidate for governor. But the party leaders decided to field no candidate for the gubernatorial election; they threw their support to DeWitt C. Senter, the decidedly more moderate of two Radical contenders.[36]

Planning carefully for its party to reclaim the Sumner County legislative delegation, the Democrats nominated Peyton for state senator from Sumner and Smith, Judge Barry for floterial representative, and J. T. Baber for direct representative. The Republicans countered with Thompson McKinley for senator, William M. Woodcock for floterial representative, and Nelson Turner for direct representative. Three weeks before the election, McKinley withdrew, leaving Peyton unopposed.[37]

The other Republican nominees remained in the contest, but to no avail. On August 6, local Democrats celebrated with the election of Peyton, Barry, and Baber.[38] The sweep in Sumner County was repeated in enough counties of the state that Democrats wrested control of both houses of the general assembly.[39] Senter was elected governor.

Three weeks later the Nashville *Union and American*, usually hostile to Peyton, printed a letter to the editor recommending him to succeed U.S. Senator Fowler, who had announced he would not stand for a second term.[40] If he should seek the office, Balie would face opposition from former President Andrew Johnson, who was generally regarded as a certain selection for it. Outside the state, a political observer noted that he was "the only prominent candidate" who could compete with Johnson for the Conservative vote. A report from Washington, however, claimed that measures had been taken "to secure Peyton's withdrawal from the canvass."[41] Recommendations, observations, and claims aside, when both houses of the general assembly met in joint session to elect the senator, Peyton's name was among the first of eight proposed. In the early balloting, he received the vote of Senator Henry Cooper of Davidson County, among others, but in successive ballots the field narrowed until Peyton withdrew and voted for Cooper, who was elected over the only other remaining nominee, former President Andrew Johnson.[42]

As the senators settled into the first session of the thirty-sixth general assembly,[43] Peyton accepted appointment to three of the standing committees of the senate: judiciary, federal relations, and public grounds and buildings. On October 28, he teamed with Barry, Baber, and others of like mind to abolish the county commission act and return county control to the quarterly courts. They next passed an act amending the charter of the city of Gallatin that eliminated provisions written in by the Radicals to disenfranchise Southern sympathizers and to assure Radical control.[44] Throughout the session Balie was remarkably quiet, a situation that at sixty-six years of age may have led to a newsman's observation that he was too old to hold "many more offices."[45]

Peyton did his best to quash rumors and correct false reports that sometimes circulated in Gallatin. On June 17, 1867, he was coauthor of a letter to the Nashville *Republican Banner* to correct a baseless report that there had been a "row" between the militia and U.S. Army regulars at Gallatin. The exaggerated story grew out of a minor disagreement between one of the militia and a physician. Peyton endorsed the regulars as "well behaved and well-disciplined . . . [who] act as soldiers should do."[46] He believed there was nothing better than truth to defuse explosive situations.

Although Balie's term in the state senate had been relatively uneventful, it had rekindled his interest in returning to the Congress. By

1870, his Unionist convictions and his undying ambition to hold high elective office united to make it deceptively easy for him to believe he could be elected to Congress as an independent, free of party nomination. And that meant leaving the Democrats he had so recently joined. He should have remembered that he had convinced Zachary Taylor to permit himself to be nominated and supported by a political party, a decision that led him directly to the White House. But the times were vastly different. Perhaps he was looking at the incumbent Congressman Prosser, who declined to submit to his party's convention two years before but was elected as an unaffiliated candidate.[47] Based on a growing Conservative momentum, Balie somehow concluded that he and the convention-nominated Conservative Democrat would have the race to themselves, with the Radical Union nominee trailing far behind.

Why did he think that he could defeat a convention-nominated candidate of essentially the same political persuasion? It was true that he had been a major player in local and regional politics wherever he had resided, but he held views that for the most part were too moderate for the early postwar years. He was not radical enough for the Radicals, nor was he conservative enough for the Conservatives. He had opposed abolition—but not as much as he opposed secession. Yet he thought that his previous experience in the Congress plus his support for the McClellan Democrats in 1864 were credentials enough to bring him a decisive number of Conservative votes.

When an even number of Sumner County Radicals and Conservatives published a request that he become a candidate for the House of Representatives from the Fifth Congressional District,[48] Peyton was eager to accommodate them. On June 3, 1870, he announced his candidacy. He would run against "the evils of centralized despotism," convinced that the House was the "forum where alone the great battle of Constitutional freedom must be fought."[49]

On June 16, the Nashville *Republican Banner* declared its opposition to nominating conventions, charging that they were generally controlled in advance by a principal candidate and did not reflect the opinions of rank-and-file members of the party. Sympathetic to Peyton, the newspaper was trying to prepare the way for him.

Unimpressed by the newspaper's denunciation of conventions, Edward L. Golladay of Wilson County posted his announcement for Congress subject to nomination by the Democratic District Convention.[50] A fortnight later the *Republican Banner* again editorialized strongly against nominating conventions and the "growing unpopularity" of such systems to select candidates.[51]

On October 19, the morning before the nominating convention, Peyton announced through the press that he would not submit to the action of that body.[52] On the next day the convention chose Golladay as the Democratic nominee for the Fifth District congressional seat, but the decision was not reached until the seventeenth ballot.[53]

Peyton had believed from the beginning that he held a trump card, and he played it on the second day after the convention. The Congress, he had been advised, would not seat Golladay because he could not take the test oath that affirmed he had been loyal to the United States throughout the Civil War and had not at any time assisted the rebellion in any fashion. Peyton was then left as the only viable Conservative candidate because he could take the oath. To prove his point, Peyton released a letter from Sam J. Randall, chairman of the National Democratic Executive Resident Committee, that firmly recommended "the nomination to Congress of such only as can take that oath." Under a date of September 15, the opinion of the committee was that "*practically*, the Radical clerk of the House would not place on the roll or permit a voice in the organization of the House one who cannot take the test oath." In conclusion the committee observed, "We all know what the Radical Party are capable of doing, and that they need but the shadow of a pretext to keep out a candidate of Democratic or Conservative tendencies."[54]

As Peyton's campaign became a serious threat to Golladay's, the editor of the *Union and American* announced he would redirect his fire from other races to focus on this one. Devoting nearly three columns of print to disparaging Peyton on October 28, he tried to tie him to the Radicals. His presence in the race would benefit the Radicals because a serious split of the Conservative vote would open the way for the incumbent candidate William F. Prosser. The newspaper opposed Balie "more in sorrow than in anger" because it recalled the time "when the name of Balie Peyton was like the white plume of Henry of Navarre; at the sight of which the ranks closed up, dissensions ceased, all knew that the cause led the man, and that the man was leader of the cause." Such was no longer the case because the editor could see "upon his flag . . . no bright emblazon of his principles, but only the name of Balie Peyton."[55]

After opening debates at Gallatin and Lebanon, Peyton and Golladay staged their first disputation in Nashville on October 26 without the Radical nominee and continued that pattern throughout most of the canvass. Golladay said that he had been chosen by the convention as the best one to fight against Radicalism whereas Peyton offered himself without the endorsement of a group of his political peers. It was a case of the regular nominee against the self-appointed, he said.[56]

The choice of candidates by a convention is not a valid procedure, Peyton contended, because such gatherings, "as a general thing, do not represent the people." He distrusted conventions and especially the most recent one, which had nominated a candidate whose Civil War record precluded his oath of office from being accepted. He reminded the voters that the seventy-five Democrats in the House had advised the Tennessee Party "to send no one there" who could not honestly take the oath.[57]

The two candidates subsequently met and debated at Franklin, Springfield, Ashland City, and several times at Nashville.[58] The Democrats staged a rally on November 3 in Nashville at the Chattanooga Depot, and the leadership granted Peyton's request to split the time allotted to his opponent. Speaking for Golladay, John C. Burch charged that Peyton was advertising himself as a "Democratic Conservative," trying to capture the Democratic vote while challenging the operation of the Democratic Party.[59]

In response to Burch, Peyton professed to be just as good a Democrat as Burch and a much "older Democrat in the party." He had been one of very few Democrats targeted by the opposition who used armed force to prevent him from speaking for the Democratic ticket in 1864.[60]

The *Republican Banner* stood by Peyton until the end. On November 5 the editor wrote:

> There are a thousand reasons for, to one against, the election of Hon. Balie Peyton to Congress. . . . He is . . . a surviving oak among the giants of the forest of that period when he was the compeer of such statesmen as the Bells, the Websters, and Clays. . . . A citizen of irreproachable character; of large experience and sagacity . . . of the highest order of manhood.

As November 8 drew nearer, Peyton and Golladay staged most of their debates in Nashville. On November 4 they appeared at the Nashville Market House, each apparently preoccupied with answering charges that the other had previously lodged.[61] They met again at the corner of Market and Broad on the evening of November 5, but their discussion degenerated into an argument that reflected little credit on either. Both candidates were nervous and exhausted.[62]

A final rally promoted by friends of Peyton was held at the Market House on election eve with a large crowd present. Two speakers summarized the case for Peyton, and one of them, William G. Brien, closed the evening with a tribute to Balie and a reassurance to the voters. He concluded: "Make Balie Peyton your standard bearer, and your banner will never trail in the dust, and if it sinks in the action, it will be crimsoned with the best blood that ever warmed the heart of mortal man."[63]

Election day passed quietly, and as the first precinct reports began to reach Nashville, there were indications that Peyton had fared poorly.

When all the votes were in, Golladay was the victor. He had even won in Sumner County, receiving fifteen more votes than Balie who, in turn, received only sixteen more than Prosser. In the district totals, Balie finished last. "A purer man was never defeated for so high a trust by such improper agencies," the *Republican Banner* declared in conceding Peyton's defeat.[64]

Democrats had turned against Balie for his unwillingness to stand for nomination at the party convention and for his determination to thwart its will. Many voted against him because of his long, strong stand for the Union, especially during the war years. Some turned away from him because they had come to regard him as a perennial candidate.

Making frequent trips to the sickbed of William Trousdale for the next several months, Peyton could tell that the former governor was gradually becoming weaker and weaker. At first Balie would entertain him with humorous stories from his vast repertoire, but by Christmas 1871 his stories fell on deaf ears. On March 27, 1872, William Trousdale died, and on the next day Balie attended the funeral service at the Presbyterian church with Fannie and John. Joined by a large delegation of attorneys and political figures from Nashville, they followed the procession to the Gallatin City Cemetery only a few blocks away. The sad occasion reminded Balie that the sands of time were running low for him just as surely as they had run out for Governor Trousdale.[65]

Not ready to slow his pace, Peyton instead enlisted in active opposition to Grant's bid for a second term in the White House. Certain that the incumbent's first term had failed miserably in reuniting the country, he made common cause with the ticket of Horace Greeley and Gratz Brown in 1872. Greeley and Brown had been nominated by a convention of Liberal Republicans at Columbus, Ohio, and by the Democratic National Convention at Baltimore. Balie agreed with delegates to both conventions who professed to want a president who could bind up the nation's wounds from the war years and turn its face to the future. They had chosen Greeley because he had embraced a federal policy of moderation toward the South.[66]

Joining both political friends and former opponents, Balie appeared before the ratification meeting for the ticket at Nashville on July 20, 1872. Acknowledging that Greeley had been an early advocate of Lincoln's Emancipation Proclamation, he recalled Greeley's "magnanimous act" of making bail for Jefferson Davis. Had the tables been turned, the only man in the South who would have had the courage to make bail for Lincoln was Robert E. Lee, Peyton said. But his primary reason for voting for Greeley was that he regarded him as "a brave, incorruptible patriot whose election would result beneficially to the whole country."[67]

Although attention to out-of-state personal business precluded political activity that might again have placed him before the voters, the ever-respected Peyton was injected into the 1874 District Congressional Convention after the 95th ballot. He and S. M. Fite, a Trousdale County judge, remained in the mix of candidates until the 109th ballot, when only the two were left, and the delegates nominated Fite by a vote of 179 to 33.[68]

But for Balie there always seemed to be one more chance. The regular election for Congress came up the very next year, and he permitted friends to propose his name to the Democrats' Fourth District Nominating Convention[69] at Carthage. After eighty-three ballots, during which his name was put up and withdrawn several times, the delegates chose H. Y. Riddle of Wilson County.[70] This time Balie understood. He was seventy-two years old, and it was time for younger persons to take over the challenging roles that had to be filled in the American political drama.[71]

Although practicing law did not hold the fascination for him that politics afforded, Peyton regarded it as his primary profession throughout the postwar years. In 1865, he and Philip Lindsley had pursued their law practice in the military and civil courts of Davidson County and advertised prompt attention to the collection claims for out-of-town creditors. The Peyton-Lindsley partners terminated their association after twelve months, and soon afterward Balie moved his office to Gallatin.[72] At the first of the year 1867, Peyton formed a law partnership there with R. A. and W. H. Bennett[73] that lasted until 1869, when he reopened his own office in Nashville at No. 1, the Porter Block. For the next two years Peyton kept an office in both Nashville and Gallatin; but beginning in 1871, he maintained an office only in Gallatin where he continued to practice for the rest of his life.[74]

Law practice and politics notwithstanding, Peyton had resumed breeding racehorses in 1866. But it was almost as if he were starting anew. Four years of war had greatly reduced the number of horses in his and other Middle Tennessee stables. Both armies had taken many of the animals. A person unknown, presumably a soldier, stole Peyton's mare Noty Price from her pasture in 1862, leaving behind an unweaned colt by Revenue called Chickahominy.[75]

In April 1866, Peyton sent horses to the stables at the Nashville track to prepare for the spring races where he entered Chickamauga, but later withdrew him.[76] For the Nashville Blood Horse Association races that opened November 6, he entered Chickamauga and Chickahominy, another chestnut colt, and watched both finish just off the pace in

Balie Peyton, circa 1875   *William Giles Harding*

each of their races.[77] He felt like going back to California to look for gold where the long odds of striking it rich appeared a better bet than his racehorses.

Peyton fielded no entries in the Nashville races from 1867 through 1870.[78] He was frequently at the track, however. A writer for the *Spirit of the Times* chose Peyton and William G. Harding from "the many distinguished turfmen present" for special mention when he reported the spring races of 1868.[79]

During these years Balie concentrated on his stud operation. He bred horses for others to own and race. Muggins, a four-year-old bright sorrel bred by Peyton at the Station Camp Creek stud, was running for others and won the Saratoga Cup race on August 8, 1867, at Saratoga, New York. Balie had sold Muggins when he was a two-year-old, and the horse's success added more to the breeder's reputation than to his treasury.[80]

In June 1868, Peyton had eleven thoroughbreds at the farm, and among them were the prize stud Gen. Rousseau, only recently retired from the track, and the proven racer Richelieu, both owned by others but boarded with Peyton. Of his own horses he considered Rapid Ann, a four-year-old chestnut filly by Jack Malone, dam Fanny McAlister, to be the "most promising animal" he ever owned. She was one of the few in training to race; the others were brood mares or at stud.[81]

Just over a year later, during the Fair and Race Week at Nashville beginning October 18, 1869, Peyton listed for sale Alboni, Panama,

Minnie Waters, Rapid Ann, Molly Bang, Chickahominy, Tom Smiley, and Richelieu. In addition he offered to sell High Constable, Carlotta Haviland, and Nickajack.[82]

One of the highlights of Balie's postbellum years as a turfman was the visit of J. H. Wallace, author of *Wallace's American Stud Book* and later editor of *Wallace's Monthly*. A few hours after he arrived in Nashville in the summer of 1868,[83] Wallace was seated in a hotel dining room where he observed "a large and remarkably fine looking gentleman enter the room and cast his eyes over the guests as if looking for someone."

When the man moved toward his table, Wallace became quite excited and described the experience in his monthly magazine of February 1876:

> The whole appearance, and especially the face, impressed me as that of a remarkable man; but I had not time for further observation till he was at my table and inquired if I was Mr. Wallace. . . . He gave his hand, and also his name, Balie Peyton . . . of all the distinguished Tennesseans then living, there was no one I was so anxious to meet as the Hon. Balie Peyton. When a boy I had read of him as a politician and statesman in the days of Jackson, and as a leader to the opposition of his administration in the counsels of the nation. At a later period I had read of him as one of the great breeders and race horse men of his generation. It appeared hardly possible that the man who had filled so large a place in public affairs, thirty or forty years before, should still possess so many of the marks of vigorous manhood.[84]

A few weeks later, Wallace visited the Station Camp farm, and he and Balie "literally filled up [every day] with racing and political reminiscences of a past generation." They rode the farm together and speculated unendingly about the future of racing in the South. In Wallace's turf world, Balie Peyton was still a man of the very highest standing.[85]

As flattered as he was by Wallace's visit, Peyton was like other Middle Tennessee breeders who kept their stables open only by sheer determination. With the exception of the Belle Meade stud, the other operators dealt daily with the inadequacy or total absence of capital funds. Assessing the situation of Sumner County breeders at midyear 1868, a visiting writer concluded that they needed help. "The present breeders are broken down and made poor by the war," he wrote, "and they will welcome gentlemen of means to come among them and help build up their once rich and beautiful country."[86]

Despite his inability to breed, sell, and race in the manner he would have chosen, Peyton was still regarded by his peers as "the Nestor of the Tennessee Turf." During "an impromptu entertainment" at Kenny and Wand's Merchant Exchange at the end of the third day of the 1868 fall races at Nashville, members of the Nashville Blood Horse Association enjoyed Peyton's comments on local turf history. In a brief speech, he "reviewed in his happiest style the history of the blooded horses of this state, and the famed contests of other days."[87]

For the next several years, Balie was unable to accomplish much with his horses. The severe blow to thoroughbred breeding in Tennessee delivered by the war was one from which it would never fully recover. Clinging to the hope that the industry might yet come back, he tried to keep a few thoroughbreds in his stables. He stayed in touch with other breeders by attending sales and races, visiting their stables, and occasionally trading horses.[88]

Fellow turfmen were pleased in January 1871, when the Nashville Blood Horse Association made Peyton an honorary member and appointed him to its rules revision committee.[89] Although he appreciated the honor, he was even more pleased when his mare Panama dropped a chestnut filly colt by Muggins on April 20 at the farm. Reporting his good fortune, he jested that when just two and a half days old, the filly had run 440 yards in the incredibly fast time of twenty-four and one-half seconds.[90] Ten days later at William Giles Harding's sale, Peyton purchased a thoroughbred chestnut colt foaled in 1869, Bengal by Blacklock.[91] Earlier in the year he had purchased two fillies from the Allman stock farm in Giles County to train at Station Camp.[92]

When time came for the Nashville spring races, Balie entered the five-year-old bay gelding Morgan Scout by John Morgan, dam Lizzie Morgan, by Imp. Glencoe in a contest of two-mile heats for all ages, but his horse was distanced.[93] He sold Morgan Scout overnight and the horse ran the next day under the colors of its new owner, W. H. Johnson, but the change did not help. Again, the gelding finished last.[94]

At the conclusion of the spring schedule in Nashville, the assembled turfmen asked Peyton to make a plea for aid of one of their number who had fallen on hard times. A reporter noted the concern of those present.

> Among the incidents of the day was a very eloquent little speech from the venerable Balie Peyton, of Sumner, in behalf of a veteran turfman, now invalided and in distressed circumstances—Uncle Berry Williams—the oldest Tennessee turfman now living—a compeer of Old Hickory in earlier times, and one of the most honorable and liberal hearted of his type. A collection was taken up . . . and a handsome fund realized for the old veteran.[95]

Peyton always looked ahead to the next racing season, although his stables offered little encouragement. He entered Nickajack for the Nashville fall races of 1871, Whitelock in the spring of 1872, and Summer Rose in the fall, but scratched all three on the day of the race.[96]

Dreaming of thoroughbred racing in Middle Tennessee restored to its prewar glory, Peyton took the lead and with six others incorporated "The Albion Jockey Club" at Gallatin in 1872. He was its first president. The declared purpose of the club was "to encourage and promote, to develop and improve the blood-stock of the county." Its charter granted shareholders the authority "to build, construct and control speed, trotting, racing and pacing tracks" in Sumner County "upon which may be tested the speed of horses."[97] Beyond the declarations of the charter, Peyton and his associates wanted to replace the defunct Gallatin Jockey Club, renew racing at the old Albion Course on Coles Ferry Pike, and gain control of public racing in the county.[98] Advertisements claimed that "the accommodation of visiting and for training . . . [could] not be surpassed."[99]

While promoting the Albion Jockey Club, Peyton began writing a series of eight articles based on his recollections of colorful turfmen and remarkable horses. All appeared under the heading "Reminiscences of the Turf" beginning on October 31, 1872, in the *Rural Sun* published at Nashville. The last article appeared on August 7, 1873. Four years later the *Spirit of the Times* printed a series of essays under the heading "Reminiscences of the Turf" that incorporated the *Rural Sun* articles in slightly altered format. Each piece was edited by Nashville turfman George W. Darden,[100] who used the pen name "Albion" in frequent contributions to the *Spirit of the Times*. He acknowledged that he had used additional information furnished by Peyton and Judge Barry to enhance the original essays.[101] James Douglas Anderson copied the Peyton essays from the *Rural Sun* with no significant changes and supplied separate titles to each in the appendix of his book, *Making the American Thoroughbred, Especially in Tennessee, 1800–1845*, published in 1916.

When the editors of the Memphis *Avalanche* heard of the renewed Middle Tennessee interest in racing exemplified by the organization of the Albion Jockey Club, they were highly critical of the undertaking. Agreeing that the club had "the countenance and support of many influential men of Middle Tennessee," the editors charged it was "ill-advised and impracticable." How could it be a profitable investment? From whence would the necessary crowds be attracted? How could they be accommodated in such a small town?

The editorial critics invited the Gallatin turfmen to redirect their efforts in favor of the Nashville Blood Horse Association. Such a change could materially benefit the semi-annual Nashville races by increasing the number of entries and races, the size of the crowds, and the size of the purses. In short, they considered good racing and small towns incompatible.[102]

Bristling at the *Avalanche*'s suggestion that the promoters of the Albion Course were not "capable of thinking and acting for themselves," Peyton issued a rejoinder on May 28, 1873. He answered the charge that a small town could not support a racetrack by pointing out that Gallatin had supported annual local races from 1804 to 1862. Responding to the suggestion that the Albion Jockey Club should use its efforts to strengthen the larger Blood Horse Association, Peyton explained, "The most effectual way of supporting the Nashville Blood Horse Association is to encourage the breeding and training of thoroughbreds by establishing race courses in the different counties, which . . . will be tributary to the great metropolitan course at Nashville."[103]

Peyton was seriously interested in both the Albion Jockey Club and the Blood Horse Association of Nashville. When the association changed a rule that governed its races, he was alarmed. Adopted in 1873, the rule made it possible for dash races ending in a dead heat to be settled by an equal division of the purse if the owners preferred that arrangement to the time-honored practice of running again to determine the winner. It was proposed as an act of humanity to spare an exhausted horse another dash when unfit to run.

Unable to block adoption of the rule when it first came before the association, Peyton attacked it by letter in the columns of the *Spirit of the Times*. Humane treatment for racehorses meant that owners should provide proper training and conditioning for them. Race fans as well as owners came to the track not just to see a short flash of speed, but to gauge "the merits and endurance of thoroughbreds," he argued. The editor supported Peyton's position and added, "Some of these gentlemen [of the association] are advocating methods of horse racing which the wisest turfmen of England have declared to be of mischievous tendency even there, and which they strenuously contend ought to be repressed."[104]

When the association met at the beginning of the spring races at Nashville, members agreed with Peyton and rejected the rule, saying that a race "must be run to its proper and natural conclusion." To win his point, Balie had come from back in the pack, a performance equaled by all too few that ran under his colors.[105]

Peyton had no entries in the Nashville spring races of 1873, but as the fall races drew near, he had horses in the stables there. Looking at the Congress Stake, the richest to be run there since the Peyton Stake, Balie entered his chestnut filly Summer Rose, but withdrew her on race day.[106] Six months later he entered Summer Rose in the Vandal Sweepstake for three-year-olds at the Nashville spring races, and this time he let her run.[107] At race time she was the favorite, but she could only win fourth place in the field of seven horses.[108] Summer Rose ran

Albion Jockey Club

AT

GALLATIN, TENNESSEE.

Stakes now open; to close Aug. 1, 1875.

The following Stakes, proposed to be run for, over the ALBION RACE COURSE, Fall Meeting, 1875:

1st Day—Murphy Stake.

For 2-year-olds, $25.00 entrance, p.p.; single dash of a mile. Club to add $100.00.

Same Day—Granger Stake!

For green 3-year-olds that have not appeared in public prior to 1st day of August, 1875; $25 entrance, p.p.; mile heats. Grangers to add $200.00.

2nd Day—Merchant's Stake!

For 3-year-olds, mile heats; $50.00 entrance, $25.00 forfeit. Merchants of Gallatin to add $100.00.

3rd Day—Ladies' Stake!

For 3-year-old fillies, $25.00 entrance, p.p.; mile heats. Ladies of Sumner County to add a Gold Cup valued at $100.00.

☞ Five or more Entries required to fill the above Stakes. To CLOSE AUGUST 1st, 1875.

Programmes will be issued immediately after the closing of the Stakes, giving the Entries in full.

Liberal Club Purses will be given during the week.

The Track has been re-graded by a competent Engineer, and is in excellent condition.

The arrangement for the accommodation of Visitors and for Training, cannot be surpassed. We have recently erected new and commodious Stands and Stables, with splendid water. For further information, address the Secretary at Gallatin, Tenn.

JAMES FRANKLIN, *President.*
W. R. TOMKINS, *Vice-President.*

D. G. JACKSON, *Secretary,* (Lock Box K.)

Albion Jockey Club

third in a contest in the fall races of 1874[109] and was far back in the pack in two races at Gallatin in 1875. In 1876, she won a dash race and led another at the Gallatin races. With only one thoroughbred in training to run, Balie looked back to earlier days for inspiration.[110]

The Gallatin *Examiner* commented on Balie's dilemma on September 3, 1875, by quoting from the New York *Sportsman*: "The fame Tennessee won on the turf with her great horses during the days of Gen. Jackson, [Green] Berry Williams, and Balie Peyton and lost by the war and its incidents, must soon return to her, if energy and capital will bring it." Balie smiled when he read the flattering notice, but he did not have the capital and his diminished energy had other calls upon it.

CHAPTER 16

CELEBRATING THE UNION
1865–1878

During the first decade after Appomattox, Peyton had been discouraged time and again by his inability to achieve any significant measure of personal political success. To elude the disappointments that beset him, he frequently permitted his favorite saddle horse, a gray, to tour him about the farm. But on most weekdays, he harnessed another to his buggy and rode into Gallatin, leaving them at a livery stable.

After a brief visit to his office, he stopped at the courthouse to join a natural gathering of fellow barristers. Their conversation usually drifted into a condemnation of the hard times that confronted them. Law practice in the county seat earned respectable fees, but collecting them was often difficult. They agreed that getting a share of the practice adequate to sustain self and family was not easy because there were more than enough lawyers to handle even the increased volume of postwar litigation.

Before the war, Peyton had never been able to attain financial success as a farmer, horse breeder, or miller, probably because he lived far from Sumner County, the site of those activities, for twenty-two consecutive years, 1837–59. His brothers and his slaves produced agricultural products, fine horses, and other livestock, and for a short period, wheat flour and cornmeal, but they could not reap meaningful profits. As a result he was generally short of funds, and to satisfy creditors, he pledged Station Camp Mills, or the farm, or both to secure his borrowings. In a last great effort to turn a profit at the mills, he borrowed to purchase wheat by the carload for flouring. In 1868, he mortgaged the mills to New York City commission firm G. Hennkin and Palmore to secure wheat credits of up to ten thousand dollars more if mutually agreeable.[1]

When the New Yorkers collected interest on the loan and claimed a commission on all the flour he sold except for local retail sales, the enlarged operation did not bring the expected results. In 1875, Balie abandoned the milling business. He sold the mills, the three and three-quarters acres of land on which they were situated, and the miller's house to his son John Bell and his one-time farm overseer James Soper.[2]

Prospects for profits from the farm were bleak as well. Devastated by the war, the farmlands lay idle, unattended and devalued. No longer in slavery, his labor force had drifted away. To reinstate agricultural production, Balie needed hired help, but he did not have the funds. The abolition of slavery had removed not only his workers but also the capital asset that they represented. No longer could he use them as collateral to borrow money for the farm and stud.

The war had delivered a measurable blow to his personal finances. In 1860, he had personal property valued at $46,850 that principally represented fifty-one slaves[3] and an unknown number of horses and cattle. He had real property, 675 acres of land, in the amount of $50,500. Eight years later his personal property, no longer including slaves, and including no cattle and next to no horses of worth, was valued at $200. The value of his real property, standing at 500 acres, was down to $12,500. The only workers living on the farm were two free black women domestic servants.[4]

Although he had been present from the beginning of the war until its end to do what he could to protect the farm, it had suffered greatly. Balie's herd of cattle was depleted and his stables nearly emptied by the occupying army. When troops came to round up horses for the Federal cavalry just before the Battle of Nashville, Peyton saved four highly prized colts by bringing them into the dining room of his house where he had covered the floor with a thick layer of straw. He completed the deception by closing and barring the window blinds and locking the doors. One colt, Blacklock, later distinguished himself on the track and at stud. The soldiers found other horses in his stables, however.[5]

Both armies had passed up and down the highway that traced the southern boundary of the farm, and neither had hesitated to appropriate fence railings for their fires. As a result, virtually no fences remained. In response to his claim for damages inflicted by the Union Army, Peyton received $2,335 from the Southern Claims Commission, far from enough to return the farm to its prewar condition.[6]

His son John Bell had urged him to present the claim directly to Congress for payment because he was a former member of that body and a Unionist. He still had friends in both houses and was a respected public figure. Balie declined, however, forfeiting the chance to realize three or four times the amount awarded. Later in the year he assisted in preparing a claim for war damages filed by Thomas Barry for Green Berry Williams. When a nominal settlement was offered by the Claims Commission, Barry sent the claim to Congress and received an award of approximately four times the commission's offer.[7] In 1871 and again in 1872, Peyton mortgaged the farm to secure ever larger obligations.[8]

During the turbulent postbellum period, Emily was a steadying influence in Balie's life. Ever loyal to her father, she supported him in his public persona but of perhaps more importance, she did what she could to assist him financially. She and an assistant, Miss Lizzie McAlister, conducted a school in the Peyton farm home in 1864 and 1865. She then taught two years in Nashville at the Shelby Female Institute before reopening her school at home in the fall of 1867 and continuing with only an occasional hiatus into the 1880s. She left the school during the session of the general assembly in 1871 to serve the state senate as engrossing clerk and returned in 1877 as assistant in the same office.[9]

In 1870, Emily contracted with her father to assume responsibility for the farm and purchased certain livestock from him for $1,258. Monsieur Waters was the only thoroughbred in the lot, and he died soon afterward. At that time she owned the thoroughbred Romping Girl that later bore three fillies and a colt for her.

Emily's responsibility did not extend to the stables that held her father's three thoroughbred horses, which increased to ten by 1878. He contracted care for them from outside the family. But Emily had other obligations. She hired and paid the servants and "purchased groceries and supplied the table." By agreement she supported her father for the last eight years of his life, and his only obligation was to pay the taxes on the farm. Her brother John Bell seems to have lost interest in the farm before 1870, perhaps because of obligations to his wife's family, the Trousdales, whose substantial farm holdings in the area required attention.[10]

Even with all that Emily did for him, Balie wrestled with debt the rest of his life. The contest was made no easier by the careless, inadequate way that he kept business records.[11]

Throughout Balie's adult life, friends made loans to him, trying to help him keep his thoroughbreds and the farm. Yet he was never the recipient of the kind of generosity that matched the experience of his fellow Whig Henry Clay. When Clay was thrown deeply in debt by a guaranty that he had made for another at Lexington, his friends raised the money and paid the debt of approximately forty thousand dollars for him.[12]

Failure to maintain records and preserve documents cost Peyton an opportunity to share in the substantial legal fees generated by the Myra Gaines lawsuit. Although he had withdrawn from the case after he became U.S. district attorney for the Eastern District of Louisiana, he had later reentered it at General Gaines's insistence. His principal contribution was a trial brief that he prepared for the U.S. Supreme Court. General Gaines recognized the importance of the brief in a letter to Balie after it had been before the court, but Balie lost the letter and earlier had lost any and all records pertaining to his part in the case.

By the time the court was reviewing claims for attorney fees, Balie had no records to sustain a fee for his considerable services. He promised son John Bell that he would check into the matter by visiting New Orleans in 1877, but warned that he doubted any claim for a fee could be enforced at that time.[13] Later developments proved his doubts true.

Seemingly indifferent toward collecting money owed to him, Peyton was so sympathetic to Middle Tennesseans for their destitute conditions that he sometimes refused to accept fees when they were presented. After he saved a die-hard rebel from General Paine's firing squad in a long military commission trial, his client "got up the money;" but when he delivered the fee of five hundred dollars, Peyton responded with tears in his eyes, "I don't want your money; I know what you have suffered; I know that you have lost your property and have a large family." The grateful client related, "It was with great effort that I got him to take one-half of his fee."[14]

In 1873, Balie welcomed news of the U.S. Centennial Exposition of 1876, brought to Nashville by his Philadelphia cousin Jesse E. Peyton. Although Jesse visited kin in Kentucky and Tennessee, he had come primarily to promote the exposition, and he wanted Tennessee to participate in it at Philadelphia. He urged Tennesseans to use the exposition to tell the story of the state's mineral deposits and other natural resources, "and be prepared to reap the golden harvest" they would yield. A veteran eastern merchant, he was warmly received in Nashville where he had long enjoyed "intimate personal and business relations" with some of the city's oldest and most substantial commercial houses.[15]

Responding to Jesse Peyton's overtures, Governor John C. Brown appointed a "Board of Commissioners and Corporators" to plan for Tennessee's participation in the exposition. On January 9, the board requested an appropriation of two thousand dollars from the legislature for preliminary expenses and requested that Balie speak to that body "in person" to support the request.[16]

Nothing could have pleased him more than the opportunity to make a patriotic speech about the reunited country he adored, and he appeared in the Hall of the House of Representatives on April 21. The exposition was important to Tennessee, Balie explained, because the state could show its natural and prospective assets, three of which were of special importance. The rich deposits of coal and iron and the potential for cotton manufacturing in the state fairly cried to be shown to the world.

Attention to these assets suggested that Peyton envisioned a new Upper South economy based on mining and manufacturing. Its development would be assisted mightily by the impending expansion of railroads already far along in Tennessee.

Declaring that Tennessee's wealth had "never been brought into market," Peyton pointed to the state's substantial coal reserves of 42,129,360,000 tons. The presence of coal undergirded the production of iron from ore that he said was plentiful in "a three-foot deep ledge of undetermined width" that began in Alabama and extended diagonally through East Tennessee into Kentucky and Virginia.

Tennessee not only had cotton fields but adjoined the major cotton-producing states of the Union, he reminded. This situation held a great potential for economical production of cotton yarn and cloth. The principal transportation costs would be reduced to those incurred transporting the finished goods to market. "A cotton factory with four thousand spindles can be put in operation here at a cost of $120,000 all told, which will work up 548,000 pounds or 1,370 bales of cotton per annum, which, at savings of transportation alone, would net a profit of $16,440 or about 14 per cent," he said.

After making the case for a Tennessee exhibit at the Centennial Exposition, Balie warmed to his lifetime theme: national unity.

> I want to see . . . the great American family meet together around the parental hearthstone at Philadelphia. I want to see them join in a great feast in the old homestead, heal all the wounds, correct all ill feelings, and there resolve again that whatever may come, this country, blessed and hallowed by sacred memories, must stand from now, henceforth and forever, one in name, one in fame, and one in greatness.[17]

Peyton's speech to the legislature did not go unnoticed in Philadelphia. His "patriotic sentiments and fraternal expressions" so impressed members of the Women's Centennial Executive Committee that they invited him to be their special guest at a mass meeting in that city at the Academy of Music on April 19. The women promised such a "warm and hearty" welcome that he would realize that "blessed are the peacemakers."[18]

But Balie could not accept the invitation. He would be engaged in the federal court at Nashville on the indicated date. Flattered, he responded by letter, remembering the dinner given to honor him in Philadelphia in 1860 "in the same beautiful building." It was the occasion when he had "united with the wise and patriotic people of Philadelphia in a vain effort to avert the impending storm of civil strife," he wrote.

Peyton believed the exposition would provide America an unusual opportunity to show the world that a free people can overcome differences and dissensions, even after they had taken them to the battlefield. He had never advocated freedom for the slave population, but at last he was ready to accept it: "Let Americans . . . show higher and nobler traits than the battlefield can boast. Let them be magnanimous and forgiving, and become one people, now, henceforth and forever."[19]

Balie's letter drew praise from the Philadelphia *Press* in its issue of July 10, 1873.

> What he has written will be read with the more pleasure as the sentiments of a distinguished Southern statesman, and we believe he only re-echoes what the great body of the people of the South will heartily approve, and earnestly strive to carry to practical results.

To sustain his positive view of the exposition, Balie had to accept President Grant's appointment of two Republicans from Tennessee to sit on the U.S. Centennial Commission, Thomas H. Coldwell of Shelbyville and former congressman William F. Prosser of Nashville. Earlier an attorney general for the state of Tennessee, Coldwell was a bank president and railroad director. He was elected first vice president of the Centennial Commission and served actively in that capacity.[20]

Balie's enthusiasm for the Centennial celebration never waned, but the death of his sister Angelina's grandson in Texas invited his participation in the settlement of a complicated estate. Valuable Texas lands constituted the bulk of the inheritance that would be split between Peyton Bell Lytle's maternal and paternal heirs. Balie, his sister Sarah Barry, the three children of their late sister Rebecca Parker and the three children of her deceased son John R. Parker, and Joseph H. Peyton's two children were the ten maternal heirs. In a memorandum prepared for the deposition he made to establish the maternal heirs, Balie referred to the death of his brother Ephriam Hamilton Peyton as having occurred in Alabama in 1825. That brief reference is the only information other than his birth date that family records offer about Ephraim.[21]

Litigation of estate related matters required Balie to spend much of the years 1874 through 1877 in the Lone Star State. Principally at issue were titles to several land tracts, originally owned by Angelina Peyton Eberly[22] when she died in 1860, but inherited by her grandson.[23]

Balie Peyton and grandson Balie Peyton III

During the early part of January 1874, Peyton journeyed to Texas to enter claims for both the maternal and the paternal heirs. The issues were sufficiently complicated by imperfect land titles that the adminis-trator recommended the paternal heirs hire an attorney of their own.[24]

Soon after arriving at Port Lavaca, county seat of Calhoun County, Balie joined the administrator and the attorney for the paternal heirs in petitions to the court seeking partition of the extensive landholdings of the estate. On February 10, the district court decreed that the lands be surveyed and divided into "two moieties," one for the maternal and the other for the paternal heirs. Naming separate sets of commissioners for lands in Calhoun and Falls Counties and instructing them to partition only those lands free of claims by others, the decree reduced the acreage of available lands significantly.[25]

The commissioners completed their assignments by May 23, 1874, and set apart the lands for both sets of heirs, apparently to their mutual satisfaction. The presence of surveyors representing for the most part heirs who lived far from the lands in question prompted a spurt of counter claims. Suddenly the titles to several of the partitioned tracts were in question.

Since much of the trouble involved 23,979 acres of land in Falls County, Balie spent much of the fall and ensuing winter in Marlin, the county seat. There his impressive bearing and quick wit made him a popular figure. When a newly made Texas friend learned that the Tennessean's congressional district was about to select a congressman to fill a vacancy caused by death, he urged voters to call Peyton from retirement and send him to Washington. Admittedly, the "noble son" of Tennessee was no longer a young man, he wrote, "yet he mounts his Texas pony with all the agility of youth, and rides the whole day over the prairies, seemingly as little fatigued at nightfall as when he started."

The writer, who signed the letter "L," observed Peyton in a week-long land title trial, and he could only conclude that Balie's questions and two-hour speech represented "one of the most vigorous intellectual efforts" he had ever heard. Tennessee owed it to her sister southern states "that this stern old patriarch should be sent to Congress, as a beacon light to guide us. . . . he belongs to the whole country."[26]

Another who heard the speech at Marlin wrote to young Balie III, encouraging him to emulate his grandfather's "great example." William R. Reagan of Reagan, Texas, said that Peyton's presentation was delivered "in a style new to our Texas bar." The speaker "pointed and backed each point he made . . . with anecdotes . . . aptly fitting and so happily related that the effect upon his adversary was perfectly stunning and overwhelming."[27]

While in Marlin, Balie received a call from Elijah Sterling Clack Robertson, son of the Texas settlement promoter Sterling C. Robertson, that resulted in "an hour of pleasant conversation" but no help with his title cases. Was his visitor a likely prospect to purchase some or all of the tracts in question? It would have been highly unlikely due to the titles squabble, but the largest single tract was in Robertson's Nashville colony. The visit was probably made to pay respects to a Tennessean of note and, in passing, to gauge the nature and extent of his interest in Texas land. In a brief memorandum of their meeting, Robertson recognized Peyton's relationship to Peyton Bell Lytle and noted that his presence in Falls County was to attend "to a lawsuit involving several leagues of fine land."[28]

Peyton remained in Texas until July 1875. Returning home, "looking hale and hearty," he made the rounds of old friends in Nashville on July 31. One wrote, "He looks good for some lively campaigning yet, be it pushing his colors to the front on the turf, or in the more enlarged area incident to a political contest."[29]

Always cultivating good relations with the press, Balie stopped in at the office of the Nashville *Daily American* on September 2, 1875, to congratulate the editors of the new journal, created by the consolidation of the *Republican Banner* and the *Union and American* the day before. They were gratified that he liked to deliver congratulations in person, "his old fashioned, hearty way."[30]

Peyton was at home again, but public calls upon his life would not let him rest. Mexican War veterans attending a daylong reunion at Gallatin on September 21 chose him to preside over their program to commemorate the Battle of Monterrey. In a brief address, he told them it was useless for him to rehash their other battles in Mexico. They would never forget them. But the attack against the city of Monterrey was of special interest to Tennesseans. He said, "No troops were ever more thoroughly tried. Seven times they passed through the 'blue blazes,' passing over heaps of their mangled and dying friends and brothers, or amid shot and canister that decimated their ranks. Through this they passed and planted their banner on the battlements of Monterrey." In that battle Tennessee soldiers "sustained the high reputation of the Volunteer State."

Concluding his remarks to hearty applause, Peyton invited a report from the resolutions committee that obviously he had engineered. Adopted unanimously, it endorsed the Centennial and called for all surviving soldiers of the war with Mexico living in Tennessee to meet together on the grounds of the exposition in Philadelphia a year hence. The state could focus national attention on her war heroes as well as upon her undeveloped resources of coal, iron, and cotton.[31] Few veterans would make the trip, however.

Resisting the temptation to work actively for the open congressional seat in his district, Peyton was convinced that successful resolution of the Texas land matter could pay off his debts, leave him comfortably situated, and contribute to the welfare of the other Lytle heirs as well. Consequently, about the middle of December he set out again for Texas, expecting to be gone "several months."[32]

It is not clear what, if anything, Peyton accomplished on this second trip to Texas. No correspondence relating to that visit has survived, except a letter from Emily written March 24 at New Orleans where he joined her from Texas in time to reach Gallatin on April 28.[33] Nine days later Balie's beloved sister Sarah Hopkins Barry died.[34] The last of his siblings, Sarah had overseen the education of Balie's children and furnished them love and a home base after their mother's death.

At home in time for the Democratic State Convention at Nashville on May 31, he attended as a delegate from the Fourth Congressional District. Addressing the convention "by general request," he said that the

Grant administration had contracted the money supply by one-half, and he was certain the country was ready to increase it substantially. As the United States had been in an economic depression since the panic of 1873, he favored making greenbacks "a lawful tender in the payment of all duties, customs—and any and everything else." He favored repeal of the resumption act and called the resumption of specie payment "the greatest humbug of the age." The government had the constitutional authority to issue paper currency, he said, and the Treasury should do it "cheaply and simply."[35]

During the summer Balie shifted his attention to the nation's Centennial Exposition. On August 14, Emily, Balie, and his eleven-year-old grandson Willie Peyton left by train for Philadelphia.[36]

For Balie the Centennial was a celebration of nationhood that reflected his devotion to the union of states. The event bespoke patriotism that he and Andrew Jackson and John Bell and many other Tennesseans understood: the nation was indivisible. It reminded all that the Union had been tested and, with human bondage eliminated, had not been found wanting. Balie had predicted correctly that the true greatness of the country could be achieved only in Union, and he had paid a high price to stand by that conviction. In a sense, the Centennial was a vindication of the hopes and dreams he had nurtured throughout his adult life, although he had carefully sidestepped the slavery question until after emancipation.

By prearrangement, the Tennessee Peytons made the home of Cousin Jesse E. Peyton of nearby Haddonfield, New Jersey, their place of residence while they attended the Exposition. Balie and Willie first visited the Exposition on August 17 and returned next, accompanied by Emily, on August 21. All were greatly excited.[37]

The array of 8 large buildings and 208 smaller ones, erected for the occasion, was impressive. Balie, Emily, and Willie had never seen anything comparable. The Main Building, as the name suggests, was usually the first stop for visitors. Within its spacious twenty-acre interior, exhibits supplied by the principal nations of the world attracted a steady flow of interested viewers. Almost as popular was the United States Government Building where the various branches of the federal government mounted displays. Exhibits prepared by the army and navy attracted large crowds, as did the Treasury Department's demonstration of coin and currency production. Other exhibits on the grounds can be inferred from the names of the other six of the larger buildings: Art Gallery, Machinery Building, Agricultural

Building, Horticultural Building, Women's Pavilion, and Judges' Hall.[38]

Few southerners attended the exposition, and "the industry of the section was meagerly represented." The North had become excited by its postbellum strides along the road to industrial revolution, but no similar excitement existed in the South. The region was still in a state of shock from the war.[39]

But as exhilarating as the Philadelphia excursion was for Balie, he knew that he had unfinished business in Texas. When Cousin Jesse procured a railway pass for him from Philadelphia to St. Louis, he was strongly tempted to leave Willie in Emily's care in Haddonfield and set out for Marlin.[40] Nevertheless he remained at the Centennial until mid-September when he, Emily, and Willie returned to Gallatin.[41] It had been a glorious trip for all three. Before leaving he paid extravagant tribute to his cousin's contribution to the success of the Centennial celebration. Jesse's efforts had "permanently established the reunion of our states," he said, "and it will so pass into history."[42]

The Exposition furnished the centerpiece of conversations for several weeks as Balie recounted Centennial experiences in entertaining detail to Gallatin friends and neighbors and compared notes with a few who had made the journey to Philadelphia. The optimism exuded by the Centennial stood in stark contrast to the pessimism and cynicism that characterized much of the prior decade in the South. Attending the Philadelphia event renewed his faith in the future of the country. It was clear to him and increasingly to others that the North and South "had turned definitely toward reconciliation."[43]

There was another celebration ahead, and it was of a much more personal nature. Balie was a guest at the golden wedding anniversary of Jo. C. and Katherine Blackmore Guild on December 19, 1876, at the Guilds' home in Edgefield.[44] It was a nostalgic evening as Peyton and his host recalled their times in the courtroom, the horse races they had attended, and the thoroughbreds they had owned individually and in partnership. There were political stories with laughter aplenty. Some of their most emotional recollections, though not articulated, were acknowledged by both. They had chosen separate political parties in the 1830s and separate loyalties in the Civil War. But all of that aside, they remembered Peyton's work with Military Governor Johnson to bring Guild home from political imprisonment at Fort Mackinac and his making bond to guarantee Guild would not participate further in acts against the Union.[45]

Asked by Guild to speak to the assembled guests, Balie first paid tribute to Mrs. Guild, and then shared a number of anecdotes dealing with his career in Congress and more recent political activities. But he never let his stories distract the guests from the purpose of the event: to

honor the Guilds and celebrate their fifty years of married life.[46] A fellow
guest, Judge Jackson B. White of Nashville, recognized Balie as "the
Chevalier Bayard of the State,"[47] and wrote that he truly graced the
occasion with his presence.

Guild spoke warmly of Balie. "My old friend . . . Peyton . . . is a man
of humor and wit," he told the guests. "I will say nothing of his age, for
he is now looking abroad for some beautiful widow or 'mountain pink,'
and I will not prejudice him on the question of age. . . . He is the only
person now alive who was at our wedding fifty years ago tonight."[48]

Six days later Peyton observed Christmas with Emily, his grandchildren,
and their parents, Fannie and John. Afterward he was ready for yet another
trip to Texas. He hoped this time to obtain a complete resolution of the
issues that continued to thwart his efforts in the land title litigation. Early in
January 1877, he appeared in Texas, prepared to stay several months.[49]

Texans who became acquainted with Balie soon recognized that he
was a highly skilled raconteur. When he told a tale, his listeners were
spellbound. Once in Austin, contributing to a late evening discussion of
the life of Sam Houston, Peyton brought up the congressional trial of
1832 that grew out of the Texan's assault on Ohio Congressman William
Stanbery. Sam had retaliated because the congressman had referred to
him on the floor of the House as one of President Jackson's bullies. The
House passed judgment on Stanbery by censuring him on July 11, 1832,
for "the use of unparliamentary language"[50] and then passed resolutions
declaring Houston guilty of contempt of Congress for his physical attack
on one of its members, and directed the Speaker to reprimand him.[51]

Before the reprimand, Houston, a former two-term congressman,
answered the charges. Stanbery had not only insulted him on the floor
of the House, but had also "slandered" him in the columns of a newspaper. Stanbery was one of the anti-Jackson crowd that, outside the
protection of the House, had made "wanton attacks" on Houston's
domestic relations. Considering the scope of the congressman's provoca-
tions, Houston believed that the summons by the House was not justified
under the Constitution. His answer availed nothing, and he stood
silently while the Speaker reprimanded him.[52]

Although the trial was reported in *Gales and Seaton's Register of Debates
in Congress*, Peyton insisted that two paragraphs had been deleted. He
recalled that Houston said:

> I ask no sympathy nor need. The thorns which I have reaped are of the
> tree I planted. They tear me and I bleed.
>
> That man Stanbery has slandered me through the columns of six
> newspapers and refused ever to answer a polite note. And I chastized
> him as I would a dog, and I will visit the same punishment on the

shoulders of anyone who insults me, even though it be one of you who now sit in judgment on my conduct.[53]

Peyton's account was so graphic that when one of his hearers, A. W. Terrell, wrote an article about it a few years later, he placed Peyton in the Congress in May 1832, fifteen months before he was elected, and embellished the tale with a drinking scene the night before the reprimand. Terrell wrote that Houston invited Senator Felix Grundy, Speaker of the House Andrew Stephenson, James K. Polk, and Balie to share his indignation at the prospect he faced. They gathered in the late afternoon and drank copious quantities of liquor, but in the early evening left him alone to drink the rest of the night away.[54]

Back in an unembellished world, Peyton worked and waited seven months trying to clear the titles, but favorable, final rulings were slow and elusive in the Texas courts. Believing there was nothing more he could do in Texas, he returned home, all the time planning to go to Washington and somehow try to get the matter before the Supreme Court.[55]

Always eager to relay news about good thoroughbreds, Balie let horse lovers in Nashville know that he had seen Rebel, a famous Texas stallion, "the sire of Sam and Ella Harper and other good ones." Coveting the horse for Middle Tennessee, he thought that Rebel's "proper place" was the Belle Meade stud.[56]

At home again by mid-August, Balie volunteered a sanguine assessment of the Texas litigation. His numerous friends, turfmen and politicians alike, hoped that resolutions of the lawsuits would retire his debts and provide a comfortable living for him. An editor reflected their sentiment:

> We are rejoiced to hear that his visit was successful, and it is probable that he will be richly remunerated. Every turfman in the country will rejoice in his success and would like to see him repose on flowery beds of ease in his declining years, for a more social, high-toned gentleman never lived than Balie Peyton.[57]

After a few weeks at home with Emily, Balie took the rail cars to Washington in pursuit of the Texas land titles. A political friend of old, Henry S. Foote, accompanied him but on an errand of his own. They reached the capital about October 1.[58]

Although facing long odds in the court case, Balie was always open for a horse trade inside or outside the courtroom. The first and only trading option available to him in Washington was the sale of all his young colts to a Kentucky turfman, and he included the sale of Emily's four yearling fillies, all at the price of four hundred dollars each.[59]

Although the land cases were not properly before the Supreme Court, Balie sought to have them called up for review. He marshaled impressive support from politicians and lawyers in the capital, but it was not enough to affect the litigation in Texas. Disappointed and nearly exhausted, he remained in Washington until the early summer of 1878. Consistent with his prior record, Balie did not take time to file a bill for his legal services in the estate matters, an omission that would be costly to his own estate.[60] Final settlement of the Peyton Bell Lytle estate would not be reached until 1883.[61]

The court fight had taken its toll on Balie, and he returned home with his health severely impaired. On August 8, in his seventy-fifth year, he collapsed while walking with a servant in the garden outside his house. It was the beginning of a ten-day period when family, friends, and his physician watched helplessly as his condition steadily worsened. He lapsed into unconsciousness three days before death overtook him at three o'clock on Sunday afternoon, August 18.[62] Emily and John Bell were at his bedside.

On the next day the largest crowd that ever followed a funeral cortege in Sumner County stood in silent respect as the Methodist pastor Burkett F. Ferrell and the Reverend John S. Arbuthnot of the Gallatin Presbyterian Church committed Peyton's body to burial in the family cemetery on the farm where he was born. He had inter- vened to free Ferrell from incarceration during the Civil War, and now in a broader sense the minister was returning the favor.[63] Many of those who attended the funeral expressed regret that there had not been enough time allowed to stage an appropriate civic or military display.[64]

Tributes flooded in. The Nashville *American* concluded a lengthy memorial essay by saying that "all in all, [he was] one of Tennessee's greatest sons."[65] The *New York Times* saluted him as "formerly one of the most prominent politicians in the country," and the San Francisco *Alta California* acknowledged that "he was a man beloved by many" and his death would "touch with sorrow many a heart that knew him in the early days of this city."[66] In Philadelphia, Cousin Jesse E. Peyton noted, "I do not think there has been born in the United States of America an individual who did more for his country than Balie Peyton."[67]

The thoroughbred racing world had lost a beloved giant. The *Spirit of the Times* was shocked. "Balie Peyton is dead! We mourn his loss," the editor wrote. He reviewed Balie's life, including his maturing years in Tennessee, "the western borders of marching civilization," and concluded, "When his friends laid him away . . . there was not a spot upon the ermine of his honor. . . . How devotedly was he loved! How ardently admired!"[68]

A year before, Dr. J. W. Weldon of New York, one of the most
prominent turfmen in America, had paid tribute to him.

> Col. Peyton is a man of rare experience, observation and intelligence,
> has been breeding and racing the thoroughbred for the past fifty years,
> and is justly regarded as high authority on all questions connected with
> the breeding, rearing, handling, and training the thoroughbred horse.
> He not only bred, trained and raced his own, and among them were
> some of the best horses in the country, but he has also witnessed the
> most brilliant racing ever seen in America.[69]

Referring to Peyton as "Tennessee's oldest and most distinguished
sportsman," Dr. Weldon said that the successful running of the Peyton
Stake in 1843 would be "a monument . . . to Col. Peyton . . . more lasting
. . . than any that the sculptor could carve from Palatine marble."[70]

At the time of his death, Balie had not given up on horses. He had a
three-year-old chestnut filly, Mary B, entered in the Maxwell House
Stake to be run at the upcoming autumn races of the Nashville Blood
Horse Association. He even had entered two two-year-olds, Louisa and
Country Girl, in the Belle Meade Stakes No. 2 to be run at Nashville in
the autumn of 1879.[71]

At home, high praise came from the members of the Gallatin bar who
remembered him as "a brilliant genius of noble and chivalrous bearing,
[and] a fiery and eloquent speaker, displaying keen wit and vivid
imagery." They had no question about his strength of character: "He was
a man of unbounded courage, of keen sensibilities, never giving or
taking an insult, kind, sympathetic, and charitable to the weak and
oppressed—a bold, candid, truthful, honest man."[72]

A local newspaper was even more eloquent in its tribute. "He was
courageous as a lion . . . valued honor more than life . . . and as a
politician . . . was free from trickery, true to his convictions, and . . .
fearless in their promulgation." In addition, Balie had stood tall for the
Union in 1861 and was "a statesman of broad and liberal views . . . and
ardently attached to our republican institutions. . . . He possessed a
quick mind . . . and an inexhaustible fund of humor, ready wit, and
tender pathos." But he was most loved as a friend and companion, the
editor believed. "A genial, warm-hearted, generous gentleman, and a
brilliant, amusing and instructive conversationalist, his companionship
was eagerly sought and universally enjoyed."[73]

At one time or another, Balie Peyton exhibited most of the fine qualities attributed to him. Even his intemperate outbursts, usually triggered
by what he regarded as unjustified questioning of his honor and
integrity, rarely besmirched an otherwise positive reputation. But he
held tenaciously to one principle every day of his life: the principle of

federal Union. Although he did not envision the extension of full civil rights to the freedmen, he coveted for the country an indivisible Union under its Constitution that guaranteed individual liberties to an extent unknown in the history of humankind. He was committed to see it survive all challenges.

Time rushed ahead; political alliances fractured; circumstances changed. But Balie's passion for keeping the Union intact was embraced by succeeding generations of Americans. And finally civil rights were extended to all.

From his first political speech to his last, and during the hundreds of speeches in between, Balie Peyton was a Unionist. That record of undeviating loyalty was even more satisfying to him than a victorious day in court or seeing his favorite thoroughbred pull away from its racing competitors and cross the finish line ahead of them all.

ABBREVIATION KEY

AJDP	Andrew Jackson Donelson Papers
ATRSM	*American Turf Register and Sporting Magazine*
CNFP	Charley Neal Family Papers
DCP	David Campbell Papers
FC	Freer Collection
HSP	Historical Society of Pennsylvania, Philadelphia
JBC	John Bell Collection
JJCP	John Jordan Crittenden Papers
LC	Library of Congress
MCOP	Murdock Collection, Overton Papers
M. Despatches	Records of the Department of State, *Despatches from United States Ministers to Chile, 1823–1906*, vol. 9, *July 20, 1849–October 2, 1851*, NA.
NA	National Archives
NARC	Notarial Archives Research Center, New Orleans, Louisiana
NBNW	*National Banner and* Nashville *Whig*
NCLR	Nashville *Commercial and Legal Reporter*
NODB	New Orleans *Daily Bee*
NODD	New Orleans *Daily Delta*
NODP	New Orleans *Daily Picayune*
NR	Nashville *Republican*
NRB	Nashville *Republican Banner*
NYST	New York *Spirit of the Times*
PFN	Peyton Family Notes
RDC	Register of Debates in Congress
RLCP	Robert L. Caruthers Papers
SCA	Sumner County Archives
SCDB	Sumner County Deed Book
SCR	Sumner County Records
S. Despatches	Records of the Department of State, *Diplomatic Instructions, Chile, 1801–1906*, vol, 15, *May 29, 1833–February 2, 1867*, NA.
SDU	Sacramento *Daily Union*
SFDAC	San Francisco *Daily Alta California*
SFDEB	San Francisco *Daily Evening Bulletin*
SHC	Southern Historical Collection
THM	*Tennessee Historical Magazine*
THS	Tennessee Historical Society
TSLA	Tennessee State Library and Archives
WPA	Works Progress Administration

NOTES

CHAPTER 1

1. Eleven children were born to John and Margaret Hamilton Peyton: Thomas Peyton died in infancy (1791); Robert Holmes (1792–1852); John Hamilton (1795–1813); William Randolph (1796–1846); Angelina (1798–1860); Evalina (1800–1852); Ephraim (1801–25); Balie (1803–78); Rebecca H. (1805–54); Joseph Hopkins (1808–45); Sarah Hopkins (1810–1876). Compiled from the Mabel Neal Collection of CNFP, a privately held collection.

2. Family records of the first Peytons in America are at variance. Some indicate that Balie Peyton was a descendant of Henry Peyton of Westmoreland County, Virginia, who left England for America about 1644. Henry died at his home "Acquia" in 1659. John Lewis Peyton, comp., *Memoir of John Howe Peyton in Sketches by his Contemporaries*. (Staunton, Va.: A. B. Blackburn & Co., 1894), 3. Another source suggests that Balie's original American ancestor was John Peyton, who sailed from England to Virginia in 1622. John had two sons, one of whom was Henry Peyton of Westmoreland County, Virginia, and Balie is said to have descended from this born-in-America Henry. Jay Guy Cisco, *Historic Sumner County, Tennessee* (Nashville: Folk Keelin, 1909), 289.

3. Peyton Family Bible, WPA Records, Sumner County, Microfilm Reel 81, TSLA.

4. John Haywood, *The Civil and Political History of the State of Tennessee* (Knoxville: Heiskell and Brown, 1823; reprint, Knoxville: Tenase Company, 1969), 414; James Douglas Anderson, *The Historic Bluegrass Line* (Nashville: Nashville-Gallatin Interurban Railway, 1913), 84.

5. Previously, John had fought in the French and Indian War at the Battle of the Big Kanawha in 1774. On each occasion, he was in the company of his twin, Ephraim. *National Banner* and Nashville *Daily Advertiser*, August 22, 1833; Haywood, *The Civil and Political History*, 134, 227; Irene M. Griffey, *The Preemptors: Tennessee's First Settlers* (Clarksville: 1989), 58;

Walter T. Durham, *The Great Leap Westward, A History of Sumner County, Tennessee, From Its Beginnings to 1805* (Gallatin: Sumner County Library Board, 1969), 95.

6. SCR, North Carolina Grant Book No. 1, April 17, 1786, 124.

7. Griffey, *The Preemptors*, 14.

8. The first public races at Gallatin were held in 1804, when he was still less than a year old. Balie Peyton, "Sumner County Races, 1804–05," *Rural Sun*, December 5, 1872.

9. James Douglas Anderson, *Making the American Thoroughbred, Especially in Tennessee, 1800–1845* (Norwood, Mass.: Plimpton Press, 1916), 240; *NYST*, November 24, 1877; Jo. C. Guild erred on page 245 of *Old Times in Tennessee* when he referred to Governor Ben Williams as governor of Virginia.

10. Anderson, *Historic Bluegrass Line*, 84.

11. PFN by Jonathan Smith, a manuscript in CNFP, 7.

12. J. Frazer Smith, *White Pillars: Early Life and Architecture of the Lower Mississippi Valley Country* (New York: Bramhall House, 1941), 31.

13. Walter T. Durham, *Old Sumner, A History of Sumner County, Tennessee, From 1805 to 1861* (Gallatin: Sumner County Library Board, 1972), 486–91; Peyton Society of Virginia, Book Committee, *The Peytons of Virginia* (Stafford: Peyton Society of Virginia, 1976), 238.

14. Anderson, *The Historic Bluegrass Line*, 84.

15. Jo. C. Guild, *Old Times in Tennessee* (Nashville: Tavel, Eastman & Howell, 1878; reprint, Gallatin: Rose Mont Foundation, 1995), 67, 81.

16. Son of Balie's Uncle Ephraim, Geoffrey Peyton was an elected district attorney in Mississippi and accepted appointment to the state supreme court in 1868. He became chief justice of the court in 1870 and served until 1875 when statewide elections swept his political party from power. James D. Lynch, *The Bench and Bar of Mississippi* (New York: E. J. Hale & Son, Publishers, 1881), 359, 361.

17. Diary of Mary Morris, 1802–1895, TSLA.

18. Nashville *Tennessean Magazine,* July 31, 1960.

19. Explanation of the hostility between the Peytons and McKain is not found in existing court records. SCA, Loose Court Records, #6067, #10107, #10108.

20. C. Richard King, *The Lady Cannoneer: A Biography of Angelina Belle Peyton Eberly, Heroine of the Texas Archives War* (Burnet, Texas: Eakin Press, 1981), 6–8.

21. Guild, *Old Times,* 83. He infrequently used his full name Josephus Conn Guild.

22. PFN, 7; Guild, *Old Times,* 72, 80.

23. Guild, *Old Times,* 85.

24. Ibid.

25. Ibid., 85–88.

26. *NCLR,* January 3, 1877.

27. George Dawson Blackmore biographical sketch, typescript, SCA.

28. Born in Smith County, Tennessee, Robert L. Caruthers (1800–82) attended Washington College, Washington County, and Greeneville College, Greene County. He began law practice at Carthage in 1823, was a Whig congressman for a single term (1841–43), and founded Cumberland University at Lebanon in 1842 and its law school in 1847. He was a justice of the Tennessee Supreme Court (1854–61). Robert M. McBride and Dan M. Robison, *Biographical Directory of the Tennessee General Assembly,* vol. 1, *1796–1861* (Nashville: Tennessee State Library and Archives and Tennessee Historical Commission, 1975), 132–33.

29. Sarah Saunders was the daughter of James and Mary Smith Donelson Saunders of Sumner County and was a granddaughter of Gen. and Mrs. Daniel Smith of Hendersonville. McBride and Robison, *Tennessee General Assembly,* 132.

30. *NCLR,* January 3, 1877.

31. Anderson, *American Thoroughbred,* 84, 86.

32. Elliott's stables were located on his Long Hollow Pike farm about two miles northeast of Peyton's place. Nashville *Republican and State Gazette,* January 1, 1831.

33. SCR, Deed Book 11, 361. The Peytons experienced interminable financial crises similar to those that Andrew Jackson and other of their planter-breeder neighbors faced.

34. Henry Alexander Wise (1806–76) studied law at Winchester, Virginia, before moving to Nashville. Back in Virginia, he was elected as a Jacksonian to the 23rd and 24th Congress, as a Whig to the 25th through the 27th Congress, and as a Democrat to the 28th

Congress. He was governor of Virginia from 1856 to 1860. *Biographical Directory of the United States Congress, 1774–1989,* bicentennial ed. (Washington, D.C.: U.S. Government Printing Office, 1989), 2075–76.

35. Henry Stuart Foote, *The Bench and Bar of the South and Southwest* (St. Louis: Soule, Thomas & Wentworth, 1876), 183.

36. *Directory of Congress,* 2075.

37. S. G. Heiskell, *Andrew Jackson and Early Tennessee History,* vol. 1 (Nashville: Ambrose Printing Company, 1918), 322–27; Barton H. Wise, *The Life of Henry A. Wise of Virginia, 1806–1876* (New York: Macmillan Company, 1899), 25–27.

38. *NBNW,* January 16, 1829.

39. King, *Lady Cannoneer,* 51.

40. *NBNW,* February 5, 1830.

41. Durham, *Old Sumner,* 193.

42. Emily T. Peyton's transcript of Balie Peyton's dictated recollections, Peyton Papers, TSLA.

43. Ibid.

44. Durham, *Old Sumner,* 198–99.

45. Her parents were Lethe and William Smith of Granville County, North Carolina. PFN, 7.

46. Peyton was "one of the most strikingly handsome men" the distinguished Chattanooga lawyer W. B. Swaney ever knew. He reminded Swaney "very much in his actions and looks, and especially his [gray] eyes, and his various accomplishments, of Edwin Booth, the famous actor." Swaney to Douglas Anderson, April 26, 1937, James Douglas Anderson Papers, TSLA.

47. Sumner County WPA Records, Reel 81.

48. Peyton to Samuel Smith Downey, March 3, 1831, Samuel Smith Downey Collection.

49. Ibid. (May 25, 1831).

50. *NBNW,* October 12, 1831.

51. Ibid. The high rates of the Tariff of Abominations were reduced in 1832, but the modifications were not acceptable to South Carolina and most other southern states until further compromises were reached in the tariff of 1833. Howard L. Hurwitz, *An Encyclopedic Dictionary of American History* (New York: Washington Square Press, 1970), 645–46.

52. *NBNW,* December 27, 1832.

53. Ibid. (August 30, 1832).

54. William Hall (1775–1856) served in the state house of representatives (1797–1805), was a member of the state senate (1821–29), and as its speaker, succeeded to the governorship upon the resignation of Sam Houston in 1829. After finishing Houston's term, he did not seek election to that office, but in 1831 was elected to the House of Representatives of the 22nd Congress.

He was a brigadier general with Maj. Gen. Andrew Jackson's army during the War of 1812. *Directory of Congress,* 1116.

55. In 1833, the Sixth Congressional District consisted of the counties of Sumner, Smith, and Jackson. Ed Speer, *The Tennessee Handbook* (Jefferson, N.C.: MacFarland and Company, 2002), 177.

56. Guild, *Old Times,* 90.

57. *NCLR,* January 3, 1877.

58. Guild, *Old Times,* 90.

59. Ibid.

60. Indian rifle fire wounded Thomas Peyton in the shoulder and broke John's arm in two places. Ephraim escaped their fire, but in the process knocked his ankle out of place. The battered Peytons were not heroes in the eyes of Chief Hanging Maw, who led the attack. A year later when John petitioned him to return his stolen horses, the chief responded that the horses were his because John had "run away like a coward and left them." John Carr, *Early Times in Middle Tennessee* (1857; reprint, Nashville: Parthenon Press, 1958), 94–95.

61. Guild, *Old Times,* 90. Nickajack, one of the lower Cherokee towns, was the base for raids into the Cumberland settlements and southern Kentucky during the early 1790s. A group of volunteer frontiersmen from both states attacked Nickajack on September 12, 1794, destroyed the village of about 150 houses, killed 55 warriors, and captured several others, including a number of women and children. Walter T. Durham, *Before Tennessee: The Southwest Territory, 1790–1796* (Piney Flats: Rocky Mount Historical Association, 1990), 179–82.

62. Guild, *Old Times,* 90.

63. Ibid., 91.

64. *NBNW,* December 27, 1832.

65. *NCLR,* January 3, 1877.

66. Civil Election Returns, 1833, United States Congress, Sixth District, Tennessee Secretary of State, TSLA.

67. The others were William M. Inge, James Standifer, W. C. Dunlap, Samuel Bunch, John B. Forester, David W. Dickinson, and John Blair. Eastin Morris, *The Tennessee Gazetteer,* 1834 (Nashville: W. Hassell Hunt and Company, 1834), 65; *Directory of Congress,* 116.

68. *NR,* November 18, 1834. John's son Ephraim Hamilton Peyton died somewhere in Alabama in 1825, but family papers offer no details of his death.

69. Will of John Peyton, *Tennessee. Sumner County. Will Book,* vol. 2, *1823–1842,* Historical Records Project, Official Record No. 65-44-1497, copied under Works Progress

Administration (May 8, 1936): 176.

70. Desha had served in the War of 1812 and was brevetted major for gallant conduct in the attempt by American forces to recapture Fort Mackinac in 1814. He returned to Gallatin in mid-1815. Elected to Congress in 1827 and again in 1829, he declined to seek a third term. Sometime after 1835 he relocated with his family to Mobile, Alabama, where he died February 8, 1849. Charles K. Gardner, *Directory of all Officers, Who Have Been Commissioned, or Have Been Appointed and Served in the Army of the United States. . . .* (New York: G. P. Putnam & Co., 1853), 14.

71. Peyton to John C. McLemore, October 5, 1832, MCOP, TSLA.

72. Desha had engaged in an inglorious fistfight with a supporter of Gen. William Hall's rival candidate for the house in 1829. Marquis James, *The Life of Andrew Jackson* (New York: Bobbs-Merrill Company, 1938), 551.

73. Peyton to John C. McLemore, October 5, 1832, MCOP, TSLA.

74. Nashville *Republican and State Gazette,* October 1, 1832.

75. *NBNW,* November 24, 1832.

76. Peyton to John C. McLemore, October 5, 1832, MCOP, TSLA.

77. *NBNW,* October 6–7, 1832; Peyton to John C. McLemore, October 5, 1832, MCOP, TSLA.

78. *NBNW,* October 8–9, 1833.

CHAPTER 2

1. According to family tradition, Balie's wife and children traveled with him en route to Washington when possible, stopping to remain with her North Carolina family until, at the end of the session, he returned on his way home to Tennessee. PFN, 8.

2. On December 9, the Speaker of the House appointed Peyton to the standing committee of elections. *RDC,* vol. 10, pt. 2 (Washington: Gales & Seaton, 1825–1837), 2159–60.

3. *RDC,* vol. 10, pt. 2 (December 17, 1833): 2204.

4. Ibid. (January 16, 1834): 2428–30, 2450.

5. Ibid. (January 16–17, 1834): 2431, 2450–52.

6. Ibid. (February 6, 1834): 2657–58.

7. Ibid., 2661.

8. Ibid., 2666–67.

9. Ibid., pt. 3 (April 21, 1834): 3744; *Congressional Globe,* vol. 1, (Washington: Blair and Rives, 1834–1874), (April 19, 1834): 330.

10. *RDC,* vol. 10, pt. 3 (April 21, 1834): 3745.

11. *Congressional Globe*, vol. 1 (April 21, 1834): 332.

12. Ibid. (June 10, 1834): 436.

13. *RDC*, vol. 10, pt. 4 (June 13, 1834): 4480.

14. Ibid. (June 19, 1834): 4596.

15. Ibid. (June 19, 1834): 4596–97.

16. Balie Peyton, "President Jackson's Orders and Reminiscences," *Rural Sun*, vol. 4 (December 19, 1872); Anderson, *American Thoroughbred*, 243–44.

17. *NYST*, December 16, 1876.

18. The election was held to fill the vacancy created by the resignation of Speaker Andrew Stevenson, a congressman from Virginia. *Directory of Congress*, 114; Joseph Howard Parks, *John Bell of Tennessee* (Baton Rouge: Louisiana State University Press, 1950), 71–72.

19. "Documents: Correspondence of John Bell and Willie Mangum, 1835," *THM*, vol. 3, no. 3 (September 1917): 119.

20. George Sellers, *James K. Polk, Jacksonian* (Princeton, N.J.: Princeton University Press, 1957), 245.

21. Cave Johnson to Polk, July 15, 1834, and W. C. Dunlap to Polk, July 26, 1834, Herbert Weaver, ed., *Correspondence of James K. Polk*, vol. 2, *1833–1834* (Nashville: Vanderbilt University Press, 1972), 440–41; Parks, *John Bell*, 73.

22. Jackson to Peyton, September 4, 1834, Thurlow Weed Collection, Rush Rhers Library, University of Rochester, Rochester, N.Y.

23. *RDC*, vol. 11, pt. 1 (December 8, 1834): 753–54.

24. The opposition to Jackson and Van Buren had coalesced in 1834 under the party name of Whig after Henry Clay had used the term approvingly in a Senate speech. Although the name had been in use for at least two years, Clay's use of it and its appearance in *Niles Register* in April 1834 fastened it on the opposition. Members of the Whig Party came from former members of the National Republican Party, supporters of John Calhoun's nullification stand, Democrats who disagreed with Jackson on the bank question, and southern planters and northern industrialists. Arthur M. Schlesinger Jr., ed., *The Almanac of American History* (New York: G. P. Putnam's Sons, 1983), 229.

25. Hugh Lawson White (1773–1840), son of General James White, founder of Knoxville, Tennessee, was an attorney who at various times held the offices of U.S. District Attorney, judge on the Tennessee Supreme Court of Law and Equity, judge on the State Supreme Court of Errors and Appeals, and state senator from Knox County. The legislature elected him to succeed Andrew Jackson in the U.S. Senate in

1825 and reelected him unanimously in 1829 and 1835. Carroll Van West, ed., *The Tennessee Encyclopedia of History and Culture* (Nashville: Tennessee Historical Society and Rutledge Hill Press, 1998), 1054–54.

26. Robert E. Corlew, *Tennessee: A Short History*, 2nd ed. (Knoxville: University of Tennessee Press, 1981), 182. The letter to White was signed by Wm. M. Inge, Balie Peyton, James Standifer, John Blair, W. C. Dunlap, Sam'l Bunch, Jno. Bell, David Crockett, John B. Forester, Luke Lea, and David W. Dickinson. *NBNW*, February 23, 1835.

27. *NR*, February 24, 1835.

28. W. R. Rucker to Polk, January 5, 1835, Weaver, ed., *Correspondence of James K. Polk*, vol. 3, *1835–1836* (Nashville: Vanderbilt University Press, 1975), 14.

29. Nashville *Union*, May 25, June 22, 1835.

30. *NR*, January 29, 1835.

31. *NBNW*, February 23, 1835.

32. Polk to James Walker, February 7, 1835, Weaver, ed., *James K. Polk*, vol. 3, 88. When he mentioned the Republican Party, Polk was referring to the party of Thomas Jefferson formed when he left President George Washington's cabinet in 1793. Next called the Democratic-Republican Party, it had been called the Democratic Party since Jackson's election in 1828. It stood for individual liberty, opposed an excessively strong central government, and upheld a strict interpretation of the Constitution. Drawing its members largely from the ranks of frontiersmen, small shopkeepers, and small farmers, the party opposed a national bank and high tariffs. Howard L. Hurwitz, *An Encyclopedic Dictionary of American History* (New York: Washington Square Press, 1970), 188–89.

33. *NBNW*, March 20, 1835.

34. Nashville *Union*, April 22, 1835.

35. *NBNW*, April 22, 1835. Although his father was involved in the Indian wars, the specific military service rendered by Balie's brother William Randolph in Jackson's army is not clear. He probably served in local militia units and may have been in volunteer call-ups under General Jackson, although existing records do not support that notion. His brother John H. died while on duty in the Creek War of 1813 and Robert Holmes volunteered for the Seminole War of 1836. Muster Rolls, War of 1812, Book 3, 231, TSLA.

36. *NBNW*, April 22, 1835.

37. Ibid. (April 1, 1835); Laughlin to James K. Polk, April 21, 1835, Weaver, ed., *James K. Polk*, vol. 3, 165.

38. Laughlin to Polk, May 30, 1835, Weaver, ed., *James K. Polk*, vol. 3, 209.

39. *NR*, August 18, 1835.

40. Ibid. (June 2, 1835).

41. Edmund Rucker, a citizen of Rutherford County, cast Tennessee's fifteen votes. An outraged Nashville editor demanded a copy of his credentials from the president of the convention, knowing there were none. *NR*, June 4, 1835.

42. Peyton to Hardy M. Cryer, May 15, 1835, Martin Van Buren Papers, Microfilm, LC.

43. *National Banner* and Nashville *Daily Advertiser*, April 22, 1835; Polk to Andrew Jackson Donelson, October 18, 1835, Weaver, ed., *James K. Polk*, vol. 3, 336–37.

44. Nashville Union, August 12, 1835; *NR*, August 18, 1835.

45. Civil Election Returns, 1835, United States Congress, Sixth District, Tennessee Secretary of State, TSLA.

46. General Marie Joseph Paul, the Marquis de Lafayette, America's invaluable French volunteer general during the American Revolution, had visited Nashville in 1825 while on his year-long tour of the United States. Arthur M. Schlesinger Jr., ed., *The Almanac of American History*, 126.

47. *NBNW*, October 9, 12, 1835; *NR*, October 13, 1835.

48. *Journal of the House of Representatives of the State of Tennessee, 21st General Assembly, 1835* (Nashville: Secretary of State, 1835), 67–73; *Journal of the Senate of the State of Tennessee, 21st General Assembly, 1835* (Nashville: Secretary of State, 1835), 21–23, 47; *Public Acts Passed at the First Session of the Twenty-First General Assembly of the State of Tennessee, 1835–6* (Nashville: S. Nye and Co., Printers—Republican Office, 1836), 213–14; *NBNW*, October 21, 26, 1835.

49. Nashville *Union*, October 9, November 24, 1835.

50. Balie Peyton to George Prentiss, September 25, 1852, George Prentiss, ed., *A Memoir of S. S. Prentiss*, vol. 2 (New York: C. Scribner's Sons, 1855), 272.

51. *ATRSM*, vol. 6, no. 5 (January 1835): 263–64, no. 7 (March 1835): 317–24.

52. *NR*, November 25, 1834.

53. Ibid. (February 3, 1835).

54. *NBNW*, June 1, October 7, 1835.

CHAPTER 3

1. S. H. Laughlin to Polk, December 1, 1835; J. N. Johnson to Polk, December 9, 1835; Weaver, ed., *James K. Polk*, vol. 3, 384–86, 390–91; Eugene Irving McCormac, *James K. Polk: A Political Biography* (Berkeley, Calif.: University of California Press, 1922), 97–98.

2. Benjamin F. Allen to Polk, January 1, 1836, Weaver, ed., *James K. Polk*, vol. 3, 420.

3. George W. Jones to Polk, June 10, 1836, Weaver, ed., *James K. Polk*, vol. 3, 658n; Polk held the speakership until December 16, 1839.

4. When making appointments to standing committees of the House two days before, Speaker Polk chose Peyton for the committee on the judiciary. *RDC*, vol. 12, pt. 2 (Washington: Gales & Seaton, 1825–1837), (December 15–16, 1835): 1959–60.

5. *NBNW*, February 5, 1836.

6. *RDC*, vol. 12, pt. 2 (December 18, 1835): 1970.

7. Ibid. (December 18, 1835): 1977, 2223.

8. *Congressional Globe*, vol. 3, *1833–1873* (Washington: Blair and Rives), December 18, 1835, 30.

9. Peyton to Robert L. Caruthers, January 8, 1836, RLCP, SHC, University of North Carolina, Chapel Hill.

10. Attorney and state legislator, Whig William B. Campbell was a member of Congress 1838–44. He had served previously in the Seminole War of 1836. When the Mexican War began, he was elected colonel of the First Regiment Tennessee Volunteers and served with distinction. In 1851, he was the successful Whig candidate for governor but did not seek reelection. He opposed secession and was elected to Congress as a Democrat in 1866, but died the following year. West, ed., *Tennessee Encyclopedia*, 121.

11. One of the few Americans to have undertaken military duty in the War of 1812, the Seminole War of 1836, and the Mexican War, Democrat William Trousdale was governor of Tennessee (1849–51) and U.S. minister to Brazil (1853–57). He practiced law in his hometown of Gallatin, where he served as an alderman (1831–35) and was elected to the state senate before leaving for the Seminole War. West, ed., *Tennessee Encyclopedia*, 994–95.

12. Peyton to Will Hart, January 1, 1836, Peyton Papers, TSLA.

13. Peyton to Caruthers, January 8, 1836, RLCP, SHC.

14. Corlew, *A Short History*, 187–88.

15. *Washington Globe*, January 23, 1836.

16. *Congressional Globe*, vol. 3, (January 7, 1836): 84.

17. Ibid. (June 29, 1836): 474–75.

18. *RDC*, vol. 12, pt. 2 (February 3, 1836): 2478–79.

19. Ibid. (February 3–4, 1836): 2,478–82.

20. Ibid. (February 4, 1836): 2,481.

21. Peyton to Campbell, March 9, 1836, DCP, microfilm, TSLA, originals in Special Collections, William R. Perkins Library, Duke University, Durham, N.C.

22. Peyton to Campbell, March 9, 1836, DCP.
23. *Congressional Globe*, vol. 3 (February 15, 1836): 184.
24. Ibid.
25. Peyton to Campbell, March 9, 1836, DCP.
26. Peyton to Caruthers, April 16, 1836, RLCP, SHC.
27. Peyton to Campbell, March 9, 1836, DCP.
28. Peyton Family Manuscript, Private Collection of Kenneth C. Thomson Jr., 19.
29. Peyton to Campbell, March 9, 1836, DCP.
30. Peyton to William Randolph Peyton, March 1, 1836, FC, the HSP.
31. *RDC*, vol. 12, pt. 3 (March 12, 1836): 2758–59.
32. Ibid. (March 26, 1836): 2,988.
33. Quoted in the *NBNW*, April 23, 1836.
34. *RDC*, vol. 12, pt. 3 (March 30, 1836): 3014.
35. Ibid. (March 29, 1836): 3,004; *Washington Globe*, January 11, 1836.
36. Reuben M. Whitney was a former director of the national bank who had resigned when the bank refused his application for a loan. He was a confidential advisor to James K. Polk in 1832–33 and worked with Amos Kendall to set up a system of deposit in selected state banks. Early in his career he had been a merchant in Philadelphia, and he maintained ties to the Girard Bank there throughout most of his later life. Arthur M. Schlesinger Jr., *The Age of Jackson* (Boston: Little, Brown, 1945), 79, 100; Robert Remini, *Andrew Jackson and the Course of American Democracy, 1833–1845* (New York: Harper and Row, 1984), 53, 109.
37. *RDC*, vol. 12, pt. 3 (April 4, 1836): 3095–97.
38. *Congressional Globe*, vol. 3 (April 6, 1836): 286–87.
39. Peyton to Robert L. Caruthers, April 16, 1836, RLCP, SHC.
40. Ibid.
41. Sellers, *James K. Polk, Jacksonian*, 316; *RDC*, vol. 12, pt. 3 (April 19, 1836): 3309–10.
42. *RDC*, vol. 12, pt. 3 (April 19, 1836): 3311.
43. Ibid., 3312–13.
44. Ibid. (April 20, 1836): 3315.
45. Ibid. (May 7, 1836): 3520.
46. May 11, 1836, DCP.
47. Martin Van Buren Papers, LC.
48. *RDC*, vol. 12, pt. 4 (July 1, 1836): 4582.
49. Ibid., 4584.
50. Ibid., 4593–94.
51. Ibid., 4594.
52. Ibid., 4596–97.
53. Ibid., 4596–4602.
54. *NBNW*, August 26, 1836.

55. Ibid.
56. Ibid.
57. Muster Roll, Capt. Jos. C. Guild's company, 2nd Regt., 1st Brigade, Tennessee Mounted Militia, War Department Records, NA. Balie's friend Guild had resigned his seat in the state house of representatives to take the field, and when the regiment elected officers, he was elevated to lieutenant colonel, relieved of the company, and made second in command to Col. William Trousdale. Durham, *Old Sumner*, 235, 266, 269; *NBNW*, September 19, 1836.
58. *NBNW*, August 30, 1836.
59. Ibid.
60. Ibid.
61. Ibid.
62. Ibid. (October 4, 1836).
63. S. H. Laughlin to Polk, September 8, 1836, Weaver, ed., *James K. Polk*, vol. 3, 719–20.
64. William Martin to William B. Campbell, September 8, 1836, DCP.
65. J. S. Brien to William B. Campbell, September 15, 1836, DCP.
66. *NBNW*, September 23, 1836.
67. Ibid.
68. B. R. Owen to William B. Campbell, September 30, 1836, DCP.
69. Quoted in Joseph Howard Parks, *John Bell of Tennessee* (Baton Rouge: Louisiana State University Press, 1950), 128.
70. *RDC*, vol. 13, pt. 1 (December 15, 1836): 1087.
71. Only Caucasian males of voting age were eligible voters in Tennessee.
72. The electoral votes totaled 170 for Van Buren; 73 for Harrison; 26 for White; 14 for Webster; and South Carolina designated its 11 for W. P. Mangum of North Carolina. Richard B. Morris, ed., *Encyclopedia of American History* (New York: Harper and Brothers, 1953), 178.
73. Harrison did not appear on Tennessee ballots. Anne H. Hopkins and William Lyons, *Tennessee Votes: 1779–1976* (Knoxville: Bureau of Public Administration, University of Tennessee, 1978), 24.
74. Corlew, *A Short History*, 189; Thomas P. Abernethy, "The Origins of the Whig Party in Tennessee," *Mississippi Valley Historical Review*, vol. 12 (1926): 522.
75. Jackson to Hardy M. Cryer, November 13, 1836, *American Historical Magazine*, vol. 4, no. 3 (July 1899): 242–43.
76. Speaker Polk reappointed Peyton to the standing committee on the judiciary on December 12, 1836. *RDC*, vol. 13, pt. 1 (December 12, 1836): 1048–49.
77. *RDC*, vol. 13, pt. 1 (December 15, 1836): 1085.

78. Ibid., 1085–86.

79. Ibid., 1085, 1088–89.

80. Speech of Mr. Peyton of Tennessee, December 15, 1836, *Niles Weekly Register*, vol. 51, January 7, 1837, 299.

81. Quoted in *NBNW*, January 4, 1837.

82. New York *Courier and Enquirer* quoted in *NBNW*, January 4, 1837.

83. Nashville *Union*, January 7, 1837.

84. Peyton to Campbell, December 30, 1836, DCP.

85. Ibid.

86. William R. Polk, *Polk's Folly, An American Family History* (New York and London: Doubleday, 2000), 191–92.

87. Harry Worcester Smith, *A Sporting Family of the Old South* (Albany, N.Y.: J. B. Lyon Company, 1936), 13.

88. Balie to William Randolph Peyton, March 1, 1836, FC, the HSP.

89. Anderson, *American Thoroughbred*, x.

90. *NYST*, vol. 6, no. 1 (April 23, 1836).

91. *ATRSM*, vol. 7, no. 6 (February 1836): 287; vol. 7, no. 10 (June 1836): 463.

92. *ATRSM*, vol. 8, no. 5 (January 1837): 229.

CHAPTER 4

1. Thomas Brown, *Politics and Statesmanship: Essays on the American Whig Party* (New York: Columbia University Press, 1985), 157.

2. *RDC, 1824–1837*, vol. 13, pt. 1 (Washington: Gales & Seaton, 1825–1837), (January 3, 1837): 1218–1219.

3. *RDC*, vol. 13, pt. 1 (January 3, 1837): 1219.

4. Ibid., 1220; *Niles Weekly Register*, November 12, 1836.

5. *RDC*, vol. 13, pt. 1 (January 3, 1837): 1223–24.

6. McCormac, *Political Biography*, 110–11; Robert Remini, *Andrew Jackson and the Course of American Democracy, 1833–1845* (New York: Harper and Row, 1984), 53.

7. S. H. Laughlin to James K. Polk, January 5, 1837; Daniel Graham to James K. Polk, January 12, 1837, Herbert Weaver, ed., *Correspondence of James K. Polk*, vol. 4, *1837–1838* (Nashville: Vanderbilt University Press, 1977), 12, 29.

8. Jackson to Donelson, January 11, 1837, John Spencer Bassett, ed., *Correspondence of Andrew Jackson*, vol. 5 (Washington, D.C.: Carnegie Institution of Washington, 1932), 449–50; Jackson to Donelson, January 24, 1837, AJDP, LC.

9. Nashville *Union*, January 14, 1837.

10. Brown, *Politics and Statesmanship*, 157; *NBNW*, January 25, 1837.

11. *Niles Weekly Register*, vol. 51, February 4, 1837. The other members of the committee were Whig Henry Johnson of Louisiana and Democrats Thomas L. Hamer of Ohio, John Fairfield of Maine, Franklin Pierce of New Hampshire, Joshua L. Martin of Alabama, and Ransom H. Gillet of New York. *RDC*, vol. 13, pt. 2, 24th Congress, 2nd Session, appendix, 179.

12. Gales & Seaton, *RDC*, vol. 12, pt. 2 (February 16, 1837): 1773.

13. *Niles Weekly Register*, vol. 51 (February 4, 1837).

14. Ibid.

15. *RDC*, vol. 13, pt. 2 (February 15, 1837): 1771.

16. Nashville *Banner* (December 13, 1899).

17. Regarded as a sharpshooter to be avoided after he killed a man in a duel in 1835, Wise depended on his friends and seconds, Peyton and S. S. Prentiss, to settle challenges before they reached the dueling ground. As he did not hesitate to issue or accept challenges, his seconds had several opportunities to negotiate face-saving settlements. One of Wise's biographers believes that pre-duel negotiations by Peyton and Prentiss more than once saved Wise from being indicted for murder. Craig M. Simpson, *A Good Southerner: The Life of Henry A. Wise of Virginia* (Chapel Hill: University of North Carolina Press, 1985), 38.

18. *RDC*, vol. 13, pt. 2 (February 4, 1837): 1756–57.

19. Ibid., 1577.

20. Ibid., 2, (February 4, 1837): 1576, 1777.

21. Ibid., 1575, 1577–78, 1582.

22. *Washington Globe*, January 30, 1837.

23. Ibid., 1837.

24. Jackson to Andrew Jackson Donelson, January 31, 1837, AJDP, LC.

25. *Washington Globe*, February 9, 1837; Nashville *Union*, March 21, 1837.

26. *RDC*, vol. 12, pt. 2 (February 13, 1837): 1735, 1738.

27. Ibid., 1739.

28. Ibid., 1741–53, 1766.

29. *RDC*, vol. 13, pt. 2 (February 16, 1837): 1782.

30. Quoted in *NBNW*, March 6, 1837.

31. Nashville *Union*, March 11, 14, 21, 1837.

32. *RDC*, vol. 12, pt. 2 (February 16, 1837): 1775–83.

33. *RDC*, vol. 13, pt. 2 (February 17, 1837): 1787–93.

34. Ibid., 1807–10.

35. Ibid. (February 18, 1837): 1858–60.

36. Ibid. (February 20–21, 1837): 1878–79, 1882; Baltimore *Patriot*, February 19, 1837.

37. Nashville *Union*, January 10, February 18, 1837.

38. February 25, 1837.

39. *RDC*, vol. 13, pt. 2 (March 4, 1837): 2076–77.

40. Ibid. (March 1, 1837): 2077–85.

41. Quoted in *NBNW*, March 8, 1837.

42. *NYST*, February 25, 1837.

43. Peyton to Jackson, February 16, 1837, Andrew Jackson Papers, LC; Jackson to Peyton, February 24, 1837, Bassett, ed., *Andrew Jackson*, vol. 5, 460–61.

44. Nancy N. Scott, ed., *A Memoir of Hugh Lawson White* (Philadelphia: J. B. Lippincott & Co., 1856), 324. Presumably the term Houstonized means to be run out of the state or out of the country, recalling Sam Houston's resignation as governor of Tennessee on April 16, 1829, after his first wife, Eliza Allen, left him and he left the state and country for Texas.

45. Peyton to Dr. B. R. Owen, February 8, 1837, DCP, microfilm, TSLA.

46. Sellers, *James K. Polk, Jacksonian*, 322–23.

47. *National Intelligencer*, March 7, 1837; *Patriot* quoted in *National Intelligencer*, March 9, 1837.

48. *NBNW*, April 17, 1837.

49. Quoted in *NBNW*, May 8, 1837.

50. Maryville (TN) *Intelligencer* quoted in *NBNW*, April 28, 1837. By referring to "the Augean stables" Peyton employed a Greek legend to suggest the need for cleaning out the corruption that existed in several federal departments. The amount of corruption was suggested by the fact that the stables of King Augeas held three thousand oxen and had remained uncleaned for thirty years.

51. Athens *Courier* quoted in the Nashville *Union*, May 18, 1837.

52. John F. Gillespy to Polk, May 5, 1837, Weaver, ed., *James K. Polk*, vol. 4, 112–13.

53. Trousdale to James K. Polk, April 27, 1837, Weaver, ed., *James K. Polk*, vol. 4, 102; *NR* quoted in *NBNW*, April 28, 1837.

54. McCormac, *Political Biography* 113; Maryville (Tenn.) *Intelligencer* quoted in *NBNW*, April 28, 1837.

55. Lawson Grifford to James K. Polk, July 26, 1837, Weaver, ed., *James K. Polk*, vol. 4, 192.

56. Jonesborough *Republican* copied in *NBNW*, May 3, 1837.

57. Quoted in the *NBNW*, July 21, 1837.

58. Nashville *Union*, July 13, 1837.

59. Peyton to Campbell, July 19, 1837, DCP.

60. Peyton to Campbell, August 5, 1837, DCP.

61. Columbia (Tenn.) *Observer* quoted in *NBNW*, September 12, 1837.

62. Texas was the location of extensive landholdings on the Red River that Balie's brother Randolph had acquired from Dr. William McKendree Gwin two years before. In the early summer Ran had advertised the land for sale in one-league tracts. *NBNW*, June 5, 1837.

63. Harold Sinclair, *The Port of New Orleans* (New York: Doubleday, Doran & Co., 1942), 193–94.

64. Nashville *Union*, August 17, 1837.

65. *NYST*, April 8, 1837.

66. *NYST*, January 28, September 9, 1837.

67. Vol. 8, no. 11, 526–27.

68. *NYST*, September 9, 1837.

69. *ATRSM*, vol. 8, no. 11 (September 1837), 527; *NYST*, July 22, 1837.

70. Youree had named his horse for Peyton hoping that, like Balie, it would run hard and win. *NYST*, October 7, 21, 1837; *ATRSM*, vol. 8, no. 12 (November 1837), 562.

71. *NYST*, October 21, 1837.

72. Charles Smith to Samuel W. Smith, October 27, 1837, DCP.

CHAPTER 5

1. By 1840, New Orleans had a population of 102,193. Martin Siegel, ed. and comp., *New Orleans: A Chronological and Documentary History 1539–1970* (Dobbs Ferry, N.Y.: Oceana Publications, 1975), 16.

2. In 1837, Breedlove, a Democrat, was collector of the port, a lucrative political appointment that terminated with the election of a Whig president in 1840. He then became president of the Atchafalaya Bank. *Gibson's Guide and Directory of the State of Louisiana, and the Cities of New Orleans and Lafayette* (New Orleans: Published and printed by John Gibson, 1838), 29, 164, 345.

3. *Michel & Co. New Orleans Annual and Commercial Directory for 1843* (New Orleans: Printed by Justin L. Sollee, 1842), 259.

4. Minutes of the Louisiana Supreme Court, January 9, 1838, vol. 5, Baton Rouge, 339.

5. *NYST*, March 10, April 14, 1838.

6. *ATRSM*, vol. 9. no. 2 (February 1838), 75–77.

7. Anderson, *American Thoroughbred*, 7.

8. *NYST*, May 12, 19, 1838; December 16, 1876.

9. Ibid. (May 19, 1838).

10. Ibid. (October 28, 1843).

11. Anderson, *American Thoroughbred*, 196.

12. *NYST*, May 19, 1838.

13. Ibid.

14. *ATRSM*, vol. 10 (January and February, 1839), 107; *NYST*, February 2, March 30, 1839.

15. Anderson, *American Thoroughbred*, 101, 108; *NYST*, June 9, 1838.

16. *NYST*, May 26, 1838.

17. *ATRSM*, vol. 10 (Mar.–April, 1839), 232.

18. *NYST*, February 2, 1839.

19. *ATRSM*, vol. 9, no. 11 (November 1838), 513, 520.

20. Ibid., vol. 9, no. 6 (June 1838): 274–75.

21. Ibid., vol. 10 (July 1839): appendix, 21.

22. Gallatin *Union*, October 4, 1839. A Sumner Countian, Youree maintained a stable near Gallatin.

23. *NYST*, November 2, 1839.

24. A wealthy Maury County planter who had married President Andrew Jackson's favorite niece Mary Eastin, Lucious J. Polk was a cousin of President James K. Polk. He broke with Jackson politically during the president's second term and became an ardent Whig. William R. Polk, *Polk's Folly, An American Family History* (New York, London: Doubleday, 2000), xiv–xv, 171–72.

25. Anderson, *American Thoroughbred*, 191–93.

26. *Southern Cultivator*, October 25, 1839.

27. *NYST*, March 7, 1839.

28. Anderson, *American Thoroughbred*, 111.

29. *ATRSM*, vol. 11 (1840), appendix, 29.

30. Ibid., vol. 10 (January–February 1839): 108; vol. 10 (March–April, 1839): 232; *NYST* (February 23, 1839).

31. For example, J. Shall Yerger had become a partner with him and Dr. Chalmers in the ownership of Black Maria, and Alexander Henderson was part owner of Maria Shepherd.

32. *NYST*, June 15, 1839.

33. Ibid. (October 26, 1839); *ATRSM*, vol. 10 (November 1839): 635.

34. *NYST*, November 23, 1839.

35. Alexander Barrow (1801–46), a native Tennessean, was admitted to the Nashville bar in 1822. Soon afterward he moved to New Orleans where he practiced law and was a prominent figure in local Whig politics. In 1840, he was elected to the U.S. Senate from Louisiana and served in that capacity until his death. He was a half brother of Washington Barrow, Nashville attorney, editor, businessman, congressman, and minister to Portugal. *Directory of Congress*, 582.

36. John Jordan Crittenden (1786–1863), a Kentucky attorney, was elected to the U.S. Senate in 1817 and resigned in 1819 but was elected to the same chamber as a Whig (1835–41, 1842–48). He returned to the U.S. Senate (1855–61) after serving as governor of Kentucky (1848–50). *Directory of Congress*, 847.

37. Peyton to Crittenden, May 23, 1841, JJCP, LC; Mortgage, Peyton to Godfrey M. Fogg and Ephraim H. Foster, trustees, April 30, 1840, Deed Book 17, 250, SCA, Gallatin. The names

and estimated ages of the slaves were listed in the deed of trust as follows: Charles, 50, and Jenny, his wife, 45; Jesse, 32, and his wife, Peggy, 30, with her 4-month-old child; Darwin, 22, and his wife, Betsy, 19, with her 8-month-old child; Fanny, 30, with her 4-month-old child; Matilda, 28; Hi, 17; Maria, 14; Eliza, 12; Louisa, 10; William, 5; Sack, 16; Lethe, 15; Dycy, 14; Tom, 12; Sam, 6; Allen, 3 months; Caswell, 14; Elizabeth, 13; Anthony, 12; and Caty, 5. All were warranted to be healthy, except Jenny who was in "feeble health" and Caty who was "deaf and dumb."

38. *ATRSM*, vol. 11 (July 1840), 362.

39. *NYST*, January 16, March 6, 1841.

40. Ibid. (November 6, 1841).

41. *ATRSM*, vol. 12 (November 1841), 637–38.

42. *NYST*, December 16, 1876.

43. *ATRSM*, vol. 12 (November 1841), 637–38.

44. Bill of Sale, February 21, 1843, SCA.

45. *NYST*, December 12, 1840, January 16, 1841.

46. Ibid. (June 5, 1841).

47. Harding was owner of the Belle Meade plantation and stud located just west of Nashville. Carroll Van West, ed., *The Tennessee Encyclopedia of History & Culture* (Nashville: Tennessee Historical Society, 1998), 407.

48. *NYST*, October 16, 1841.

49. Ibid. (October 1, 1842).

50. Ibid. (June 3, 1843).

51. Ibid. (September 3, 1842).

52. J. P. Gatlin to John H. Gatlin, May 13, 1843, author's collection.

53. Adolphe Mazureau to Crittenden, January 4, 1842, and Peyton to Crittenden, February 22, 1842, JJCP, LC; Albert Dennis Kirwan, *John J. Crittenden: The Struggle for the Union* (Lexington: University of Kentucky Press, 1962), 158.

54. Peyton to Crittenden, February 22, 1842, JJCP, LC.

55. *NYST* (December 12, 25, 1841).

56. Ibid. (November 19, 1842).

57. Six of the nominees were dead by this time. *ATRSM*, vol. 12 (August 1841): 459.

58. Vol. 12 (August 1841), 459.

59. *NYST* (July 30, August 13, 1842).

60. Ibid. (July 29, September 2, 1843).

61. *Daily Nashville American* (December 11, 1877) quoting Dr. J. W. Weldon in *NYST*.

62. *NYST* (April 15, 1843).

63. Ibid. (August 6, October 29, 1842).

64. SCDB 19 (October 7, 1844): 357, SCA.

65. *NRB*, October 11, 1843.

66. *NYST*, October 28, 1843.

67. Ibid. (October 18, 1843).
68. *ATRSM*, vol. 14 (November 1843), 678.
69. *NODP*, March 13, 22, and 24, April 12, 1844.
70. *NYST*, April 6, 1844.
71. Ridley Wills II, *The History of Belle Meade: Mansion, Plantation, and Stud* (Nashville: Vanderbilt University Press, 1991), 58–59.
72. *NYST*, March 30, 1844; January 4, 1845.
73. Ibid. (June 22, 1844).
74. *NODP*, December 15, 1844.
75. *NYST*, June 2, 1845.
76. Ibid. (January 11, 1845).
77. *NODP* (May 23, June 7, 1845).
78. Ibid. (May 27, 1845).
79. *NYST*, October 18, 1845; *NODP*, October 19, 1845; *NODD*, October 24, 1845.
80. *NODP*, November 15, 19, 21, 1845.
81. *NYST*, February 14, 1846.
82. *NODP*, April 7, 1846.
83. Ibid. (April 4, 7, 1846).
84. *NYST*, March 28, 1846.
85. *NODP*, December 18, 1847.
86. Sumner County Clerk Records, Miscellaneous Bills of Sale, vol. B, 1844–1851, 316, SCA

CHAPTER 6

1. Gallatin *Union*, January 20, 1837.
2. Peyton to William B. Campbell, March 2, 1838, DCP, microfilm, TSLA.
3. Fourteen banks in the city had suspended payment in specie the prior year, and each of the three municipalities issued its own currency. Martin Siegel, ed. and comp, *New Orleans: A Chronological and Documentary History 1539–1970* (Dobbs Ferry, N.Y.: Oceana Publications, 1975), 16.
4. Peyton to William B. Campbell, March 2, 1838, DCP. Had he not been so busy he would probably have seen some of the autumn performances staged in New Orleans in 1837 by the Brichta Italian Opera Company at the St. Charles Theatre and at the Theater d'Orleans. Or he could have attended presentations of other music and dance groups that frequented the city, many scheduling stops after performing at Havana, Cuba. Alfred E. Lemmon, "Across the Gulf: From New Orleans to Havana," *Historic New Orleans Collection Quarterly*, vol. 16, no. 4 (fall 1998): 6–7.
5. November 24, 1838.
6. John M. Sacher, "The Sudden Collapse of the Louisiana Whig Party," *Journal of Southern History*, vol. 65, no. 2 (May 1999): 222–25.
7. Peyton to Wise, June 17, 1838, Miscellaneous Collection, HSP.
8. Ibid.

9. Peyton to William B. Campbell, March 2, 1838, DCP.
10. Catron to James K. Polk, April 18, 1838, Weaver, ed., *James K. Polk*, vol. 4, 431.
11. *NODP*, September 13, 15, 25, 1839.
12. A conviction under Louisiana law carried a fine of no more than one thousand dollars and/or a prison sentence of no more than two years. *NODP*, July 4, 1839.
13. *NODP*, July 4, 1839.
14. Ibid.
15. Ibid. (July 6, 1839).
16. Ibid. (July 9, 10, 1839).
17. Ibid. (July 13, 1839).
18. Ibid. (April 26, 30, 1840).
19. It was identified as Township Twenty-Four, Range Number 30, lot number eight. H. B. Cenas, vol. 33, 529–30, May 22, 1845, NARC.
20. John S. Preston endorsed the note signed on February 11, 1837, by its makers Jesse Strong, William Gilmore, and Jacob Hollingsworth, and later assumed by five other investors. March 30, 1839, Act #252, T. Seghers, vol. 31, NARC.
21. Joseph Hopkins Peyton to William B. Campbell, October 26, 1839, DCP.
22. J. H. Peyton to William B. Campbell, January 10, 1840, DCP.
23. Peyton to William B. Campbell, November 26, 1840, DCP.
24. *NODP*, January 5, 1840.
25. Ibid. (January 8–10, 1840).
26. John S. Bassett, ed., *Correspondence of Andrew Jackson, 1839–1845*, vol. 6 (Washington, D.C.: Carnegie Institution of Washington, 1931), 49–51.
27. *NODP*, February 14, 1840.
28. Gallatin *Union*, April 18, 1840.
29. New Orleans *Advertiser*, May 11, 1840; *NODP*, May 5, 1840.
30. *NODP*, June 27, 1840.
31. The discussions nationwide were so stimulating that the voter turnout in 1840 reached 80.2 percent, up from 57.8 percent in 1836. Michael F. Holt, *Political Parties and American Political Development from the Age of Jackson to the Age of Lincoln* (Baton Rouge and London: Louisiana State University Press, 1992), 151, 153.
32. *NODP*, July 4, 1840; *NODB*, July 4, 1840.
33. Foote was later U.S. Senator and governor of Mississippi. He had moved to Nashville by 1861 when he was elected to represent the Nashville District in the Confederate Congress. Nashville *Daily American*, May 21, 1880.

34. *NODP*, August 14, 1840.

35. Henry Stuart Foote, *Texas and the Texans, or the Advance of the Anglo Americans to the South-West*, vol. 1 (Philadelphia: Thomas Copperthwart & Co., 1841), iv.

36. *NRB*, August 13, 18–19, 1840.

37. Nashville *Whig*, August 19, 1840.

38. *NRB*, August 22, 1840.

39. Ibid. (September 3, 1840).

40. Virginia Campbell to Mrs. Mary Hamilton Campbell, October 16, 1840, DCP.

41. *NRB*, October 1, 1840; J. M. Davis et al. to William B. Campbell, October 1, 1840, DCP.

42. *NODP*, November 15, 17, 1840.

43. During his own term of office, 1889–93, President Benjamin Harrison recounted the story to John Bell Peyton, Balie's son. Unidentified, undated Nashville newspaper clipping, Vertical Files, TSLA.

44. Chinn to Crittenden, December 26, 1840, JJCP, LC.

45. Lyon G. Tyler to John B. Peyton, June 19, 1889, correspondence by author, TSLA.

46. Peyton to William B. Campbell, March 4, April 18, 1841, DCP.

47. Certificate of Appointment, Peyton Papers, TSLA; Washington *National Intelligencer*, April 20, 1841.

48. *NODP*, April 19, 1841.

49. Peyton to Crittenden, May 23, 1841, JJCP.

50. August 15, 1841, Wayne Cutler, ed., *Correspondence of James K. Polk*, vol. 5, 1839–1841 (Nashville: Vanderbilt University Press, 1979), 725.

51. Lyon G. Tyler to John B. Peyton, June 19, 1889, correspondence by author, TSLA.

52. Ibid.; James Grant Wilson and John Fiske, eds., *Appleton's Cyclopedia of American Biography*, vol. 4 (New York: D. Appleton and Company, 1888), 748.

53. *NODP*, May 8, 1841.

54. Ibid.

55. Nolan B. Harmon Jr., *The Famous Case of Myra Clark Gaines* (Baton Rouge: Louisiana State University Press, 1946), 235, 237; *NODP*, May 8, 1841. Litigation over all aspects of the Myra Gaines case continued until after her death in 1885. The U.S. Supreme Court made a final ruling in 1891 that provided for a settlement of $576,707.92 in favor of her estate. Harmon, *The Famous Case of Myra Clark Gaines*, 451, 453.

56. New Orleans *Daily Orleanian*, February 7, 1848.

57. *NODB*, July 3, 1841; *NODP*, July 3, 1841.

58. *NODB*, July 6, 1841.

59. Ibid. (July 7, 1841).

60. Ibid.; *NODP*, July 7, 1841.

61. Report by the chargé d'affaires of the French Legation in Texas, Dubois de Saligny, June 1, 1841, in Nancy Nichols Barker, ed. and trans., *The French Legation in Texas*, vol. 1 (Austin: Texas State Historical Association, 1971), 248. In Texas, Chalmers became secretary of the treasury of the republic under President Mirabeau B. Lamar. C. Richard King, *The Lady Cannoneer: A Biography of Angelina Belle Peyton Eberly, Heroine of the Texas Archives War* (Burnet, Tex.: Eakin Press, 1981) 112.

62. Book 30, 582, Office of the Register of Conveyances, Parish of Orleans, New Orleans, Louisiana.

63. Clerk of Wayne County, Kentucky, to author, February 1, 2000; Clerk of Pulaski County, Kentucky, to author, February 3, 2000.

64. Book 29, 215, May 1, 1841, Office of the Register of Conveyances, Parish of Orleans, New Orleans, Louisiana.

65. Book 30, 644, November 17, 1841, Office of the Register of Conveyances, Parish of Orleans, New Orleans, Louisiana.

66. *NODP*, January 16, 1842.

67. Ibid.

68. Ibid. (April 20, 1842).

69. April 22, 1842.

70. *NODP*, May 27, 1842.

71. *NODB*, June 19, 20, 22, 1842.

72. Ibid. (June 22, 1842).

73. *NODP*, June 18, 1843.

74. Ibid. (April 18, 27; June 4, 7, 14–15, 1844); New Orleans *Commercial Bulletin*, March 30, 1847.

75. *NODP*, May 9, 10, 1843.

76. It was the state-chartered successor to the Bank of the United States that Jackson had finally overcome in 1834.

77. *NODB*, April 23, 1843; *NODP*, May 23, 1843.

78. Balie to Joseph Hopkins Peyton, January 28, 1844, Peyton Papers, TSLA.

79. John R. Grymes, P. Anderson, C. Roselius, and Thomas Slidell to the Commercial Court of New Orleans, December 5, 1843, JJCP, LC.

80. Peyton to Charles B. Penrose, Solicitor of the Treasury, August 12, 1844, JJCP, LC.

81. *NODP*, March 3, April 3, 10, December 18, 1844.

82. Ibid. (June 29, 1844).

83. Joseph Hopkins Peyton to William B. Campbell, January 5, April 6, 1841, DCP.

84. A political and personal protégé of Andrew Jackson, Robert Armstrong attracted the general's attention as a heroic artilleryman in the Creek War of 1813. He was an unsuccessful candidate for governor of Tennessee in 1837, even with the backing of Whigs Campbell

and Bell. Marquis James, *Andrew Jackson: Portrait of a President* (New York: Garden City Publishing Co., 1940), 383, 442, 472.

85. Robert Armstrong to James K. Polk, December 20, 1842, Wayne Cutler, ed., *Correspondence of James K. Polk*, vol. 6, *1842–1843* (Nashville: Vanderbilt University Press, 1983), 153; Thomas Barry to Governor James C. Jones, June 17, 1842, Governors Papers, TSLA.

86. Joseph Hopkins Peyton to William B. Campbell, January 29, November 20, December 10, 1843, DCP.

87. The thirty-five-year-old mother's children were Caroline, age six, and John, four. Sumner County Clerk Records, Miscellaneous Bills of Sale, vol. B, 1844–1851, SCA, 41.

88. Sumner County Clerk Records, Misc. Bills of Sale, vol. B, 1844–1851, SCA, 82.

89. Barton H. Wise, *The Life of Henry A. Wise of Virginia, 1806–1876* (New York: MacMillan Company, 1899), 97.

90. *NODP*, February 20, 1844.

91. Ibid. (February 23–24, 1844).

92. Oscar T. Shuck, ed., *History of Bench and Bar of California* (Los Angeles: Commercial Printing House, 1901), 282–83.

93. H. B. Cenas, vol. 26A, 465–66, June 22, 1842, NARC.

94. Senate Document 257, 29th Congress, First Session, *Public Documents Printed by Order of the Senate of the United States*, vol. 5 (Washington: Ritchie & Heiss, 1846); *Reports of Committees, Thirtieth Congress, First Session, Senate, Rep. Com. 49*; Balie Peyton to Joseph Peyton, January 28, 1844, Peyton Papers, TSLA.

95. H. B. Cenas, vol. 33, 529–30, May 22, 1845, NARC.

CHAPTER 7

1. Balie Peyton to Joseph Hopkins Peyton, January 28, 1844, Peyton Papers, TSLA.

2. *Congressional Globe*, vol. 13, *1833–1873* (Washington: Blair and Rives, 1844), 96; *Appendix to the Congressional Globe for the First Session Twenty-eighth Congress [1843–1844]* (Washington: Blair and Rives, 1844), 46.

3. Balie Peyton to Joseph Hopkins Peyton, January 28, 1844, Peyton Papers, TSLA.

4. Thomas Brown, *Politics and Statesmanship: Essays on the American Whig Party* (New York: Columbia University Press, 1985), 167; Joseph Hopkins Peyton to William B. Campbell, January 13, March 6, May 29, 1844, DCP, microfilm, TSLA.

5. Joseph Hopkins Peyton to William B. Campbell, May 29, 1844, DCP.

6. Joseph Hopkins Peyton to William B. Campbell, February 16, 1845, DCP.

7. Balie Peyton to Joseph H. Peyton, June 30, 1845, DCP; *NRB*, June 21, 1844; Nashville *Banner*, April 16, 1886.

8. Balie Peyton to Joseph H. Peyton, June 30, 1845, DCP.

9. Ibid.; *NODP*, January 15, 1845.

10. Loose Court Records, Lawsuits 7316, 10326, SCA; John S. Brien brief book, Buell-Brien Papers, TSLA. Lewis died at Gallatin of natural causes, December 8, 1862. Margaret Cummings Snider and Joan Hollis Yorgason, comps., *Sumner County, Tennessee, Cemetery Records* (4–7) (Owensboro, Ky.: McDowell Publications, 1981), 4–6.

11. *NRB*, June 24, July 10, 1844.

12. John Patterson to William B. Campbell, July 8, 1844, DCP.

13. *NRB*, September 16, 1844.

14. Jackson to Polk, December 16, 1844, Wayne Cutler, ed., *Correspondence of James K. Polk*, vol. 8, *September–December, 1844* (Knoxville: University of Tennessee Press, 1993), 438.

15. *NODP*, May 24, 1845.

16. Martin Siegel, ed. and comp., *New Orleans: A Chronological and Documentary History 1539–1970* (Dobbs Ferry, N.Y.: Oceana Publications, 1975), 17, 19.

17. *NODP*, March 29, 1844.

18. John Magill, "Facets of Childhood in Nineteenth-Century New Orleans," *Historic New Orleans Collection Quarterly*, vol. 16, no. 4 (fall 1998), 2–3; Donald E. DeVore and Joseph Logsdon, *Crescent City Schools: Public Education in New Orleans, 1841–1991* (New Orleans: Center for Louisiana Studies, University of Southwestern Louisiana, 1991), 5, 10, 18.

19. *NODP*, January 14, 1845.

20. Peyton Family Manuscript, 115, Private Collection of Kenneth C. Thomson Jr.; *NODP*, January 14, 1845.

21. Balie Peyton to Joseph H. Peyton, June 30, 1845, DCP.

22. B. R. Howard to William B. Campbell, November 11–12, 1845. DCP.

23. *NODB*, August 10, 1846; *NODP*, August 9, 1846.

24. Nashville *Whig*, August 10, 1844.

25. Allan Nevins, ed., *Polk: The Diary of a President, 1845–1849* (New York: Longman, Green, and Co., 1929), 8–9.

26. Ibid., 9, 269.

27. *NODD*, May 13, 1846; Harold Sinclair, *The Port of New Orleans* (New York: Doubleday, Doran & Company, 1942), 195.

28. Peyton to William B. Campbell, June 26, 1846, DCP.

29. Order dated May 13, *NODD*, May 21, 1846; *NODP*, September 2, 1846.

30. *NODD*, May 15, 1846.

31. May 25, 1846.

32. He hung the flag on the balustrade of the New Commercial Exchange until he and his men sailed. "On the one side is the motto of the regiment—*Conquer or Die*—and underneath, in a circle, 'Presented to the Orleans Regiment by the ladies of New Orleans.' On the reverse are the arms of the state—the pelican feeding her young—and underneath, the motto, *Union and Confidence*," reported the *Daily Delta*, May 23, 1846.

33. A protégé of Andrew Jackson, William McKendree Gwin (1803–84) held lucrative appointments in Mississippi and Louisiana. He later moved to California and became that state's first full-term U.S. senator. He and Peyton were acquaintances, but political differences kept them from developing the friendship one might expect from two second-generation Tennessee frontiersmen born only a few miles apart. Walter T. Durham, *Volunteer Forty-Niners: Tennesseans and the California Gold Rush* (Nashville and London: Vanderbilt University Press, 1997), 122, 124.

34. The staff included Lt. Col. H. W. Dunlap; W. T. Fortson, Adjutant; T. H. Hayes, Quartermaster; A. C. Hunter, Sergeant-Major; John Shannon, Quartermaster Sergeant; J. L. Satterfield, Surgeon; J. B. Henderson, Assistant Surgeon; C. B. Buckner, 2nd Assistant Surgeon; and J. W. Wilson, Paymaster. *NODD*, May 26, 1846.

35. Charles K. Gardner, *Dictionary of all Officers, Who Have Been Commissioned, or Have Been Appointed and Served in the Army of the United States* . . . (New York: G. P. Putnam and Company, 1853), 414, 537.

36. *NODP*, May 27–28, June 9, 16, 1846.

37. The secretary assigned Gen. George M. Brooks to command the Western Division. *NODP*, June 11, September 8, 11, 1846.

38. The camp was on high ground overlooking the Rio Grande about eight air miles from the Gulf but about twenty-five by the meanders of the river. Burita was a tiny village, "a cluster of huts." Justin H. Smith, *War with Mexico*, vol. 1 (New York: Macmillan & Co., 1919), 159, 162, 206.

39. Peyton to Campbell, June 29, 1846, DCP; *NODP*, June 20, 1846.

40. Peyton to Campbell, June 29, 1846, DCP.

41. *NODD*, August 2, 1846.

42. Ibid.; *NODP*, August 2, 1846.

43. *NRB*, August 14, 1846.

44. It was reported erroneously in New Orleans that he had joined a Tennessee regiment as its second in command. *NODP*, August 9, 1846.

45. August 22, 1846.

46. Compiled Military Service Records for the Mexican War, NA.

47. Bounty Land Files, Claim dated February 4, 1847, NA.

48. This and subsequent paragraphs about the Battle of Monterrey are based on and/or quoted from Peyton's account of the part played by General Worth's regular army division and Jack Hays's Texas Mounted Riflemen. Detailing that part of the battle in which he participated as an aide to General Worth and about which he was thoroughly informed, he added a tribute to the First Regiment of Tennessee Volunteers whose assault on the enemy was not within his view. He wrote the account from Monterrey on September 25 in the form of a letter published in the *NODP*, October 23, 1846, and afterward copied widely in other newspapers.

49. Jack Hays's mother was Elizabeth Cage, whose family lived about five miles from Peyton's farm in Sumner County. Her father, like Balie's, was an early settler in the area. The career of Jack Hays, born in adjoining Wilson County, Tennessee, was well known to Peyton. Jay Guy Cisco, *Historic Sumner County, Tennessee* (Nashville: Folk Keelin, 1909), 191–92.

50. *NODP*, October 23, 1846.

51. Anderson, *American Thoroughbred*, xi; Peyton to Crittenden, October 2, 1846, JJCP, LC.

52. Peyton to Crittenden, October 2, 1846, JJCP, LC.

53. *NODP*, October 3, 1846.

54. Peyton to Crittenden, October 2, 1846, JJCP, LC.

55. *NODP*, February 18, 1847.

56. Nashville *Tri-Weekly Union*, November 14, 1846.

57. Peyton Family Manuscript, 13.

58. Milo Milton Quaife, ed., *The Diary of James K. Polk, During His Presidency, 1845–1849*, Chicago Historical Society Collections, vol. 2 (Chicago: A. C. McClurg & Co., 1910), 236.

59. Peyton to Crittenden, November 5, 1846, JJCP, LC.

60. *NODP*, October 21, 1846; *NRB*, October 30, 1846.

61. Nashville *Tri-Weekly Union*, November 10, 1846. Feeling his honor threatened at the moment, he turned to the ultimate nineteenth-century example of manhood: a willingness to put his life on the line. Bertram Wyatt-Brown, *Honor and Violence in the Old South* (New York and Oxford: Oxford University Press, 1986), viii.

62. Peyton to Gen. Albert S. Johnston, October 11, 1846, four o'clock P.M.; Marshall to Peyton, October 11, 1846, six o'clock P.M.;

Peyton to Crittenden, November 5, 1846, JJCP, LC.

63. *NODB*, October 30, 1846.

64. Peyton to Crittenden, October 2, 1846, JJCP, LC.

65. Jefferson Finis Davis (1808–89) was a West Point graduate and was an army officer until 1835, when he moved to Mississippi to become a planter, Democratic congressman (1845–46), and U.S. senator (1847–51; 1857–61). He was a colonel commanding the First Regiment Mississippi Riflemen in the Mexican War; U.S. Secretary of War (1853–57); and president of the Confederate States of America (1861–65). *Directory of Congress*, 879.

66. Davis to Peyton, November 1, 1846, DCP.

67. Peyton to Davis, November 3, 1846, DCP.

68. Prentiss had moved to New Orleans the year before. *NODP*, October 19, 1845.

69. Peyton to Campbell, November 5, 1846, DCP.

70. Davis to Peyton, November 14, 1846, DCP.

71. Nashville *Tri-Weekly Union*, November 17, 1846; Nashville *Whig*, November 17, 1846.

72. Ephraim H. Foster (1794–1854) was a Nashville attorney and Whig political leader, serving briefly in the U.S. Senate (1838–39) and the House of Representatives (1843–45). He was a presidential elector for state-at-large on the 1840 Whig ticket of William Henry Harrison and John Tyler and was an unsuccessful candidate for governor of Tennessee in 1845. Robert M. McBride and Dan M. Robison, *Biographical Directory of the Tennessee General Assembly, 1796–1861*, vol. 1 (Nashville: Tennessee State Library and Archives and Tennessee Historical Commission, 1975), 257–58.

73. Nashville *Union and American*, December 3, 1846.

74. Office of the Register of Conveyances, Parish of Orleans, New Orleans, Louisiana, Book 42, January 27, 1847, 353.

75. Minutes of the Monument Public Meeting at Gallatin, November 21, 1846, DCP.

76. Ibid.

77. Ibid.

78. The citizens of Lawrence County also raised a Mexican War monument at Lawrenceburg, the only other memorial to Mexican War soldiers erected in Tennessee. Only seven other monuments commemorating the war were erected in the entire United States. *The Tennessean Magazine*, December 9, 1934; Cisco, *Historic Sumner County, Tennessee*, 46–55.

79. Colonel Davis's speech at Vicksburg, Mississippi, extracted from the Vicksburg *Sentinel* by the Nashville *Whig*, December 5,

1846; James T. McIntosh, Lynda L. Crist, and Mary S. Dix, eds., *The Papers of Jefferson Davis*, vol. 3, July 1846–December 1848 (Baton Rouge and London: Louisiana State University Press, 1981), 79, 83n.

80. Peyton to Campbell, December 8, 1846, DCP.

81. Ibid.

82. Nashville *Union*, December 3, 1846.

83. Peyton to William B. Campbell, February 20, 1847, DCP.

CHAPTER 8

1. *NODP*, December 15, 1846.

2. Peyton to Campbell, December 12, 1846, DCP, microfilm, TSLA.

3. A Democrat, Anderson was second in command to Colonel Campbell in Mexico. Durham, *Old Sumner*, 229.

4. Democrat Aaron V. Brown was the incumbent governor.

5. Peyton to Campbell, December 12, 1846, DCP.

6. PFN; *NODP*, January 8, 1847.

7. Peyton to Campbell, February 20, 1847, DCP; *NODP*, February 18, 1847; *The Jeffersonian*, March 30, 1847.

8. *NODP*, February 18, 1847.

9. Ibid. (March 31, 1847).

10. Caleb Cushing (1800–1879) was a Massachusetts attorney, legislator, congressman, and jurist; minister to China; brigadier general, Mexican War; U.S. Attorney General; minister to Spain; holder of various presidential appointments and assignments. *Directory of Congress*, 861.

11. *NODP*, April 1, 1847.

12. Ibid. (May 9, 27, 1847); Nashville *Daily American*, December 11, 1877, quoting Dr. J. W. Weldon in *NYST*.

13. The power specifically directed him to secure a debt of $1,498.38 owed to one John M. Henley at Gallatin, which he did by conveying title to six slaves. Barry listed the slaves as "Letty, aged 31 years; Jane, 31 years; Cosswell, aged 21 years; Henry Clay, aged 4 years; Lizzy, aged 2 years; and Martha, aged 10 years." SCDB 20, 179–80, SCA.

14. Arthur M. Schlesinger Jr., ed., *The Almanac of American History* (New York: G. P. Putnam's Sons, 1983), 253–54.

15. Judah Philip Benjamin (1811–1884) was a New Orleans attorney, state legislator and, in 1853, Whig U.S. senator. He was reelected to the Senate in 1859 as a Democrat, but withdrew in 1861. He served the Confederate States of America as attorney general, secretary of war, and secretary of state. He moved to England in 1865, practiced law there, and was appointed the

queen's counsel in 1872. In 1883, he retired and moved to Paris, France. *Directory of Congress*, 607.

16. General Taylor was called "old rough and ready" by his soldiers. *NODP*, July 12, 30, 1847.

17. *NODP*, August 24, 1847.

18. Ibid. (July 11, 1847).

19. Ibid. (November 4–5, 16, 18, 1847).

20. Ibid. (December 1, 5, 1847).

21. Peyton to Crittenden, January 25, 1848, JJCP, LC.

22. Ibid.

23. Peyton to Reuben Chapman, December 30, 1847, American Diplomats, HSP.

24. George Washington Barrow to William B. Campbell, January 6, 1848, DCP.

25. Daniel Walker Howe, *The Political Culture of the American Whigs* (Chicago: University of Chicago Press, 1979), 300.

26. Holman Hamilton, *Soldier in the White House* (Indianapolis and New York: The Bobbs-Merrill Company, 1951), 66.

27. *NODP*, January 22, 1848. A few days before, Peyton was gratified to learn that both houses of the Tennessee General Assembly had passed resolutions recommending Taylor for president. *NODB*, January 18, 1848.

28. *NODD*, January 23, 1848; *NODP*, January 23, 1848.

29. Ibid.

30. *NODD*, January 25, 1848.

31. Ibid. (January 28, 1848).

32. Louisiana *Courier*, January 28, 1848.

33. *NODP*, January 29, 1848.

34. Ibid. (January 30, 1848).

35. Quoted in Louisiana *Courier*, February 8, 1848.

36. Louisiana *Courier*, February 8, 1848.

37. *NODP*, February 23, 1848.

38. Ibid. (March 15, 1848).

39. Ibid. (April 23, 1848).

40. W. C. C. Claiborne to Henry Clay, April 25, 1848, Henry Clay Papers quoted in William H. Adams, *The Whig Party of Louisiana* (Lafayette: University of Southwestern Louisiana, 1973), 169.

41. *NODP*, April 25, 1848; Hamilton, *Soldier in the White House*, 77–79. Unknown to Peyton and the Taylor men of New Orleans, a group of "Washington Taylorites" had prepared a similar letter and dispatched it to Baton Rouge by Maj. William Bliss. The major arrived after Taylor had signed the Hunton-Love-Peyton letter. Michael F. Holt, *The Rise and Fall of the American Whig Party, Jacksonian Politics and the Onset of the Civil War* (New York and Oxford: Oxford University Press, 1979), 309.

42. K. Jack Bauer, *Zachary Taylor, Soldier, Planter, Statesman of the Old Southwest* (Baton

Rouge: Louisiana State University Press, 1985), 233, 243.

43. Brown, *Politics and Statesmanship*, 218.

44. *NODP*, May 12, 1848.

45. Hamilton, *Soldier in the White House*, 91.

46. *NODP*, May 31, June 1, 13, 1848.

47. Hamilton, *Soldier in the White House*, 65.

48. Schlesinger, ed., *The Almanac of American History*, 255.

49. *NODB*, June 26, 1848.

50. *NODP*, June 25, 1848; *NODB*, June 26, 1848.

51. *NODP*, June 25, 1848.

52. *NODD*, June 25, 1848.

53. *NODP*, June 25, 1848.

54. Ibid.; New Orleans *Daily Crescent*, June 26, 1848; *NODB*, June 26, 1848.

55. Quoted in Louisiana *Courier*, July 19, 1848.

56. Bauer, *Zachary Taylor, Soldier, Planter, Statesman*, 186–87.

57. New Orleans *Daily Crescent*, July 19, 1848.

58. Ibid. (July 25, 1848).

59. *NODP*, July 12, 1848.

60. July 25, 1848.

61. Louisiana *Courier*, July 19, 1848.

62. Michael F. Holt, *The Rise and Fall of the American Whig Party, Jacksonian Politics and the Onset of the Civil War*, 397; August 29, 1848, JJCP, LC.

63. George Rawlings Poage, *Henry Clay and the Whig Party* (Gloucester, Mass.: Peter Smith, 1965), 175.

64. Peyton to Crittenden, August 29, 1848, JJCP, LC.

65. Baton Rouge *Weekly Gazette*, August 12, 1848, quoted in Dallas C. Dickey, *Seargent S. Prentiss, Whig Orator of the Old South* (Baton Rouge: Louisiana State University Press, 1945), 325; Plaquemine *Southern Sentinel*, September 4, 21, 1848, quoted in William H. Adams, *The Whig Party of Louisiana*, 177.

66. *NODD*, September 5–6, 1848; New Orleans *Daily Crescent*, September 5, 1848; Peyton to Crittenden, August 29, 1848, JJCP, LC.

67. Nashville *Whig*, September 19, 1848.

68. Louisiana *Courier*, September 9, 1848.

69. Ibid. (October 2, 1848).

70. Nashville *Whig*, October 10, 12, 17, 1848.

71. *Presbyterian Record*, December 9, 1848.

72. Nashville *Whig*, October 17, 1848; Nashville *Daily Union*, October 11, 1848.

73. Nashville *Daily Union*, October 11, 1848.

74. Nashville *Whig*, October 17, 26, 1848; Nashville *Daily Union*, October 19, 1848.

75. Nashville *Whig*, October 17, 1848.

76. Lebanon *Packet* quoted in Nashville *Whig*, October 26, 1848.

77. Peyton to Crittenden, October 22, 1848, JJCP, LC.

78. Memphis *Daily Eagle*, October 30, 1848.

79. Ibid. (October 30; November 1, 1848).

80. Hamilton, *Soldier in the White House*, 130; *NODP*, November 1, 1848, quoted in Adams, *The Whig Party of Louisiana*, 190.

81. New Orleans *Daily Crescent*, November 10, December 4, 1848.

82. The lines that differentiated the parties became blurred by 1852 when they "seemed more alike than different." By that time both major parties were committed to accepting the Compromise of 1850. Michael F. Holt, *The Political Crisis of the 1850s* (New York: John Wiley and Sons, 1978), 102–104.

83. Louisville *Journal* quoted in *NODP*, December 20, 1848.

84. A friend and correspondent of J. J. Crittenden, Burnley was a wealthy Whig who furnished the money to start a Taylor administration newspaper in Washington. He had lived in Kentucky, Louisiana, and Texas. Albert D. Kirwan, *John J. Crittenden: The Struggle for the Union* (Lexington: University of Kentucky Press, 1962), 255–56.

85. Holt, *The Rise and Fall of the American Whig Party*, 398; Poage, *Henry Clay and the Whig Party*, 191.

86. Louisville *Journal* quoted in *NODP*, January 31, 1849.

87. Brainerd Dyer, *Zachary Taylor* (Baton Rouge: Louisiana State University Press, 1946), 303–304.

88. Ibid., 303.

89. Nashville *Whig*, February 8, 1849.

90. William B. Campbell to Governor David Campbell, February 23, 1849, DCP.

91. Ibid.

92. Nashville *Whig*, February 10, 1848.

93. Ibid. (February 17, 1849).

94. Hamilton, *Soldier in the White House*, 141.

95. Dyer, *Zachary Taylor*, 304; *National Intelligencer*, February 21, 1849.

96. *National Intelligencer*, February 24, 1849.

97. Dyer, *Zachary Taylor*, 306.

98. Ibid., 398.

99. Peyton to William M. Meridith, May 28, 1849, Huntington Library, San Marino, California.

100. The last Congress had raised the diplomatic mission to Chile to the level of a ministry presided over by a minister plenipotentiary who had full authority to speak and act for his government. *NODP*, November 14, 1849.

101. L. E. Mitchell to William B. Campbell, June 5, 1849, DCP.

CHAPTER 9

1. Quoted in Nashville *Daily American*, June 24, 1849.

2. Office of the Register of Conveyances, Book 48 (July 6, 1849): 674, Parish of Orleans, New Orleans, La.

3. West Tennessee *Whig*, October 24, 1849.

4. Fifteen of the thirty-four slaves were under the age of fourteen. *U.S. Census 1850*, Slave Census, Civil District No. 6, Sumner County, Tennessee.

5. Peyton to John M. Clayton, July 20, 1849, M. Despatches; K. Jack Bauer, *Zachary Taylor: Soldier, Planter, Statesman of the Old Southwest* (Baton Rouge: Louisiana State University Press, 1985), 270.

6. New Orleans *Daily Crescent*, September 24, 1849.

7. Clayton to Peyton, September 16, 1849, S. Despatches.

8. Peyton to John M. Clayton, September 27, October 8, 1849, M. Despatches; Clayton to Peyton, October 3, 11, 1849, S. Despatches.

9. Peyton to Clayton, October 30, 1849, M. Despatches; Peyton to H. W. Poynor, November 4, 1849, Harding-Jackson Papers, TSLA.

10. Peyton to William B. Campbell, November 7, 1849, DCP, microfilm, TSLA.

11. Balie's concern for the welfare of the Whig Party in Louisiana was well placed. Soon after Taylor's victory, the party began its terminal decline in that state. Perry A. Howard, *Political Tendencies in Louisiana* (Baton Rouge: Louisiana State University, 1971), 57.

12. Peyton to William B. Campbell, November 7, 1849, DCP.

13. Peyton to H. W. Poynor, November 4, 1849, Harding-Jackson Papers, TSLA; Memphis *Daily Enquirer*, November 21, 1849; *NODP*, November 13, 1849; Peyton to John M. Clayton, November 29, 1849, M. Despatches.

14. Panama *Star*, December 4, 1849, quoted in Memphis *Daily Eagle*, December 31, 1849. Most of those emigrating were en route to the California gold fields.

15. Nashville *Daily Gazette*, March 22, 1850.

16. Peyton to John M. Clayton, December 26, 1849; February 22, 1850, M. Despatches.

17. Simon Collier and William F. Sater, *A History of Chile, 1808–1994* (New York: Cambridge University Press, 1996), 98–99.

18. Ibid., 94, 98–99, 101; Henry Clay Evans Jr., *Chile and Its Relations with the United States* (Durham, N.C.: Duke University Press, 1927), 60–61.

19. Coastal shipping remained useful as a method of passenger transportation well into the twentieth century, sometime after a network of

railroads had been developed in the South.
Evans Jr., *Chile and Its Relations with the United States*, 59.

20. Leslie Bethel, ed., *Chile Since Independence* (New York: Cambridge University Press, 1993), 6.

21. Ibid., 1.

22. Diego Barros Arana, *Un decenio de la historia de Chile*, vol. 2 (Santiago: 1906), 553.

23. *Brownlow's* Knoxville *Whig and Independent Journal*, May 4, 1850; *NODP*, April 16, 1850.

24. *Daily Union*, City of Washington, June 28, 1850.

25. Within five years American millers and shipowners overcame that advantage by kiln drying the flour so it could withstand the rigors of crossing the equator twice and by constructing larger, faster schooners that could deliver flour from the eastern United States to San Francisco cheaper than conventional merchant ships sailing from ports in Chile. Evans Jr., *Chile and Its Relations with the United States*, 74.

26. *Brownlow's* Knoxville *Whig and Independent Journal*, May 4, 1850.

27. *NODP*, April 16, 1850.

28. Peyton to Clayton, February 22, 1850, M. Despatches.

29. J. S. Holliday, *The World Rushed In* (New York: Simon and Schuster, 1981), 400–401.

30. Collier and Sater, *A History of Chile, 1808–1994*, 81.

31. Earlier the State Department had agreed that Peyton could make his residence at either Valparaiso or Santiago, but once on the ground, he seems to have considered only the latter. John M. Clayton to Peyton, October 11, 1849, S. Despatches.

32. Peyton to John M. Clayton, March 24, April 28, May 27, June 24, 1850, M. Despatches; Deposition of Emily T. Peyton, May 28, 1883, Loose Court Records, Case #2078, SCA.

33. John M. Clayton to Peyton, June 15, 1850, S. Despatches; Peyton to Daniel Webster, September 24, 1850, M. Despatches.

34. Peyton to Webster, November 23, 1850; January 12, 1851; M. Despatches.

35. Deposition of Emily T. Peyton, May 28, 1883, Loose Court Records, Case #2078, SCA.

36. Peyton to Daniel Webster, January 23, 1852; J. B. Holman to Daniel Webster, January 24, 1852, M. Despatches.

37. Peyton to Daniel Webster, July 13, 1852; J. B. Holman to William L. Marcy, May 14, 1853; Peyton to Marcy, May 26, June 11, 1853; M. Despatches.

38. John M. Clayton to Peyton, September 17, 1849, S. Despatches.

39. Andrés Bello (1781–1865), Venezuelan-born poet, philosopher, and statesman, played an

important role in postindependence Chile. He is considered one of the foremost Latin American intellectual and political leaders of his day. *New Encyclopedia Brittanica*, 15th ed. (Chicago: Encyclopedia Brittanica, 1993), 79.

40. Clayton to Peyton, September 16, 1849, S. Despatches.

41. Peyton to Clayton, February 22, 1850, M. Despatches.

42. Peyton to Clayton, March 24, April 28, 1850, M. Despatches.

43. Peyton to Clayton, May 27, 1850, M. Despatches.

44. Peyton to Clayton, June 27, 1850, M. Despatches.

45. Peyton to Clayton, June 27, July 4, 1850, M. Despatches.

46. Peyton to Clayton, August 2, 1850, M. Despatches.

47. JJCP, LC, September 25, 1850.

48. Peyton to Daniel Webster, September 24, 1850, M. Despatches.

49. Daniel Webster to Peyton, August 19, 1850; William S. Derrick, Acting Secretary of State, to Peyton, November 9, 1850; S. Despatches; Peyton to Daniel Webster, January 25, February 22, 1851, M. Despatches.

50. Peyton to Daniel Webster, February 22, 1851, M. Despatches.

51. Ibid. (May 23; June 21, 1851).

52. Ibid. (August 23, 1851).

53. Ibid. (August 13, 1852).

54. John M. Clayton to Peyton, September 16, 1849, S. Despatches.

55. Campbell was elected governor in 1851 in a contest with the Democratic incumbent William Trousdale. At the end of his term, he declined to stand for reelection. Robert H. White, *Messages of the Governors of Tennessee, 1845–1847*, vol. 4 (Nashville: Tennessee Historical Commission, 1957), 403.

56. Peyton to Campbell, July 24, 1851, DCP, microfilm, TSLA.

57. Loose Court Records, Case 9865, SCA; Franklin (TN) *Weekly Review*, October 10, 1851.

58. Thomas Barry to Balie Peyton, January 13, 1852, JBC, LC, microfilm, TSLA.

59. Indicted for the murder of Robert Holmes Peyton, McElwrath was convicted of manslaughter by the circuit court of Sumner County in February 1852 and sentenced to serve ten years in the state penitentiary. The Tennessee Supreme Court of Error and Appeals heard the case on the first Monday in December 1852, and remanded it to the lower court for a new trial because of an error by the prosecuting attorney. The absence of further court records suggests that the defendant was never incarcerated. Loose

Court Records, Case 6999, State vs John McElwrath, SCA.

60. The following account of Peyton's match race in Chile is based on an article by J. H. Wallace following his interview of Peyton in 1868 at Station Camp Creek farm. He published the article in the February 1876 issue of *Wallace's Monthly*, 385–88. It was reprinted in the *Rural Sun* (Nashville, TN) on February 17, 1876, and the story was verified by Peyton at that time. Anderson, *American Thoroughbred*, 224–27.

61. *Wallace's Monthly*, February 1876, 388.

62. Nashville *Daily True Whig*, May 21, 1852.

CHAPTER 10

1. Peyton to John M. Clayton, June 27, November 23, 1850, M. Despatches.

2. Peyton to Webster, April 19, 1851, M. Despatches; Washington *Union*, June 6, 1851.

3. Peyton to Daniel Webster, April 23, 1851, M. Despatches.

4. Ibid.

5. Ibid. (April 19, 23, 1851).

6. Ibid. (April 23, 1851).

7. Ibid. (June 21, 1851).

8. Ibid. (April 23, 1851).

9. Ibid. (May 23, 1851).

10. Ibid.

11. Montt was the first civilian president in the history of Chile. He was chosen by the Conservatives in part because of a perceived threat from the Liberal Party to offer a more moderate administration. Henry Clay Evans Jr., *Chile and Its Relations with the United States* (Durham, N.C.: Duke University Press, 1927), 65; Leslie Bethel, ed., *Chile Since Independence* (New York: Cambridge University Press, 1993), 8.

12. Peyton to Daniel Webster, June 23, 1851, M. Despatches.

13. Peyton to Daniel Webster, September 24, 1851, M. Despatches; Simon Collier and William F. Sater, *A History of Chile, 1808–1994* (New York: Cambridge University Press, 1996), 109.

14. Peyton to Daniel Webster, September 24, 1851, M. Despatches.

15. Ibid.

16. Ibid.

17. Lieutenant Gilliss was superintendent of the U.S. Naval Astronomical Expedition at Santiago, 1849–52. *Executive Document No. 121*, 33rd Congress, 1st Session, House of Representatives, vol. 1 (Washington: A. O. P. Nicholson, Printer, 1855), 184.

18. *Executive Document No. 121*, 483.

19. Ibid., 484.

20. Peyton to Daniel Webster, September 24, 1851, M. Despatches. Emily traveled from Chagres to New Orleans in the company of George Love of Gallatin and other returning disappointed forty-niners. Emily Peyton to "My dear brothers," November 12, 1851, William Trousdale Papers, TSLA; Thomas Barry to Peyton, January 13, 1852, JBC, LC, microfilm, TSLA.

21. Collier and Sater, *A History of Chile, 1808–1994*, 108; Peyton to Daniel Webster, October 3, 1851, M. Despatches.

22. Emily T. Peyton to "My dear brothers," November 12, 1851, William Trousdale Papers, TSLA.

23. Collier and Sater, *A History of Chile, 1808–1994*, 108.

24. Peyton to Daniel Webster, November 20, 24, December 22, 1851, M. Despatches.

25. When Bulnes began preparations for further action a few days after the Battle of Loncomilla, General Cruz agreed to a peace treaty giving up whatever gains the rebels had made. It had been speculated that Cruz yielded to Bulnes because as a landowner himself he was worried that the revolution was about to be hopelessly discredited by unbridled guerrilla activity and banditry then surfacing in the South. Collier and Sater, *A History of Chile, 1808–1994*, 108.

26. Peyton to Daniel Webster, December 22–23, 25, 1851, M. Despatches.

27. Samuel E. Eckel to Peyton, December 13, 1851; Peyton to Eckel, December 10, 17, 1851, M. Despatches.

28. Peyton to Eckel, December 17, 1851, M. Despatches.

29. Eckel to Peyton, January 27, 1852, M. Despatches. Eight months later, the government dismissed some of its own army officers who had been compromised by the rebellion. A revolt followed in a regiment in Santiago, but it was put down quickly, and the president ordered nine of the mutineers put to death. Peyton to Daniel Webster, September 13, 1852, M. Despatches.

30. Peyton to Everett, January 13, 1853, M. Despatches.

31. President Montt never granted the general amnesty that the treaty provided. Collier and Sater, *A History of Chile, 1808–1994*, 111.

32. Varas to Peyton, December 30, 1851, January 12, 1852; Peyton to Varas, January 13, 1852; Peyton to Webster, October 28, 1852, M. Despatches.

33. Collier and Sater, *A History of Chile, 1808–1994*, 109.

34. Admiral Moresby was in command of the British fleet in the eastern Pacific. Peyton to Daniel Webster, February 22, 1852, M. Despatches.

35. Daniel Webster to Peyton, April 13, 1852, S. Despatches.

36. John M. Clayton to Peyton, September 17, 1849; Daniel Webster to Peyton, March 24, 1851; W. L. Marcy to Peyton, June 25, 1853, S. Despatches.

37. Peyton to Daniel Webster, February 20, 1851, M. Despatches.

38. Daniel Webster to Peyton, March 10, 1851, S. Despatches.

39. Peyton to Clayton, June 24, 1850, M. Despatches.

40. Peyton to Daniel Webster, April 19, 1851, M. Despatches.

41. Ibid.

42. A member of the U.S. Naval Astronomical Expedition to the Southern Hemisphere, 1849–52, Lieutenant McRae was stationed in Santiago and served informally as military attaché to the American legation. *Executive Document No. 121*, 33rd Congress, 1st Session, House of Representatives, vol. 1 (Washington: A. O. P. Nicholson, Printer, 1855).

43. Peyton to Daniel Webster, April 24, October 3, 1851, M. Despatches.

44. Peyton to Daniel Webster, April 26, 1852; Peyton to Varas, March 16, 1852; Varas to Peyton, March 19, April 29, 1852, M. Despatches.

45. Peyton to Varas, May 17, June 16, 23, 1852; Peyton to Daniel Webster, June 28, 1852, M. Despatches.

46. Varas to Peyton, July 29, 1852, M. Despatches.

47. Peyton to Daniel Webster, September 29, 1852, M. Despatches.

48. Peyton to Daniel Webster, November 23, 1850, M. Despatches.

49. Peyton to Daniel Webster, January 21, February 22, 1852, M. Despatches; Peyton to McCauley, January 13, 1852, M. Despatches.

50. Admiral Fairfax Moresby to Peyton, January 14, 1852; Peyton to Moresby, January 15, 1852, M. Despatches.

51. Peyton to Daniel Webster, September 29, 1852; McCauley to Peyton, September 29, 1852; Peyton to Edward Everett, December 13, 1852, M. Despatches.

52. Peyton to John M. Clayton, March 24, 27, June 27, 1850; Peyton to Edward Everett, December 20, 1852, January 13, 1853; Peyton to Varas, January 10, 1853; Peyton to William L. Marcy, June 13, 1852, M. Despatches.

53. Peyton to John M. Clayton, May 27, June 24, July 4, 1850, M. Despatches.

54. Peyton to Daniel Webster, September 24, 1851, M. Despatches.

55. William Duer to Peyton, August 27, 1852, M. Despatches.

56. An attorney born and educated in New York City, who had lived in New Orleans the four years prior to Peyton's locating there, Duer (1805–79) represented New York State for two terms in the U.S. Congress as a Whig, 1847–51. *Directory of Congress*, 933.

57. Duer to Peyton, August 27, 1852, M. Despatches; Peyton to Daniel Webster, August 28, 1852, M. Despatches.

58. Peyton to Webster, October 12, 1852, M. Despatches.

59. Peyton to Webster, November 13, 28, 1852; Varas to Peyton, November 11, 1852; Peyton to Varas, December 8, 1852; Peyton to Everett, December 28, 1852, M. Despatches.

60. Peyton to Clayton, March 24, 1850; Peyton to Webster, September 24, 1850; March 22, 1852, M. Despatches.

61. Peyton to Webster, April 26, 1852, M. Despatches.

62. Charles I. Bevans, comp., *Treaties and Other International Agreements of the United States of America, 1771–1949*, vol. 6 (Washington: Department of State, 1971), 535.

63. Peyton to Webster, June 25, 1852, M. Despatches.

64. Peyton to Marcy, June 11, 1853, M. Despatches.

65. Peyton to John Bell, February 3, 1856, JBC, microfilm, TSLA.

66. Thomas Barry to Peyton, January 13, 1852, JBC, microfilm, TSLA.

67. Peyton Society of Virginia, Book Committee, *The Peytons of Virginia* (Stafford: Peyton Society of Virginia, 1976), 238.

68. Zachary Taylor, Millard Fillmore, and Franklin Pierce were the presidents; John M. Clayton, Daniel Webster, Edward Everett, and William L. Marcy were the secretaries of state.

69. According to family tradition, President Pierce offered Peyton another four-year term as envoy and minister plenipotentiary to Chile, but he declined to accept it. CNFP.

70. Peyton to Marcy, April 30, June 11, 1853, M. Despatches; Marcy to Peyton, May 28, July 15, July 29, 1853, S. Despatches; *Republican Banner and* Nashville *Whig*, September 21, 1853.

71. *Republican Banner and* Nashville *Whig*, September 21, November 18, 1853.

72. Diego Barros Arana, *Un decenio de la historia de Chile*, vol. 2 (Santiago: 1906), 567.

73. Agustin Edwards, *Cuatro presidentes de Chile*, vol. 1 (Valparaiso, 1932), 25.

74. William Roderick Sherman, *The Diplomatic and Commercial Relations of the United States and Chile, 1820–1914*, (Boston: Richard G. Badger, Publisher, Gorham Press, 1926), 61.

75. Peyton to Marcy, August 6, 1853, M. Despatches.

76. Peyton to Marcy three days after he embarked, September 26, 1853, M. Despatches; Marcy to Peyton, September 20, 1853, M. Despatches.

77. Marcy to David Starkweather, July 8, 1854, S. Despatches.

CHAPTER 11

1. *SFDAC*, November 8, 10, 1853.

2. Oscar Lewis, *San Francisco: Mission to Metropolis* (San Diego: Howell-North Books, 1980), 64–65, 70, 83.

3. Robert M. Senkewicz, *Vigilantes in Gold Rush San Francisco* (Stanford, Calif: Stanford University Press, 1985), 14, 17–18.

4. Lewis, *San Francisco: Mission to Metropolis*, 93.

5. Nashville *Daily True Whig*, December 16, 1853.

6. Nashville *Daily Gazette*, May 30, 1854.

7. *SFDAC*, July 22, 1854.

8. July 25, 1854.

9. Winfred J. Davis, *History of the Political Conventions in California, 1849–1892* (Sacramento: California State Library, 1893), 34, 37.

10. Quoted in Nashville *Daily True Whig*, June 21, 1854.

11. Sacramento *Daily Democratic State Journal*, July 27, 1854.

12. Thomas Brown, *Politics and Statesmanship: Essays on the American Whig Party*, 225; Sacramento *Daily Democratic State Journal*, July 27, 1854; Michael F. Holt, *The Rise and Fall of the American Whig Party, Jacksonian Politics and the Onset of the Civil War* (New York and Oxford: Oxford University Press, 1979), 857–58.

13. Sacramento *Daily Democratic State Journal*, July 27, 1854.

14. *Republican Banner and* Nashville *Whig*, September 5, 1854.

15. Ibid.

16. Ibid.

17. September 5, 1854.

18. Peyton to Bell, February 4, 1857, JBC, LC, microfilm, TSLA.

19. Senkewicz, *Vigilantes in Gold Rush San Francisco*, 131, 134; Peyton Hurt, "The Rise and Fall of the 'Know Nothings' in California," *California Historical Society Quarterly*, vol. 9, no. 1 (March 1930): 18–19, 24, 29, 45, 106–7, 118–19.

20. *SFDAC*, September 5, 1854.

21. Ibid. (September 9–10, 1854).

22. Lewis, *San Francisco: Mission to Metropolis*, 79, 84, 88, 98.

23. Ibid., 70.

24. *SFDAC*, June 1, 1855.

25. Ibid. (June 1, 16, 1855).

26. PFN, 18–19; Law Department Register, 1859, University Archives, Cumberland University, Lebanon, Tennessee.

27. A guyascutus is an imaginary animal of a very ferocious kind with a voice characterized by ominous, terrifying sounds. Mitford Mathews, ed., *Dictionary of Americanisms*, vol. 1 (Chicago: University of Chicago Press, 1951), 761.

28. Hurt, "The Rise and Fall of the 'Know-Nothings' in California," 38–39.

29. Ibid., 39.

30. *SFDAC*, September 3, 1855.

31. Ibid. (September 5, 1855).

32. Hurt, "The Rise and Fall of the 'Know-Nothings' in California," 45–46.

33. *SFDAC*, June 1, 1855.

34. Nashville *Daily Republican Banner*, October 23, 1855.

35. Ibid.

36. Peyton to John Bell, February 3, 1856, JBC, microfilm, TSLA.

37. *SFDAC*, January 16, 24, 1856; Peyton to John Bell, February 3, 1856, JBC, microfilm, TSLA.

38. Peyton to John Bell, February 4, 1857, JBC, microfilm, TSLA.

39. *SFDAC*, November 22, 1855.

40. Lewis, *San Francisco: Mission to Metropolis*, 86–87.

41. *SFDAC*, September 1, October 1, 1855; March 23, 1856.

42. San Francisco *Daily Herald*, March 25–26, 30, 1856.

43. Ibid. (May 8, 1856).

44. Dorothy H. Huggins, comp., "Continuation of the Annals of San Francisco," *California Historical Society Quarterly*, vol. 16, no. 4 (December 1937): 339.

45. Ibid., vol. 17, no. 2 (June 1938): 169.

46. *SDU*, December 18, 1854.

47. Ibid. (December 20, 1854).

48. Lewis, *San Francisco: Mission to Metropolis*, 71.

49. Ibid., 71–72.

CHAPTER 12

1. Oscar Lewis, *San Francisco: Mission to Metropolis* (San Diego: Howell-North Books, 1980), 71.

2. Doyce B. Numis Jr., ed., *The San Francisco Vigilance Committee of 1856: Three Views* (Los Angeles: Los Angeles Westerners, 1971), 31n; *SFDEB*, May 20, 1856; Lewis, *San Francisco: Mission to Metropolis*, 72.

3. *SFDEB*, May 19, 23, 1856; *SFDAC*, May 23, 1856.

4. Lewis, *San Francisco: Mission to Metropolis*, 75.

5. San Francisco *Daily Herald*, June 15, 1856.

6. *SFDEB*, June 9, 1856.

7. [James O'Meara], *The Vigilance Committee of 1856* (San Francisco: James H. Barry, Publisher, 1887), 18–19.

8. The conciliators specifically recalled by General Sherman were Peyton, Crockett, Ritchie, Thornton, Foote, Donohue, and Kelly. *Memoirs of General William T. Sherman by Himself* (Bloomington: Indiana University Press, 1957), 128.

9. *SFDEB*, June 9, 1856.

10. Peyton and G. W. P. Bissell to Governor John Neely Johnson, June 12, 1856, John Neely Johnson Papers, Bancroft Library, University of California, Berkeley.

11. *SFDEB*, June 9, 1856.

12. *Memoirs of General William T. Sherman by Himself*, 130–31.

13. *SFDEB*, June 13, 1856.

14. Ibid.

15. Ibid.

16. Local newspapers disagreed about the precise number attending, but agreed that it was the largest mass meeting ever gathered in the city. *The Wide West*, 15,000; *Daily Alta California*, 10,000; the *Herald*, 3,000; and the *Daily Evening Bulletin*, 15,000. Philip J. Ethington, *The Public City: The Political Construction of Urban Life in San Francisco, 1850–1900* (New York: Cambridge University Press, 1994), 140.

17. *SDU*, June 16, 1856.

18. San Francisco *Daily Herald*, June 15, 1856.

19. San Francisco *Chronicle* copied in *SDU*, June 16, 1856.

20. San Francisco *Daily Herald*, June 15, 1856.

21. *SFDEB*, June 16, 1856; San Francisco *Chronicle* copied in *SDU*, June 16, 1856.

22. San Francisco *Daily Herald*, June 15, 1856; *SFDEB*, June 14, 16, 1856; San Francisco *Chronicle* copied in *SDU*, June 16, 1856.

23. Ethington, *The Public City*, 140–41.

24. Senkewicz, *Vigilantes in Gold Rush San Francisco*, 176–77; *SFDEB*, July 25, 30, 1856; San Francisco *Daily Herald*, July 25–26, August 2, 1856.

25. *SFDEB*, August 18, 1856; *Wide West*, August 17, 31; November 9, 1856.

26. Peyton to John Bell, February 4, 1857, JBC, LC, microfilm, TSLA.

27. Peyton to Bell, May 5, 1856, JBC, microfilm, TSLA.

28. *Wide West*, August 3, 10, 1856; *SFDEB*, August 8, 1856.

29. *SDU*, August 18, 1856.

30. Ibid.

31. Ibid.

32. Ibid.

33. Ibid.

34. Ibid. (September 1, 1856).

35. The other three electors were R. N. Wood of Amador County; Jessie S. Pitzer of Trinity County; and O. C. Hall of Sierra County. Hurt, "The Rise and Fall of the 'Know-Nothings' in California," 102–103.

36. *SDU*, September 4–5, 1856.

37. Ibid. (September, 5, 1856).

38. Ibid.

39. *SFDAC*, September 27, 1856.

40. San Francisco *Daily Herald*, October 5, 1856.

41. Ibid. (October 11, 1856).

42. October 14, 1856.

43. *SDU*, November 1, 1856.

44. *SFDAC*, November 4, 18, 1856.

45. Quoted in *SFDAC*, November 12, 1856.

46. His associates were William Duer, Dallas Lake, and Julius K. Rose. He remained with the firm until 1858, when he left to practice alone with an office in the Express Building. *San Francisco Directory*, 1856, 174; 1857, 174; 1858, 225; 1859, 223.

47. *SFDAC*, July 19, 1857.

48. Ibid. (July 29, 1857).

49. Ibid. (July 30, 1857).

50. Hurt, "The Rise and Fall of the 'Know-Nothings' in California," 116.

51. At first erroneously identified in court records as L. H. Bateman. *SFDAC*, August 24, 1854.

52. *SFDAC*, July 4, 6–7, 1854.

53. Ibid. (August 16, 24, 30, 1854).

54. Ibid. (August 30–31; September 1, 1854).

55. Ibid. (August 31; September 2, 9, 1854).

56. *SFDAC*, July 7, 1854.

57. Ibid. (July 9, 1854).

58. *SFDAC*, July 7, 9, 1854; Oscar T. Shuck, ed., *History of the Bench and Bar of California* (Los Angeles: Commercial Printing House, 1901), 282.

59. July 26, 1854.

60. *SFDAC*, December 12, 1855; July 17, 21, 1856; November 2, 1857.

61. *SFDEB*, February 24, 1859.

62. November 16, 1858.

63. *SFDAC*, October 31, 1859.

64. John Myers Myers, *San Francisco Reign of Terror* (Garden City, N.Y.: Doubleday & Company, 1966), 230–31.

65. *Constitution and Bylaws, Officers and Members, The Pacific Club, 1886*, Annual Members Handbook, n.p.

66. SCDB 24, 593, SCA.

67. Sumner County Loose Records, Deed #1780, SCA.

68. Early in January 1854, Thomas Barry, acting for him, had increased the size of his land-holdings by purchasing 175 acres of land that adjoined Balie's Station Camp Creek farm along its eastern boundary. He paid James Douglass the sum of $5,758.50 in cash. SCDB 23, 298–99.

69. *SFDAC*, November 11, 1859.

CHAPTER 13

1. Philadelphia *Daily Evening Bulletin*, November 28, 1859.

2. *NYST*, December 3, 1859.

3. Jesse E. Peyton, *Reminiscences of the Past* (Philadelphia: Printed by J. B. Lippincott, 1895), 28; Joseph Howard Parks, *John Bell of Tennessee* (Baton Rouge: Louisiana State University Press, 1950), 344–345; Peyton to John Bell, December 17, 1859, JBC, LC, microfilm, TSLA.

4. Peyton, *Reminiscences of the Past*, 28.

5. Philadelphia *Daily Evening Bulletin*, December 8, 1859; *Harper's Weekly*, January 7, 1860.

6. Peyton to William B. Campbell, December 17, 1859, DCP, microfilm, TSLA.

7. December 16, 1859.

8. Peyton to John Bell, December 17, 1859, JBC, microfilm, TSLA.

9. Peyton to John Bell, December 17, 1859, JBC, microfilm, TSLA.

10. The eighteen were Henry C. Carey, James Millikin, John Grigg, Wm. D. Lewis, Morton McMichael, Alexander Henry, Alger S. Roberts, J. Edgar Thomas, J. R. Ingersoll, Robert Hare Powel, James Traquair, D. Haddock Jr., A. Browning, Geo. N. Eckett, James C. Hand, James Dundas, William Elder, and Henry M. Fuller. Philadelphia *Daily Evening Bulletin*, January 12, 1860.

11. Philadelphia *Daily Evening Bulletin*, January 12, 1860.

12. Ibid.

13. Ibid. (December 16, 1859).

14. Philadelphia *American* copied in *Daily National Intelligencer*, January 16, 1860.

15. *NRB*, January 22, 1860.

16. James Vaulx Drake, *Life of General Robert Hatton* (Nashville: Marshall and Bruce, 1867), 194, 306.

17. Philadelphia *American* copied in *Daily National Intelligencer*, January 16, 1860.

18. *New York Times*, January 16, 1860.

19. Ibid.

20. *NRB*, January 14, 1860.

21. Ibid.; Philadelphia *Daily Evening Bulletin*, January 16, 1860.

22. Ibid.

23. *NRB*, January 14, 1860.

24. Ibid.; Philadelphia *Daily Evening Bulletin*, January 16, 1860.

25. Ibid.

26. Parks, *John Bell*, 349; *New York Times*, January 16, 1860.

27. *New York Times*, January 16, 1860.

28. Philadelphia *Daily Evening Bulletin*, January 16, 1860.

29. Construction of the Tennessee State Capitol was nearing completion, and Wood and Perot of Philadelphia were in the final process of supplying an iron stairway for the cupola and the iron galleries and stairways for the state library portion of the building. For the exterior of the building, the iron fabricators were furnishing a series of elaborate lamp supports of fluted Corinthian columns twelve and one-half feet high, each surrounded by three life-sized figures representing morning, noon, and night. Philadelphia *Daily Evening Bulletin*, January 18, 1860.

30. Peyton, *Reminiscences of the Past*, 31.

31. Peyton to Crittenden, February 25, 1860, JJCP, LC.

32. Philadelphia *Daily Evening Bulletin*, January 28, 1860.

33. Tennessee Governor Isham G. Harris avoided the trip because he favored secession and evinced virtually no interest in trying to bridge the widening gap between North and South.

34. *Republican Banner and* Nashville *Whig*, January 25, 28–29, 1860.

35. *Nashville City and Business Directory for 1860–61* (Nashville: L. P. Williams & Co., Publishers and Proprietors, 1860), 296; Gallatin *Examiner*, February 11, 1860.

36. Unidentified Nashville newspaper clipping dated June 6, 1860, vertical files, TSLA.

37. *NRB*, January 5–6; January 12–February 23, 1860.

38. Parks, *John Bell*, 347.

39. *NRB*, January 12, 21, February 5, 11–12, 14, 16–18, 21, l860.

40. Gallatin *Examiner*, February 11, 1860.

41. *NRB*, February 5–23, 1860; *Brownlow's Knoxville Whig*, February 18, March 2, 1860.

42. *NRB*, February 23, 1860; Stanley J. Folmsbee, Robert E. Corlew, and Enoch L. Mitchell, *Tennessee: A Short History* (Knoxville: University of Tennessee Press, 1969), 326.

43. Philip M. Hamer, ed., *Tennessee—A History, 1673–1932*, vol. 1 (New York: American Historical Society, 1933), 516.

44. Peyton to Crittenden, February 25, 1860, JJCP, LC.

45. Gallatin *Examiner*, February 11, 1860.

46. Drake, *Life of General Robert Hatton*, 274.

47. The Archives War was fought at the beginning of 1843 over possession of the Texas State Archives then situated in Austin. Governor Sam Houston, fearing a Mexican move on Austin, ordered Rangers to remove the archives to Houston for safekeeping. Believing the governor was about to move the capital from their city, some Austin citizens formed a committee to resist the order. Initially caught off guard, they did not detect the actual loading of the records, but rallied and overtook the wagon train transporting them. After a few shots were fired, the Rangers surrendered their cargo to avoid further bloodshed. Alexander Peyton fell in the brief exchange of gunfire. Louis Wilz Kemp, "Mrs. Angelina B. Eberly," *Southwestern Historical Quarterly*, vol. 36 (January 1933): 196–97.

48. Peyton Society of Virginia, Book Committee, *The Peytons of Virginia* (Stafford: Peyton Society of Virginia, 1976), 238; Texas Farm and Ranch, February 1, 1890, 12.

49. *New York Times*, May 10–11, 1860; Hamer, *Tennessee—A History, 1673–1932*, vol. 1, 516.

50. Paul H. Buck, *The Road to Reunion, 1865–1900* (Boston: Little, Brown and Company, 1937), ix.

51. Daniel W. Crofts, *Reluctant Confederates: Upper South Unionists in the Secession Crisis* (Chapel Hill and London: University of North Carolina Press, 1989), 79.

52. Nashville *Daily Gazette*, August 17, 1860.

53. *NRB*, August 2, 22–24, 29.

54. Ibid. (August 23, 29, 1860).

55. Ibid. (September 1, 1860); Nashville *Union and American*, September 1, 1860.

56. Memphis *Daily Enquirer*, September 12, 1860.

57. Memphis *Daily Appeal*, September 12, 1860. An advocate of secession, Yancey was a former Alabama congressman.

58. *NRB*, September 19, 1860.

59. Herschel Gower and Jack Allen, eds., *Pen and Sword: The Life and Journals of Randal W. McGavock*, (Nashville: Tennessee Historical Commission, 1959), 579.

60. Nashville *Union and American*, September 29, 1860.

61. Ibid. (September 29; October 5–6, 14, 1860).

62. Ibid. (September 29, 1860).

63. Ibid. (October 17, 1860).

64. Gower and Allen, eds., *Pen and Sword*, 581.

65. Both Peyton and Haynes had missed some appointments, but local speakers substituted for them. Peyton's absences were usually

caused by the demands of his law practice. *NRB*, September 23, October 12, 16–17, 1860.

66. Nashville *Union and American*, October 18, 1860.

67. *Brownlow's Knoxville Whig*, November 3, 1860.

68. Nashville *Patriot*, November 26, 1860.

69. John Lewis Peyton, comp., *Memoir of John Howe Peyton in Sketches by his Contemporaries* (Privately published, Staunton, Va: A. B. Blackburn & Co., 1894), 276; Crofts, *Reluctant Confederates*, 220–21.

70. *NRB*, December 6, 1860.

71. Quoted in *NRB*, November 11, 1860.

72. *Senate Journal of the Thirty-Third General Assembly of the State of Tennessee* (Nashville: J. O. Griffith and Company, Public Printers, 1861), 52; *House Journal of the First Extra Session of the Thirty-Third General Assembly of the State of Tennessee* (Nashville: J. O. Griffith and Company, Public Printers, 1861), 53.

73. L. E. Chittenden, *A Report of the Debates and Proceedings in the Secret Session of the Conference Convention for Proposing Amendments to the Constitution of the United States, Held at Washington, D.C., in February A.D. 1861* (New York: D. Appleton & Co., 1864), 26, 440–50, 452.

74. The other two Sumner delegates were his brother-in-law, by then a Unionist, Thomas Barry, representing the county and J. J. Turner the floterial district. Nashville *Weekly Patriot*, January 30, 1861.

75. *NRB*, March 5, 1861.

76. Gallatin *Courier*, April 3, 17, 1861.

77. *NRB*, October 30, 1860, May 28, 1861; Walter T. Durham, *Rebellion Revisited, A History of Sumner County, Tennessee, From 1861 to 1870* (Gallatin: Sumner County Museum Association, 1982), 15, 26, 59.

78. *NRB*, April 19, 1861; Knoxville *Whig*, April 27, 1861.

79. Philip M. Hamer, ed., *Tennessee—A History, 1673–1932*, vol. 2 (New York: American Historical Society, 1933), 540–41; *NRB*, April 19, 1861.

80. Bate to Leroy P. Walker, April 26, 1861, U.S. War Department, *The War of the Rebellion: A Compilation of the Official Records of the Union and Confederate Armies*, series 1, vol. 52, pt. 2 (Washington: Government Printing Office, 1880–1901), 74.

81. *NRB*, May 4, 1861.

82. Allen Johnson, ed., *Dictionary of American Biography*, vol. 12 (New York: Charles Scribner's Sons, 1928), 510–11.

83. Nashville *Daily Gazette*, May 9, 1861.

84. Gallatin *Tennessean*, August 24, 1878.

85. Ibid.

86. Ibid.

87. *NRB*, June 9, 11, 1861.

88. Peyton to Campbell, May 3, 1861, DCP.

89. February 18, 1860.

90. *NYST*, February 18, March 3, 1860.

91. Ibid. (May 26, 1860; January 19, 1861).

92. Ibid. (May 26, 1860).

93. Deposition of Emily T. Peyton, May 28, 1883, Loose Court Records, Lawsuit #2078, SCA. Emily's funds probably came from a small inheritance from her mother.

94. June 9, 1860.

95. *NYST*, June 9, 1860.

96. Ibid. (January 26, 1861).

97. At the Albion Course stables, in addition to Fannie McAlister, he had three two-year-olds and one a few months younger. *NYST*, June 8, 1861.

98. *NYST*, June 8, 1861.

99. Ibid.

100. Ibid. (February 6, 1875).

101. Peyton to William B. Campbell, August 9, 30, 1861, DCP.

102. They were William Peyton, b. 1865; Balie Peyton, b. 1867; Mary Bugg Peyton, b. 1871; and Louise Allen Peyton, b. 1876.

103. Deed of Gift, William Trousdale Collection, THS, TSLA.

CHAPTER 14

1. First Lt. Balie Peyton Jr., Company A, 20th Tennessee.

2. George Baber to Peyton, January 23, 1862. CNFP.

3. E. G. Squier, ed., *Frank Leslie's Pictorial History of the American Civil War*, vol. 1 (New York: Frank Leslie, 1862), 276. This citation incorrectly identifies the Second Minnesota Regiment as the Second Massachusetts.

4. Raymond E. Myers, *The Zollie Tree* (Louisville: Filson Club Press, 1964), 101.

5. Nashville *Union and American*, February 1, 1862; New York *Herald*, January 21, 26, February 3, 1861; Myers, *The Zollie Tree*, 126–28; Memphis *Commercial Appeal*, February 26, 1862, quoted in Sumner County *News*, March 18, 1937.

6. *House Journal 1861–62 of the First Session of the Thirty-Fourth General Assembly of the State of Tennessee which Convened at Nashville, on the First Monday in October, A.D. 1861 and Adjourned in Memphis, March 20, 1862* (Nashville: Tennessee Historical Commission, 1957), 357, 395; *Nashville Union and American*, February 1, 1862.

7. Tuttle to Peyton, February 6, 1907, and Peyton to Tuttle, February 14, 1907, *Confederate Veteran*, May 1907, 230; Peyton Papers, TSLA.

8. Nashville *Daily Gazette*, February 4, 1862.

9. Memphis *Commercial Appeal*, February 26, 1862, quoted in Sumner County *News*, March 18, 1937.

10. The body of General Zollicoffer was buried in the Nashville City Cemetery on February 2. Myers, *The Zollie Tree*, 129.

11. Durham, *Rebellion Revisited*, 61–65; Durham, *Nashville The Occupied City, The First Seventeen Months–February 16, 1862, to June 30, 1863* (Nashville: Tennessee Historical Society, 1985), 1–20.

12. Peyton to Crittenden, May 4, 1862, JJCP, LC.

13. George Fort Milton, *The Age of Hate: Andrew Johnson and the Radicals* (New York: Coward-McCann: 1930), 110.

14. Nashville *Daily Union*, April 29–30, May 4, 1862.

15. Ibid. (May 4, 14, 1862).

16. Ibid. (June 17, 1862).

17. Unlike other federal judges in the South, Humphreys did not resign his office when he assumed a similar responsibility in the judicial system of the Confederate States. Kermit L. Hall, "West H. Humphreys and the Crisis of the Union," *Tennessee Historical Quarterly*, vol. 34 (1975), 56, 67–69.

18. Nashville *Daily Union*, July 1, 1862.

19. Radical Unionists wanted to preserve the Union; they generally favored abolition and, in some cases, punishment of slaveholders. Conservative Unionists were committed to preserving the Union but most believed slavery should be addressed through the political process at the state level.

20. Nashville *Daily Union*, July 8, 1862.

21. As an example of what others could expect if they continued to resist returning their allegiance to the United States, Johnson had banished Guild along with William Giles Harding, wealthy Nashville planter and owner of Belle Meade plantation, and George Washington Barrow, former editor, congressman, and one of the state commissioners chosen the year before by the legislature to negotiate Tennessee's relationship with the Confederate States of America. Walter T. Durham, "The Arrest: North to Fort Mackinac," *Tennessee Historical Quarterly*, vol. 55, no. 4 (winter 1996): 336.

22. Guild to Peyton and Robert A. Bennett, June 20, 1862, Johnson Papers, LC.

23. Leroy P. Graf and Ralph W. Haskins, eds., *The Papers of Andrew Johnson*, vol. 4, *1860–1861* (Knoxville: University of Tennessee Press, 1976), 14.

24. Nashville *Daily Times and True Union*, October 12, 1862.

25. U.S. War Department, *The War of the Rebellion: A Compilation of the Official Records of the Union and Confederate Armies*, vol. 32, pt. 2 (Washington, D.C.: Government Printing Office, 1880–1901), 90–91, 103, 292; Peyton to A. R. Wynne, February 13, 1864, George Wynne Collection, Wynne Family Papers, THS, TSLA.

26. Sumner County Unnumbered Deed Book, Civil War Period, 1860–69, 168, SCA.

27. Peyton to Crittenden, November 12, 1862, JJCP, LC; Ezra J. Warner, *Generals in Blue: Lives of the Union Commanders* (Baton Rouge: Louisiana State University Press, 1964), 100–101, 569–70; Warner, *Generals in Gray: Lives of the Confederate Commanders* (Baton Rouge: Louisiana State University Press, 1959), 65–66.

28. *National Intelligencer*, May 26, 1863; Nashville *Dispatch*, May 31, 1863.

29. Nashville *Daily Union*, July 4, 1863.

30. Nashville *Daily Press*, December 30, 1863.

31. John S. Brien was a former legislator, judge of the Davidson County Chancery Court, and presidential elector on the Whig ticket of Taylor and Fillmore in 1848. Robert M. McBride and Dan M. Robison, *Biographical Directory of the Tennessee General Assembly, 1796–1861*, vol. 1 (Nashville: Tennessee State Library and Archives and Tennessee Historical Commission, 1975), 78–79.

32. Nashville *Daily Press*, December 30, 1863.

33. Nashville *Dispatch*, March 11, 1864.

34. *Official Records of the War of the Rebellion*, series 2, vol. 8, 421.

35. *NRB*, July 28, 1867.

36. Peyton to A. R. Wynne, February 13, 1864, George Wynne Collection, Wynne Family Papers, THS, TSLA.

37. Nashville *Daily Times and True Union*, September 1, 1864; Chicago *Tribune*, August 26–28, September 1, 1864.

38. Richard B. Morris, ed., *Encyclopedia of American History* (New York: Harper and Brothers, 1953), 244.

39. James Welch Patton, *Unionism and Reconstruction in Tennessee, 1860–1869* (Gloucester, Mass.: P. Smith, 1966), 46.

40. The complete electoral ticket for McClellan and Pendleton included William B. Campbell of Wilson County and T. A. R. Nelson of Washington, state at large; James P. T. Carter of Carter; John Williams of Knox; A. Blizzard of McMinn; Henry Cooper of Bedford; Peyton of Sumner; John Lellyett of Davidson; Emerson Etheridge of Weakley; and John D. Perryman of Shelby. Nashville *Daily Press*, September 30, 1864.

41. Stokes to Campbell, September 24, 1864, DCP, microfilm, TSLA; Nashville *Daily Press*, September 30, 1864.

42. Nashville *Daily Press*, October 3, 1864.

43. Ibid.

44. Ibid.; *National Intelligencer* quoted in Nashville *Daily Press*, October 17, 1864; Louisville *Daily Journal*, October 15, 1864.

45. Jordan Stokes to William B. Campbell, October 5, 1864, DCP.

46. New York *Herald*, October 15, 1864.

47. Nashville *Daily Press*, October 21, 1864.

48. Ibid. (October 31, 1864).

49. Ibid. (October 22, 1864).

50. October 25, 1864.

51. Philip M. Hamer, *Tennessee—A History, 1673–1932*, vol. 2 (New York: American Historical Society, 1933), 590.

52. Nashville *Daily Press*, October 25, 1864.

53. Peyton to Campbell, October 25, 1864, DCP; Nashville *Daily Press*, October 31, 1864.

54. Nashville *Daily Press*, October 31, 1864.

55. Hamer, *Tennessee—A History, 1673–1932*, vol. 2, 590.

56. Nashville *Dispatch*, October 6, 9, 1864.

57. Stanley F. Horn, *The Decisive Battle of Nashville* (Baton Rouge: Louisiana State University Press, 1956), 16, 19, 21.

58. Ibid., 159.

59. Lindsley had read law in Peyton's office during the war. In 1868, President Johnson appointed him U.S. District Attorney for Middle Tennessee, and in 1873 he was elected to the House of Representatives of the state legislature. In 1875, he moved to Dallas, Texas, where he lived for the rest of his life. Robert M. McBride and Dan M. Robison, *Biographical Directory of the Tennessee General Assembly, 1861–1901*, vol. 2 (Nashville: Tennessee State Library and Archives and Tennessee Historical Commission, 1979), 534–35.

60. E. Doug. King, comp., *Singleton's Nashville Business Directory for 1865* (Nashville: R. H. Singleton, Publisher, 1865), 15, 154.

61. Nashville *Dispatch*, April 24, 1865.

62. Ibid. (April 21, 1865).

63. Milligan, a native of Greene County, Tennessee, and graduate of Tusculum College, was an attorney, legislator, justice of the Tennessee Supreme Court (1864–68), and judge of the federal court of claims thereafter. McBride and Robison, *Biographical Directory of the Tennessee General Assembly*, vol. 1, 522.

64. Milligan to Johnson, April 29, 1865; Leroy P. Graf, ed., *The Papers of Andrew Johnson*, vol. 7, 1864–1865 (Knoxville: University of Tennessee Press, 1986), 665.

65. Peyton to Campbell, June 23, 1865, DCP.

66. John Lellyett to William B. Campbell, June 19, 1865; Jordan Stokes to Campbell,

June 21, 1865; J. C. Golladay to Campbell, June 23, 1865, DCP.

67. Peyton to Campbell, July 5, 1865, DCP.

68. Nashville *Daily Union*, June 25, 1865.

69. *NYST*, September 16, October 28, 1865.

70. Peyton to Campbell, December 5, 1865, DCP.

71. Ibid.

72. Ezra J. Warner, *Generals in Blue*, 413.

73. Paul H. Buck, *The Road to Reunion, 1865–1900* (Boston: Little, Brown and Company, 1937), vii.

74. Ibid., 5.

CHAPTER 15

1. DCP, microfilm, TSLA.

2. Paul H. Bergeron, Stephen V. Ash, and Jeanette Keith, *Tennesseans and Their History* (Knoxville: University of Tennessee Press, 1999), 163.

3. William B. Campbell to John Baxter, June 24, 1866, DCP.

4. Corlew, *A Short History*, 357.

5. Nashville *Daily Press and Times*, September 17, 1866.

6. November 5, 1866.

7. Peyton to Campbell, January 22, 1867, DCP.

8. Ibid.

9. Ibid. (March 24, 1867).

10. Corlew, *A Short History*, 354.

11. Lellyett to William B. Campbell, June 25, 1867, DCP.

12. Campbell to John Baxter, June 24, 1866, DCP.

13. Corlew, *A Short History*, 358–59.

14. *NRB*, June 19, July 7, 1867.

15. Ibid. (July 7, 10, 1867).

16. Ibid. (July 7, 1867).

17. Ibid. (July 10, 19, 1867).

18. Nashville *Union and Dispatch*, July 7, 1867.

19. July 8, 1867.

20. T. G. Moss, Adjutant General's Office, Candidate Oaths, Smith-Sumner, 19–1, TSLA.

21. Nashville *Daily Press and Times*, August 3, 1867.

22. Ibid. (August 3, 17, 1867).

23. Bergeron, Ash, and Keith, *Tennesseans and Their History*, 166.

24. *NRB*, August 20, 1867.

25. *Reports of the Cases Argued and Determined in the Supreme Court of Tennessee, During the Year 1868*, Thomas H. Coldwell, State Reporter (Nashville: S. C. Mercer, Printer to the State, 1869), 589; Nashville *Daily Press and Times*, March 11, 1868.

26. Nashville *Daily Press and Times*, March 11, 1868.

27. Ibid. (March 31; April 9, 1868).

28. Ibid. (March 31, 1868).

29. *Reports of the Cases Argued and Determined in the Supreme Court of Tennessee, During the Year 1868*, 598–99; Lebanon Democrat, March 13, 1869.

30. Johnson was impeached by the House; the Senate conducted the first trial of an American president and on May 26 voted to dismiss all charges. David M. DeWitt, *The Impeachment and Trial of President Andrew Johnson* (New York: Macmillan Company, 1903), 554.

31. Sumner County *Republican*, June 13, 1868.

32. Nashville *Daily Press and Times*, September 30, 1868.

33. Ibid.

34. Born in Pennsylvania, Prosser spent the years 1854–61 in California. During the Civil War he became a colonel in the Union Army, and after the war he lived near Nashville. *Directory of Congress*, 1667.

35. Nashville *Daily Press and Times*, November 4, 1868; *NRB*, November 10, 1868.

36. Durham, *Rebellion Revisited*, 329.

37. *NRB*, August 17, 1869; Nashville *Daily Press and Times*, July 16, 1869.

38. Hiram S. Patterson must have waged a write-in campaign in Smith County because that county reported it had given him 553 votes to Peyton's 1,962. As Peyton had no opposition on the ballot, little attention was paid to vote totals for him, and only the Smith County report was published. *NRB*, August 7–8, 1869. The state of Tennessee Archives has no returns for the senatorial contest in its files.

39. Durham, *Rebellion Revisited*, 331–32.

40. August 26, 1869.

41. Cincinnati *Commercial* quoted in *NRB*, August 10, 1869.

42. *Senate Journal of the First Session of the Thirty-Sixth General Assembly of the State of Tennessee, which convened at Nashville, on the first Monday in October, A.D. 1869* (Nashville: James Purvis & Co., Printers to the State, 1869), 54–66.

43. There were three sessions of the 36th General Assembly. The first was from October 4, 1869, to March 7, 1870; the next was May 9, 1870, to July 11, 1870; and the third was December 5, 1870, to February 6, 1871.

44. *Acts of the State of Tennessee, Passed by the First Session of the Thirty-Sixth General Assembly, for the Years 1869–70* (Nashville: Published by Authority, 1870), 7–8, 182–83.

45. An unidentified 1869 newspaper clipping in the Peyton Papers, TSLA.

46. *NRB*, June 18, 1867; Nashville *Daily Press and Times*, June 20, 1867.

47. Nashville *Daily Press and Times*, September 30, 1868.

48. The Fifth District consisted of six counties: Davidson, Sumner, Robertson, Cheatham, Williamson, and Wilson.

49. *NRB*, June 3, 1870.

50. Ibid. (August 31, 1870).

51. September 13, 1870.

52. Nashville *Union and American*, November 4, 1870.

53. *NRB*, October 21, 1870.

54. Randall to Peyton, *NRB*, September 22, 1870.

55. Nashville *Union and American*, October 28, 1870.

56. *NRB*, October 27, 1870.

57. Ibid.

58. Nashville *Union and American*, October 23, 1870.

59. Ibid. (November 4, 1870).

60. Ibid.

61. *NRB*, November 5, 1870.

62. Nashville *Union and American*, November 6, 1860; *NRB*, November 6, 1870.

63. *NRB*, November 8, 1870; Nashville *Union and American*, November 8, 1870.

64. *NRB*, November 9–10, 1870.

65. Robert M. McBride and Dan M. Robison, *Biographical Directory of the Tennessee General Assembly, 1796–1861*, vol. 1 (Nashville: Tennessee State Library and Archives and Tennessee Historical Commission, 1975), 740.

66. Paul H. Buck, *The Road to Reunion, 1865–1900* (Boston: Little, Brown and Co., 1937), 91–92.

67. *NRB*, July 21, 1872.

68. The convention was called to nominate a candidate to fill the unclaimed seat of the late congressman-elect John W. Head of Sumner. *NRB*, December 19, 1874.

69. The Fourth District counties were Sumner, Smith, Wilson, Robertson, Jackson, Macon, Clay, Trousdale, Putnam, Fentress, and Overton.

70. Gallatin *Examiner*, December 10, 1875.

71. Ibid.

72. *Singleton's Nashville Business Directory for 1865* (Nashville: R. H. Singleton, 1865), 154, 227.

73. *NRB*, January 20, 1867.

74. *King's Nashville City Directory, 1868* (Nashville: E. Doug King, 1868): 314, (1869): 196, (1870): 180; *The Nashville City Directory, 1871* (Nashville: Marshall and Bruce), xlix, (1872): 318, (1873): 323, (1874): 338, (1875): 338, (1876): 359, (1877): 327, (1878): 378.

75. *NYST*, February 6, 1875.

76. Nashville *Daily Union*, April 22, 1866; *NYST*, March 31, 1866.

77. Nashville *Daily Press and Times*, November 7, 1866.

78. *NYST*, May 18, 22, November 2, 1867; May 16, October 31, 1868; March 18, October 10, 1869; May 21, October 22, 1870.

79. May 16, 1868.

80. *NRB*, August 9, 1867.

81. Among the other thoroughbreds, Chickahominy was at stud. In training to run was Tom Smiley, four-year-old chestnut colt by Jack Malone, dam Daisy Derby. The brood mares were Benicia, four-year-old chestnut mare by Jack Malone, dam Alboni; Molly Bang, one-year-old chestnut filly by Blacklock, dam Capitola; Alboni, twelve-year-old chestnut mare by Imp. Albion, dam Noty Price; Capitola, nine-year-old chestnut mare by Imp. Albion, dam by Wagner; Minnie Waters, eight-year-old black mare by Imp. Albion, dam Kate Shelby; and Panama, three-year-old chestnut filly by Meteor, dam Alboni. *NYST*, June 27, 1868.

82. Handbill, September 17, 1869, Gallatin *Examiner* Print, CNFP.

83. Wallace's visit was made in 1868, but the Peyton article appeared in *Wallace's Monthly* eight years later. The lapse can be attributed to the fact that the first issue of the monthly did not appear until October 1875. Apparently, Wallace kept the notes made on his visit and wrote the account of it in time for the fifth issue of his monthly, February 1876.

84. *Wallace's Monthly*, vol. 1, no. 5 (February 1876): 385–86.

85. Anderson, *American Thoroughbred*, 224–25.

86. *NYST*, June 27, 1868.

87. Ibid. (October 31, 1868).

88. Ridley Wills II, *The History of Belle Meade: Mansion, Plantation, and Stud* (Nashville: Vanderbilt University Press, 1991), 164; *NYST*, May 21, 1870; Gallatin *Examiner*, May 5, 1876.

89. *NRB*, January 7, 13, 1871.

90. Ibid. (April 27, 1871).

91. Ibid. (May 7, 1871).

92. Ibid. (March 26, 1871).

93. Ibid. (May 11, 1871).

94. *NYST*, May 20, 1871.

95. *NRB*, May 14, 1871.

96. Ibid. (March 17, 23; June 4, 1872).

97. Petition for Charter, Lawsuit #8187, Loose Court Records, SCA.

98. *NRB*, December 12, 1872.

99. Walter T. Durham, James W. Thomas, and John F. Creasy, *A Celebration of Houses Built Before 1900 in Sumner County, Tennessee* (Gallatin: Sumner County Historical Society, 1995), 119.

100. George W. Darden was secretary of the Nashville Blood Horse Association in 1876. Wills II, *The History of Belle Meade: Mansion, Plantation, and Stud*, 171.

101. *NYST*, November 24, December 1, 8, 15, 29, 1877.
102. *NRB*, May 27, 1873.
103. Ibid. (June 4, 1873).
104. *NYST*, April 26, 1873.
105. Ibid. (May 24, 1873).
106. *NRB*, September 28–29, 1873.
107. Ibid. (March 5, 1874).
108. Ibid. (May 19–20, 1874).
109. Ibid. (October 7, 9, 19, 1874).
110. *NYST*, March 13, 1875; *Wallace's Monthly*, vol. 1, no. 1 (October 1875): 70–71; vol. 1, no. 3 (December 1875): 247–48; vol. 2, no. 7 (December 1876): 639; *NYST*, October 30, 1875.

CHAPTER 16

1. Sumner County Unnumbered Deed Book, Civil War Period, 1860–69, 582–83, SCA.
2. SCDB 30 (February 27, 1875): 239, SCA.
3. Twenty-four of the slaves were male and twenty-seven female. Thirteen of the males and ten of the females were over nineteen years of age. U.S. Census, Sumner County, Tennessee, 1860, NA Microfilm, SCA, Roll 1275, 206.
4. U.S. Census, Sumner County, Tennessee, 1870, Roll 1566, 657; Slave Census, Sumner County, 1860, District 6, Roll 1286, 13; Sumner County Tax List, 1868, Roll 335, 2905.
5. Anderson, *American Thoroughbred*, xiii. Anderson stated that the mare Noty Price was one of those taken by the army, but Balie's son John Bell said that she was "stolen" two years before. *NYST*, February 6, 1875.
6. U. S. Treasury, General Records of the Department of the Treasury, Records of the Commissioners of Claims (Southern Claims Commission), NA Record Group 56, CMSN #1150F, March 20, 1873, Settlement #2362.
7. John Bell Peyton Deposition, March 28, 1902, Lawsuit #9492, Loose Court Records, SCA.
8. SCDB 28 (December 17, 1871): 322–23; Deed Book 30 (July 29, 1872): 238, SCA. Peyton's co-sportsman William Giles Harding of the Belle Meade plantation in Nashville was one of the few with financial resources adequate to maintain an active stud and stable; Durham, *Nashville The Occupied City*, 167.
9. Deposition of Emily T. Peyton, May 28, 1883, Lawsuit #2078, Loose Court Records, SCA; *Senate Journal of the First Session of the Thirty-Ninth General Assembly of the State of Tennessee* (Nashville: Tavel, Eastman & Howell, 1875), 30–33.
10. Deposition of Emily T. Peyton, May 28, 1883, Lawsuit #2078, Loose Court Records, SCA.

11. Peyton to Wynne, August 24, 1866, George W. Wynne Collection, Wynne Family Papers, THS, TSLA.
12. Jesse E. Peyton, *Reminiscences of the Past* (Philadelphia: J. B. Lippincott Co., 1895), 23. Balie's Philadelphia cousin Jesse was one of the contributors to Clay's fund.
13. Balie to John Bell Peyton, July 18, 1877, Collection of Kenneth C. Thomson Jr.
14. *NRB*, July 28, 1867.
15. Ibid. (January 1; February 22, 1873).
16. Ibid. (January 10, 1873).
17. Ibid. (February 22, 1873); *Rural Sun*, February 27, 1873.
18. *Rural Sun*, July 24, 1873.
19. Ibid.
20. *Directory of Congress*, 1667; William S. Speer, *Sketches of Prominent Tennesseans* (Nashville: Albert B. Tavel, 1888), 14–15; United States Centennial Commission, *Grounds and Buildings of the Centennial Exposition, Philadelphia, 1876*, vol. 9, Dorsey Gardner, ed. (Washington: Government Printing Office, 1880), 10–11, 112.
21. CNFP.
22. Calhoun County, Texas, Probate Records, Journal B, 126–27.
23. Order granting partition and appointing commissioners, February 12, 1874, Calhoun County, Texas, Probate Records, Book C, 368–69.
24. William T. Peyton to Balie Peyton, January 27, 1874, CNFP; Nashville *Daily American*, August 28, 1878; Deposition of Emily T. Peyton, May 28, 1883, Lawsuit #2078, Loose Court Records, SCA.
25. Calhoun County, Texas, Probate Records, Book 3, 368–69.
26. *NRB*, December 16, 1874.
27. William R. Reagan to Balie Peyton III, December 26, 1874, CNFP.
28. C. Richard King, *The Lady Cannoneer: A Biography of Angelina Belle Peyton Eberly, Heroine of the Texas Archives War* (Burnet, Tex.: Eakin Press, 1981), 154, 159.
29. *NRB*, July 31, 1875.
30. Nashville *Daily American*, September 3, 1875.
31. Ibid. (September 22, 1875).
32. Gallatin *Examiner*, December 17, 1875; William T. Peyton to Balie Peyton, December 19, 1875, CNFP.
33. Emily T. Peyton to William T. Peyton, March 24, 1876, CNFP; Gallatin *Examiner*, May 5, 1876.
34. Margaret Cummings Snider and Joan Hollis Yorgason, comps., *Sumner County Tennessee, Cemetery Records* (Owensboro, Ky.: McDowell Publications, 1981), entry 4-111.

35. Nashville *Daily American*, June 1, 1876.

36. Gallatin *Examiner*, August 18, 1876.

37. Balie Peyton to Frances Trousdale Peyton, August 22, 1876, William Trousdale Papers, 1803–1907, TSLA.

38. United States Centennial Commission, *Grounds and Buildings of the Centennial Exposition, Philadelphia, 1876*, vol. 9, 34, 41–54, 125–31, 143, 149.

39. Paul H. Buck, *The Road to Reunion, 1865–1900* (Boston: Little, Brown and Co., 1937), 138–39.

40. William Trousdale Peyton to John Bell Peyton, September 12, 1876, William Trousdale Papers, 1803–1907, TSLA.

41. J. E. Peyton to Willie Peyton, October 15, 1876, Private Collection of Herbert Harper; Gallatin *Examiner*, September 22, 1876.

42. Jesse E. Peyton, *Reminiscences of the Past* (Philadelphia: J. B. Lippincott Co., 1895), 66.

43. Buck, *The Road to Reunion*, 143.

44. Located on the east bank of the Cumberland River directly opposite downtown Nashville, Edgefield became a part of the city of Nashville in February 1880.

45. Jo. C. Guild, *Old Times in Tennessee* (Nashville: Tavel, Eastman & Howell, 1878; reprint, Gallatin: Rose Mont Foundation, 1995), 356; Durham, *Rebellion Revisited*, 4–5, 75–78, 84–85.

46. *NCLR*, January 3, 1877.

47. White attributed to Peyton the noble characteristics of Lord Pierre Terrail Bayard, a fifteenth- and early-sixteenth-century French military hero known as *le chevalier sans peur et sans reproche*, translated "the knight without fear and without reproach." *New Encyclopedia Britannica*, 15th ed., vol. 1 (Chicago: Encyclopedia Britannica), 978–79.

48. Guild, *Old Times in Tennessee*, 359.

49. Gallatin *Examiner*, January 12, 1877.

50. *Directory of Congress*, 1860.

51. *RDC*, vol. 8, *1824–1837*, pt. 3 (Washington: Gales & Seaton, 1825–1837), 3014–15, 3017, 3021.

52. Ibid., pt. III, 3020–21.

53. A. W. Terrell, "Recollections of General Sam Houston," *Southwestern Historical Quarterly*, vol. 16 (October 1912): 127.

54. Ibid., 124.

55. Nashville *Daily American*, August 28, 1878.

56. Ibid. (August 11, 1877).

57. Ibid. (August 26, 1877).

58. Ibid. (October 16, 1877).

59. Peyton to Emily T. Peyton, December 19, 1877, Deposition of Emily T. Peyton, May 28, 1883, Lawsuit #2078, Loose Court Records, SCA.

60. Deposition of Emily T. Peyton, May 28, 1883, Case #2078, Loose Court Records, SCA.

61. At that time the surviving maternal heirs were John Bell Peyton and Emily Peyton; Thomas, J. B., David H., L. W., Peytona, and James Barry; Margaret Collier; Susan M. Butler, A. P. Butler; Clare, Washington, and John R. Parker; Kate H. S. Stewart and Sallie B. Parker, all of Sumner County, Tennessee. Probate Files, Angelina Belle Peyton Eberly and Peyton Bell Lytle, County Clerk's Office, Calhoun County, Texas.

62. Nashville *Daily American*, August 28, 1878.

63. Gallatin *Tennessean*, April 24, 1878; Nashville *Daily American*, August 20, 1878.

64. Nashville *Daily American*, April 20, 1878.

65. August 20, 1878.

66. Ibid.

67. Peyton, *Reminiscences of the Past*, 33.

68. August 24, 1878.

69. *NYST* quoted in Nashville *Daily American*, December 11, 1877.

70. Ibid.; Dr. Weldon died a week after Balie, August 25, 1878, at Saratoga Springs, New York. *NYST*, August 31, 1878.

71. *NYST*, August 31, 1878.

72. Resolutions of the Bar at Gallatin, Nashville *Daily American*, April 28, 1878.

73. Gallatin *Tennessean*, August 24, 1878.

BIBLIOGRAPHY

BOOKS

Acts of the State of Tennessee, Passed by the First Session of the Thirty-Sixth General Assembly, for the Years 1869–70. Nashville: Published by Authority, 1870.

Adams, William H. *The Whig Party of Louisiana.* Lafayette: University of Southwestern Louisiana, 1973.

Anderson, James Douglas. *The Historic Bluegrass Line.* Nashville: Nashville-Gallatin Interurban Railway, 1913.

_____. *Making the American Thoroughbred, Especially in Tennessee, 1800–1845.* Norwood, Mass.: Plimpton Press, 1916.

Appendix to the Congressional Globe for the First Session Twenty-eighth Congress [1843–1844]. Washington: Blair and Rives, 1844.

Barker, Nancy Nichols, ed. and trans. *The French Legation in Texas.* Vol. 1. Austin: Texas State Historical Association, 1971.

Barros Arana, Diego. *Un decenio de la historia de Chile.* Vol. 2. Santiago, Chile: N.p., 1906.

Bassett, John Spencer, ed. *Correspondence of Andrew Jackson.* Vol. 6. Washington, D.C.: Carnegie Institution of Washington, 1932.

Bauer, K. Jack. *Zachary Taylor: Soldier, Planter, Statesman of the Old Southwest.* Baton Rouge: Louisiana State University Press, 1985.

Bergeron, Paul H., Stephen V. Ash, and Jeanette Keith. *Tennesseans and Their History.* Knoxville: University of Tennessee Press, 1999.

Bethel, Leslie, ed. *Chile Since Independence.* New York: Cambridge University Press, 1993.

Bevans, Charles I., comp. *Treaties and Other International Agreements of the United States of America, 1771–1949.* Vol. 6. Washington: Department of State, 1971.

Biographical Directory of the United States Congress, 1774–1989. Bicentennial ed. Washington, D.C.: U.S. Government Printing Office, 1989.

Brown, Thomas. *Politics and Statesmanship: Essays on the American Whig Party.* New York: Columbia University Press, 1985.

Buck, Paul H. *The Road to Reunion, 1865–1900.* Boston: Little, Brown and Company, 1937.

Carr, John. *Early Times in Middle Tennessee.* 1857; reprint, Nashville: Parthenon Press, 1958.

Chittenden, L. E. *A Report of the Debates and Proceedings in the Secret Session of the Conference Convention for Proposing Amendments to the Constitution of the United States, Held at Washington, D.C., in February A.D. 1861.* New York: D. Appleton & Co., 1864.

Cisco, Jay Guy. *Historic Sumner County, Tennessee.* Nashville: Folk Keelin, 1909.

Collier, Simon, and William F. Sater. *A History of Chile, 1808–1994.* New York: Cambridge University Press, 1996.

Congressional Globe, vols. 1, 2, 3, and 10: *1833–1873.* Washington: Blair and Rives, 1834–1874.

Constitution and Bylaws, Officers and Members, The Pacific Club, 1886. Annual Members Handbook.

Corlew, Robert E. *Tennessee: A Short History.* 2nd ed. Knoxville: University of Tennessee Press, 1981.

Crofts, Daniel W. *Reluctant Confederates: Upper South Unionists in the Secession Crisis.* Chapel Hill and London: University of North Carolina Press, 1989.

Cutler, Wayne, ed. *Correspondence of James K. Polk.* Vol. 5, *1839–1841.* Nashville: Vanderbilt University Press, 1979.

_____. *Correspondence of James K. Polk.* Vol. 6, *1842–1843.* Nashville: Vanderbilt University Press, 1983.

_____. *Correspondence of James K. Polk.* Vol. 8, *September–December, 1844.* Knoxville: University of Tennessee Press, 1993.

Davis, Winfred J. *History of the Political Conventions in California, 1849–1892.* Sacramento: California State Library, 1893.

DeVore, Donald E., and Joseph Logsdon. *Crescent City Schools: Public Education in New*

Orleans, 1841–1991. New Orleans: Center for Louisiana Studies, University of Southwestern Louisiana, 1991.

DeWitt, David M. *The Impeachment and Trial of President Andrew Johnson*. New York: Macmillan Company, 1903.

Dickey, Dallas C. *Seargent S. Prentiss, Whig Orator of the Old South*. Baton Rouge: Louisiana State University Press, 1945.

Drake, James Vaulx. *Life of General Robert Hatton*. Nashville: Marshall and Bruce, 1867.

Durham, Walter T. *Before Tennessee: The Southwest Territory, 1790–1796*. Piney Flats: Rocky Mount Historical Association, 1990.

_____. *The Great Leap Westward, A History of Sumner County, Tennessee, From Its Beginnings to 1805*. Gallatin: Sumner County Library Board, 1969.

_____. *Nashville The Occupied City, The First Seventeen Months—February 16, 1862 to June 30, 1863*. Nashville: Tennessee Historical Society, 1985.

_____. *Old Sumner, A History of Sumner County, Tennessee, From 1805 to 1861*. Gallatin: Sumner County Library Board, 1972.

_____. *Rebellion Revisited, A History of Sumner County, Tennessee, From 1861 to 1870*. Gallatin: Sumner County Museum Association, 1982.

_____. *Volunteer Forty-Niners: Tennesseans and the California Gold Rush*. Nashville: Vanderbilt University Press, 1997.

_____. *Wynnewood, Bledsoe's Lick, Castalian Springs, Tennessee*. Castalian Springs: Bledsoe's Lick Historical Association, 1994.

Durham, Walter T., James W. Thomas, and John F. Creasy. *A Celebration of Houses Built Before 1900 in Sumner County, Tennessee*. Gallatin: Sumner County Historical Society, 1995.

Dyer, Brainerd. *Zachary Taylor*. Baton Rouge: Louisiana State University Press, 1946.

Edwards, Agustin. *Cuatro presidentes de Chile*, vol. 1. Valparaiso, Chile: N.p., 1932.

Ethington, Philip J. *The Public City: The Political Construction of Urban Life in San Francisco, 1850–1900*. New York: Cambridge University Press, 1994.

Evans, Henry Clay, Jr. *Chile and Its Relations with the United States*. Durham, N.C.: Duke University Press, 1927.

Executive Document No. 121, 33rd Congress, 1st Session, House of Representatives. Vol. 1. Washington: A. O. P. Nicholson, Printer, 1855.

Folmsbee, Stanley J., Robert E. Corlew, and Enoch L. Mitchell. *Tennessee: A Short History*. Knoxville: University of Tennessee Press, 1969.

Foote, Henry Stuart. *The Bench and Bar of the South and Southwest*. St. Louis: Soule, Thomas & Wentworth, 1876.

_____. *Texas and the Texans, or the Advance of the Anglo Americans to the South-West*. Vol. 1. Philadelphia: Thomas Copperthwart & Co., 1841.

_____. *War of the Rebellion; or Scylla and Charybdis*. New York: Harper and Brothers, 1866.

Gardner, Charles K. *Dictionary of all Officers, Who Have Been Commissioned, or Have Been Appointed and Served in the Army of the United States. . . .* New York: G. P. Putnam and Company, 1853.

Gibson's Guide and Directory of the State of Louisiana, and the Cities of New Orleans and Lafayette. New Orleans: John Gibson, 1838.

Gower, Herschel, and Jack Allen, eds. *Pen and Sword: The Life and Journals of Randal W. McGavock*. Nashville: Tennessee Historical Commission, 1959.

Graf, Leroy P., ed. *The Papers of Andrew Johnson*. Vol. 7, *1864–1865*. Knoxville: University of Tennessee Press, 1986.

Graf, Leroy P., and Ralph W. Haskins, eds. *The Papers of Andrew Johnson*. Vol. 4, *1860–1861*. Knoxville: University of Tennessee Press, 1976.

Griffey, Irene M. *The Preemptors: Tennessee's First Settlers*. Clarksville: 1989.

Guild, Jo. C. *Old Times in Tennessee*. Nashville: Tavel, Eastman & Howell, 1878; reprint, Gallatin: Rose Mont Foundation, 1995.

Hamer, Philip M., ed. *Tennessee—A History, 1673–1932*. Vols. 1 and 2. New York: American Historical Society, 1933.

Hamilton, Holman. *Soldier in the White House*. Indianapolis and New York: Bobbs-Merrill Company, 1951.

Harmon, Nolan B., Jr. *The Famous Case of Myra Clark Gaines*. Baton Rouge: Louisiana State University Press, 1946.

Haywood, John. *The Civil and Political History of the State of Tennessee*. Knoxville: Heiskell and Brown, 1823; reprint, Knoxville: Tenase Company, 1969.

Heiskell, S. G. *Andrew Jackson and Early Tennessee History*. Vol. 1. Nashville: Ambrose Printing Company, 1918.

Holliday, J. S. *The World Rushed In*. New York: Simon and Schuster, 1981.

Holt, Michael F. *The Political Crisis of the 1850s*. New York: John Wiley and Sons, 1978.

_____. *Political Parties and American Political Development from the Age of Jackson to the Age of Lincoln*. Baton Rouge and London: Louisiana State University Press, 1992.

_____. *The Rise and Fall of the American Whig Party, Jacksonian Politics and the Onset of the Civil War*. New York and Oxford: Oxford University Press, 1979.

Hopkins, Anne H., and William Lyons. *Tennessee Votes: 1779–1976*. Knoxville: Bureau of Public Administration, University of Tennessee, 1978.

Horn, Stanley F. *The Decisive Battle of Nashville*. Baton Rouge: Louisiana State University Press, 1956.

House Journal 1861–62 of the First Session of the Thirty-Fourth General Assembly of the State of Tennessee which Convened at Nashville, on the First Monday in October, A.D. 1861 and Adjourned in Memphis, March 20, 1862. Nashville: Tennessee Historical Commission, 1957.

House Journal of the First Extra Session of the Thirty-Third General Assembly of the State of Tennessee. Nashville: J. O. Griffith and Company, Public Printers, 1861.

Howard, Perry A. *Political Tendencies in Louisiana*. Baton Rouge: Louisiana State University, 1971.

Howe, Daniel Walker. *The Political Culture of the American Whigs*. Chicago: University of Chicago Press, 1979.

Hurwitz, Howard L. *An Encyclopedic Dictionary of American History*. New York: Washington Square Press, 1970.

James, Marquis. *Andrew Jackson: Portrait of a President*. New York: Garden City Publishing Co., 1940.

_____. *The Life of Andrew Jackson*. New York: Bobbs-Merrill Company, 1938.

Johnson, Allen, ed. *Dictionary of American Biography*. Vol. 12. New York: Charles Scribner's Sons, 1928.

Journal of the House of Representatives of the State of Tennessee, 21st General Assembly, 1835. Nashville: Secretary of State, 1835.

Journal of the Senate of the State of Tennessee, 21st General Assembly, 1835. Nashville: Secretary of State, 1835.

King, C. Richard. *The Lady Cannoneer: A Biography of Angelina Belle Peyton Eberly, Heroine of the Texas Archives War*. Burnet, Tex.: Eakin Press, 1981.

King, E. Doug., comp. *Singleton's Nashville Business Directory for 1865*. Nashville: R. H. Singleton, 1865.

King's Nashville City Directory, 1868–1870. Nashville: E. Doug King, 1869–70.

Kirwan, Albert Dennis. *John J. Crittenden: The Struggle for the Union*. Lexington: University of Kentucky Press, 1962.

Lewis, Oscar. *San Francisco: Mission to Metropolis*. San Diego: Howell-North Books, 1980.

Lynch, James D. *The Bench and Bar of Mississippi*. New York: E. J. Hale & Son, Publishers, 1881.

Malone, Dumas, ed. *Dictionary of American Biography*. Vol. 17. New York: Charles Scribner's Sons, 1935.

Mathews, Mitford, ed. *Dictionary of Americanisms*. Vol. 1. Chicago: University of Chicago Press, 1951.

McBride, Robert M., and Dan M. Robison. *Biographical Directory of the Tennessee General Assembly, 1796–1861; 1861–1901*. Vols. 1 and 2. Nashville: Tennessee State Library and Archives and Tennessee Historical Commission, 1975, 1979.

McCormac, Eugene Irving. *James K. Polk: A Political Biography*. Berkeley: University of California Press, 1922.

McIntosh, James T., Lynda L. Crist, and Mary S. Dix, eds. *The Papers of Jefferson Davis*. Vol. 3, *July 1846–December 1848*. Baton Rouge and London: Louisiana State University Press, 1981.

Memoirs of General William T. Sherman by Himself. Bloomington: Indiana University Press, 1957.

Michel & Co. New Orleans Annual and Commercial Directory for 1843. New Orleans: Justin L. Sollee, 1842.

Milton, George Fort. *The Age of Hate: Andrew Johnson and the Radicals*. New York: Coward-McCann, 1930.

Morris, Eastin. *The Tennessee Gazetteer*. Nashville: W. Hassell Hunt and Company, 1834.

Morris, Richard B., ed. *Encyclopedia of American History*. New York: Harper and Brothers, 1953.

Myers, John Myers. *San Francisco Reign of Terror*. Garden City, N.Y.: Doubleday & Company, 1966.

Myers, Raymond E. *The Zollie Tree*. Louisville: Filson Club Press, 1964.

Myers, William Starr, ed. *The Mexican War Diary of George B. McClellan*. Princeton: Princeton University Press, 1917.

Nashville City and Business Directory for 1860–61. Nashville: L. P. Williams & Co., Publishers and Proprietors, 1860.

Nashville City Directory, 1871–1878. Nashville: Marshall and Bruce, 1872–1879.

Nevins, Allan, ed. *Polk: The Diary of a President, 1845–1849*. New York: Longman, Green, and Co., 1929.

New Encyclopedia Brittanica. 15th ed. Chicago: Encyclopedia Brittanica, 1993.

Numis, Doyce B., Jr., ed. *The San Francisco Vigilance Committee of 1856: Three Views*. Los Angeles: Los Angeles Westerners, 1971.

[O'Meara, James]. *The Vigilance Committee of 1856*. San Francisco: James H. Barry, 1887.

Parks, Joseph Howard. *John Bell of Tennessee*. Baton Rouge: Louisiana State University Press, 1950.

Patton, James Welch. *Unionism and Reconstruction in Tennessee, 1860–1869*. Gloucester, Mass.: P. Smith, 1966.

Peyton, Jesse E. *Reminiscences of the Past.*
Philadelphia: J. B. Lippincott Co., 1895.

Peyton, John Lewis, comp. *Memoir of John Howe
Peyton in Sketches by his Contemporaries.*
Staunton, Va.: A. B. Blackburn & Co., 1894.

Peyton Society of Virginia, Book Committee.
The Peytons of Virginia. Stafford: Peyton Society
of Virginia, 1976.

Poage, George Rawlings. *Henry Clay and the
Whig Party.* Gloucester, Mass.: Peter Smith,
1965.

Polk, William R. *Polk's Folly: An American Family
History.* New York and London: Doubleday,
2000.

Prentiss, George, ed. *A Memoir of S. S. Prentiss.*
Vol. 2. New York: C. Scribner's Sons, 1855.

*Public Acts Passed at the First Session of the Twenty-
First General Assembly of the State of Tennessee,
1835–6.* Nashville: S. Nye and Co., Printers—
Republican Office, 1836.

Public Acts of the State of Tennessee, 1859–60.
Nashville: E. G. Eastman & Co., 1860.

*Public Documents Printed by Order of the United
States, First Session, 29th Congress.* Vol. 5.
Washington: Ritchie & Heiss, 1846.

Quaife, Milo Milton, ed. *The Diary of James K.
Polk, During His Presidency, 1845–1849.*
Chicago Historical Society Collections, Vol. 2.
Chicago: A. C. McClurg & Co., 1910.

Register of Debates in Congress, vols. 10, pts. 2–4;
11, pt. 1; 12, pts. 2–4; 13, pts. 1–2:
1824–1837. Washington: Gales & Seaton,
1825–1837.

Remini, Robert. *Andrew Jackson and the Course of
American Democracy, 1833–1845.* New York:
Harper and Row, 1984.

*Reports of the Cases Argued and Determined in the
Supreme Court of Tennessee, During the Year 1868.*
Thomas H. Coldwell, state reporter. Nashville:
S. C. Mercer, 1869.

*Reports of Committees, Thirtieth Congress, First
Session, Senate, Rep. Com. 49.*

San Francisco Directory, 1856–1859. San
Francisco: N.p., 1856–1859.

Schlesinger, Arthur M., Jr. *The Age of Jackson.*
Boston: Little, Brown, 1945.

———, ed. *The Almanac of American History.* New
York: G. P. Putnam's Sons, 1983.

Scott, Nancy N., ed. *A Memoir of Hugh Lawson
White.* Philadelphia: J. B. Lippincott & Co.,
1856.

Sellers, George. *James K. Polk, Jacksonian.*
Princeton: Princeton University Press, 1957.

*Senate Journal of the First Session of the Thirty-
Ninth General Assembly of the State of Tennessee.*
Nashville: Tavel, Eastman & Howell, 1875.

*Senate Journal of the First Session of the Thirty-Sixth
General Assembly of the State of Tennessee, which*
convened at Nashville, on the first Monday in
October, A.D. 1869. Nashville: James Purvis &
Co., 1869.

*Senate Journal of the Thirty-Third General Assembly of
the State of Tennessee.* Nashville: J. O. Griffith
and Company, 1861.

Senkewicz, Robert M. *Vigilantes in Gold Rush San
Francisco.* Stanford, Calif: Stanford University
Press, 1985.

Sherman, William Roderick. *The Diplomatic and
Commercial Relations of the United States and Chile,
1820–1914.* Boston: Richard G. Badger,
Publisher, 1926.

Shuck, Oscar T., ed. *History of the Bench and Bar of
California.* Los Angeles: Commercial Printing
House, 1901.

Siegel, Martin, ed. and comp. *New Orleans: A
Chronological and Documentary History
1539–1970.* Dobbs Ferry, N.Y.: Oceana
Publications, 1975.

Simpson, Craig M. *A Good Southerner: The Life of
Henry A. Wise of Virginia.* Chapel Hill:
University of North Carolina Press, 1985.

Sinclair, Harold. *The Port of New Orleans.* New
York: Doubleday, Doran & Co., 1942.

Smith, Harry Worcester. *A Sporting Family of the
Old South.* Albany, N.Y.: J. B. Lyon Company,
1936.

Smith, J. Frazer. *White Pillars: Early Life and
Architecture of the Lower Mississippi Valley Country.*
New York: Bramhall House, 1941.

Smith, Justin H. *War with Mexico.* Vol. 1. New
York: Macmillian & Co., 1919.

Snider, Margaret Cummings, and Joan Hollis
Yorgason, comps. *Sumner County, Tennessee,
Cemetery Records.* Owensboro, Ky.: McDowell
Publications, 1981.

Speer, Ed. *The Tennessee Handbook.* Jefferson,
N.C.: MacFarland and Company, 2002.

Speer, William S. *Sketches of Prominent Tennesseans.*
Nashville: Albert B. Tavel, 1888.

Squier, E. G., ed. *Frank Leslie's Pictorial History of
the American Civil War.* Vol. 1. New York: Frank
Leslie, 1862.

*Tennessee. Records of Sumner County. Marriage
Records, 1787–1838.* Nashville: Historical
Records Survey, 1939.

U.S. War Department. *The War of the Rebellion: A
Compilation of the Official Records of the Union and
Confederate Armies.* 70 vols. in 128. Washington:
Government Printing Office, 1880–1901.

United States Centennial Commission. *Grounds
and Buildings of the Centennial Exposition,
Philadelphia, 1876.* Vol. 9. Dorsey Gardner, ed.
Washington: Government Printing Office, 1880.

Warner, Ezra J. *Generals in Blue: Lives of the
Union Commanders.* Baton Rouge: Louisiana
State University Press, 1964.

_____. *Generals in Gray: Lives of the Confederate Commanders*. Baton Rouge: Louisiana State University Press, 1959.

Weaver, Herbert, ed. *Correspondence of James K. Polk*. Vol. 2, *1833–1834*. Nashville: Vanderbilt University Press, 1972.

_____. *Correspondence of James K. Polk*. Vol. 3, *1835–1836*. Nashville: Vanderbilt University Press, 1975.

_____. *Correspondence of James K. Polk*. Vol. 4, *1837–1838*. Nashville: Vanderbilt University Press, 1977.

West, Carroll Van, ed. *The Tennessee Encyclopedia of History & Culture*. Nashville: Tennessee Historical Society and Rutledge Hill Press, 1998.

White, Robert H. *Messages of the Governors of Tennessee*. Vol. 4, *1845–1847*. Nashville: Tennessee Historical Commission, 1957.

Wills, Ridley, II. *The History of Belle Meade: Mansion, Plantation, and Stud*. Nashville: Vanderbilt University Press, 1991.

Wilson, James Grant, and John Fiske, eds. *Appleton's Cyclopedia of American Biography*. New York: D. Appleton and Company, 1888.

Wise, Barton H. *The Life of Henry A. Wise of Virginia, 1806–1876*. New York: Macmillan Company, 1899.

Wyatt-Brown, Bertram. *Honor and Violence in the Old South*. New York and Oxford: Oxford University Press, 1986.

ARTICLES

Abernethy, Thomas P. "The Origins of the *Whig* Party in Tennessee." *Mississippi Valley Historical Review*, vol. 12 (1926).

American Historical Magazine, vol. 4, no. 3 (July 1899).

"Documents: Correspondence of John Bell and Willie Mangum, 1835." *THM*, vol. 3, no. 3 (September 1917).

Durham, Walter T. "The Arrest: North to Fort Mackinac." *Tennessee Historical Quarterly*, vol. 55, no. 4 (winter 1996).

Hall, Kermit L. "West H. Humphreys and the Crisis of the Union." *Tennessee Historical Quarterly*, vol. 34 (1975).

Huggins, Dorothy H., comp. "Continuation of the Annals of San Francisco." *California Historical Society Quarterly*, vol. 16, no. 4 (December 1937).

_____. "Continuation of the Annals of San Francisco." *California Historical Society Quarterly*, vol. 17, no. 2 (June 1938).

Hurt, Peyton. "The Rise and Fall of the 'Know Nothings' in California." *California Historical Society Quarterly*, vol. 9, no. 1 (March 1930).

_____. "The Rise and Fall of the 'Know-Nothings' in California." *California Historical Society Quarterly*, vol. 9, no. 2 (June 1930).

Kemp, Louis Wilz. "Mrs. Angelina B. Eberly." *Southwestern Historical Quarterly*, vol. 36 (January 1933).

Lemmon, Alfred E. "Across the Gulf: From New Orleans to Havana." *Historic New Orleans Collection Quarterly*, vol. 16, no. 4 (fall 1998).

Magill, John. "Facets of Childhood in Nineteenth-Century New Orleans." *Historic New Orleans Collection Quarterly*, vol. 16, no. 4 (fall 1998).

Peyton, Balie. "President Jackson's Orders and Reminiscences." *Rural Sun*, vol. 4 (December 19, 1872).

_____. "Sumner County Races, 1804–05." *Rural Sun*, vol. 4 (December 5, 1872).

Sacher, John M. "The Sudden Collapse of the Louisiana Whig Party." *Journal of Southern History*, vol. 65, no. 2 (May 1999).

Terrell, A. W. "Recollections of General Sam Houston." *Southwestern Historical Quarterly*, vol. 16 (October 1912).

UNPUBLISHED MATERIALS

American Diplomats. Collection. Historical Society of Pennsylvania, Philadelphia.

Anderson, James Douglas. Papers. TSLA.

Bell, John. Collection. Library of Congress, Microfilm, TSLA.

Blackmore, George Dawson. Biographical Sketch. Typescript, SCA.

Bounty Land Files, NA.

Brien, John S. Brief Book. Buell-Brien Papers, TSLA.

Calhoun County, Texas, Records. Probate Records, Book C, Journal B, Book 3, Probate File.

Campbell, David. Papers. Microfilm, TSLA. Originals in Special Collections, William R. Perkins Library, Duke University.

Caruthers, Robert L. Papers. SHC, University of North Carolina, Chapel Hill.

Cenas, H. B. Vols. 26A, 33. NARC

Civil Election Returns, 1835. United States Congress, Sixth District, Tennessee Secretary of State, TSLA.

Civil Election Returns, 1833. United States Congress, Sixth District, Tennessee Secretary of State, TSLA.

Compiled Military Service Records for the Mexican War, NA.

Correspondence by author. TSLA.

Crittenden, John Jordan. Papers. Library of Congress.

Donelson, Andrew Jackson. Papers. Library of Congress.

Downey, Samuel Smith. Collection. William R. Perkins Library, Duke University, Durham.

Durham, Walter T. Private Collection.
Eaton, John. Collection. Special Collections, University of Tennessee, Knoxville.
Falls County, Texas, Records. Probate File.
Freer Collection. Historical Society of Pennsylvania, Philadelphia.
Governors Correspondence (Tenn.). TSLA.
Harding-Jackson Papers, TSLA.
Harper, Herbert. Private Collection.
Jackson, Andrew. Papers. Library of Congress.
Johnson, Andrew. Papers. Library of Congress.
Johnson, John Neely. Papers. Bancroft Library, University of California, Berkeley.
Lauderdale Papers. TSLA.
Law Department Register, 1859, University Archives, Cumberland University, Lebanon, Tenn.
Minutes of the Louisiana Supreme Court, vol. 5. Baton Rouge.
Miscellaneous Collection. Historical Society of Pennsylvania, Philadelphia.
Morris, Mary. Diary, 1802–1895. TSLA.
Muster Roll, Capt. Jos. C. Guild's company, 2nd Regt., 1st Brigade, Tennessee Mounted Militia. War Department Records, NA.
Muster Rolls, War of 1812, Book 3, TSLA.
Neal, Charley. Family Papers compiled from the Mabel Neal Collection of Charley Neal Family Papers. Private Collection.
Overton Papers. Murdock Collection. TSLA.
Parish of Orleans, New Orleans, Louisiana, Office of the Register of Conveyances, Books 29–30, 42, 48.
Peyton Family Bible. WPA Records, Sumner County, Microfilm Reel 81, TSLA.
Peyton Family Notes by Jonathan Smith, a Manuscript. CNFP.
Peyton Papers. TSLA.
Pulaski County, Ky., Records.
Records of the Department of State, Despatches from United States Ministers to Chile, 1823–1906, vol. 9, July 20, 1849–October 2, 1851, NA.
Records of the Department of State, Diplomatic Instructions, Chile, 1801–1906, vol. 15, May 29, 1833–February 2, 1867, NA.
Seghers, T. Vol. 31. NARC.
Sumner County Records, Sumner County Archives.
Bills of Sale, 1840–1843, 1844–1851.
Deed Books 11, 17, 19–21, 23–24, 28, 30.
Loose Court Records.
North Carolina Grant Book No. 1.
Slave Census, Sumner County, 1860, District 6, Microfilm Roll 1286.
Sumner County Tax List, 1868, Microfilm Roll 335.
Sumner County WPA Records, Microfilm Roll 81.

U.S. Census 1850, Slave Census, Civil District No. 6, Sumner County, Tenn. Series 432, Microfilm Roll 907.
U.S. Census, Sumner County, Tenn., 1860, NA Series 432, Microfilm Roll 1275.
U.S. Census, Sumner County, Tenn., 1870, Microfilm Roll 1566.
Unnumbered Deed Book, Civil War Period, 1860–69.
Will Book, 1823–1842.
Thomson, Kenneth C., Jr. Private Collection.
Trousdale, William. Collection. THS, TSLA.
Trousdale, William. Papers, 1803–1907. TSLA.
U.S. Treasury. General Records of the Department of the Treasury. Records of the Commissioners of Claims (Southern Claims Commission), NA Record Group 56.
Unidentified Nashville newspaper clippings, Vertical Files, TSLA.
Van Buren, Martin. Papers. Microfilm, Library of Congress.
Wayne County, Kentucky, Records.
Weed, Thurlow. Collection. Rush Rhers Library, University of Rochester, Rochester, N.Y.
Williamson County Records. Chancery Court Minutes, vol. A, May 1825–1829.
Wynne, George W. Collection. Wynne Family Papers, THS, TSLA.

TENNESSEE NEWSPAPERS
Brownlow's Knoxville *Whig*.
Brownlow's Knoxville *Whig and Independent Journal*.
Clarksville *Jeffersonian*.
Franklin *Weekly Review*.
Gallatin *Courier*.
Gallatin *Examiner*.
Gallatin *Tennessean*.
Gallatin *Union*.
Hartsville *Vidette*.
Knoxville *Whig*.
Lebanon *Democrat*.
Memphis *Daily Appeal*.
Memphis *Daily Eagle*.
Memphis *Daily Enquirer*.
Nashville *Banner*.
Nashville *Commercial and Legal Reporter*.
Nashville *Daily American*.
Nashville *Daily Gazette*.
Nashville *Daily Press*.
Nashville *Daily Press and Times*.
Nashville *Daily Republican Banner*.
Nashville *Daily Times and True Union*.
Nashville *Daily True Whig*.
Nashville *Dispatch*.
Nashville *Patriot*.
Nashville *Republican*.
Nashville *Republican Banner*.

Nashville *Republican and State Gazette.*
Nashville *Tennessean Magazine.*
Nashville *Tri-Weekly Union.*
Nashville *Union.*
Nashville *Union and American.*
Nashville *Union and Dispatch.*
Nashville *Weekly Patriot.*
Nashville *Whig.*
National Banner and Nashville *Daily Advertiser.*
National Banner and Nashville *Whig.*
Presbyterian Record.
Republican Banner and Nashville *Whig.*
Rural Sun (Nashville).
Sumner County *Republican.*
West Tennessee *Whig.*

OTHER NEWSPAPERS
Baltimore *Patriot.*
Chicago *Tribune.*
Clarksville (Tex.) *Northern Standard.*
Louisiana *Courier.*
Louisville *Daily Journal.*
New Orleans *Advertiser.*
New Orleans *Commercial Bulletin.*
New Orleans *Daily Bee.*
New Orleans *Daily Crescent.*
New Orleans *Daily Delta.*
New Orleans *Daily Orleanian.*
New Orleans *Daily Picayune.*
New York *Herald.*

New York *Spirit of the Times.*
New York Times.
Philadelphia *Daily Evening Bulletin.*
Philadelphia *Public Ledger and Daily Transcript.*
Plaquemine (La.) *Southern Sentinel.*
Pointe Coupee (La.) *Echo.*
Sacramento *Daily Democratic State Journal.*
Sacramento *Daily Union.*
San Francisco *Daily Alta California.*
San Francisco *Daily Evening Bulletin.*
San Francisco *Daily Herald.*
Ubiquitous, formerly the *Phoenix* (San Francisco).
Washington *Daily Union.*
Washington *Globe.*
Washington *National Intelligencer.*
Washington *Union.*

PERIODICALS
The Bud of Thought. Gallatin, Tenn.: Howard
 Female Institute, 1860. SCA.
American Turf Register and Sporting Magazine.
Confederate Veteran.
Harper's Weekly.
Niles Weekly Register.
Smithsonian Magazine.
Southern Cultivator.
Texas Farm and Ranch.
Wallace's Monthly.
The Wide West.

PHOTO ACKNOWLEDGMENTS

The author wishes to thank the following individuals and organizations for granting permission to reproduce the illustrations and photographs in this work on the indicated pages:

Clark Chapter No. 13, United Daughters of the Confederacy, Gallatin, Tennessee, 93.
Nathan Harsh, 18.[*]
Allen Haynes (photo of painting in Rose Mont Collection), 62.
Jean and Alexander Heard Library of Vanderbilt University, 65.
The Historic New Orleans Collection (acc.no. 1995.29.1), 60, 104.
Jim Hoobler Collection (*Harper's Weekly*, March 8, 1862), 206.
Library of Congress, 173, 176.
National Archives, 211.
Mrs. Mabel Neal, Indian Trail, North Carolina, cover, 11, 205, 232, 245.
Sumner County Archives, 123, 204, 237.
Tennessee Historical Society, frontispiece, chapter openers, 31, 190, 209.
Tennessee State Library and Archives, 22, 81, 97, 141, 221, 232.
Tennessee State Museum, 106.
Kenneth C. Thomson Collection, Gallatin and Cross Plains, Tennessee, 98.

Images on pages 13, 34, and 101 are from the author's collection.

[*] The painting of Andrew Jackson on page 18 is an oil painting on wood panel owned by Nathan Harsh of Gallatin. It is thought to be one of two copy portraits, painted circa 1830 by an unknown artist, of the undated original by Nathan W. Wheeler which is in the collection of the Pennsylvania Historical Society.

INDEX